Gleanings of Freedom

THE WORKING CLASS
IN AMERICAN HISTORY

Editorial Advisors
James R. Barrett
Alice Kessler-Harris
Nelson Lichtenstein
David Montgomery

Gleanings of Freedom

*Free and Slave Labor along
the Mason-Dixon Line,
1790–1860*

MAX GRIVNO

University of Illinois Press

URBANA, CHICAGO, AND SPRINGFIELD

Publication of this book is supported
by the Richard T. Farrell Award, given
by the Department of History at the
University of Maryland.

The Library of Congress cataloged the cloth edition as follows:
Grivno, Max L.
Gleanings of freedom : free and slave labor along
the Mason-Dixon Line, 1790–1860 / Max Grivno.
p.   cm. — (The working class in American history)
Includes bibliographical references and index.
ISBN 978-0-252-03652-1 (hardcover : alk. paper)
ISBN 978-0-252-09356-2 (e-book)
1. Slave labor—Maryland—History—19th century.
2. Slavery—Maryland—History—19th century.
3. Freedmen—Maryland—History—19th century.
4. Agricultural laborers—Maryland—History—19th century.
5. Mason-Dixon Line. I. Title.
E445.M3G74   2011
305.5'63—dc23   2011041224
PAPERBACK ISBN 978-0-252-08047-0

Does not man have hard service on earth?
Are not his days like those of a hired man?

Like a slave longing for the evening shadows,
or a hired man waiting eagerly for his wages,

so I have been allotted months of futility, and
nights of misery have been assigned to me.

—Job 7:1–3

Look! The wages you failed to pay the workmen who mowed your fields are crying out
against you. The cries of the harvesters have
reached the ears of the Lord Almighty.

—James 5:4

Contents

Illustrations

Acknowledgments

These are the last passages that I will write in a project that has been a part of my life for the past decade. It is, therefore, something of a bittersweet experience. Looking back, however, I am struck with a profound sense of gratitude to the many people who made these years some of the happiest and most rewarding of my life.

Leslie Rowland was this project's staunchest defender and its most demanding critic. I cannot describe Leslie's utter dedication to the historian's craft and to her students in such a small space, but one example might suffice. In the summer of 2007, Leslie tumbled down the steps of a subway station and shattered the wrist of her writing hand. Despite these painful injuries, she read a draft and scrawled detailed comments on over 300 pages—with the wrong hand! Whatever merits this work possesses are hers; its shortcomings stem from my stubbornness.

I have been fortunate to work with many excellent historians. I spent four years with the Freedmen and Southern Society Project. The editors' passionate engagement with questions surrounding emancipation, rural labor, and the meanings of freedom was a constant source of inspiration, and their exacting research and careful attention to the sources provided an example that I have constantly emulated. I would like to acknowledge the project's director, Leslie Rowland, and former and current editors Anthony Kaye, Kate Masur, Steven Miller, and Susan O'Donovan for their help over the years.

Many other scholars lent their skills to this project. The study traces its roots back to a Historical Resources Survey commissioned by the National Park Service. I am indebted to the historians at Antietam National Battlefield and the Chesapeake and Ohio Canal for their assistance with the early stages of my research. At the University of Maryland, Ira Berlin, Clare Lyons, James Henretta, and Mark Leone made this project immeasurably better. I am especially grateful to Ira, who saw the project's potential at an early stage and constantly goaded me to ask bigger questions of a small slaveholding society. Mike Fitzgerald has been a steadfast friend and mentor since my days as an undergraduate at St. Olaf College. I hope that seeing this book in print will, in some way, reward him for the years he spent helping me grow as a historian. Many people have read portions of the manuscript and provided useful comments. Here, I would like to acknowledge Alex Lichtenstein, T. Stephen Whitman, Eva Sheppard Wolf, David Montgomery, my colleagues at the University of Southern Mississippi, and the anonymous readers for the University of Illinois Press.

Numerous archivists have assisted me with my research, but special thanks are due to Robert Barnes of the Maryland Hall of Records, who guided me through the warren of county court records and provided constant good cheer. I would also like to thank the Archivist of Maryland, Edward C. Papenfuse, who guided me to collections I would not have otherwise found. At the University of Maryland, Lauren Brown, Jennie Levine, and the staff of the Archives and Manuscripts Department fielded my requests for what must have seemed an endless stream of documents. Finally, I would like to thank the many archivists and librarians at the Maryland Historical Society for the countless hours of assistance they provided me over the years.

I could not have completed this work without generous financial support. In 2006, I received a Mary Savage Snouffer fellowship from the College of Arts and Humanities at the University of Maryland. The 2008 Richard T. Farrell Award from the Department of the History at University of Maryland came with a subvention that helped underwrite this cost of producing this volume. Likewise, the 2008 C. Vann Woodward Award from the Southern Historical Association helped me complete the final stages of research on *Gleanings of Freedom*. I am deeply grateful to these award committees for their encouragement, for their confidence in this project, and for their thoughtful comments and questions.

Completing a study of Maryland while beginning a career in southern Mississippi presented challenges that I could never have overcome on my own. The revisions to this book would not have been possible without the assistance of several graduate students at the University of Maryland. Thanayi Jackson, Mark A. Johnson, and Mary-Elizabeth Murphy answered my sometimes arcane research requests with alacrity and aplomb. I am also indebted to the librarians at the University of Southern Mississippi. They consistently amazed me with their knack for wrangling obscure pamphlets, newspapers, and manuscripts on microfilm.

The staff at the University of Illinois Press has made preparing the book manuscript and seeing it through production not only painless, but actually enjoyable. Laurie Matheson was an enthusiastic supporter of this project and steered me around the innumerable snares and pitfalls that might derail a young writer. My copyeditor, Ellen Goldlust-Gingrich, spared me from many embarrassing errors and made my prose clearer, stronger, and more direct than I ever could have.

My parents, Steve and Connie Grivno, instilled in me a love of history and made tremendous sacrifices to guarantee that I would be the first in my family to attend college. The pluck they showed raising a family in the rural Midwest during the farm crisis of the 1980s has, in many ways, shaped my understanding of the past. Still, my greatest debts are to my wife, Traci. She stood beside me during the long and leans years of graduate school, waded through moldering documents at county courthouses and historical societies, and evinced a deep, abiding confidence in this study and its author. Traci, this book is dedicated to you with boundless love and immeasurable gratitude.

Gleanings of Freedom

INTRODUCTION

Sharpsburg, Maryland, 1803

On 17 September 1862, the Union's Army of the Potomac and the Confederacy's Army of Northern Virginia clashed on the corn and wheat fields, pastures, and woodlots surrounding Sharpsburg, Maryland. When the smoke cleared, upward of twenty-three thousand men had been killed or wounded and the "irrepressible conflict" between societies built on slavery and free labor had taken a radical turn.[1] Emboldened by the triumph of northern arms, President Abraham Lincoln issued a preliminary Emancipation Proclamation that transformed the war into a crusade against slavery. In so doing, he etched Sharpsburg and the Battle of Antietam into the nation's historical memory.[2]

The sleepy village had witnessed other struggles over slavery. One of these battles erupted on the night of 31 December 1803, when the barn and stables on George Carey's farm burst into flames. While the buildings burned, free black Edward "Ned" Ford; his enslaved wife, "Negro Nancy"; and Ludwick Speice's slave, "Negro Anthony," took advantage of the confusion to break into a nearby store and steal a chest that contained eighteen hundred dollars in banknotes and silver and several yards of cloth. Within a week, the three suspects were apprehended and lodged in the Washington County jail. Under pressure from county authorities, who needed his assistance to convict Ford and Nancy, the twenty-five-year-old Anthony confessed to arson and burglary and testified against his codefendants. Although his testimony was inadmissible in Ford's trial for arson, it was sufficient to secure his conviction for theft, which translated into a six-year stint laboring on the public roads and a six-year prison sentence. For receiving stolen merchandise, the court sentenced Nancy to be "burnt on the crown of the thumb." In recognition of Anthony's services, the court petitioned Governor Robert Bowie for a pardon, arguing that "it was necessary to make use of Anthony as a witness for the state" and that he had been "directed and influenced by Ned." Bowie agreed. On 26 March 1804, he issued a pardon "on the express condition that the master of the said Anthony do within one hundred days . . . sell [him] to some person residing out of the State of Maryland." Speice had purchased his only slave a mere three years earlier but raised no objections to the governor's decision. On 3 May, Speice removed Anthony from the county jail and sold him to Benjamin Dorsey, a slave trader who was driving a coffle overland to Georgia. The human chattels had not marched more than thirty miles when Anthony struck for freedom. Eager to be reunited with his wife, also a slave, Anthony slipped from Dorsey's clutches near Winchester, Virginia, and fled to the neighborhood of his wife's master, near Sharpsburg. Anthony's freedom was short-lived. On 24 July, Sheriff Nathaniel Rochester recorded Anthony's arrest and imprisonment in the county gaol. But Anthony was not done fighting. After being auctioned in September, he "immediately" escaped and disappeared, leaving the frustrated sheriff to conclude that "it is probable he is now lurking about . . . Sharpsburg."[3]

Anthony was not alone in challenging slavery on the farms and small plantations that dotted the countryside around Sharpsburg. Decades before the Mumma farmstead was embroiled in some of the heaviest fighting of the Battle of Antietam—fighting that reduced its barn to smoldering ruins—Jacob Mumma Sr. and his family fought a series of skirmishes with their slaves. Despite or perhaps because of the small size of their slaveholding, which never exceeded four slaves, the Mumma family had a tenuous grasp on their bondspeople. In 1799, the elder Mumma provided Harry with a pass ("written in German") to visit Frederick. With few opportunities for family or community life on his home place, Harry may have been visiting kinfolk. He seized this opportunity to flee, possibly with the assistance of "a free black woman, by the name of Nancy." Harry was captured but remained unbowed. In March 1801, he made another unsuccessful bid for freedom. Tensions must have been running high on the Mumma place, for the slow drumbeat of escapes continued over the following years. A "deformed leg" and "half worn shoes" did not prevent George Amos from decamping in June 1806. In April 1807, Mumma announced the escape of a "negro man named Perry." By the end of the summer, he was advertising for the return of Sarah, a young woman who spoke "tolerable good German and English" and who had escaped with a "mulatto fellow at Hughes's forge." Yet another slave fled in 1814. That August, a "remarkably strong built" blacksmith, Sam Tilman, ran away. The slaves may have struck their most decisive blow on 2 January 1822, when fire consumed the Mumma barn along with between four thousand and five thousand dollars' worth of grain and livestock. Suspicion soon focused on a slave. "It is supposed," reported a newspaper, "that it was set by a negro who belonged to Mr. Mumma." Mumma fingered the truculent Harry as the arsonist, but the bondsman once again defied his master's authority by pleading not guilty and beating the charges.[4]

I began *Gleanings of Freedom* with the simple goal of shedding some light on these and other enslaved people who lived, worked, and fought for their freedom along Mason and Dixon's Line. After a decade of research and writing, I have come to appreciate that their lives were but one string in an often tangled skein. As I fumbled with (and occasionally cursed at) this knotted mess, the threads of other stories emerged. It soon became apparent, for example, that the histories of "Negro Anthony" and Harry were inseparable from those of other workers. Indeed, the hallmark of northern Maryland's workforce was its diversity. The region's slaves toiled alongside "term slaves," free blacks, sharecroppers and tenant farmers, itinerant and often impoverished white hirelings, artisans, and displaced urban workers. Together, they formed a motley crew that one historian has likened to a whirling kaleidoscope or "an ever-changing mosaic of unfree and free laborers."[5] To tell their stories well, *Gleanings of Freedom* became a history of the entire rural workforce.

One need only glance at the ledgers of Harford County farmer, miller, and tavern keeper John Mitchell to sense the myriad bonds that developed between labor regimes and among workers. Between 1807 and 1830, Mitchell's crew included his family, his modest slaveholding of two people, and an ensemble of twenty-seven wage laborers, including free blacks, hired slaves, unskilled white laborers, and a smattering of artisans. Mitchell's various enterprises required a diverse, multifaceted workforce whose ranks expanded and contracted with the changing seasons and the varied fortunes of the economy. Among his workers were two hired slaves and at least four free blacks, among them "Negro Clem," who erected a post-and-rail fence in June 1811, and "Negro Wapping Talbot" and his son, Joe, who labored intermittently between April and November 1808. They toiled alongside poor, semiskilled whites such as Vinson Rickets. From April through July 1807, Rickets worked as a farmhand, reaping oats, wheat, and a monthly wage of between eight and ten dollars. Rickets, who may have lacked a permanent home, resurfaced in Mitchell's account book during the winter of 1808, when he accrued debts for room and board. Artisans, too, made their homes with Mitchell. Cooper Matthias Havern lived on his employer's property from 1808 to 1810. In exchange for lodging, tobacco, brandy, clothing, and tools, Havern knocked together 474 fish and flour barrels, which Mitchell sold to merchants in Havre de Grace and Baltimore. Mitchell further augmented his workforce by swapping labor with nearby families. These transactions were enmeshed in networks of exchange and reciprocity that knitted together his rural neighborhood. For example, Mitchell loaned money to farmer John Fulton and provided him with flaxseed, corn, bacon, and cider. Fulton repaid some of these debts with cash and wheat, but he squared most of his accounts by cutting wheat, cleaning flax, and weaving cloth. For large undertakings, such as raising a barn or husking corn, Mitchell mobilized the entire neighborhood by hosting "frolics" that featured drinking, dancing, and more than a little sweat.[6] To succeed as a farmer and merchant, Mitchell needed to be something of an alchemist, blending together workers who were enslaved and free, black and white, skilled and unskilled.

Laborers forged economic partnerships, friendships, and romances at workplaces and at the fairgrounds, taverns, and rural crossroads where they gathered to dance, drink, gamble, and peddle their wares. These often raucous gatherings brought together people of diverse races and statuses. In 1786, a Frederick newspaper cautioned townsfolk to be "upon their guard" against the "great concourse of blacks, yellows, and whites" who spent their evenings cockfighting and "the rest of the night stealing what they get." For poor whites eking out livings, these frolics provided opportunities to do business with slaves. In 1801, Francis Clark ran afoul of county authorities for peddling liquor in small quantities (and without a license), for purchasing a box of window glass from a slave, and for "receiving from Negro George, the slave of Francis Thomas, seven geese and six eggs." The bonds between blacks and whites were not always born of necessity. During the revolutionary and early national decades, the workers on the bottom rungs of the ladder sometimes formed close, long-standing relationships. In 1778, Sarah, a "lusty" and "likely molatto wench," and her son escaped from George Fox's plantation in Frederick County. Sarah's master believed that this bondswoman, who spoke "good English and Dutch," had fled with Valentine Lind, an itinerant tailor who plied his trade in the neighborhood. "'Tis supposed they have one or more horses with them," he continued, "and may possibly attempt to pass for man and wife." Washington County slave owner Charles Darnel similarly suspected that his runaway bondswoman, Peggy, was "lurking" around Funkstown, Maryland, where she "co-habits with a certain white man, named John Carr, an Irishman," who "may conceal her, and be accessory towards her making her escape."[7]

At times, the alliances between workers undercut or even overturned the arithmetic that equated whiteness with freedom and blackness with slavery. Although a century had passed since the "giddy multitude" of indentured servants and slaves last challenged the power of the Chesapeake planters, whites and blacks continued to find common cause.[8] White servants and black slaves sometimes found a rough equality among themselves. In 1778, Frederick County master Basil Dorsey offered a $150 reward for the capture of his "likely active Negro man . . . Charles," who had escaped with Dorsey's "English convict servant lad," John Barnham. A vast difference existed in these workers' legal statuses, not least because the convict would be free in four years, but their material conditions were sometimes quite similar.[9] Dorsey noted that Barnham wore "nearly the same dress as the slave" and warned any would-be captor that both of these "great villains" should be "well ironed." When whites and blacks mingled, the white servants sometimes found themselves in the inferior legal position. For example, after surrendering with the British at Yorktown, Thomas Salmon bound himself as a carpenter at Roger Johnson's iron furnace in Frederick County. There, Salmon married a free black woman, fathered several children, and incurred his master's wrath by escaping to Baltimore. The subversive potential of such relationships haunted masters. Whenever possible, those who commanded laborers attempted to sever the connections among those on society's lowest rungs. In 1819, planter John Thomson Mason accused John Duncan of selling liquor without a license, harboring a slave, purchasing stolen merchandise from a slave, and "keeping a disorderly house and permitting negro slaves and others to gamble."[10]

The story that unfolded on the sectional border affirms, at least partially, Marx's dictum that "labor cannot emancipate itself in the white skin where in the black skin it is branded."[11] Free labor and free workers, including many who wore black skin, were shaped by the presence of the peculiar institution, just as slavery and the enslaved were influenced by the wage laborers in their midst. Sometimes we can glimpse these connections in the lives of individual families. From 1810 to 1820, "Negro Stephen" worked as a carpenter and farmhand on the Frederick County plantation where his wife and their three children were enslaved. In 1810, Stephen purchased and liberated his wife, Will, who occasionally worked alongside her husband. By 1814, they had scrimped and saved enough to hire their daughters Polly (age twenty-one) and Sarah (age eleven), but the couple's young son, Stephen (age five), and an unnamed infant remained with their master. The slave owner's decision to retain control of Stephen's namesake and the baby may have reflected an unwillingness to loosen his grip on the family. It is also possible, however, that these transactions were guided by Stephen and Will's shrewd calculations about their children's potential value on the labor market. Unlike their younger siblings, Polly and Sarah could make immediate contributions toward the family's freedom.[12] Stephen, Will, and their children had gleaned an essential lesson about slavery and freedom in this corner of the Upper South:

Employers' need for hired help might crack open the door to freedom, but slavery cast a long shadow over the emerging free labor market.

The worlds of "Negro Stephen" and of the enslaved and free workers who toiled alongside him in the Maryland countryside have received scant attention from scholars. This historical silence is especially deafening when attempting to understand the lives of free black and white farmhands. Despite their newfound interest in unskilled "common" laborers, most scholars attending to these workers have focused on canals, cities, or other modernizing sectors of the economy.[13] Few historians have examined the men and women who tilled the nation's fields. A similar trend prevails in the historiography of southern free blacks, where scholars have fixated on cities to the virtual exclusion of rural black communities.[14] The few social histories that focus on antebellum farmhands are primarily descriptive.[15] Those scholars who have attempted more rigorous examinations of agricultural laborers have been primarily interested in tracing the evolution of a rural proletariat, a pursuit that is often subsumed under larger questions about the roots of capitalism in the countryside.[16] Much ground remains unbroken, and this field of inquiry is fertile and promises great yields. The lives of the men and women who worked the land along the Mason-Dixon Line open a window onto the evolution of race, class, and labor regimes in the early national and antebellum United States.

While casting about for a theoretical framework that would allow me to make sense of the stories of "Negro Anthony," "Negro Stephen," and their white counterparts, I was drawn to the work of anthropologist and historian Sidney Mintz. Although best known for his work on slave and postslave societies in the Caribbean, Mintz has made observations about the profound linkages between labor regimes that seem germane to northern Maryland. In 1974, Mintz argued that an economy could "only be fully understood when slavery, contract labor, forced labor, and all other means of relating to the instruments of production are seen in relation to one another."[17] He was convinced that different systems "were not interchangeable, each representing a variant response to labor needs, nor was it accidental or random that they usually occurred in combined forms." Mintz insisted that the various segments of a workforce were distinct, complementary, and interdependent, a conclusion that has been echoed in studies of such disparate settings as ancient Rome and the Panama Canal.[18]

Most historians of American workers have examined particular segments of the workforce in isolation, excising forms of labor extraction from their larger contexts and then teasing apart the various elements of workers' experiences. To the extent that other regimes and laborers are discussed, it is for comparative purposes alone. Still, the handful of scholars who have attempted integrative histories of the workers and labor regimes in a given industry have reached conclusions that tend to confirm Mintz's observations. John Bezís-Selfa's meticulous study of the iron industry in the colonial and early national Middle Atlantic demonstrates that foundry owners purchased slaves to reduce dependence on indentured servants and wage laborers. By creating an artificial labor surplus, iron masters depressed wages and made hired workers more tractable, thus spurring the development of "a wage-labor regime."[19] Decades later, the managers of Richmond's Tredegar Iron Works pursued a similar strategy. In 1847, white ironworkers struck over the management's decision to employ more slaves in skilled positions. Worried that a protracted labor struggle would expose economic and political fissures in southern society and that a victory for the strikers would threaten the slaveholders' property rights, the firm's managers replaced the white ironworkers with slaves. The crackdown on white workers was, according to one historian, needed to buttress "the social and political order necessary to upholding the slave regime."[20] The links between bound and free labor were no less important in the countryside. In antebellum North Carolina, Wayne K. Durrill has found that hired hands "served as a labor reserve for planters" and that an underground economy flourished between slaves and poorer whites.[21] Even the staunchest defenders of slavery conceded that certain segments of the southern economy would grind to a halt without wage laborers. Fire-eater Edmund Ruffin admitted that his wheat harvests could not be "executed very perfectly" because his "limited force" of slaves was not equal to the labor demands of the harvest season and because hired hands were either unavailable or ungovernable. "No laborers, either reapers or binders, worth having, can be hired," he grumbled, "and all who seek for such employment in harvest, studiously avoid all farms where there is any heavy growth . . . and no whiskey is permitted."[22] In certain settings, unfree and free labor balanced each other; slaves could be used to bring unwieldy free workers to heel, and hired help was needed to keep the relatively inflexible system of slavery running smoothly.

Northern Maryland was no exception to this pattern. Its different forms of labor control were sometimes locked in competition, but they could also complement one another. For example, the landowners of the early republic used indentured servants to augment their slaves. In 1784, a Frederick County planter bequeathed to his son eight slaves and ordered his executor to purchase "two indentured farming white servants . . . who have four to five years to serve" for his son.[23] Five years later, Elie Williams described how wage labor, slavery, and tenancy worked together on his Washington County plantation. "In order to enable Dutch John & my negro men to clean up & sow in good order" and "make other necessary and profitable improvements," he needed to bolster his crew with a tenant who would "work the fields, which are not in grain on a share."[24] Although the composition of the workforce changed over time, employers never stopped splicing together crews from different segments of the labor pool. In 1829, Sharpsburg planter John Blackford harvested his wheat with the assistance of his five enslaved men, four free blacks (three men and a woman who raked), at least ten white farmhands, and a hired slave woman who cooked.[25]

By reconstructing and reintegrating the histories of northern Maryland's free and enslaved farmhands, *Gleanings of Freedom* bridges the gulf separating two literatures and charts a course toward a broader, more inclusive history of American workers. Treating the workforce as a single, unified whole illuminates not only how laborers and labor regimes interacted but also how they evolved. The need for such a holistic approach has grown more pressing as historians begin to reassess the relationship between slavery and free labor, a relationship that was once presented as a stark and static dichotomy. Historians have recognized that these systems were not always polar opposites; they existed along a spectrum of free and unfree labor regimes whose parameters shifted over time. Examining the sources of this historiographical turn, Bezís-Selfa identifies three important developments that have "narrowed the conceptual gap between the two systems." First, some historians have discovered that "masters and employers posed fundamentally similar challenges to slaves and employees, who in turn fashioned similar tactics to accomplish similar objectives." Second, scholars have become more attuned to those settings where slavery operated in conjunction with a myriad of labor regimes. Finally, historians have shown that the growth of free labor was a halting, uneven process. As the system matured during the eighteenth and nineteenth centuries, many nominally free workers found themselves laboring under a constellation of legal constraints and forms of discrimination that circumscribed their freedom.[26]

When viewed as an economic, legal, or political abstraction, the slave-free divide seems precise and unambiguous. In practice, however, the distinctions were sometimes blurred. As historian O. Nigel Boland notes, labor regimes seldom conform to their legal ideals. Slavery could mimic its ostensible opposite. The enslaved occasionally earned cash wages and engaged in petty production, while their owners embraced elements of bourgeois modernity and attempted to imbue the institution with the flexibility usually associated with free labor. If slavery's daily operations bore little resemblance to the norms prescribed in southern law, neither was the institution the archaic, outmoded form of production described by abolitionists. Like free labor, slavery proved adaptive, malleable, and able to flourish in a variety of industries.[27]

Such interpretations have muddied the waters separating slavery and free labor but have not gone unchallenged. Edmund S. Morgan offers a forceful rejoinder to those seeking to narrow the distance between slavery and free labor: "There could be grades of status within slavery, some slaves winning more privileges than others, but there was no halfway house between slavery and freedom, no set of steps that led progressively from one to the other."[28] In a similar vein, Tom Brass has challenged those who "seek either to dissolve the free-unfree distinction or else to dismiss its significance." Brass contends that a fundamental, unbending difference existed between slavery and free labor. While conceding that the definitions of and distinctions between free and unfree labor were historically constructed and that these forms of labor extraction might operate in tandem, Brass insists that these machinations neither blurred nor undermined the boundary between slavery and freedom.[29]

The debates about slavery's relationship with free labor have been complicated by an outpouring of local studies that document the almost endless variations of slavery. "It is increasingly clear," observes Peter Kolchin, "that we must come to grips not so much with slavery as with slaveries."[30] A distinction clearly existed between slavery and free labor, but the sharpness of that divide varies with one's vantage point. Indeed, we might liken the relationship between slavery and freedom to an image viewed through a lens that is shifting in and out of focus. The lines between slavery, wage labor, and the other forms of labor discipline become either clear or blurred as one proceeds through time. Moreover, the clarity of the image changes as one progresses downward from the level of ideological and legal debates through the operation of labor markets and finally to the level of individual workers.

Gleanings of Freedom is set in a narrow swath of territory near the Mason-Dixon Line. More specifically, it focuses on six Maryland counties that abutted the sectional border (Baltimore, Carroll, Cecil, Harford, Frederick, and Washington). Agriculture was the bedrock of the area's economy from the colonial decades through the Civil War. The earliest employment figures from Frederick County reveal that in 1820, approximately 68 percent of the free men whose occupations were recorded were engaged in agriculture. That figure was even higher in Washington County, where 74 percent of the workers earned their livings from the land.[31] The percentage of Frederick County's workforce engaged in agriculture remained constant through 1840, but in Washington County, that number dropped to 57 percent.[32] By 1860, approximately 26 percent of Frederick County's free workforce consisted of farmers, with an additional 41 percent composed of rural artisans (blacksmiths, coopers, and millers) and of laborers, a slippery term that encompassed farmhands, canal workers, and factory operatives.[33]

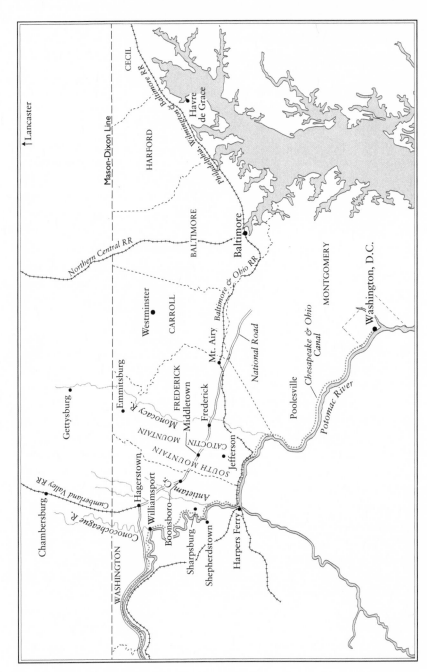

Map. The Upper South

Small farms dominated the countryside. In 1792, Governor Thomas Johnson wrote that land in Frederick County was "generally in small farms of 100 to 250 acres," while Englishman John Palmer observed that "the size of farms, near Hagerstown, is 200 acres, often half in wood."[34] This pattern seems to have persisted in subsequent decades. In 1835, Frederick County's tax assessment revealed that 90 percent of farms consisted of fewer than 300 acres.[35] By 1860, all but 16 of the county's 2,365 farms were less than 500 acres in size, as were 1,033 of the 1,038 farms in Washington County.[36]

The farms, plantations, and shops where "Negro Anthony," Harry, and their enslaved and free coworkers spent their lives were embedded in what historian Ira Berlin has dubbed a society with slaves. Like other areas where slavery was of little economic value, northern Maryland was a region where "slavery was just one form of labor among many" and where "no one presumed the master-slave relationship to be the social exemplar."[37] At the dawn of the nineteenth century, slaves constituted only 17 percent of northern Maryland's total population (see table 1 in chapter 1). A few miles away, Pennsylvania's Gradual Abolition Act of 1780 was further thinning the already sparse ranks of slaves and slave owners. In the counties north of the Mason-Dixon Line, the number of slaves plummeted from 6,855 in 1780–82 to a mere 795 in 1810.[38]

Northern Maryland was a checkerboard of farms and plantations tucked among rolling hills. Slavery may have been marginal to the local economy, but the institution lost none of its malignancy. At the dawn of the twentieth century, the few antiquarians and amateur historians who bothered to discuss slavery in northern Maryland concluded that it either withered or at least sprouted fewer thorns along the sectional border. "Property in man must have been very precarious," concluded a passenger on a train rumbling across the sectional border near Hagerstown, "for it required no superhuman effort for the slave to spring across this Mason & Dixon's Line and breathe the air of liberty." By the dawn of the twentieth century, many antiquarians had embraced the somewhat dubious notion that slave owners stayed their hands and lashes because they feared the specter of their chattels making the short dash to freedom. Explaining why slavery in his native Washington County was "necessarily of a mild character," Thomas J. C. Williams suggested that "any harsh treatment . . . resulted in a flight to Pennsylvania, and the recovery from that state, with many of its people in sympathy with the fugitives, was difficult." James Helman echoed these sentiments in his 1906 history of Emmitsburg, a tiny community located a mere mile south of Pennsylvania: "We were too near the Mason and Dixon line for slavery to exist. It was only by the kindest treatment [that slaves] could be kept."[39]

"Negro Anthony" would have known better. He and his fellow bondsmen and -women came of age during a time when the counties along the Mason-

Dixon Line were becoming dangerous terrain. The American Revolution may have shaken the foundations of slavery along the sectional border, but the institution retained its terrible vigor in Georgia, South Carolina, and the emerging plantation societies west of the Appalachians.[40] Indeed, the trader who bought "Negro Anthony" for the Georgia market was one of many kidnappers and speculators who prowled the Upper South looking for unfortunate victims to feed the Deep South's growing appetite for labor. Although it is difficult to gauge the extent of this trade during the 1790s and 1800s, it seems clear that northern Marylanders were feeling its effects. As early as 1792, two Frederick County slaves struck their master in a "fit of desperation or madness" after learning that he intended to take them to Kentucky and then "to New Orleans [and] sell them to the Spaniards."[41] By 1807, the traffic had reached such levels that a Hagerstown newspaper published a poem decrying "the inhuman practice of negro buying, which is so unfortunately prevalent in this county." In the piece, a slave is snatched away by "a despot fierce, [who] has marked him for his prey; and though his cries the heavens pierce, he bears him far away."[42]

Northern Maryland also felt the repercussions of the domestic trade that was gouging the slave communities of the Chesapeake. By 1800, tobacco planters on the Eastern Shore and in southern Maryland were reeling from stagnant markets and had begun hemorrhaging slaves to the Deep South. The trade spawned rumors of revolt, a spike in the number of runaway slaves, and wave of resistance that spilled into the counties on the Mason-Dixon Line. In 1800, the sheriff of Washington County arrested a slave from Kent County who had recently been purchased by "a gentleman in Savannah in the state of Georgia." John Gassaway slipped away from his master during the long march from Kent Island to Natchez and briefly eluded his captors in Frederick County. "Negro Bob" was more successful. This Caroline County bondsman escaped from "a dealer in negroes, living in North or South Carolina" and spent fourteen months lurking about Washington County.[43]

As the trade gained momentum, many enslaved and free blacks on the sectional border learned that the door between slavery and freedom swung not only violently and unpredictably but also both ways. People freed by Pennsylvania's Gradual Abolition Act or by Maryland slave owners who took advantage of their state's liberalized manumission laws were among those spirited to the Deep South. In 1802, for example, Matthew Patton of Chester-Town, Maryland, notified the Pennsylvania Abolition Society that freedman Abraham Green had been abducted by "Georgia Men" and sold to a resident of Hagerstown, who subsequently held him "a long time as a slave." Patton was, however, optimistic that Green could be freed and "paid for what time he has been there" if a copy of his manumission could be secured.[44] That same year, the grand jury of Alexandria, Virginia, complained that traders "from distant parts of the United States" were prowling the town for slaves. Not only did the jurors lament seeing "parents being wrested from their offspring and children from their parents," they also bemoaned the "practice of persons making sale of black people who are by will of their masters designed to be free at the expiration of a term of years."[45] The threats that emerged during the early national period became more dangerous over the following decades. Indeed, the intertwined evils of kidnapping and sale to the Deep South loomed over African Americans through the early years of the Civil War.[46]

In this chaotic and sometimes violent setting, the crude geography that pointed north to freedom and south to slavery was sometimes unreliable. As sectional differences emerged and hardened in the 1790s and 1800s, free and enslaved blacks crisscrossed the Mason-Dixon Line in ways that muddied sectional differences. A few enslaved and free blacks from Pennsylvania sought refuge in Maryland. In 1800, for example, Sheriff John Waggoner of Washington County arrested "Negro Joseph," an aged bondsman who claimed to be the property of Samuel Lukings of York County, Pennsylvania. Authorities in neighboring Frederick County imprisoned "Gregg," who confessed to his jailers that "he belongs to Mr. McPherson, living about two miles from Gettysburg."[47]

While slavery went through its death throes north of the Mason-Dixon Line, a few Pennsylvania slave owners and slaves trickled into northern Maryland. Reluctant to surrender their bondsmen and -women, some masters spirited them south. In 1791, for example, John McPherson transported his slave, Cyrus, from Pennsylvania to Frederick County. Fearful that his home state's abolition statute would deprive him of the services of a valuable farmhand, McPherson agreed to manumit his twenty-two-year-old slave provided that he "indenture himself to serve the said John McPherson for the term of seventeen years."[48] Cyrus was not the only bound laborer to cross the Mason-Dixon Line. In 1804, Frederick County farmer Philip Dietrich sold Thomas, a young slave, to another Marylander for two hundred dollars. In the bill of sale, Dietrich explained that Thomas had been born near Lancaster around 1786 and had been sold to five different masters in southern Pennsylvania before being purchased by Dietrich. Dietrich stipulated that Pennsylvania's laws must be honored and that Thomas would therefore "be free at age twenty-eight."[49]

Pennsylvanians who settled in northern Maryland sometimes brought their slaves with them. When Mary Brown arrived from Adams County, Pennsylvania, she brought along "Negro Phillis," then aged twenty-five.[50] Brown safeguarded the young woman's prospective freedom by registering her with the Frederick

County court, but others were less scrupulous. In 1785, Pennsylvanian William Kelso ignored the provision of his state's gradual abolition law that required masters to register their slaves with county officials and sold "Negro Diana" as a slave for life in Montgomery County, Maryland, where she was subsequently resold to Frederick County resident Thomas West.[51] Pennsylvanian Abraham Green suffered a similar fate.

Enslaved Marylanders who reached Pennsylvania found that free soil offered no reprieve from slavery. Both the Pennsylvania Gradual Abolition Act of 1780 and the federal Fugitive Slave Law of 1793 allowed slaveholders to reclaim their human chattels, and at least some Pennsylvanians were more than willing to assist in the recovery process. In July 1816, the *Chambersburg Democratic Republican* announced in a Hagerstown paper, "Out of 15 runaway negroes advertised in [the Chambersburg] paper, since February last, 12 have been recovered."[52] Others, however, were less supportive of slaveholders' rights. The Pennsylvania Abolition Society offered legal assistance to fugitive slaves and some local officials were unsympathetic toward slaveholders. In a 1796 petition to the Maryland General Assembly, William Handy of Worcester County complained that "the abolition society, in conjunction with the civil officers of Pennsylvania, have deprived him of his negroes, and arrested his person."[53] "Negro Anthony" and the black people who lived along the Mason-Dixon Line were caught in the undertow of two currents, one that pulled them north toward an uncertain freedom and another that wrenched them toward slavery. The tension between these forces never went away but continued to spark desperate flights to freedom and pitched battles between blacks and their enslavers until the Civil War.[54]

Freedom may have beckoned across the Mason-Dixon Line, but the short passage from slavery was fraught with dangers. Indeed, Frederick Douglass believed that "the nearer were the lines of a slave state to the borders of a free state the greater was trouble" confronting runaways. Slave catchers and their associates were a constant danger, but a weak grasp of the terrain beyond their neighborhoods also hobbled many slaves. To readers who found it "quite absurd" that his escape from the Eastern Shore of Maryland was a "formidable undertaking," Douglass retorted, "The real distance was great enough, but the imagined distance was, to our ignorance much greater. . . . Our notions of the geography of the country were very vague and indistinct." The border between free and slave territory was unmarked, and freedom seekers sometimes lost their bearings. In 1842, for example, twenty-six fugitives from Anne Arundel County, Maryland, became "bewildered" near York, Pennsylvania, and began walking south. Washington County slave James W. C. Pennington confronted similar obstacles when he resolved to flee from his master in the autumn of 1827. "How can I expect to succeed," he fretted, when "I have no knowledge of distance or direction—I know that Pennsylvania is a free state, but I know not where its soil begins or that of Maryland ends." Pennington's fears were not groundless. After creeping along northern Maryland's roads for several days, he was dismayed to learn that he had traveled east, not north, and was eighteen miles west of Baltimore. His uncertainty lingered as he pressed northward. "I know not at what point I should strike Pennsylvania," he wrote, "or when I should find a friend."[55]

The confusion that gripped Pennington and other fugitives reflected something more than mere ignorance of "distance and direction." The Mason-Dixon Line may have figured prominently on maps and in slaves' imaginations, but it was invisible to those on the ground. Travel narratives from the early republic suggest that the distinctions between slave and free territory were imperceptible when one stood near the border; the differences appeared gradually as people traveled deeper into the South. Describing his southward journey from Pennsylvania to Frederick and Montgomery Courthouse in Maryland, Englishman Isaac Weld noted that "the change in the face of the country after leaving Frederick is gradual, but at the end of a day's journey a striking difference is perceptible." The "well cultivated fields, green with wheat," were replaced by vast tracts of abandoned and exhausted tobacco fields. As he neared his destination, Weld sensed a more profound transformation. Frederick's yeoman farmers disappeared, and "the eye is assailed in every direction with the unpleasant sight of gangs of . . . slaves toiling under the harsh command of the overseer." As Weld's account suggests, the Mason-Dixon Line sometimes appeared as more of a smudge, leading one scholar to dub the region the "Chesapeake borderlands."[56]

Northern Maryland bore the indelible marks of the societies whose collision and confluence during the eighteenth century had created a setting where slavery and free labor jostled, mingled, and merged. Pennsylvania Germans settled much of this borderland and left their marks on everything from farm management to folk architecture.[57] The diffusion of crops and farming practices blurred the border between Maryland and Pennsylvania; the primary crops grown by farmers on both sides of the Mason-Dixon Line were wheat, oats, and rye, along with a variety of garden crops. Not surprisingly, agricultural writers treated the Middle Atlantic as a single, unified whole. "Jersey, Pennsylvania, Delaware, and Maryland may be classed together, from a resemblance of climate, soil, and mode of cultivation," argued one writer, while President George Washington lumped together several Maryland and Pennsylvania counties, declaring them "inferior in their natural state to none in America."[58]

The rhythms of agricultural production and the movement of commodities, manufactured goods, and people bound together the counties of northern Maryland and southern Pennsylvania. Throughout the early national and antebellum decades, a fierce struggle between the merchants of Baltimore and Philadelphia for the region's surplus prompted the construction of an extensive network of turnpikes, canals, and railroads that fused the border counties into a series of "overlapping hinterlands."[59] By 1800, wagons hauling produce across the Mason-Dixon Line had become a common sight on country roads. Improvements in the transportation network strengthened interstate connections. In 1823, the completion of turnpikes and canals across the Susquehanna River allowed an "abundant supply of fine Pennsylvania butter, poultry, eggs, [and] pork" from Lancaster County to flood Baltimore's markets.[60] Later that decade, a writer from Gettysburg announced that two turnpikes made Baltimore "the nearest market for the products of our soil." Wheat, rye, corn, barley, and oats were the main products that Pennsylvanians carted to Maryland, "in addition to which a large quantity of pork is annually hauled to said city for sale."[61] In 1835, the completion of the Chesapeake and Ohio Canal to Williamsport attracted produce from farmers in Franklin County, Pennsylvania, who proclaimed the Maryland entrepôt their "natural outlet."[62]

Whatever similarities existed between Maryland and Pennsylvania, the counties of the Upper South differed fundamentally from their northern neighbors because they were embedded in a slave state. Yet slavery's roots ran shallow along the Mason-Dixon Line. The area's farmers and planters raised some tobacco but otherwise grew none of the traditional slave staples. Wheat, corn, cattle, and dairy products were the foundation of the region's agricultural economy. Slaves never accounted for more than a quarter of the area's population, and by 1860, their presence had been whittled down to a numerical and statistical nub. Slaveholders who met the conventional definition of *planters* (owning twenty slaves) were few and far between. In 1820, 32 of the 1,520 slave owners in Frederick County were planters, while a mere 13 of the 732 masters and mistresses in Washington County could claim the title.[63] Manumission and sale winnowed the ranks of planters over the following decades. In 1860, the census recorded only 8 planters among the 794 slaveholders in Frederick County; 2 among the 398 slave owners in Washington County; and only a single case among the 208 masters and mistresses in Carroll County.[64] Masters had little sense of themselves as a distinct class and seldom flexed their political muscle in defense of the peculiar institution.

One of the more frustrating aspects of this study has been the difficulty of tracking change over time. Certain demographic, economic, and legal developments can be traced with relative ease. The dwindling slave population, the stagnation of farm wages, and the worsening legal climate for free blacks can be documented with certainty, but other parts of this history do not lend themselves to a linear narrative. Northern Maryland's history had few decisive turning points during the early national and antebellum periods, though I do not mean to suggest that this historical terrain was flat and undifferentiated. Maryland's economy was volatile. Farmers basked in prosperity during the Napoleonic Wars, felt the sharp pangs of uncertainty during the Panic of 1819, and spent the 1820s and 1830s languishing under "hard times." These upheavals had real consequences, influencing manumission rates, the interstate slave trade, and attitudes toward free labor. Significant strands of continuity are, however, apparent in this book. For example, whether they lived in 1790 or 1860, rural laborers were dogged by seasonal unemployment and haunted by the specter of disease and injury. The task of measuring change is further complicated by the marginality of the workingmen and -women whose experiences lie at the heart of this study. Reconstructing their lives has been akin to weaving a tapestry from short, often disparate strands. The snippets—mere glimpses—of their lives found in almshouse records, in court papers, in plantation ledgers, and occasionally in newspapers have yielded a composite biography that is both unrelentingly grim and at times regrettably static.

The opening chapter, "'The Land Flows with Milk and Honey': Agriculture and Labor in the Early Republic," examines northern Maryland's economy and workforce from the 1790s through the 1810s. These were prosperous times. The Napoleonic Wars disrupted farming and trade in Europe and the Caribbean, creating a void that allowed Americans to reap a windfall by supplying the belligerents and their colonies with foodstuffs. As commodity prices soared, northern Marylanders waded deeper into export markets and were drawn more closely into Baltimore's commercial orbit. In these heady decades, many people cast caution to the wind, speculating in land, purchasing consumer goods on credit, and amassing fortunes in dubious notes issued by rural banks and turnpike companies.

To keep their farms, mills, and ships running, employers stitched together workforces from whatever pieces were available. Experimentation and opportunism were the hallmarks of labor arrangements; farmers eager to increase production purchased slaves, engaged indentured servants, and hired wage laborers. No consensus existed on the relative merits of different labor regimes, and few believed that free and unfree labor were incompatible. Moreover, the boundaries, definitions, and future of the region's labor regimes remained unsettled. Indentured servitude was waning and coming under increased scrutiny, but bound whites continued to toil alongside enslaved blacks. Having weathered the American Revolution, slavery seemed poised to expand from Maryland's tobacco-producing counties to its northern reaches. In the years following independence, tobacco planters on the Eastern Shore and in southern Maryland staggered under the combined weight of debts and flagging markets. Many farmers switched from tobacco to grain, thereby creating a surplus of slave labor that was partially absorbed by farmers and planters in the prosperous counties along the Mason-Dixon Line. In some northern Maryland counties, the growth of the slave population outpaced that of the white population between 1790 and 1820. Still, slavery's long-term future was uncertain. Maryland had liberalized its manumission laws after the revolution, and the free black population of the state's northern counties dramatically increased during the early republic. The expansion of slavery was, to a certain extent, a product of employers' ambivalence toward hired laborers. Farmers often balked at hirelings, who commanded high wages and possessed greater legal freedoms in the postrevolutionary decades. Stripped of the legal compulsions they had once wielded over hired laborers and denied the right to punish free workers physically, many employers doubted whether hirelings could be molded into an efficient workforce.

The constellation of labor arrangements in northern Maryland began to realign during the 1810s and 1820s. The ideological and legal borders between free and unfree labor hardened and became increasingly rigid as the antebellum decades progressed. Chapter 2, "'A Strange Reverse of Fortune': Panic, Depression, and the Transformation of Labor," examines the causes of this transformation and considers why many of northern Maryland's farmers and planters abandoned slavery and embraced free labor. The roots of this momentous change lie in both national trends and developments specific to northern Maryland. A variety of national as well as local economic, legal, and political forces conspired against indentured servitude in the decades following the revolution, thus obliterating an important halfway house between slavery and free labor. Without indentured servitude, labor arrangements were increasingly divided into a dichotomy of slavery and free labor. The strains on northern Maryland's economy during the lean years that followed the end of the Napoleonic Wars widened the chasm between slavery and free labor. The return of peace brought the region's decades of prosperity to a crashing halt. Stagnating commodity markets, financial panics, crop failures, and increased competition from western farmers combined to create an economic malaise that lasted from the 1820s to the 1840s.

Hard times forced landowners to scrutinize their operations and to reconsider the composition of their workforces. Eager to resurrect northern Maryland's fortunes, agricultural reformers and political economists implored landholders to rid themselves of slaves and to employ wage laborers, a move reformers believed would foster agricultural innovation and promote European immigration. Farmers struggling to regain their footing became convinced that slavery was an outmoded, inefficient form of labor extraction and, perhaps more important, an impediment to recovery. A growing chorus of writers posited a stark dichotomy between slavery and free labor that locked these institutions in an almost Manichaean struggle for supremacy.

Not only was slave property deemed unprofitable, it was becoming untenable. During the late eighteenth and early nineteenth centuries, Pennsylvania was transformed into free soil and a haven for runaway slaves through the workings of its gradual emancipation act and the implementation of anti-kidnapping statutes and a personal liberty law. Faced with an economy that was in the doldrums and fearful that their slaves would escape northward, slaveholders on the sectional border began to rid themselves of their human chattels. The number of manumissions climbed during the 1820s as owners grew more apprehensive about the security of slave property and more confident in their ability to command free laborers. The decision to abandon slavery did not necessarily entail financial loss, for the onset of hard times in northern Maryland coincided with slavery's expansion into the Deep South. Eager to mend finances that had been torn during the 1810s and 1820s, northern Maryland's slave owners consigned hundreds, perhaps thousands, of bondspeople to the South's cotton and sugar plantations. Growing involvement in the interstate trade accelerated slavery's decline within the region. The constant threat of sale drove the enslaved to greater acts of resistance, which, in turn, compelled more slave owners to manumit their chattels, sell them south, or risk the total loss of their financial value and labor through flight. The combined effects of manumission, flight, and sale were soon apparent in census returns: Between 1820 and 1860, northern Maryland's slave population dropped precipitously.

Yet the turn from slavery to wage labor did not result in a sudden, complete restructuring of the rural workforce. Unlike the Deep South, where freedom struck with a thunderclap amid the Civil War, northern Maryland experienced emancipation as a long, extended process. While slavery lingered, farmers continued to cobble together workforces from slaves, free blacks, and hired whites. Their strategies for recruiting and disciplining these often diverse crews are examined in chapter 3, "'There Are Objections to Black and White, but One Must Be Chosen': Managing Farms and Farmhands in Antebellum Maryland." Regardless of the composition of their workforces, landowners labored under certain imperatives: They needed to eliminate or at least trim the cost of supporting their workers' dependent kin and to rid themselves of surplus hands during slower seasons while guaranteeing a workforce adequate for harvesting wheat. As Barbara Jeanne Fields has observed, Marylanders "wanted to have it

both ways. They wanted labor readily available when they needed it and prepared to serve on terms they found acceptable—something that slavery could
guarantee. But they did not want the charge upon their operating capital of
maintaining that labor when they did not need its services—something that
slavery required."[65] To balance these competing imperatives, employers of free
labor winnowed workers they perceived as unproductive—women, children,
the elderly—from their rolls and crafted economic and legal stratagems to
bring hired farmhands to heel. For their part, slave owners grafted the most
attractive elements of free labor onto the peculiar institution. They offered
cash payments to induce the enslaved to work harder at harvest. They found
additional chores to occupy their slaves during slack times. They dangled
the promise of freedom to guarantee bondspeople's obedience. And they
began shifting the burden of slaves' support and reproduction onto their
free black relatives. Likewise, all landowners struggled to break their free and
enslaved workers of the excessive drinking and other preindustrial habits that
characterized farmwork. Thus, when viewed from the perspective of northern
Maryland's farmers and planters, the distinction between slavery and free labor
appears murky: The seasonal rhythms of wheat production shaped both.

Yet efforts to transplant slavery to the Maryland Piedmont exposed the
limits of the institution's flexibility. On the most basic level, masters found that
slavery and grain farming were an imperfect fit because women and children
were incapable of performing many essential tasks. Most women and children lacked the upper-body strength to swing cradles and scythes during the
harvest, and few could steer the heavy double-shovel plows used for planting.
While landowners could refuse to support their free workers' dependents,
those who owned enslaved men and their families were burdened with supporting workers whose productive labor was sometimes of little immediate
value to them. In a larger sense, northern Maryland provided poor soil for
slavery because the daily routines of wheat production diluted slaveholders'
mastery. Unlike their counterparts in the Deep South, who toiled in gangs
under overseers' watchful eyes, slaves in northern Maryland often worked
alone or in small squads alongside free blacks and white hirelings. In such
settings, slaves attempting to escape found innumerable opportunities to steal
a march on their pursuers and sometimes discovered allies among their free
black coworkers.

Although slavery and free labor coexisted on northern Maryland's farms,
the boundary between slavery and freedom was neither obscured nor undermined. When viewed through the lens of individual slaves and slaveholders,
the distinctions between slavery and freedom snap into sharp relief. Both
masters and their bondspeople were mindful that their remote corner of

slavery's empire was enmeshed in a larger plantation complex. The interstate slave trade cut broad swathes through northern Maryland's slave communities and spurred the enslaved to seek freedom through flight, the threat of which sometimes prodded slaveholders toward manumission.

Chapter 4, "' . . . How Much of Oursels We Owned': Finding Freedom along the Mason-Dixon Line," continues the examination of manumission, the interstate slave trade, and resistance begun in the preceding chapters but devotes particular attention to the unequal negotiations between masters and mistresses eager to preserve slavery and bondspeople desperate to escape. Both parties confronted two central and inescapable realities: The enslaved could inflict grievous financial losses on their owners by escaping to Pennsylvania, and slaveholders could destroy black families and communities by selling slaves south. Located hard against free soil, slaveholders had to wield the instruments of their power with restraint: A flogging or the threat of sale might send slaves fleeing into Pennsylvania. To restore a tenuous peace and to eliminate the intertwined threats of flight and sale, slaveholders and their chattels hammered out delayed manumission or term slavery agreements whereby slave owners promised to free their slaves after a certain date, a pledge that was contingent on the slaves' continued obedience. Bondsmen and -women who entered into such agreements received not only the promise of freedom but also a legal guarantee that they would not be sold outside Maryland. Slave owners thus negated the threat of flight and found a new means of extracting years of labor from their slaves, while the enslaved secured protection from the ravages of the interstate trade.

The wall separating slavery and freedom may have been the most prominent feature in northern Maryland's labor market, but the terrain of free labor was neither stable nor unvaried. Indeed, the rocky ground trod by free black and white farmhands belied the idealized image of free labor that abolitionists and liberal economists had forged as a counterpoint to slavery.[66] Chapter 5, "'Chased Out on the Slippery Ice': Rural Wage Laborers in Antebellum Maryland," examines how landless workers survived in an economy whose defining characteristics were scarcity and uncertainty. Unskilled and unorganized, rural free laborers faced a desperate struggle for survival; they were buffeted by seasonal and cyclical unemployment, and their nonwage economic activities were constricted by a legal system that was designed to maintain slaveholders' authority. Single women's prospects were especially dismal. Unable to perform the heavier types of agricultural labor and confronting a labor market that pegged their wages lower than men's, women eked out a living on the margins of the rural economy. At the same time, the growing number of African Americans who escaped slavery discovered that the institution cast a long shadow. Denied the labor of relatives who remained in bondage and hindered by laws that circumscribed their movements and limited their economic options, free blacks found themselves in a legal shadow land. In the end, these workers were often left with the mere gleanings of freedom.

The conclusion examines the interplay among the multiple boundaries between slavery and freedom. Northern Marylanders lived on slavery's tattered margin, a circumstance that profoundly influenced how workers experienced both slavery and free labor. Not all of the forces shaping the fault lines were local. Northern Maryland was part of a slaveholding state whose legal and political apparatuses were forged by and for Chesapeake planters. Moreover, residents of the area were inextricably linked to the vibrant slave societies developing along the South's cotton frontier. The tangled intersection where labor systems collided and where local and national forces converged was the setting where the slavery–free labor boundary emerged.

1. "The Land Flows with Milk and Honey"

Agriculture and Labor in the Early Republic

Northern Maryland's landscape was inspiring. In 1776, traveler John F. D. Smyth found that "the land around Frederick-Town is heavy, strong, and rich, well calculated for wheat, with which it abounds." It was, he believed, "as pleasant a country as any in the world." To Polish nobleman Julian Ursyn Niemcewicz, the counties on the Mason-Dixon Line seemed less like the heart of Baltimore's hinterlands and more like a vision of the biblical Canaan. "There is nothing more fertile than this land," he exclaimed as his stagecoach rattled toward Frederick. The fields "groan under the weight of indian corn, wheat, [and] rye," the meadows were "covered with clover," and the roads were choked with wagons hauling farmers' bounty to markets and mills in Baltimore. "In a word," the excited nobleman concluded, "the land flows with milk and honey." Both men hit the mark.[1]

At the dawn of the nineteenth century, artists working in northern Maryland captured some of its fertility, vibrancy, and wealth. In 1791, celebrated painter and museum curator Charles Willson Peale offered a glimpse of Baltimore County's bucolic splendor in his portrait of Mr. and Mrs. James Gittings and their granddaughter (figure 1). The massive canvas laid bare the intertwined roots of the planter's fortunes and of the county's prosperity. Gittings sits confidently in the foreground overlooking his Long Green plantation, whose golden fields recede gently toward the horizon. In the distance sits Gittings's flour mill, which ground his wheat for sale in Baltimore and thence to markets in Europe and the Caribbean. As if to underscore his mastery of the scene, Gittings holds several shafts of wheat, the region's most valuable staple. Artist Francis Guy also drew inspiration from Maryland. His 1805 rendering of Perry Hall, the Baltimore County seat of Harry Dorsey Gough, shows fields thick

Figure 1. Mr. and Mrs. James Gittings and Granddaughter, 1791. Oil on canvas by Charles Willson Peale. Image courtesy of the Maryland Historical Society, Baltimore. MA 8754.

with wheat shocks tucked among rolling hills and forests (figure 2). Guy's painting is, in many ways, an homage to Gough's talents as an agriculturalist; his prizewinning bulls dominate the foreground of the tiny canvas, while Gough, seen in the distance, directs a harvest crew.

The landscapes that Peale and Guy painted were of a region in the throes of an almost unbridled economic expansion. In 1793, the French Revolution flared into a series of wars that disrupted both European agriculture and international trade. Into this void stepped the Middle Atlantic's farmers and merchants, who scrambled to supply the warring empires with American foodstuffs, especially flour. Baltimore's merchants and their competitors in other seaport cities constructed a dense web of canals and turnpikes that crisscrossed the Mason-Dixon Line and cemented growers into larger markets. Far from being worried about these developments, farmers greeted them with enthusiasm. By 1800, northern Marylanders were confidently wading deeper and deeper into the international commodity markets, waters that seemed warm, inviting, and tranquil.[2]

But what of the workers who harvested the wheat, ground the flour, and labored on the turnpikes? We know little about these men and women. The

Figure 2. Perry Hall Slave Quarters with Fieldhands at Work, ca. 1805. Oil on canvas by Francis Guy. Image Courtesy of the Maryland Historical Society, Baltimore. 1986.33.

paintings by Peale and Guy suggest a compelling and useful metaphor for their historical invisibility. In Peale's sprawling canvas, the harvesters are mere pinpricks. Guy shows farmhands cutting, raking, and binding the plantation's wheat, but individual workers remain faceless; some are black, some are white, but all are subsumed in a work meant to impress viewers with Gough's wealth. Scholars have treated rural laborers with similar indifference.[3] This omission is in part a product of the painfully thin records these workers left behind. Rural workers are an elusive quarry; they flit through a fugitive slave advertisement or across the pages of a farm ledger, then recede into a historical fog. For example, we know nothing about "Flying Adam," a farmhand on Gideon Denison's Lion Hill plantation in Harford County, except that he was "mulatto," as evidenced by the word scrawled next to his name in Denison's account book, and that between the spring and early fall of 1795, "Flying Adam" spent five months working Denison's land, receiving a monthly

wage of seven dollars. There is no information regarding his age, his family
and friends, or his legal status. "Flying Adam" stopped drawing steady wages
in late 1795 but seems to have remained in the neighborhood, appearing
intermittently in Denison's ledger the following year, when he earned credits
for cutting wood and working in the wheat harvest. It is, however, unclear
how he supported himself during the remainder of 1796. Denison charged
"Flying Adam" for grazing livestock and renting a plow, so we know that he
owned animals and had access to a parcel of land, but the full range of his
economic activities remains a mystery. In January 1797, "Flying Adam" squared
his accounts and then receded into anonymity, becoming, one imagines, one
of the nondescript harvesters in a landscape painting.[4]

The poor artistic renderings of workers may be read as a metaphor for their
historical obscurity, but these hazy images might be an accurate reflection
of how employers viewed the working people of the Middle Atlantic. When
it came to recruiting laborers, those seeking help showed a marked indifference toward the ethnicity, race, and legal status of their hands. Bosses viewed
their laborers, whether bought or hired, as an interchangeable commodity.
As historian Seth Rockman observes in his discussion of Baltimore's labor
market, employers "calculated the virtues of some workers over others, juggled
different kinds of workers within the same endeavor, and made rapid switches
between types of workers when doing so seemed advantageous."[5] The same
could be said of their rural counterparts.

Farmers were remarkably promiscuous when it came to finding laborers.
Workforces were often patchwork affairs stitched together from farmhands
whose varied backgrounds and legal statuses defied or at least muddied the
neat distinctions between slavery and freedom, black and white. During his
tenure on Denison's plantation, "Flying Adam" worked alongside slaves, free
blacks, and an array of artisans that included tailors, shoemakers, coopers,
and distillers. Employers were constantly fiddling with the composition of
the workforces. In Frederick County, planter and Revolutionary War general
Otho Holland Williams spent the 1780s and 1790s groping for a workforce
that was efficient and tractable and that squared with his ethnic and racial
concerns. Not only were individual hands hired and fired, but Williams intro-
duced, modified, and scrapped entire labor regimes. In 1791, he informed
his manager that he intended to purchase "three or four stout men" from the
next shipment of German redemptioners. They must have proved unsatisfac-
tory, for the following spring his manager ended an appeal for additional
workers by imploring, "I wish for no more of your doche [Dutch] men."[6]
Williams's discontent with indentured servants was matched by his mounting anger with his "helpless worthless sett" of tenants, whom he evicted in

1794. Despite his misgivings about slavery, Williams resolved to restructure his workforce around a resident manager who would oversee an expanded force of slaves.[7]

The fluidity apparent in the labor arrangements of individual farms and plantations was symptomatic of larger transformations in the economy of the Middle Atlantic. The American Revolution unleashed waves of economic, legal, and political change that fundamentally altered the terrain of labor. Indentured servitude showed a renewed burst of life in the 1790s but soon became a moribund institution. While bound Europeans were becoming increasingly scarce, the number of enslaved blacks in northern Maryland soared (see table 1). Yet slavery's future was uncertain. Even as the slave population ballooned, liberalized manumission laws were fueling the explosive growth of a free black population. The clouds on slavery's horizon thickened with the passage of Pennsylvania's Gradual Abolition Act in 1780, which placed slavery in that state on the path to extinction and made the counties north of the Mason-Dixon Line a potential haven for runaway bondsmen and -women.

The future may not have augured well for slavery, but the portents also were not promising for free labor. Political economists ranted against slavery and urged farmers to embrace the more efficient and rational system of wage labor, but employers remained wary of free labor. Hired workers were probably scarce, for the white populations of Cecil, Frederick, and Washington Counties either declined or stagnated between 1790 and 1810 (see table 1). Farmers lucky enough to find unemployed hands may have balked at the price because wages posted dramatic increases during the 1790s (see figure 3). The shortage of hired farmhands and the spike in their earnings tipped the field against their bosses. "The labourers, owing to their small numbers in proportion to those in Europe, have it in their power to prescribe their own prices, instead of submitting to those of proprietors," observed a German traveler in 1796. He was astonished to find that harvesters near Lancaster, Pennsylvania, had demanded daily wages of $1.25, "a pint of Madeira wine, and a half-pint of rum a day, and received it."[8]

Many landowners doubted whether free laborers could be brought to heel. The egalitarian impulse of the American Revolution had narrowed the legal and social gap between workers and their employers. The assertiveness—the presumptuousness—of American farmhands shocked Englishman John Parkinson, who rented a farm in Baltimore County in 1799. "It is very common," he observed, "if you step out of your house into the garden, to find a man of any description (black or white) when you come in, to have lighted his pipe and [sat] down in a chair, smoking, without apology." Those who chastised their workers were viewed as enemies "of the rights of man" and "infringer[s]

Table 1. Population of Northern Maryland, 1790–1860 (Percentage Change over Previous Decade)

County	1790	1800	1810	1820	1830	1840	1850	1860
Carroll*								
White						15,521	18,667	22,525
						(n/a)	(+20%)	(+21%)
Slave						1,122	975	783
						(n/a)	(−13%)	(−20%)
Free Black						898	974	1,225
						(n/a)	(+08%)	(+26%)
Cecil								
White	10,055	6,542	9,652	14,723	11,478	13,329	15,472	19,994
		(−35%)	(+48%)	(+53%)	(−22%)	(+16%)	(+16%)	(+29%)
Slave	3,407	2,103	2,467	2,342	1,705	1,352	844	950
		(−38%)	(+17%)	(−5%)	(−27%)	(−21%)	(−38%)	(+13%)
Free Black	163	373	947	1,783	2,249	2,551	2,623	2,918
		(+128%)	(+154%)	(+88%)	(+26%)	(+13%)	(+3%)	(+11%)
Frederick								
White	26,937	26,478	27,893	31,997	36,706	28,975	33,314	38,391
		(−2%)	(+5%)	(+15%)	(+15%)	(n/a)†	(+15%)	(+15%)
Slave	3,641	4,572	5,671	6,685	6,370	4,445	3,913	3,243
		(+26%)	(+24%)	(+18%)	(−5%)	(n/a)	(−12%)	(−17%)
Free Black	213	473	783	1,777	2,716	2,985	3,760	4,957
		(+122%)	(+71%)	(+127%)	(+53%)	(n/a)	(+26%)	(+32%)
Harford								
White	10,784	12,018	14,606	11,207	11,314	12,041	14,413	17,971
		(+11%)	(+21%)	(−23%)	(+01%)	(+6%)	(+20%)	(+25%)
Slave	3,417	4,264	4,431	3,320	2,947	2,643	2,166	1,800
		(+25%)	(+4%)	(−25%)	(−12%)	(−10%)	(−18%)	(−17%)
Free Black	775	1,344	2,221	1,367	2,058	2,436	2,777	3,644
		(+73%)	(+65%)	(−38%)	(+51%)	(+18%)	(+14%)	(+31%)
Washington								
White	14,472	16,108	15,591	19,247	21,277	24,724	26,930	28,305
		(+11%)	(−3%)	(+23%)	(+11%)	(+16%)	(+09%)	(+05%)
Slave	1,286	2,200	2,656	3,201	2,909	2,546	2,090	1,435
		(+71%)	(+21%)	(+21%)	(−9%)	(−12%)	(−18%)	(−31%)
Free Black	64	342	483	627	1,082	1,580	1,828	1,677
		(+434%)	(+41%)	(+30%)	(+73%)	(+46%)	(+16%)	(−8%)

Source: U.S. Census, 1790–1860.

* Carroll County was carved from portions of eastern Frederick County and western Baltimore County in 1837.

† It is difficult to determine the extent to which the population losses recorded in Frederick County in 1840 were caused by the creation of Carroll County.

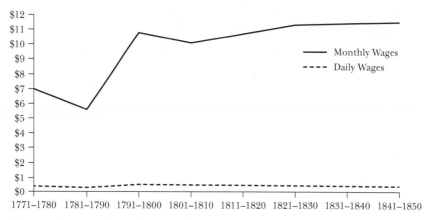

Figure 3. Average Agricultural Wages in Maryland, 1771–1850

Source: Donald R. Adams, Jr., "Prices and Wages in Maryland, 1750–1850," *Journal of Academic History* 46 (Sept. 1986): 625–45.

of the rights which they and their fathers fought for."[9] Workers were further emboldened by legal developments that expanded their freedoms. Throughout the nation, a series of court decisions and laws redrew the boundaries between voluntary and involuntary labor and stripped employers of older forms of compulsion—physical punishment, criminal sanction, and specific performance clauses—that had long been brandished over workers.[10]

"A Rage for Mills": Farmers and Markets in the Early Republic

Commercial agriculture had deep roots along Mason and Dixon's Line. The farmers of southern Pennsylvania had begun producing surpluses for local and regional markets by the mid-1700s.[11] Landowners in northern Maryland had taken a similar plunge into the emerging commodity markets, expanding production to meet the Continental Army's demands during the American Revolution and becoming more involved in national and international markets after independence. During the late eighteenth century, northern Maryland's farmers moved more extensively into the grain market, with Frederick County posting a 300 percent increase in wheat production between 1770 and 1800.[12] Most of this wheat found its way to market as flour. In 1785, German immigrant Christian Boerstler observed that "much grain was planted" in Washington County and that "almost all farmers have their wheat ground into flour that is packed into barrels . . . and taken to port cities."[13] The deepening commitment to commercial agriculture manifested itself in a bifurcated market, with stagnant local demand standing in stark contrast to thriving export markets. In 1793, a Frederick editor noted that farmers in the county's more remote districts needed better access to markets because "wheat or flour does not command cash" inside the county. David Shriver concurred. Explaining why he needed to transport his wheat to Baltimore or the District of Columbia, the Frederick County farmer stated bluntly, "I can't sell it at home."[14]

The intensification of commercial production gave rise to a thriving milling industry in rural Maryland. In 1792, Governor Thomas Johnson was astounded by Frederick County's "rage for mills," an observation seconded in 1798 by a Frederick editor who counted "upwards of 80 grist mills, busily employed in the manufacture of flour."[15] While touring Washington County in 1806, geographer Joseph Scott found no slackening in the milling industry. Antietam Creek alone turned fourteen mills that sent "large quantities of flour" to merchants in Alexandria, Georgetown, and Baltimore.[16] By 1810, Frederick County was home to 101 flour mills with an annual production of 84,080 barrels, while Washington County's 52 mills produced an impressive 86,250 barrels.[17]

Although wheat was, in Governor Johnson's reckoning, "a cash article and therefore the chief that we cultivate for market," farmers' commercial activities were not confined to small grains.[18] Joseph Scott found that Washington County's farmers distilled "large quantities of whiskey" for coastal markets. In 1810, census enumerators recorded that the county's ninety-two distilleries produced 200,043 gallons of alcohol.[19] Landowners also continued to raise tobacco, but the extent and duration of their involvement in its culture remains unclear.[20] Animal herding rounded out farmers' market activities. In 1792, a French traveler reported that landowners in Frederick and Washington Counties "raise much livestock, which they drive to Baltimore."[21] In addition to marketing their own stock, farmers sold fodder to backcountry drovers who were herding cattle and swine to Baltimore and Philadelphia.[22]

Before the construction of canals and turnpikes, most northern Marylanders marketed their produce on Potomac River flatboats, which carried large shipments of flour along with whiskey, deerskins, venison, and maple syrup. Anecdotal evidence suggests that the river trade flourished at the turn of the century. In 1789, a traveler in Old Town, one of Washington County's largest Potomac River entrepôts, declared that "the place puts me very much in mind of a seaport," with crowds of sailors and masters "running up and down, disposing of their cargoes of rum, wine &c., and purchasing wheat and bacon to take down again."[23] Surveyor Tobias Lear offered a similar description of the Potomac trade in 1793: "Boats, carrying from one hundred and fifty to two hundred barrels of flour already pass from Cumberland to Great Falls;

and many thousands of barrels of flour have been brought in boats . . . during the present year."[24] John Thomson Mason's accounts with the owners of several barges provide another barometer of the flour trade. Between 1806 and 1808, the Washington County planter increased the number of barrels of flour he shipped annually from 615 to 1,045.[25] Mason's barrels would have joined a massive cascade of flour descending the Potomac that sometimes overwhelmed draymen and merchants. In 1796, a Georgetown trader advised an associate that their firm's flour should remain in warehouses at Great Falls because the volume of flour shipped that spring had driven carriage rates "uncommonly high."[26]

While farmers in Frederick and Washington Counties concentrated on small grains, those in the immediate vicinity of Annapolis, Baltimore, Georgetown, and Washington City devoted considerable resources to truck farming. Quaker Zephaniah Buffinton, who visited several estates near Annapolis and Baltimore in 1813, was astonished by the variety of garden crops raised for urban markets. Beets, cabbages, celery, onions, parsnips, pumpkins, tomatoes, turnips, and watermelons "all fetch a great price," he observed, for "demand is twice as much as they can probably raise." In a single year, a farmer with an orchard of five hundred apple and peach trees cleared one thousand dollars in cider and fruit, while another boasted that he had received exorbitant prices for hens, turkeys, and lambs. Farmers also responded to the growing urban demand for firewood and staves. "Find a good cooper," advised Buffinton, "as there is want for more barrels than they can get made—fish barrels, thousands of them wanted, and flour barrels the quantity of them wanted is immense."[27] As butter and dairy products became mainstays of the local economy, farmers grew more attuned to changing urban markets. In 1811, Harford County landowner Mark Pringle informed his manager that butter was "at an extraordinary price—$3 per pound" in Baltimore and ordered his dairymaids and tenants to "make all [they] can to be sent down."[28] A successful farmer could reap handsome rewards by producing for urban markets. Between 1822 and 1824, Gough made numerous forays into Baltimore's markets, selling apple cider ($776), peaches and pears ($603), butter ($416), and a diverse array of fruits, vegetables, and livestock.[29]

Northern Maryland's integration into larger national and international markets triggered concern that producers would become dependent on foreign wares and foodstuffs. Some observers worried that farmers risked losing their independence and self-sufficiency in their reckless pursuit of profits. In 1786, an anonymous writer from Frederick County begged his neighbors to "remit something of our rage for raising wheat for exportation," a dangerous trend that had "changed and enervated our whole system" and "led us to the brink of ruin." The author chastised farmers and planters for devoting all their fields to wheat and importing "malt, hops, beer, soap, candles, even beef, pork and potatoes in considerable quantities."[30] These fears may have been exaggerated. The evidence suggests that most farms conformed to the "composite farm" model described by historian Richard Bushman, integrating both market-oriented and subsistence agriculture into their overall economic strategies.[31] This seems to have been the case in Frederick County, where Governor Johnson observed that farmers raised large quantities of wheat for export but also tended orchards and cultivated beans, cabbages, carrots, corn, potatoes, and turnips "for family consumption . . . seldom with a view towards sale."[32] In 1819, an Englishman traveling through Frederick County reported that farmers continued to mix market and nonmarket activities. "On farms of 300 acres," he wrote, "100 is in wood, 100 in corn and rye, for the support of the farm establishment, and 100 is in wheat, clear gain, which might be put in the pocket every year."[33]

Far from being concerned about the disruptive potential of commercial agriculture, most producers sought improved access to commodity markets. Farmers selling their land boasted that their estates offered easy access to market. "Four of the farms [are] immediately on the turnpike," noted Eleanor and William Potts, who added that the other plots were "not more than three quarters of a mile" from the road.[34] Archibald Chisholm noted that his land was "particularly valuable to the man that understands the cultivation of Hemp and Flax" and assured potential buyers that the product could "at small expense . . . be transported down the Potomac to Georgetown where he is always sure of a ready sale."[35]

The periodic disruption in river transportation occasioned by droughts and freshets prompted some farmers to seek more efficient, dependable means of marketing their produce. The need for improved transportation was made more urgent by the poor state of the roads, which were left in a shambles by the heavy volume of wagons carrying flour. As early as 1787, the Maryland General Assembly had complained that roads between Baltimore and the western counties were "rendered almost impassible during the winter season" by "the great number of wagons" that traversed them.[36] In 1802, a writer from Frederick County complained that he had "driven my wagon regularly to Baltimore for several years and must confess that the roads are now in the worst condition I ever knew them."[37] The poor condition of the roads was still a concern in 1817, when residents of Washington County called the legislature's attention to the turnpikes between Baltimore and Frederick, "many parts of which are often out of repair, to the great injury and inconvenience of all traders."[38]

Whether by canal or by turnpike, farmers clamored to participate in larger commodity markets and the cash economy. In 1793, a resident of Frederick

County complained that the shoddy roads and unpredictable rivers rendered transportation costs prohibitively high and prevented farmers and millers from taking advantage of "sudden advances" in the Baltimore market.[39] In 1803, a farmer in Washington County encouraged Baltimore's merchants to finance a turnpike through the western counties, reminding them that "it is in our interest to have as many avenues to market as possible; it is in yours to promote the easiest communication with the agricultural part of the community."[40] For their part, coastal merchants assured farmers in the hinterlands that their produce would command stable prices, paid promptly in cash. In a letter promoting improvements to the Potomac, a Georgetown merchant attested to the almost insatiable demand for flour: The sudden arrival of fourteen thousand barrels could not dampen the price, which "still continues the same!" Not only could the market absorb this surge, merchants stood ready to make cash payments. "It is almost a matter of wonder," he continued, "that the merchants of George Town have been able to purchase such quantities; for, a few years ago, two or three wagon loads could be disposed of for cash."[41]

The agitation for a more robust transportation system soon prodded the state legislature into action. Between 1796 and 1801, Maryland's General Assembly incorporated five turnpike companies. All of these ventures had foundered by 1804, prompting the legislature to charter three additional companies to build a network of turnpikes connecting Baltimore with communities in western Maryland and southern Pennsylvania. Public enthusiasm for turnpikes remained high into the 1810s. In 1809, construction began on a turnpike from Frederick to Harpers Ferry, Virginia, followed in 1813 by a road linking the Frederick County villages of Westminster, Taneytown, and Emmitsburg.[42]

Farmers and planters rallied behind schemes to improve navigation in the Potomac watershed. In 1804, residents of the Monocacy River Valley advanced money to the struggling Potomac Canal Company to "improve navigation . . . into the Heart of Frederick County."[43] The successful completion of internal improvement projects and the prosperity they brought to northern Maryland were causes for celebration. In 1803, a Georgetown merchant gushed about the improvements made to navigation on the Potomac River. When fourteen thousand barrels of flour had descended the Potomac in twelve days, he reminded an associate in Washington County that "had it been sent by land, [it] would have required nearly one thousand wagons—one thousand men, and four or five thousand horses."[44]

By the end of the Napoleonic Wars, the farmers and millers of northern Maryland were fully integrated into Baltimore's commercial orbit; they kept a weather eye on fluctuations in the city's economy and viewed the local economy through the prism of Baltimore's flour markets. As early as 1787, farmers near Liberty-Town in Frederick County were gathering to toast "the success of the plough" and to "enquire [about] the price of Wheat and Flour, at Baltimore."[45] Millers courted farmers by emphasizing that their operations were geared to the Baltimore trade. In 1811, a Frederick County miller advertised that his mill was "built to manufacture flour for the Baltimore market," while another boasted that his prices were "within a few cents" of those offered by the city's millers.[46] Mindful that their flour's price would in part be determined by the grade it received from inspectors in Baltimore, rural millers prided themselves on receiving high marks. In 1817, rumors that his flour had been condemned in Baltimore sparked a furious response from Frederick miller Jacob Cronise, who threatened to sue his "slanderers."[47]

Northern Marylanders also kept abreast of domestic and foreign intelligence, especially as it concerned their bottom lines. In 1787, Washington County planter Elie Williams weighed his decision to market flour against trends in the Baltimore market. "I have two loads of flour," he wrote to his brother, "but from the accounts of the low price of flour in Balto, shall decline sending it at present in hopes of a greater demand and of course a better price."[48] Likewise, Baltimore merchant William Lee kept Sharpsburg farmer Joseph Chapline apprised of trends in the city's markets and of the latest rumors of war. In 1803, Lee reported that flour prices remained low with "no likelihood of rising" but cautiously added, "You no doubt have heard the report of war between England & France." "Should such take place," he continued, "it will no doubt have some effect upon the produce of this country however its thought to be only speculator's news."[49]

The speculative fever that gripped northern Maryland did not break during the early national period. Farmers and planters had plunged headfirst into the churning but rising waters of the international commodity market, paying little heed to their growing dependence on foreign markets and their lengthening lines of credit. Nor were they terribly concerned about who would harvest their wheat, grind their flour, and drive their wagons to Baltimore. In their headlong dash for wealth, Marylanders took whatever help they could find.

"We Are Week Handit": Labor in the New Nation

In 1795, Abraham Shriver purchased a farm in York County, Pennsylvania, on short credit. Desperate to begin planting, Shriver appealed to his father in Frederick County, Maryland, for additional workers. "We are week handit," his father replied, explaining that the family's indentured servant had recently received his freedom and that the hired farmhand was "going home next week." Disappointed, Shriver asked an associate to scour Baltimore's wharves for indentured servants. These efforts, too, met with no success. "Yesterday arrived a ship from Bremen, went on Bord to look out for a servant but there was only one which was a stone worker and did not like to keep from his trade," his disappointed partner reported. Shriver's fortunes improved in March 1796, when he contracted with farmhand Andrew Kenna. In exchange for one year's service, Shriver agreed to furnish Kenna with clothing, room and board, a twenty-dollar advance, and an additional thirty dollars on completion of the contract. Shriver also secured the services of Jennett Franklin, a young indentured servant. Unfortunately for Shriver, his hold on Franklin proved tenuous; in 1797 or 1798, she abandoned him and married. Rather than press his claims to the remainder of her term of service, Shriver nullified the agreement. By 1801, Shriver had relocated closer to his father's farm in Frederick County, where, perhaps soured by his experiences with indentured servants, he began to assemble a workforce of slaves. In November, Shriver's attorney promised "the first chance I get in procuring [a slave] of the kind you want I shall purchase, if even at a high price." It is unclear whether the lawyer found a slave, for the following spring Shriver's brother, Andrew, bought him an enslaved family consisting of a woman, Minta, and her three children. "The husband of the woman, an old man named Sam, a freeman . . . would be glad to be employed by you," Andrew noted, "but of this you will know more by conversing with the old man."[50]

While Shriver was muddling through, other landowners were experimenting with the region's diverse labor regimes. Irish immigrant Clotworthy Birnie tinkered with both indentured servitude and slavery after he settled in Frederick County in 1810. While contemplating his move, Birnie had received advice from his uncle, Annapolis physician Upton Scott, who encouraged Birnie to ponder the relative merits of indentured servants, hired workers, and slaves. Scott warned that hired farmhands were scarce and commanded "enormous wages" and that slaves were unreliable: "I can, from my own experiences, assure you, that unless you strictly supervise [slaves'] conduct and rigidly enforce the performance of their duties, you will not earn from their labors enough to feed and clothe them." In Scott's opinion, the best solution was to purchase indentured servants.[51] Birnie heeded his uncle's advice. After arriving in Maryland, he requested that his associates in Ireland begin contracting with indentured servants. In particular, he asked that they secure the services of a carpenter (who would serve three years) and of Jonathan Maxwell, a farmhand, and his three adolescent sons, who would serve terms ranging from three to seven years.[52] Yet finding laborers willing to indenture themselves was something of a challenge. An agent in Belfast managed to find two servants but reported "a good deal of trouble with the laborers," while an associate in Northampton avoided discussing the character of the servant he had secured, noting simply that he "shall go without being bound hand and foot."[53]

While awaiting the arrival of his indentured servants, Birnie searched Frederick and Prince George's Counties for slaves. He purchased at least two slaves during his first months in Maryland and subsequently purchased another between 1810 and 1814.[54] Still, neither Birnie nor his uncle was convinced that slaves offered the best solution. When Birnie wrote that his slaves Pompey and Jenny had run away, Scott lamented the "necessity we are under of employing Negroes" and declared it "one of the most disagreeable circumstances attending a residence in this country." But as "servants of a different nature cannot be gotten when wanted," he suggested that his nephew "mix young women amongst your servants" and encourage them to establish families. The children born of these unions could be inculcated with "the habits of industry," "a kind affection for your family," and a sense of his "magisterial authority."[55] Once again, Birnie heeded his uncle's advice. In 1815, the "Profit and Loss" column of his account book included credits for children born to Molly and Bett.[56] By 1820, Birnie had expanded his force to include fourteen slaves, nine of whom were children or adolescents.[57]

Shriver's and Birnie's winding route through northern Maryland's labor market illuminates the contingency and experimentation that marked labor arrangements in the early republic. Frustrated by the unavailability of wage laborers and dissatisfied with indentured servants, Shriver and Birnie had, perhaps reluctantly, embraced slavery as an imperfect solution to their chronic labor shortages. Such adaptability was not unusual, for in the three decades following the American Revolution, artisans and farmers cobbled together workforces that included apprentices, indentured servants, slaves, tenants, and wage laborers. In 1810, an employer in Frederick captured the opportunism that characterized labor arrangements in early national Maryland when he advertised for a hostler. Either "a white man, a free black, or slave," would suffice, provided that he had a reputation for "industry, sobriety, and honesty."[58] Likewise, the contractor responsible for building the Cumberland Turnpike Road in 1817 announced that he "*WANTED TO HIRE BY THE YEAR*, from twenty to thirty good, stout Negro Men, and two or three Women." A month later, he advertised for "a number of Labouring Men" who would "find constant employment and good wages" on the turnpike.[59] Decisions concerning the composition of individual crews were determined less by doctrinaire beliefs in the relative merits of different labor regimes than by a constellation of economic and political forces—and a certain amount of chance. No consensus existed on the relative merits of the myriad labor regimes. Few commentators thought that slavery was an impediment to economic growth. With an ingenuity that would have shocked antebellum free labor ideologues, slaveholders proved remarkably adept at harnessing bound labor to a variety of agricultural and industrial pursuits.[60] While some employers were beginning to voice a preference for free laborers, others groused about the mercurial and expensive hirelings who toiled in the fields and factories. On this shifting and uneven terrain, employers often had little recourse but to corral workers haphazardly.[61]

The uncertainty that characterized labor arrangements in early national Maryland was a product of the American Revolution. Among the conflict's unintended consequences was a profound reordering of labor arrangements on both the local and national levels: Slavery, wage labor, and indentured servitude were fundamentally altered in the wake of the war. The revolution had unleashed a wave of emancipations that swept across New England and the Middle Atlantic before crashing against the rocks of slaveholder resistance and receding. Between 1777 and 1804, every state north of the Mason-Dixon Line abolished slavery through constitutional amendment or judicial fiat or set it on the road to extinction through the enactment of gradual emancipation laws. Although antislavery forces also floated schemes for gradual emancipation in Delaware, Maryland, and Virginia during the 1780s and 1790s, these proposals gained little traction and soon stalled. Slavery thus remained firmly entrenched in these states, but it did not survive unscathed. Yielding to a combination of slave resistance, economic pressures, and political and religious concerns, the Chesapeake states liberalized their manumission laws. In 1782, Virginia allowed private acts of manumission without legislative approval. Five years later, Delaware stopped requiring that slave owners post bonds before freeing their slaves. Maryland's General Assembly caught the spirit in 1790 when it legalized manumission by last will and testament.[62]

In parts of northern Maryland, slavery became a moribund institution in the decades following the revolution. In Cecil and Harford Counties, the transition from tobacco to mixed agriculture and truck farming, along with the concomitant increase in the number of manumissions, heralded slavery's collapse. Harford's slave population posted a dramatic increase between 1790 and 1800, then plummeted 22 percent over the next two decades. Although the number of slaveholding households in the county increased between 1790 and 1810, the average number of slaves owned by each household slipped to under five.[63] The slave population of neighboring Cecil County followed the same downward spiral, declining 31 percent between 1790 and 1820. Slaves were a diminishing presence in both counties' overall populations during these decades: The percentage of Harford's population composed of slaves fell from 23 to 21 percent, while the share of Cecil's population in bondage dropped from 25 to 16 percent (see table 1).

At the same time, slavery was developing along a different track in Frederick and Washington Counties, both of which registered increases in their slave populations that either equaled or outpaced the growth of their white populations. The percentage of slaves in the overall population also grew, rising from 12 to 17 percent in Frederick and from 8 to 14 percent in Washington. The number and percentage of white slaveholding households posted similar increases; by 1820, about one-quarter of white households included slaves. The geographical distribution of slave ownership was uneven. In Frederick County, the largest concentrations of slaves and slaveholders were found in its eastern and southern reaches, which enjoyed the best access to markets in Baltimore and the District of Columbia. Although geographical disparities were less pronounced in Washington County, masters and slaves clustered in the districts bordering the Potomac River.[64]

Slavery's expansion into northern Maryland was driven by the migration of planters from the tobacco counties of the Chesapeake. Some of the most prominent families from the Eastern Shore and southern Maryland, including the Barneses, Tilghmans, and Ringgolds, responded to soil exhaustion and flagging tobacco markets by abandoning their worn-out plantations and seeking new beginnings in northern Maryland.[65] The estates they established became nodes for distributing slaves throughout their neighborhoods. This process occurred on Colonel Richard Barnes's Washington County plantation. After Barnes's death, his executor, John Thomson Mason, assumed responsibility for the colonel's 104 slaves scattered across St. Mary's and Washington Counties. Barnes's will freed many of them, but Mason needed to find hirers or purchasers for those too young to be freed and those whose age or disability precluded legal manumission. Between 1804 and 1807, he sold 16 of Barnes's slaves to farmers and manufacturers in Washington County. He hired out another 41 to employers scattered throughout northern Maryland, many of whom retained these slaves for several years.[66] Mason tailored his advertisements to nonslaveholders who may have been wary of managing and disciplining enslaved workers. He assured prospective hirers that the aging but "honest, well-disposed, and orderly" servants would be "very useful to persons who have few or no slaves."[67]

Those Chesapeake planters who remained on their lands and attempted to revive their fortunes by making the transition from tobacco to wheat soon found themselves with labor surpluses.[68] While some fed these unneeded chattels into the yawning maw of the interstate trade, others sold them into northern Maryland. A handful of enterprising businessmen saw tremendous potential in the slave trade between the Chesapeake and the northern counties. In 1790, Nathaniel Rochester and three associates, including Charles Carroll, pooled £1,933 to purchase slaves from the struggling planters on the Eastern Shore and sell them to farmers along the Mason-Dixon Line who were eager to expand production but were starved for laborers. The partners bought forty-one people and had little trouble selling them in Frederick and Washington Counties. When they squared their accounts later that year, Rochester and his associates had grossed £2,556, a 32 percent return on their original investment.[69] Although the scale of the trade between Maryland's tobacco plantations and its upcountry wheat plantations is difficult to gauge, the numerous fugitive slave advertisements from the 1800s and 1810s describing slaves from northern Maryland attempting to reunite with kin on the Eastern Shore and in southern Maryland bespeak a brisk market and a large forced migration. When Elijah escaped from a farm near Hagerstown, his disgruntled master noted that "he was purchased of a certain William Evans of St. Mary's County, Md., and probably may have taken that course." Washington County farmer Coleman Combs had similar suspicions about his fugitive slave "Negro Luke," who was raised "about 15 miles from Port Tobacco, in St. Mary's County, and may, perhaps bend his course that way." Likewise, a Hagerstown master suspected that "Negro Winny" might attempt to return to her previous homes on the Eastern Shore or in St. Mary's County.[70]

Other masters and mistresses in the tobacco-growing counties found outlets for their unneeded slaves by hiring them to northern Marylanders. In 1800, a Washington County farmer advertised for the return of Luke, whom he described as "the property of a Mr. Lock of St. Mary's County, hired by George Lock of this county to me." Edward Price of St. Mary's County took a similar approach with an unneeded slave: In 1808, he hired "Negro Harry" to a farmer near Hagerstown. Not every bondsman hired out by slave owners from the Eastern Shore and southern Maryland was destined to work the land. Charles County master Robert Brent hired "Negro James" to John Hughes's ironworks in Washington County.[71]

For the unscrupulous, the growing appetite for laborers in northern Maryland created opportunities to defraud slaves who had been promised their freedom and to pocket a handsome profit. In 1792, "Negro Rachel" petitioned the Frederick County court for her freedom, claiming that her former master had reneged on her manumission and "resolved to take her to the back country and sell her." Rachel's master had spirited her to Frederick County, where he quickly sold her to Richard Truman, who, according to the bondswoman's petition, "not only refuses to permit your petitioner to come to court but also holds your petitioner in slavery."[72] Three years later, Walter Butler lodged a similar petition. Born to free parents, Butler had been apprenticed by his mother to Charles County farmer John Hugeford. Upon Hugeford's death, Butler was sold to a succession of masters within Charles and St. Mary's Counties, the last of whom rechristened him Stephen and sold him into Frederick County "as a slave." Butler's pleas fell on receptive ears at the Frederick County court, and the judges ordered him released from bondage.[73]

How northern Maryland's whites greeted the expansion of slavery into their region remains uncertain. The growing number of slaveholding households in Frederick and Washington Counties suggests that many people welcomed the additional help. For some, the decision to purchase slaves bespoke temporary expediency more than an abiding commitment to the institution. Washington County farmer William Ford depended on slaves while his children were maturing, but by 1800 they had reached working age, and Ford found that he had "no occasion for slaves," offering to "sell them for ready money."[74] Farmer and gunpowder manufacturer Christian Boerstler managed his operations on Antietam Creek with the assistance of his son, but when the young man was badly burned, Boerstler was "forced to buy a negro for $300 who attended to the mill."[75]

Maryland did not follow the states north of the Mason-Dixon Line in placing slavery on the path to gradual extinction following the American Revolution, but a few whites challenged the institution in the decade immediately following independence. In 1791, Dr. George Buchanan of the Maryland Society for Promoting the Abolition of Slavery condemned slavery as un-Christian and inconsistent with the nation's republican ideals. He chastised his fellow Marylanders for having obtained "the blessings of peace" only to become "apostates to their principles, and riveted the fetters of slavery upon the unfortunate Africans." Not only was slavery a glaring inconsistency in the young republic, it hobbled economic development. "One freeman is worth almost two slaves in the field," he declared, "which makes it in many instances cheaper to have hirelings; for they are excited to industry by the hopes of reputation and future employment."[76] Buchanan's arguments resonated with at least some northern Marylanders. While touring the countryside near Hagerstown, Ferdinand Bayard asked an overworked farmwife why her husband had not purchased slaves. "Even if we were richer I would not want any of them," she replied. "These poor negroes, receiving none of the fruits of their labor, do not love work," and "if we had slaves, we should have to . . . beat them to make use of them."[77]

Religion stoked the fires of freedom. Although recent studies have drawn attention to the economic and disciplinary considerations behind private manumissions, the importance of slave owners' religious convictions cannot be dismissed. A few masters and mistresses cited religious motives when freeing their slaves. In 1792, for example, Abner Ritchie of Frederick County declared that God had placed him "in a land of liberty" and had convinced him that slavery was "derogatory to Humanity," "incompatible to a free and candid mind," and a blemish upon "the Blessings of Liberty, civil and religious." The religious impulse behind manumissions was clearest among Methodists and Quakers, who encouraged their brethren to free their slaves. While some members of the sects reconciled their religious beliefs with chattel slavery, many chose to liberate their bondsmen and -women. In May 1787, for example, a Pennsylvanian reported that a Methodist itinerant, Wolman Hickson, had after "many years labour & application" secured the freedom of 229 slaves in the Baltimore Circuit. The Methodists took formal action to limit the spread of slavery among their ranks in 1796, when they declared that any member who sold slaves would be "immediately . . . excluded from the society." Those who bought slaves were expected to submit the transactions to the next quarterly meeting to "determine the number of years in which the slave so purchased would work out the price of his purchase." After the meeting fixed a term of service, masters and mistresses who failed to "execute a legal instrument for the manumission of such slave" faced expulsion. The Methodists further required slave owners to make additional provisions for children born during their female slaves' terms; the deed of manumission must stipulate that any daughters born to an enslaved woman would be freed at twenty-one, while sons were to liberated at twenty-nine. In 1804, the Methodists expanded the scope of these rules, declaring that any congregant who purchased "a slave with a certificate of future emancipation" must submit the transaction to the quarterly meeting for review.[78]

Compliance with the decrees of the Methodist Church was far from universal, but its strictures were not toothless. The records of the quarterly meetings from northern Maryland contain a smattering of manumissions. Between 1794 and 1816, for example, the quarterly meeting of the Baltimore Circuit oversaw the gradual liberation of twenty-six people, while the Harford Circuit managed fourteen delayed manumissions between 1799 and 1830. To determine how long a slave must serve, the quarterly meetings weighed the bondsman's or -woman's age, health, sex, and, perhaps most important, purchase price. The arithmetic that guided their deliberations snapped into sharp relief in the case of Greenbury Crook and "Negro Perry." In October 1813, Crook paid seventy-five dollars for Perry, who was not yet three years of age, and brought him before the Baltimore Circuit to determine how long the boy should serve to "make full compensation." Noting that the child was "imperfect in one of his arms," the meeting declared that Perry should serve Crook and his heirs until his thirtieth birthday. In addition to negotiating manumissions, the quarterly meetings punished those who sold or mistreated their human chattels. In February 1803, the Baltimore Circuit expelled Thomas Bennett for selling a slave for life. That November, the circuit suspended preacher and class leader Benjamin Bowen for "whipping a negro man immoderately."[79]

Religion may have chipped away at slavery's foundations, but the heavy blows that gave the house of bondage a decided lean came from other, more earthly directions. Whatever misgivings Marylanders harbored about slavery's economic benefits and morality paled in comparison to the workaday problems of managing bondsmen and -women in an economy built on diversified agriculture. In wedding slavery to mixed farming, masters and mistresses surrendered a measure of control over their chattels. The tensions inherent in these adaptations were apparent in the employment of slave wagoners. With the intensification of commercial agriculture and the expansion of the Middle Atlantic's transportation networks, many slaveholders began employing the enslaved as drovers and wagoners during slower seasons. After visiting with a Frederick County master, Englishman William Faux described how these arrangements defrayed transportation expansions by creating side employments when slaves might otherwise be idle. The farmer "finds living 40 miles from market of no importance," Faux explained, "as the carrying is done when men and horses have nothing else to do."[80] By the early 1800s, driving wagons had become an essential skill for field hands, and enslaved teamsters were becoming commonplace on northern Maryland's roads.[81] Experienced wagoners fetched hefty prices, and slaveholders commonly boasted when they had a bondsman who was an "excellent wagoner" or "possessed of few equals as a wagoner."[82]

Assigning slaves to drive wagons to distant markets was a dangerous proposition. The bondsmen who hauled northern Maryland's bounty worked without supervision and soon learned that some roads led to freedom. A slave named Isaac may have capitalized on this knowledge when he fled from George Carter's plantation in Loudoun County, Virginia. Unable to speculate on his slave's whereabouts, the frustrated Carter explained that Isaac had an extensive knowledge of local geography. "He has driven my wagon several times to Baltimore, and is very-well acquainted with Alexandria."[83] A Frederick County master found himself in a similar bind, for his slave, Peter, had been employed to drive a team from Baltimore to Tennessee.[84] Slaveholders whose people seldom ventured beyond their home farm or plantation might find their authority compromised by black wagoners. Montgomery County slave owner Benjamin Jones suspected that Sally had escaped with "a person of color who drove a wagon," as did a Virginian whose runaway slave was seen "in company with some Negro wagoners driving . . . for Baltimore."[85] Even white wagoners posed a threat. In 1816, a white man hauling wares to Pittsburgh aided Washington County slave Barney Mason. Mason's bid for freedom failed, but his master remained suspicious of wagoners. When Mason escaped again in 1818, his master believed it "probable he may get in with some wagoner . . . and make for Pennsylvania."[86]

The simmering problems in the unhappy marriage of slavery and diversified agriculture flared during the summer wheat harvest. To make slavery more responsive to the season's pressing labor demands, masters relinquished some of their power at harvest. They plied their slaves with whiskey and wages, hired unneeded slaves to neighbors, and, perhaps most important, allowed slaves to seek outside employment. This loosening of the shackles occurred with the state's blessing. Recognizing that wheat required a more flexible and mobile workforce, the Maryland General Assembly stipulated in 1787 that although slaves were not generally allowed to hire themselves or "act as free," such behavior would be permitted for ten days at harvest.[87] In 1818, the legislature expanded this concession to twenty days.[88] Both laws buttressed slaveholders' authority by imposing fines on those employing slaves without their owners' consent, but enforcement of this provision seems to have been sporadic.

Allowing the enslaved to seek outside employment may have imbued slavery with a measure of plasticity needed for wheat production, but it also cracked open the door to freedom. Harvest provided an ideal opportunity for slaves to melt into the motley bands of roaming harvesters and make their escape. The generous pay offered at harvest may have emboldened those contemplating escape: With work abundant and wages high, fugitives could purchase food, lodging, transportation, and new clothing. Fugitive slave advertisements illuminate how harvesting loosened slaves' shackles. A Frederick County master advertised for the capture of Arch after concluding that he had followed the harvest to freedom: "He is a fast reaper and no doubt will procure a sickle and attempt to pass as a freeman."[89] After "Negro Ned" escaped, his anxious owner speculated that he had fled under cover of harvest, for he "understands felling, mowing, [and] cradling."[90] On rare occasions, women also made bids for freedom at harvest. Henry Cooley suspected that "Negro Hannah" was funding her escape by harvesting because she was "only used to plantation work."[91]

The passage of Pennsylvania's gradual emancipation act in 1780 further eroded slavery's foundations in northern Maryland. The transformation of Pennsylvania into free soil made the Mason-Dixon Line a widening chasm along which fissures erupted that threatened slaveholders' authority in Maryland. Before 1780, owners had moved their human chattels across the Mason-Dixon Line with impunity. The 1780 statute retained some of this fluidity. Masters and mistresses could still bring their slaves into Pennsylvania, provided they remained in the state for less than six months. Slaveholders who intended to settle in Pennsylvania were required to manumit their slaves, but they could retain the services of their erstwhile bondsmen and -women by indenturing adults for seven years and minors until age twenty-eight. In 1788, a series of abuses led the Pennsylvania legislature to restrict the movement of slaves across the state's borders. Although travelers were still permitted to bring their slaves for six months, the new statute declared that slave owners who intended to settle in Pennsylvania must immediately and unconditionally manumit their slaves.[92]

Those enslaved south of the Mason-Dixon Line were quick to take advantage of Pennsylvania's changing legal climate. Slave owners whose businesses spanned the Maryland-Pennsylvania border continued crossing and recrossing the border with their slaves, but their chattels now used Pennsylvania's courts to test their chains. Among the records of Lancaster County is an undated deposition sworn by Louisa Smith, who "claims to be a free woman" because her owner, John Ritsell, had moved from Hagerstown to Lancaster County "about two years ago with his family and brought the said Louisa with him." Smith remained with Ritsell "about four months" and then abandoned him after "being well assured that she was free according to the laws of Pennsylvania."[93]

Frederick County farmer Robert Crawford discovered that the Mason-Dixon Line had become treacherous territory for slaveholders when he moved his enslaved woman, Hannah, and her children, George and Nancy, to York County, Pennsylvania. Crawford remained in Pennsylvania longer than six months without registering or manumitting his slaves, which prompted Hannah to launch a freedom suit. Crawford's neighbors testified on Hannah's behalf. William Cochran swore that Crawford had moved to York County in "the winter after Cornwallis was taken, at York in Virginia" (the winter of 1781–82). He further averred that "from the time that said Crawford came into the county . . . I new the s[d] Negro Wench to be in the service of s[d] Crawford as a slave, which was above six months." William Askew collaborated Cochran's testimony. Although he admitted that he did not remember when Crawford brought Hannah and her children into Pennsylvania, Askew swore that "I do know and well remember that I calculated . . . that the aforesaid Negroes were held as Crawford's slaves by him in Pennsylvania . . . more than six months." Based on the testimony, Pennsylvania Supreme Court justice Thomas McKean issued a writ of habeas corpus demanding that Roberts surrender Hannah and her children. Roberts responded that Hannah was not in his possession. "Sundry designing persons have spirited away the said Negro Wench from me," he explained, "and she for sometime past hath been in York Town." Justice McKean promptly declared Hannah free, having "become so by having resided in this State with her former Master above six months unregistered." Hannah's children may not have been as lucky. Roberts rebuffed the writ for them to be delivered to York County, noting that he had purchased the slaves in Maryland "where they are now detained, & have been so detained for a long time past."[94]

Maryland courts were sympathetic to slaves who claimed their freedom under the 1780 and 1788 statutes. In 1799, for example, the General Court heard the petition for freedom of "Negro David," an enslaved man from Frederick County. Although the precise grounds for his petition remain unclear, David alleged that his master, Richard Coale, had hired him to a Pennsylvanian named McLean sometime in 1788. The court ruled that David, who had subsequently been returned to Maryland and remained in his master's possession, was entitled to his freedom.[95]

To the chagrin of Maryland slaveholders, Pennsylvania became a haven for runaway slaves. Despite the legislature's stipulation that the 1780 statute "shall not give any relief or shelter" to runaway slaves from neighboring states and despite assurances that a master "shall have like right and aid to demand, claim and take away his slave . . . as he might have had in case this act had not been made," the enslaved leaped at the chance to escape into Pennsylvania and disappear in its burgeoning free black community. Throughout the 1780s and 1790s, a growing number of slave owners suspected that their fugitive slaves were lurking among Pennsylvania's freemen and -women. Reuben Meyer was uncertain whether his slave, Harry, would flee to his childhood home in Virginia, escape to Baltimore, or "endeavour to get into Pennsylvania, and there pass as a freeman." Slaveholder William Gordon nursed similar fears. When Dick and Ned escaped in 1785, the Baltimore County master noted that "they were heard to say they intended [to go] a little beyond Philadelphia, where they would be free." Before long, Maryland masters were condemning the corrosive effects of the Pennsylvania statute. Slave owner James Hutchings growled that his two fugitives were probably in Pennsylvania "under the cover of a law, fraught with great mischiefs and inconvenience to her sister States."[96]

Marylanders complained that the lingering death of slavery in Pennsylvania heralded the institution's demise in their state. In 1815, Washington County masters bemoaned "the facility with which Negro Slaves get into [Pennsylvania] and the great difficulty which attends regaining them, owing, in great measure, to the Laws of Pennsylvania."[97] The complaint was not unusual: Between 1816 and 1822, the members of the Maryland General Assembly peppered their northern neighbor with five resolutions criticizing Pennsylvanians for harboring fugitive slaves and impeding efforts to recover them.[98] Pennsylvania's legislature raised the stakes in 1820 by enacting a statute that increased to twenty-one years the maximum prison sentence for abducting free blacks and prohibited local officials from assisting in the recovery of fugitive slaves. Six years later, Pennsylvania passed a personal liberty law stipulating that suspected fugitives must receive due process and that masters must obtain a certificate of removal from a judge before returning suspected fugitives to bondage.[99] The laws incensed slaveholders below the Mason-Dixon Line, who worried that their already tenuous hold on their slaves would be further weakened. In 1828, masters in Frederick County complained that they had sustained "serious losses" from slaves escaping into Pennsylvania and cautioned that "the evil seems to be growing, and unless a speedy stop can be put to [it], much greater evils can be anticipated."[100]

Pressed by the revolution's ideological challenge to slavery and the growing realization that their mastery was crumbling, some slaveholders relented and freed their bondsmen and -women. Frederick County's slave owners manumitted 630 people between 1790 and 1819 but did so out of motives that were far from altruistic. For most masters and mistresses, manumission was a desperate attempt to shore up their authority, not an expression of political or religious sentiments. Instead of beating a hasty retreat from the institution, they committed themselves to a rearguard action that tightened their grip on their chattels and extended slavery's life.[101] Delayed manumission or "term slavery" agreements were common, accounting for 395 of the manumissions recorded in Frederick County (63 percent). In the hands of slaveholders such as Ignatius Davis, delayed manumission was an instrument of control. In 1793, Davis freed Kate outright but specified that her husband, Robert, and son, Sam, would remain enslaved until 1799 and 1814, respectively. In addition, their freedom was hemmed by clauses to guarantee the family's continued obedience. Davis stipulated that Kate "shall not be free unless she finds her husband . . . in good and sufficient clothing from this time and during the term of six years." If the couple ran, their terms would be extended "three years, three months, and three days."[102] Two years later, Davis concocted a similar scheme for freeing several other slaves, stating that "all the children that may be born of them during their time of servitude be forever free as soon as they attain the age . . . of twenty-eight and the children of the said children and their children's children forever." He added that if any members of the succeeding generations "run away or unlawfully absent themselves," their terms would be extended.[103]

Slave owners excelled at lengthening the path to freedom and encumbering those laboring along the tortuous road with conditions. Delayed manumission promised that freedom would come, but only if bondsmen and -women continued to labor faithfully. In 1816, for example, John Knox manumitted

Sal and her son, Silas, whose freedom would commence in 1824 and 1853, respectively, if they "continue to serve me as heretofore" and comport themselves as "faithful and obedient" slaves.[104] Likewise, in 1817, Jacob Smith bequeathed his slave, Charles, to Smith's widow with the promise that Charles would "be a free man on May 8, 1830, if he . . . obeys his mistress's orders and conducts himself well at all times." If Charles proved disobedient, Smith authorized his widow to revoke the promise and sell the slave.[105]

Slave owners were not rushing to free their bondsmen and -women. Indeed, the prevalence of delayed manumission agreements suggests that most were groping for new, stronger purchases on their chattels. The Faustian bargains struck between slaveholders and slaves guaranteed that whites would continue to enjoy the prerogatives of mastery and that black families would linger in slavery's shadow. In 1793, Lenix Martin promised his seven slaves their freedom between 1797 and 1819 but specified that their offspring must continue serving his family until age twenty-five, "so *totius quotius infinitum*."[106] Thomas Rigg outlined similar terms when he freed Jenny and her infant daughter, Beck, in 1813. Not only would mother and child remain in bondage until 1817 and 1832, respectively, but their children would remain enslaved "until they arrive to the full age of thirty and so on, the children of such children in like manner forever."[107] The repercussions of such agreements reverberated through several generations. In 1801, for example, the executors of Frederick County master Upton Sherridine manumitted Kate (age thirty-two), whose freedom had been slated to commence when she turned forty. The deed further stipulated that Kate's descendants would remain in bondage until their thirty-first birthdays.[108] Decades later, her grandchildren and great-grandchildren were still laboring toward freedom. In 1842, a Frederick County master sold Juliet Gooding and her infant daughters, Sarah Jane and Minerva, whom he noted were "descendents of Kate, to be freed at 31."[109]

For the enslaved, accepting the attenuated and deferred freedom that their masters and mistresses proffered was a bitter draft, but it may have been their only hope of escape from bondage. Having emerged from slavery with nothing but their freedom, most African Americans lacked the resources to liberate their spouses and children. Only seventeen of the people manumitted between 1790 and 1819 were ransomed with cash. Slaveholders were quick to capitalize on freedpeople's desire to purchase their kin, a drive that could be used to ensnare former slaves and expand workforces. Slave owners accepted free blacks' offers to indenture or reenslave themselves—that is, to mortgage their freedom—in exchange for loved ones' releases. Thus, on 29 December 1809, John Cregar bought "Negro Nace" and provided for his eventual freedom in 1817. In exchange, Nace's wife, Hannah Burgee, indentured herself to Cregar for eight years. Moreover, she pledged that "if she should turn out to be a slave" or if she or her husband absconded, Cregar could retain Nace in slavery for an indefinite period to compensate Cregar for his loss.[110]

To secure a relative's purchase, free blacks entered into complex negotiations with slaveholders and with third parties who provided financial backing in exchange for labor. Long before he authored the infamous *Dred Scott* decision, Roger Brooke Taney intervened on behalf of enslaved blacks. In 1819, Taney and an associate bought Clarissa from Woodward Evitt for $350. That same day, Clarissa's husband, Harry Peter, drafted a $350 note, which he secured by indenturing himself to the attorneys for ten years. During his service, Peter was to receive clothing, food, and lodging "suitable for a slave." If, at any point, Peter discharged the debt, Taney promised that he and his wife would be manumitted.[111] Ann Koon and her infant son entered into a similar agreement with Henry Keller, who had purchased them from Richard Temper for $60 and provided for their freedom. To compensate Keller, Koon agreed to work for "50¢ per week, clear of sickness, time lost, etc." until her debt was retired.[112]

While some slave owners were learning to manipulate their human chattels' yearnings for freedom, others were discovering that the threat of sale to the Deep South's expanding cotton and sugar plantations was a potent weapon for controlling truculent slaves. Clotworthy Birnie wielded this lash with great effect during the winter of 1811–12, when Pompey and Jenny made separate, unsuccessful bids for freedom. After their capture, Birnie lodged them in a local prison and began making preparations to sell them to a Baltimore trader. Birnie's uncle, Upton Scott, advised his nephew to make "speedy measures to remove Jenny from the expenses attending her being lodged in prison" but confessed that he felt "much uneasiness" about selling her. Because Jenny's husband and daughter remained with Birnie, Scott believed that it "would be inhumane to separate them." He was, however, quick to add that if Birnie could sell the entire family and if "he deem[ed] such a measure prudent, I shall not object thereto." Unmoved by Jenny's family ties, Birnie continued with his plans. Faced with the threat of imminent sale, Pompey buckled on the road to Baltimore. "He and I came to an understanding," Birnie noted, "he preferred coming home and promised to behave well." Birnie accepted Pompey's promise, had him flogged by a constable, and sent him home. Jenny was less fortunate. "I preceded to B. More.," he scrawled in his diary. "Sold Jenny." Scott approved of his nephew's handling of the situation, although he believed that Jenny's sale price ($435) was "less than her real value." Pompey's conversion and the anguish that he must have witnessed on the part of Jenny's husband and daughter taught Birnie a powerful lesson: The threat of the auction block was as effective as the scourge in controlling slaves.[113]

The challenges of maintaining slavery did not automatically translate into enthusiasm for free wage labor. To the extent that political economists imagined a binary relationship between bound and free labor, it was constructed around slaveholding plantations and family farms. Farmers' increased participation in commodity markets had not undermined the importance of family labor; the family farm or freehold remained the dominant form of land tenure and labor extraction in New England and the Middle Atlantic through the early nineteenth century.[114] Republicanism strengthened the rhetorical significance of small farmers by declaring that independent yeomen—Jefferson's "chosen people of God"—were both repositories of virtue and bulwarks against tyranny. The laboring poor, whether employed in agriculture or industry, occupied an undesirable position in this cosmology. Pointing to the miserable plight of European workers, American political economists cited a large population of permanent wage laborers as a harbinger of social decay.[115]

Whether performed by family members, apprentices, indentured servants, or slaves, household labor formed the backbone of the agricultural workforce, but farmers and planters did have periodic recourse to hired laborers. We glimpse farmers' need for hired help in a 1770 agreement between Frederick County farmer George Dillenher and his son, John, in which the father relinquished control of the family's Buck Lodge farm. Recognizing that wage laborers would be essential to the farm's operation, Dillenher agreed to pay half the wages of "all ye laborers or workmen which he, sd. John, would be necessitated to hire or employ to assist . . . in working and managing sd. plantation to advantage in a proper and regular manner from to time to time."[116] The need for hired laborers was most acute during hay making and the grain harvests. When Peter Weedle divided his Frederick County farm between his son and his widow, he specified that the son must assist his mother by paying "half of all expenses in hiring labourers in hay making and harvesting."[117] Farm account books underscore the need for hired laborers at harvest. Despite owning twenty-four slaves, Harford County planter Nathan Rigbie employed free black and white farmhands for 242 days between 1772 and 1780. The vast majority of those days (216) were devoted to cutting hay or harvesting rye and wheat.[118]

Whether these harvesters and farmhands were permanent wage laborers or members of landowning families making temporary forays into the labor market is uncertain. Many contemporaries complained that permanent hired laborers were scarce during the early national period. In 1792, Philadelphian Richard Peters reckoned that "the class of people merely laborers is not very numerous, and by no means stationary or collected." The causes of this shortage, Peters argued, were the uncertainty of farmwork and the abundance of inexpensive frontier land. With workers thin on the ground, most farmers exchanged labor with their neighbors during the busiest seasons. "Many who have small farms," Peters noted, "can spare a portion of their time to assist their neighbors for hire."[119]

Despite or perhaps because of the scarcity of wage laborers, employers on both sides of the Mason-Dixon Line voiced numerous complaints and misgivings about hired hands. In 1787, Alexander Coventry, a farmer in New York's Hudson River Valley, bemoaned the "insolence of what is called hired help, who must be humored like spoiled children, or they will leave at their own will."[120] Pennsylvanians shared these sentiments. "The Germans seldom hire men to work upon their farms," wrote Benjamin Rush, because "the feebleness of that authority which masters possess over hired servants, is such that their wages are seldom procured from their labor."[121] Dissatisfaction with hirelings led some Marylanders to express a preference for bound laborers. In 1785, for example, Governor Thomas Johnson encouraged George Washington to employ indentured servants and slaves on the Potomac Canal. Johnson thought it "desirable to hire Negroes as well as purchase servants" for the canal, believing that "their labor will be more valuable than that of common white hirelings."[122] That same year, Baltimore County farmer Thomas Jones grew frustrated with his white hands and decided to harvest his wheat with slaves.[123]

Marylanders' dissatisfaction with hired laborers stemmed from many sources. Some complained about employees' irregular work habits, penchant for drinking, and disagreeable habit of demanding high wages. Niemcewicz bemoaned the shiftless behavior of northern Maryland's itinerant laborers, who punctuated brief stints of work with long bouts of drinking. "Why not?" he sneered. "After all, three days work is enough for a week's drinking." Boerstler shared this contempt for the region's pampered and often besotted hirelings. In 1785, he complained that harvesters were plied with liquor, paid generous wages, fed meals that were "like a wedding feast," and were otherwise "treated well for the terrible job they do." The farmhands and apprentices who attended horse races attracted their share of criticism from those concerned about workers' habits. One moralist chided those who "crowd to the booths, drink to intoxication, and proceed to quarrelling, and frequently to murder" before returning to their workplaces "unfit for any industry." Others simply viewed footloose laborers as threats to the region's peace and stability. In 1807, the sheriff of Frederick County denounced the "disorderly and riotous conduct of laborers" on a road and warned that the "military authority" would quell future disturbances.[124]

Concerns about free laborers' unruly habits were inextricably linked with fears of a breakdown of authority and a further weakening of poor people's work ethic. Northern Maryland's commercial expansion had spawned an underclass of impoverished whites and free blacks who worked intermittently, drank and gambled persistently, and seldom lived under the watchful eyes of bosses or masters. For free labor to become a useful implement, free laborers would need to be broken of their preindustrial habits. But doing so was a daunting task, for the countryside was a raucous place. In 1798, the Frederick County court lamented the growing number of "ill-regulated taverns" that were fast "becoming the haunts, of not only the idle and dissipated but also . . . of negroes and other ill-disposed people." The court urged constables to take action against tippling houses and other places where "the lower class of people" gathered for "shooting matches, frolics, and merry making," lest the county's residents abandon their "industry and prudent habits."[125]

Throughout the early national period, Maryland's state, county, and municipal governments constructed an imposing legal edifice designed to discipline the workforce. Vagrancy laws were the cornerstone of this policy, which, as historian Seth Rockman notes, often mixed Christian charity and a steely determination to control workers.[126] In 1796, the General Assembly authorized the Washington County overseers of the poor to commit any "vagrants, vagabonds, beggars, and other dissolute and disorderly persons . . . who follow no labor, trade, occupation, or business" to the workhouse for "any time not exceeding three months." There, the overseers would break the poor of intemperate habits and inculcate in them a work ethic and a strong sense of shame. To keep the inmates sober, the state authorized the overseers to impose a forty-dollar fine on peddlers who sold "any strong liquor" on the workhouse grounds. Inmates capable of working were to be kept "at hard labor." In an effort both to stigmatize the workhouse's denizens and to prevent their escape, the poor were required to wear shirts or hats bearing blue or red badges with the letters *P.W.* Those inmates who refused could have their rations reduced or be sentenced to additional stints at hard labor.[127] Municipalities wielded similar authority. Frederick's 1816 charter allowed aldermen to impose a twenty-dollar fine on "vagrant and loose and disorderly persons" or to lodge them in the municipal workhouse for thirty days.[128] Hagerstown followed suit the following decade. In 1824, the town council declared that all "vagrant, loose and disorderly persons, lewd women, keepers of bawdy houses, and persons having no visible means of support" were subject to arrest and examination by justices of the peace. People who violated this ordinance faced fines and confinement in the county workhouse, where they could be "kept at hard labor for any time not exceeding thirty days."[129] Despite the range of laws arrayed against the poor, it remains unclear whether the vagrancy ordinances disciplined the poor and drove recalcitrant laborers into the workforce. The records of aldermen, justices of the peace, and sheriffs who were responsible for enforcing these policies are not extant, but anecdotal evidence suggests that the measures were not dead letters. In 1822, for example, five "idle and dissolute" women escaped from the Hagerstown workhouse.[130] While it is difficult—even impossible—to determine how vigorously county authorities enforced the vagrancy ordinances, their rationale and intent remains clear—to use legal compulsion to compel otherwise ungovernable free, landless laborers to work.

The numerous challenges confronting those attempting to forge an efficient, tractable workforce from hired laborers were made apparent to English agriculturist Richard Parkinson, who rented Orange Hill farm on the outskirts of Baltimore from 1799 to 1800. So disastrous were his dealings with American domestics and farmhands that the Englishman concluded, "If I was compelled to live in that country I would not wish to have more land than myself or my family could cultivate . . . for all the white men I employed ate much and worked little." Parkinson's woes were exacerbated by the labor shortages gripping early national Maryland, which forced employers to compete for workers. It was not uncommon, Parkinson recalled, for neighboring farmers to "offer wages, before your face, to induce the white men who are working with you to go with them, which makes them very saucy." Workers soon recognized their power and acted accordingly: They demanded advances, refused to engage except by the month, and spent weeks "frolicking" in Baltimore.[131]

The American legal and political systems compounded Parkinson's troubles. To his dismay, he had discovered that American workers enjoyed greater legal freedom than their English counterparts. "There is no power given you, as a master, to confine a hired servant by law," Parkinson lamented, "nor is there any compulsion by the whip." Worse, the radical egalitarianism unleashed by the American Revolution had emboldened laborers, rendering them ungovernable. "The idea of liberty and equality there destroys all rights," Parkinson complained, "and every one does as he likes." Parkinson attempted to disabuse his farmhands of their republican beliefs but soon learned that "any man that obstructs these liberties is looked upon as a bad subject, and an enemy of the rights of man." Indeed, Parkinson's attempts to enforce verbal agreements and discipline his workers often ended in disaster. When he chastised a German farmhand for careless mowing, the worker "threw down his hat and scythe, stamped upon his hat, damned me and all Englishmen, and went his way."[132]

Parkinson's narrative must be approached with skepticism. An ardent conservative, he despised the "wild chimeras of fallacious equality" that had swept through the United States and France. Parkinson hoped that an "unadorned relation" of his bitter disappointment in North America would stem the tide of English emigration and spare his country "the loss of many a valuable though humble member."[133] Not surprisingly, American critics ridiculed Parkinson's account of his tribulations. "So cautiously is every consolatory topic avoided, that we are at a loss how, in the midst of all sorts of calamity and vexation, he could either have paid his rent or preserved his reason," opined Charles Brockden Brown, editor of the *Literary Magazine and American Register*. Still, Brown conceded that Parkinson's depiction of American workers contained a kernel of truth: Hired workers were expensive and often difficult to manage. Brown was, however, optimistic that servants and farmhands would become more tractable over time, predicting "that as numbers increase in America, the evil complained of will wear out"; laborers, "like all other dealers in articles of growing supply, will become more and more courteous to their employers."[134]

If some writers were optimistic about the future of free labor, the form that the emerging labor regime would take remained unclear. Slavery might have been an unwieldy tool, but employers remained wary of the undisciplined landless workers who tramped around the Middle Atlantic. In 1801, former Maryland slaveholder John Beale Bordley captured this uncertainty about the future of labor in the young nation. "When slavery shall cease or be inhibited," he pondered, "where or how are means of cultivating the southern and middle states to be found?" The question was especially vexing for those engaged in wheat production. They needed help at critical junctures in the growing season, which created short-term labor shortages that drove wages upward. "The farmer is fortunate who can find then hands for his purposes," Bordley observed, "for, generally, when one farmer wants additional aid, others also want it." While engaging slaves or workers under annual contracts could guarantee enough hands for harvest and planting, farmers with large standing forces might find themselves saddled with idle, unproductive hands during much of the year.

For Bordley, cottagers were the solution to this dilemma. Landlords engaged these tenants and their families under annual contracts and provided them with houses, small plots, and periodic advances of cash or credit. In exchange for these wages, they demanded that cottagers and their dependents assist with the harvest and other chores. During the slack seasons, however, landlords expected cottagers to support themselves and allowed them to seek other work. Such agreements offered many benefits to both tenants and landlords. The cottagers received homes, land, and a measure of stability. Their employers received a tractable workforce, for the debts cottagers accrued could be used to drive them into the harvest fields. Moreover, a landlord could command the services of tenants' wives and children but was not responsible for their maintenance: The cost of supporting dependent spouses and children remained squarely on the cottagers' shoulders.[135]

Large landowners along Mason and Dixon's Line followed this advice and made cottagers a mainstay of their workforces. Indeed, farm and plantation ledgers reveal that planters were learning to harness the productive energies of entire households. Cobbler and farmhand Edward Moland and planter Roger Johnson of Frederick County, for example, spun a complex web of credits and debits. Between 1816 and 1818, Moland amassed debts totaling $133.97 for rent, foodstuffs, and wool. He squared these accounts by making shoes, binding wheat, and having his wife spin thread. His fellow tenant, Robert Campbell, repaid Johnson for $49.62 in store credits, cash advances, rent, and provisions with the assistance of his wife, who earned $8.25 as a harvester. Neither Campbell nor Moland was fully employed by Johnson, which suggests that they, like the cottagers Bordley idealized, were exchanging credit and a stable residence for periodic labor.[136]

Employers discovered other strategies for tapping the labor power of rural households. Outwork allowed merchants and planters to profit from the labor of women who never entered the fields. Between 1810 and 1812, farmer and storekeeper Aquilla Hall of Harford County advanced raw flax to seventeen women, including eight free blacks, who spun the fibers into thread. In exchange for a share of the thread produced (they worked "on halves"), Hall provided women such as "Negro Easter Rice," "Negro Nancy York," and Fanny Johnson with small cash payments, credits, and foodstuffs. The web of exchange between Hall and his workers at times included an array of domestic manufactures. In addition to making thread worth twelve cents, Mrs. George Taylor sold him three dozen chickens, fourteen shirts, and five suits of "Negroes Clothes."[137]

Contracts stipulating that workers' families were to work, at least periodically, in exchange for credit, rent, and various supplies became a mainstay of labor agreements during the early national period. In 1819, a Frederick County farmer advertised for "an industrious, steady man" with a "small family to work on the farm."[138] The following year, Baltimore County farmer Robert N. Carman made similar demands of laborer Leven Hall. In their contract, Carman agreed to give Hall, his wife, and his sons "the sum of $200 a year, and also to find his sons in common working clothes and provide his wife with a half bushel of corn meal per year and one pound of bacon or pork or beef per day, also with milch or cider for their breakfasts and suppers, and they all to labor faithfully in and about any work upon the farm and conduct themselves in a sober, orderly, and industrious manner."[139]

Such agreements were not confined to agricultural employments; hirers also demanded that the families of rural artisans and factory operatives assist with their businesses. When Thomas Reed commenced as a blacksmith at Mt.

St. Mary's Seminary, the institution made his wife's board and lodging conditional on her raising poultry for the college.[140] The owners of a Frederick County paper factory expressed a preference for "a person with a family of children from eight years and upward" and promised a "house and garden [to] be given rent free and employment in the mill to all children who may be capable of doing anything."[141] As the nineteenth century progressed, more and more employers along the Mason-Dixon Line began hiring men with the understanding, either implicit or explicit, that their families would engage in domestic production, such as weaving or tending dairy cows and poultry, or trudge into the harvest.[142]

The terrain of the emerging market for family labor was uneven, fracturing along sometimes overlapping lines of gender and legal status. Employers wanted to control the labor of their free workmen's dependents but had little interest in either enslaved or free single women who brought children in tow. Those seeking domestic servants or dairymaids preferred single, unattached women, because workers in these positions often became part of their employers' households. Both masters and employers feared that their female workers' children and spouses might disturb their homes or distract women from their chores. Moreover, the pervasive notion of female dependency made free single mothers seem strangely out of place in a labor market increasingly dominated by male-headed households.[143] County officials—and a good many gossips—assumed that these women were a burden to the community. In 1793, the wagging tongues of her neighbors compelled a woman known only as Elizabeth to submit a petition denying that she had abandoned an illegitimate child on the butcher's doorstep in Frederick. Through her attorney, Elizabeth insisted that she was a "good, true, faithful, pious, chaste, and honest citizen" and vehemently denied rumors that she was "a whore and had many bastard children and would have them again if they . . . were to be supported by the county."[144]

Given the assumptions made about women workers, it not surprising that when Rebecca Phillips announced that she wanted to hire or purchase "a middle aged Negro Woman, who is a good cook and washer," she specifically asked for one "unincumbered with children." Such advertisements were not unusual. In 1816, a resident of Frederick County advertised for a slave "who has been accustomed to house work and who is unincumbered with a husband or children." Enslaved domestics with too many children might become a burden to their owners. Explaining why he was selling a "strong and healthy [woman] of honest, industrious, and sober habits" along with her three young children, a Frederick County slaveholder noted that this otherwise "excellent house servant . . . does not suit the present owner on account of her children."

Another slave owner assured buyers that he was selling his "NEGRO WOMAN and her four female children" for no fault "but for want of room to keep such a growing family."[145] Just as some masters and mistresses spurned slaves with families, bosses had neither use nor sympathy for free single mothers. This viewpoint became painfully clear to Sarah Woolford when her husband, John, was convicted of burglary and sentenced to nine years in the penitentiary. Sarah had been a dairymaid on the Frederick County plantation of Baker Johnson, where her husband worked as a cobbler, farmhand, and wagoner. Despite Sarah's "honest and industrious" character, Johnson was unwilling to keep her and her four children after John's imprisonment. In a statement that reveals a complete lack of either compassion or a sense of irony, Johnson noted that the Woolford family "appear to be in great poverty" and were "chiefly supported by the bounty of friends."[146] The marginalization of women in northern Maryland's labor market would become even more pronounced over the following decades.

If the future of free, wage labor was clouded, that of indentured servitude became increasingly clear—and grim—during the early national period. Despite enjoying a brief revival after the American Revolution, the institution had become moribund by 1820. Although historians debate the scale of the trade in bound immigrants, indentured servants or "redemptioners" continued to arrive in the United States from the 1780s until the 1810s. Advertisements for European servants peppered the papers along the Mason-Dixon Line during the early national decades. In 1787, for example, a merchant in Georgetown informed readers in Frederick County that he had "about sixty Redemptioners and Servants, whose time of service will be disposed of . . . for cash or any kind of country produce.[147] After the War of 1812, a large number of German servants arrived in Philadelphia, where they were sold to rural employers in southeast Pennsylvania. In the summer of 1817, a Baltimore newspaper reported heavy immigration from Switzerland and the German states, which had traditionally been leading sources of redemptioners. Later that year, readers in Hagerstown learned that the *Hersteller* had arrived from Amsterdam with "a number of German Emigrants, who are desirous of binding themselves to good masters for their passage." As late as 1819, a newspaper in Frederick announced the arrival of a ship from Bremen carrying "a number of persons of both sexes, who are willing to serve a certain time for their passage—the men are principally tradesmen and farmers."[148] It is unclear how many of these servants made their way to northern Maryland, although the number may have been quite small. An examination of 110 inventories recorded between 1786 and 1790 in Frederick County revealed only three indentured servants.[149]

The traffic in indentured servants or redemptioners came under increased scrutiny in the 1810s. European nations took measures to stem the tide of emigration, both free and unfree, and to regulate the traffic in indentured servants. Great Britain forbade the emigration of skilled laborers (1794) and limited the number of passengers on ships sailing for America to one person for every five tons of the vessel (1817), a restriction that made it almost impossible for captains or merchants to profit from the market for indentured servants. Other states cracked down on the abuses endemic to the trade. In 1817, for example, Holland and Switzerland began investigating the trade in servants and enacted laws to protect emigrants. The Dutch dispatched an ambassador to study measures that would protect emigrants, while the Swiss refused to grant passports to anyone who could not present a note of two hundred florins, a measure that prevented poor people from leaving the country.[150]

Indentured servitude was besieged on both sides of the Atlantic. Beginning in 1817, the newly formed German Society of Maryland began campaigning against the abuses and frauds perpetrated against redemptioners. The Maryland General Assembly had already created some daylight between indentured servitude and slavery in 1790, when the legislature declared that indentured service could not be made hereditary. Believing it "contrary to the dictates of humanity and the principles of the Christian religion to inflict penalties on the children for the offenses of the parents," the legislature declared without irony that the offspring of black men and free or indentured white women would no longer be forced into servitude.[151] In 1818, having proclaimed that white women could not under any circumstances pass their unfree status to succeeding generations, the General Assembly responded to pressure from the German Society and further distanced indentured servitude from slavery by enacting legislation that limited masters' authority over bound immigrants. Noting that German and Swiss servants were "frequently exposed to cruel and oppressive impositions," the legislature required state-appointed registers to review and record all indentures. Terms of service for adults were limited to four years, and those of minor children were capped at ages eighteen for girls and twenty-one for boys. Children's rights were protected in other ways as well: They could not be bound out by anyone except their parents, next of kin, or the state register; their masters were required to provide two months of education annually; and they could not be held responsible for debts incurred by their parents or relatives. Moreover, the law stipulated that a ship's master could not detain immigrants longer than sixty days. If labor contracts were not made within that period, the immigrants' transportation costs would be transformed into a simple debt, recoverable through collection actions but not through forced labor.[152]

The death knell for indentured servitude came in 1829, when a Baltimore city court annulled the contracts of bound workmen on the Chesapeake and Ohio (C & O) Canal. The company's managers had attempted to address its chronic labor shortages by importing indentured servants from Great Britain. By August, the C & O had brought over about five hundred workmen, but controlling them proved difficult. Many servants bolted soon after arriving in the United States. The company captured and imprisoned some of the fugitives but could retain only a tenuous hold on the servants. Two of the runaways appealed to a federal court for a writ of habeas corpus, claiming that they "could not make themselves slaves" and were therefore "under no obligation to serve the company." The judge disagreed. Although he declared that indentured servitude was "repugnant" and "opposed to the principles of our free institutions," he upheld the 1715 Maryland statute that required the servants to complete their contracts. Other workmen sought redress in the Baltimore court, whose judges were more sympathetic to their plight. The court declared that the C & O could sue workers for debt but could not compel them to complete their contracts. By the 1820s, indentured servitude had become a legal relic.[153]

Most people seem to have been sympathetic to indentured servants who challenged their masters. Clotworthy Birnie discovered how his neighbors' unwillingness to support his claim on a fugitive indentured servant, Betty, could render him powerless. In December 1811, Birnie attempted to reclaim Betty, who was being sheltered at the nearby home of Mr. and Mrs. Cowers. Birnie "reasoned" with Betty and asked her to return voluntarily, then flourished her indenture before the Cowerses and demanded that they surrender the runaway. Birnie seized Betty but was immediately confronted by the Cowerses and another couple, the Gildeas, who had rallied to Betty's defense. A tussle soon erupted. Amid the melee, Birnie threatened violence against Betty and Mrs. Gildea and warned that he would prosecute the Cowerses and Gildeas. Undeterred, Mr. Gildea growled that Birnie "should feel the weight of his hand (or fist)" if he "would lay a hand on her," while Mr. Cowers declared "it was his house & that [Birnie] should not take her away." Birnie retreated, but the following summer he brought his complaint before the Frederick County court. The court upheld the indenture and authorized Birnie to "use reasonable force to enforce her return to my service," but Birnie seems to have been unwilling to risk another confrontation: There is no evidence that Betty returned to his household.[154]

The gradual disappearance of indentured servitude clarified racial distinctions that were sometimes murky during the colonial period. Maryland had been a thoroughgoing slave society since the seventeenth century, and white servants had long been granted privileges and spared abuses, distinguishing whites from blacks. Still, whites sometimes found themselves subjected to harsh treatment. In 1788, William Boswell petitioned the Frederick County court for redress, claiming that his master, Nathan McGruder, had held him "under the most rigid government," kept him "almost naked," and "compelled your petitioner to receive a few old rags, a pr. of old shoe buckles, and a pr. of good shoes for his *freedom dues*." The punishments inflicted on indentured servants made a powerful impression on one Carroll County slaveholder, who decades later remembered seeing an Irish servant whipped and placed in an iron collar. Working and suffering alongside slaves also fostered friendships and intimate relationships between indentured immigrants and slaves. In 1773, John Fletcher hauled his servant, Ann Grimes, before the Frederick County Court, where she stood accused of bastardy for bearing a "Child begot by a Negro." White servants continued to find common cause with slaves. In 1792, for example, a slaveholder in Baltimore County advertised for the return of Bob, "a country born, young negro man" who had escaped with an Irish indentured servant.[155] Still, such moments would become increasingly rare as indentured servitude withered, as service became equated with blackness, and as poor whites began to defend their racial prerogatives.

The legal dismantling of indentured labor was both cause and consequence of the rising popular disdain for the institution. In the aftermath of the American Revolution, servitude steadily became the reserve of Africans and African Americans. While traveling through Maryland and Virginia in the 1790s, Englishman Thomas Cooper complained of the "impossibility of procuring any servants but Negro-slaves." As the links between blackness and servility grew stronger, poorer whites began asserting their independence by kicking against the goads of inequality and servitude. Englishman Isaac Weld was dismayed to discover that the "lower classes of people will return rude and impertinent answers . . . and will insult a person that bears the appearance of a gentleman . . . to show how much they consider themselves on an equality with them." As a result of this leveling spirit, "none but those of the most indifferent characters ever enter into service, which they consider as suitable only to negroes." This climate had a chilling effect on masters attempting to hold on to their servants. In 1819, Clotworthy Birnie Jr. informed his father that an English immigrant who had arrived in Frederick with fourteen indentured servants had soon lost them. "They are all leaving him," the younger Birnie reported.[156]

As the chasm between bound and free labor widened, the beatings and public humiliations that had previously been inflicted on both black and white criminals came under increased scrutiny. In August 1803, the Washington County court sentenced Peter Light, a white man from Sharpsburg, to "be whipt, pilloried, and cropt" for making counterfeit money. Such punishments were not unusual and were inflicted with little regard to the criminals' race. Light was probably still recuperating from his wounds in February 1804, when the Washington County court ordered two more whites to the whipping post. John Murdoch was to receive "thirty lashes on his bare back, well laid on, and stand ten minutes in the pillory" for stealing an axe, while John Saunders received twenty lashes for theft. They were joined by "Negro Bob," a free black who was sentenced to fifteen stripes for stealing a few pieces of iron. By the 1810s, though, physical punishments were increasingly reserved for indentured servants. In 1817, for example, Frederick's aldermen declared that "any slave or imported servant" convicted of violating municipal ordinances would suffer "any number of stripes, not exceeding thirty-nine." The dwindling number of white servants, combined with a republican ideology that celebrated equality among whites, guaranteed that whites would bristle at anything that smacked of slavery. In 1819, the Washington County court sparked a firestorm when it sentenced a poor white man to be flogged for profane swearing. "We can scarcely believe that such proceedings should have taken place in Maryland," thundered one writer, who insisted that whipping a white man was "repugnant to humanity . . . and inconsistent with the spirit of free government."[157]

The Odysseys of Romulus Ware and Charity Butler

Like the hazy images in the landscapes painted by Peale and Guy, most of the workingmen and -women who built the economy of the young republic dwelled in obscurity. For more than two centuries, they have remained small figures in the distant backgrounds of paintings, entries in plantation ledgers, and the "artful villains" of runaway servant and slave advertisements. There are, however, times when we can piece these fragments into a fuller if still incomplete mosaic of individual laborers. One of these rare moments occurred on 22 June 1807, when HMS *Leopard* attacked and boarded USS *Chesapeake* off Norfolk, Virginia. Among the seamen impressed by the British was an alleged deserter from HMS *Melampus,* William (alias Romulus) Ware. Were it not for his capture, we would have scant knowledge of Ware. But in the aftermath of the *Chesapeake*'s surrender, the identities of her imprisoned crewmen—their backgrounds, citizenship, and legal status—became questions of national significance. Hoping to hasten the release of the prisoners, the friends of neighbors of the Ware and his shipmates gathered depositions proving that they were native-born Americans. These affidavits throw light upon the winding path that brought Ware to the *Chesapeake* and illuminate a great deal about the economic and social transformations being wrought in early national Maryland.[158]

William Ware was born into slavery in Frederick County, where his master, Norman Bruce, owned a farm near the flour mills on Pipe Creek. The most striking feature of the young bondsman was his color, which witnesses described as "like a very dark white man" and "approaching nearer to white than any mulatto." The source of his complexion was no mystery. According to his master's son, Upton Bruce, Ware was "universally admitted" to be the offspring of a "dark mulatto" slave, Phillis, and Andrew Ware, a white man. "This fact was never questioned," Bruce averred. "The children passed for, and were admitted to be his, and assumed his name." There was, however, no doubt about the young man's status. Ware was "raised with the children of other slaves, and stood upon the same footing" until his twentieth birthday, when the younger Bruce granted him a measure of freedom. Moved by his affection for the now deceased Andrew Ware and by "the desire expressed by [my] father to have [his] children liberated," Bruce allowed William "to go at large" with the promise that he would "make some compensation, which was never done." Bruce never filed a deed of manumission, and people in the neighborhood understood that Ware's legal standing remained murky. One witness testified that Ware was not free but had "made some agreement with his master, by which he was suffered to go at large," while another remembered that he "left the service of his master by some permission or some agreement, I suppose." Unconcerned by these technicalities, Ware carried himself as a freedman. He shed his past by adopting the name Romulus and earned a living by "working about the country . . . sometimes as a waggoner, driving a team to and from Baltimore" and later going to sea. Ware may have found something akin to freedom, but his life ended in shackles. In 1807, an admiralty court sentenced him and his mates, David Martin and John Strachan, to five hundred stripes for desertion. Although the British spared the Americans from being flogged, Martin and Strachan did not return home until 1812. Ware was less fortunate. He died in a Royal Navy hospital in 1809.[159]

While Romulus Ware sought freedom on the high seas, another slave belonging to Norman Bruce was seeking her freedom in the courts. In 1821, the Supreme Court of Pennsylvania heard the case of Charity Butler and her daughters, Harriet and Sophia, who claimed their freedom under the state's gradual emancipation act of 1780. The long, twisting road that brought them before the Supreme Court began in 1782, when Bruce leased his farm and a "number of slaves" to a man named Cleland. Soon after signing the contract, Cleland hired one of the young bondswomen included in the lease to a man named Gilleland. In exchange for Charity's services, Gilleland was "to feed and clothe her until her arrival at sixteen years of age." At some point, Gilleland's marriage soured, and he abandoned his wife, leaving her "destitute [and] obliged to support herself and an infant child." Mrs. Gilleland then moved into her mother's house and supported herself as a seamstress. In 1788 and 1789, Mrs. Gilleland "occasionally went into Pennsylvania to work, taking the child and Charity with her to nurse it." The trips back and forth across the Mason-Dixon Line became the foundation of the Butler family's suit. If their attorneys could prove that Charity had lived on free soil for more than six months and that she had done so with the consent of her master or his lessees, then Charity would receive a kind of retroactive manumission effective in 1788 or 1789. If she were free at this early date, then Harriet and Sophia, who were later born slaves in Maryland, would follow their mother into freedom. After being rebuffed by the lower courts, the Butlers appealed to the Supreme Court, whose justices affirmed that the Butlers were not entitled to their freedom because their owner, Bruce, had never authorized Cleland or Gilleland to remove them from Maryland.[160]

Tragic and unusual in their particulars, the odysseys of Ware and Butler were products of profound shifts shaking the economic and political landscapes of the Middle Atlantic. Like a growing number of African Americans in Maryland and Pennsylvania, Ware and Butler moved—fitfully and unevenly—toward an uncertain freedom. Some, like Ware, took advantage of the buoyant economy to find work and a measure of freedom on the Middle Atlantic's farms, turnpikes, and waterfronts. Others, like Butler and her family, sensed the changes to the region's legal landscape and fought for their freedom in courts. The commercial expansion of the early republic invigorated slavery along the Mason-Dixon Line, but the institution rested on unsound foundations, and the enslaved were determined to test their chains.

The lives of workingmen such as Romulus Ware bore the indelible marks of the Middle Atlantic's unpredictable international commodity markets. Ware spent his early years nears the mills in Frederick County, and the wagons he drove between Pipe Creek and Baltimore were undoubtedly crammed with barrels of flour. Ware probably began his maritime career in Baltimore, then emerging as one of the nation's leading commercial entrepôts. Baltimore's merchants and the farmers in its hinterlands followed the conflicts that engulfed Ware and his shipmates on the *Chesapeake,* for continued warfare meant steady demand and high prices for their foodstuffs. It was, however, a dangerous game. In late 1807, the *Chesapeake* affair, combined with continued assaults on the nation's merchantmen, led President Thomas Jefferson to call for a suspension of foreign trade. Congress responded with the Embargo Act of 1807, which brought northern Maryland's prosperity to an abrupt halt.

The farmers and planters along the Mason-Dixon Line had reaped bountiful harvests and tidy profits because of strong international demand for their foodstuffs during the Napoleonic Wars. The embargo turned off the spigot. Northern Marylanders now learned that their products were worthless without access to European and Caribbean markets. "To say that the wheat and other grain shall not go out of the country is the same thing as to tell us that we shall not sell them at all," declared an anonymous writer from Frederick County.[161] "With good crops, and our grain ready for market, we are not able to sell it for more than the expense of carrying it down and must . . . let it remain at home, and rot in our fields," moaned another writer.[162] The region's dependence on foreign markets was underscored during the War of 1812. With foreign trade disrupted, producers once again saw demand for their wheat and flour evaporate. The farmers of Frederick County can "sell to Baltimore for *domestic use*, only 6,000 barrels of their 100,000," wailed one farmer, and prices became depressed to the point where "our flour would probably not bring more than would pay for the carriage of an empty barrel!"[163] The Embargo Act and the War of 1812 were painful reminders that the heady prosperity rested on shaky footings. Yet these upheavals were mere tremors. In 1819, northern Maryland would feel an economic earthquake that shook its foundations to the core and forever altered the landscape of slavery and freedom.

2. "A Strange Reverse of Fortune"

Panic, Depression, and the
Transformation of Labor

In 1831, John P. Thompson of the *Frederick-Town Herald* climbed the "High Knob" of Catoctin Mountain. There, he was confronted with a glorious vision. "I have stood upon the mountain high in the air, and witnessed on all sides, as far as the eye can reach, an almost unbroken line of yellow grain, which reflected in the sun, like the shining bed of *Paetolus*."[1] Thompson's appreciation was shared by other commentators, including the acerbic travel writer Anne Royall, who toured Maryland in the 1820s. Although she spared few criticisms in her description of the Middle Atlantic, Royall was enthralled by Frederick County, which "exhibits a uniform representation of beautiful farms and mansions." "Nothing like poverty shows its head, in or near Frederick," she gushed, "all is flowing with wealth, health, and beauty."[2] Such effusive praise suggests that little had changed in the decades since Polish traveler Julian Ursyn Niemcewicz's visit. But a great deal had changed, and those changes had left indelible marks on the countryside.

For those who cared to notice, there were abundant signs that northern Maryland had weathered numerous storms during the 1820s. In 1832, Englishman Thomas Hamilton found that "the appearance of poverty seemed to increase" outside Hagerstown. "Here and there a ragged negro slave was seen at work near the wretched hovel of his master," but many farms were abandoned and the fields allowed to "relapse into a state of nature."[3] For James W. C. Pennington, an enslaved blacksmith living near Hagerstown, nothing embodied the fundamental and wrenching changes more than Fountain Rock, the former seat of Washington County planter Samuel Ringgold. As Pennington wrote his autobiography in the 1840s, he remembered a bleak night twenty years earlier when he had crossed the yard of the abandoned plantation and witnessed its overgrown walks, rusting fences, sagging ceilings, and a silence broken only by "the crying cricket and cockroaches." "I could but pause a moment and recur in silent horror to the fact, that a strange reverse of fortune had lately driven from that proud mansion a once opulent family," Pennington recalled.[4]

Pennington intended his remarks as a cautionary tale about slavery's corrosive effects on whites, but the crumbling plantation represented something larger. It attested to the agricultural and financial upheavals that by 1830 had left northern Maryland's economy in ruins and placed slavery on the path to gradual extinction. This "strange reverse of fortune" represented a dramatic departure from the decades immediately following the American Revolution, when slavery and free labor had mingled without creating serious dissonance among employers. The misgivings that landowners harbored about slavery were, to a large extent, balanced by their ambivalence toward wage laborers, and most were content to cobble together a workforce from the ranks of both free and unfree workers. In the decades following the Panic of 1819, the fluidity that had characterized earlier labor arrangements gradually hardened. A growing chorus of agricultural reformers and political economists crafted a new dialectic between slavery and free labor, locking these labor regimes in a mortal struggle for supremacy. How these transformations came about and what they portended for free and enslaved laborers are the subjects of this chapter.

"The Day of Retribution": The Panic of 1819

"We have been rioting and reveling in the blood of Europeans," declared Frederick merchant and publisher Mathias Bartgis. Writing in the aftermath of the Panic of 1819, Bartgis reckoned that his countrymen were experiencing God's retribution for "basking in the sunshine of good times" while thousands died. "Alas, human nature shudders, it never occurred how we should be scourged for our inequities; and, not until the day of retribution had come, did we think of our past follies."[5] Others also saw the hand of Providence in the economic crises. In 1822, the mayor of Hagerstown proclaimed a "day of humiliation and prayer" for deliverance from the depression, a protracted drought, and a cholera outbreak.[6] Bartgis and his neighbors had not missed the mark, for the region's farmers and merchants were suffering the consequences of decisions made during the Napoleonic Wars, when robust commodity markets and the rapid expansion of credit networks had buoyed the economy and encouraged many people to become dangerously overextended.

The return of peace presaged great hardship for northern Marylanders. In 1815, England enacted a more restrictive corn law that made it difficult for American produce to compete in that country's flour markets. Poor 1816 harvests in both Europe and North America sent flour prices rocketing upward, but northern Maryland's farmers were unable to capitalize because their crops had failed. Over the following years, expanding domestic markets and growing demand for foodstuffs in the West Indies and South America softened the impact of restrictive trade measures and the resumption of European agriculture, but flour prices never regained their wartime levels.[7]

Disruptions in the financial system dovetailed with the weakening commodity markets to exacerbate northern Maryland's woes. By the 1810s, signs indicated that the unstable banking and credit systems that had emerged and flourished during the Napoleonic Wars were beginning to collapse. During the 1790s and 1800s, banks throughout the Middle Atlantic had pursued a reckless course, issuing currency and extending loans under the assumption that commodity markets would continue their upward march. When the wars ended, Baltimore's bankers and the farmers in the city's hinterlands began losing confidence in the small, undercapitalized institutions in rural communities. In 1815, a Washington County editor warned local distillers, farmers, and millers to "be on their guard" when selling produce in Baltimore, for "the merchants of that city have paid you in the notes of distant country banks, and when the same notes are carried back and offered to them, they will not receive them, unless you make a large deduction." Washington County legislator Thomas Kennedy concurred. Although many of his neighbors thought they "were doing wonders when they get a few more cents per barrel for their flour" by taking worthless "western paper," he believed it "a losing business to them in the end." Northern Marylanders believed their financial institutions were secure, but Baltimoreans were less sanguine. Some of the city's bankers and merchants began refusing currency issued by banks in Hagerstown and Frederick, while others imposed drastic discounts.[8]

The resulting confusion sent shock waves through the countryside. As early as 1813, Frederick County planter Thomas S. Lee fretted that growers had become too dependent on commercial flour production and the increasingly scarce currency issued by banks in Baltimore. "Flour is almost the only article that will command money," he wrote, "but money seems to have vanished from the mountains." The potentially disastrous consequences of a financial constriction alarmed many residents of the countryside. "Much vexation and some loss have been and will be experienced in this and other counties by the refusal of the Baltimore banks to receive any but their own paper," warned a Frederick editor in 1815. Two years later, Frederick's businessmen conceded that much of the currency in circulation was unsound. At a public meeting, fifty-four merchants and millers resolved not to receive "the notes of any bank, corporation, road company, or private association, under one dollar" and to "seek opportunities to transmit them to the institutions where they are redeemable." In January 1818, a Hagerstown merchant echoed these complaints, noting that "small notes are constantly getting out of credit" and that "much trouble arises from their circulation." That summer, farmers and millers gathered at Hagerstown to condemn the "sort of paper, *purporting* to be bank notes" and to warn that unless these bills were removed from circulation, "a most serious loss and heart-breaking distress will and surely must be soon felt."[9]

The prediction proved remarkably prescient. In 1818, the Baltimore branch of the Bank of the United States attempted to rein in the unstable credit markets and shore its foundations by collecting some of its twenty million dollars in outstanding loans. The resulting depreciation and contraction of credit reverberated through the countryside. In January 1819, Hancock merchant Samuel Gregory described a "great stagnation of business—banks all thro' this country shutting up and failing."[10]

The financial panic soon spread to the commodity markets. Baltimore's flour markets tumbled so rapidly that one of the city's agricultural journals expressed "great embarrassment in attempting to state the price of anything," a task that the editor equated to measuring "the height of a tree in the midst of a passing tornado."[11] Farmers nervously watched the collapsing markets. From Frederick County, Clotworthy Birnie Jr. wrote that "the harvest has commenced here & it certainly is as luxurious as has ever been known, but if prospects do not mend the farmers may feed their wheat & distill their rye."[12] When the dust settled, flour fetched a mere fraction of its previous value: Between 1817 and 1821, prices plummeted from $14.00 per barrel to a paltry $3.62.[13] Rural merchants and millers, whose fortunes were inextricably linked to commodity markets in Baltimore, felt the impact of the collapse. In 1820, Frederick County miller Ignatius Davis traced the decline of the flour market for a census taker. "During 1815, the price varied from $10 to 9 [per barrel]," he reported; "1819, from $7 to 6; the present year, $5 to 4."[14] The depression did not dissuade manufacturers from producing large quantities of flour and whiskey, but the flagging markets yielded meager profits. "The demand for flour not great—sales considerable—but the price very low," griped Jonathan Hoover, also a miller, while a neighboring whiskey distiller complained of producing "as much as ever" but making "a small profit."[15]

Property values were dragged down in the undertow of commodity prices. "Times here . . . begin to wear an alarming aspect," worried Gregory. "Property, I do believe, within a month, has fallen 25 pr. cent."[16] Kennedy concurred, noting that "land which cost sixty or seventy dollars will not bring twenty" and that most of the farms seized for debts during the previous year remained "unsold for want of bidders."[17] The twin collapses of the commodity and land markets had disastrous consequences for overextended farmers and merchants. Farmland in Frederick County had tickled $125 per acre during the previous decade, and many speculators found themselves caught in a terrible bind. They "stupidly thought it would continue to rise in the same way," observed immigrant J. Jakob Rutlinger. "Then the peace came, and the price fell unbelievably. There they were, the rogues."[18]

Others found themselves staggering under consumer debts. As he traveled along the Mason-Dixon Line attempting to collect on his debts, Bartgis lamented that during "the good times of Dress and Fashion," many farmers "possessing not more than one hundred acres of land" had accrued debts of more than fifteen hundred dollars that "would take their all at the rate property is selling."[19] County court records reveal the consequences of indebtedness. In November 1819, the Washington County court heard 411 cases involving debts or ejectments, a dramatic increase from earlier sessions. In October 1810, for example, the court tried 144 cases involving debts or ejectments, while in October 1814 it heard 131 such cases.[20] In 1820, at the urging of delegates from the state's northern counties, the Maryland General Assembly stanched the bleeding by enacting a stay law that suspended the execution of existing debts until 30 November 1821.[21]

Domestic and foreign competition added to the region's troubles. Northern Maryland's undercapitalized industries felt the strain of competition from more efficient operations in New England and Europe. In 1820, Frederick County tanner John Mantz received discouraging news from a Richmond merchant, who feared that he would be unable to sell Mantz's leather "so long as we are glutted with such quantities of sole leather from the North, which altho' greatly inferior to yours [is] more desirable on account of its cheapness."[22] Mantz also felt pressure from overseas. "Leather has considerably declined these two years," he complained, "owing no doubt, in some measure, to severe competition from the Brasil."[23] Textile mills, too, were swamped in the tempest. In 1819, Bartgis visited a struggling factory outside Hagerstown that possessed "water power sufficient to give employment to two hundred hands" but had only enough work for twenty.[24] The Frederick County textile mill of G. J. Conradt was also foundering. "The immense influx of foreign goods [has] glutted and depressed the market to a ruinous extent," Conradt grumbled, leaving his fledgling operation at the mercy of "foreign competitors of immense wealth, long established in business."[25]

The weakening demand for flour did not prevent farmers from sending their produce to Baltimore and Georgetown. In the spring of 1819, the *Frederick-Town Herald* reported that forty-five hundred barrels of flour had been inspected at Georgetown and that an additional ten thousand barrels had arrived at the city's wharves. "This quantity came down the river in two days, and great quantities more are on the way."[26] The following winter, the *Herald* noted that the "badness of the roads and the low price of produce" had not prevented flour from "pouring into Baltimore."[27] While traveling between Frederick and Baltimore in May 1821, tailor Jacob Englebrecht counted 102 wagons "all going to Baltimore with flour."[28] Warnings from Baltimore's merchants and millers did not dissuade farmers from sending their produce to market. The cruel arithmetic that compelled farmers to send their worthless produce to market was delineated by Washington County planter John Blackford in 1824: "Our markets keep down, [and] the calculation is that the market will be glutted this winter." Worse, there remained "a large quantity of flour in this section of the country to go out—and out it must go—the people must have money."[29] Unwilling or unable to withdraw from commercial production, some farmers sought ways to manipulate the markets. "Delay grinding what wheat you may have on hand, as long as you can," advised one farmer, "and when you have your flour ready, *never, never* store it at any market, as it has a direct tendency of keeping down the price."[30]

The depression abated somewhat in 1824, but the reprieve proved brief. The Hessian fly, an insect whose larvae destroyed maturing wheat, assaulted the region with particular intensity during the 1820s and 1830s.[31] The infestations combined with recurring droughts and unstable commodity markets to devastating effect. In 1832, a harsh winter and a cold, dry spring "totally blasted" the crops. "The wheat fields present a bleak and barren appearance, with scarcely a green spot upon the surface to delight the eye," lamented one writer, who added that in addition to damaging the crops "almost past recovery," the inclement weather had destroyed the meadows and forced farmers to feed their livestock with surplus grain or drive undersized animals to market.[32]

Farmers not only gathered meager harvests in 1833 but also found their efforts undercut by flagging commodity markets. The following spring, the directors of the Washington County Bank painted a bleak portrait of the local economy. The "immensely diminished products of the earth in this section of the country" had not stopped the "rapid and continuing decline" in commodity prices. Property values were plummeting at an "alarming" rate, with some land commanding a mere quarter of its purchase price.[33] Northern Marylanders limped through 1834 and 1835 before disaster struck in the summer of 1836. The Hessian fly descended with renewed ferocity, destroying most of the wheat. "The ravages of the fly are very obvious in many fields," reported one newspaper. "It is much to be feared that there will not be half the usual product."[34]

These dire prophecies proved accurate. By June 1836, farmers were offering their blighted wheat fields as pastures to drovers, while others desperate to provide for their families were retrieving from the warehouses flour that had been intended for export.[35] Flour prices on the local market climbed to unprecedented levels that fall, and some residents became temporarily dependent on imported food.[36] The situation worsened during the following winter and spring. "The prospect of the wheat crop is exceedingly unfavorable," warned one newspaper. Many farmers abandoned their fields, and those who persevered did not expect more than one-third the usual harvest.[37] A series of terse entries in the harvest rolls of Hagerstown farmer George F. Heyser illustrates the calamities that befell the region's farmers during the 1830s. In 1835, he recorded, "Nothing more than a good half crop this year." The following year, his workers gathered a mere forty bushels because "the wheat [had been] killed by the fly." A slight improvement occurred in 1837, but the situation remained grim: "Two fields in wheat this year . . . very bad crops."[38]

"Could Not Beg—Could Not Obtain Employment": The Realignment of Labor

The tempest unleashed by the Panic of 1819 slammed all segments of the rural workforce, but free and enslaved workers experienced the hard times differently. The economic collapse made hired farmhands' hardscrabble existence even more difficult: Unemployment became more frequent, and those fortunate enough to find work found their wages cut. The enslaved fared worse. While the financial pressure weighing on slave owners led some to manumit their slaves, others responded by selling them south. These responses contributed to larger transformations that redrew the landscape of slavery and freedom. Amid the economic crisis, northern Maryland's landowners haltingly and sometimes grudgingly embraced free labor.

The precipitous collapse of commodity markets pulled wages downward. In 1819, a Frederick newspaper reported, "We have it from unquestionable authority that mowers have this season been hired at less than half the wages they had the last seven years."[39] Workers fared no better in Pennsylvania. There, English traveler William Faux recorded a conversation with a farmer who lamented that there were "many more [workers] than could be employed." "The excess of laborers," he warned, presaged "much distress in the coming winter."[40] Those fears were soon realized. The following winter and spring brought little relief: Labor markets remained unsteady and wages low. Although he retained most of his workforce, Clotworthy Birnie demanded concessions from his farmhands and tenants "in case the markets do not improve." Other workers were less fortunate. Among those Birnie considered hiring in 1820 was a young wagoner whose previous employer had defaulted on his entire year's wages.[41] Some people found the chronic unemployment and grinding poverty unbearable. Hagerstown miller James Huston explained why he was committing suicide in a terse note tucked inside his vest: "Could not beg—could not obtain employment."[42]

The plight of northern Maryland's farmhands was exacerbated by the sudden arrival of displaced urban workers seeking employment in the country. The Panic of 1819 brought Baltimore's commercial and industrial sectors to a screeching halt and spawned widespread unemployment. One of the city's newspapers lamented that many "manufactures have stopped or are about to stop, and every branch of mechanical industry is reduced from one-third to one-half," a situation that had plunged "many thousands of productive workers" into poverty.[43] Baltimore's crisis soon reverberated throughout the hinterlands. In Washington County, Samuel Gregory found that "tradesmen of all descriptions are seeking refuge and employment in the countryside. I can now hire hands at $10 a month, whereas in May and June I gave $14.50."[44] Urban laborers continued to scour the countryside looking for work the following year. In July 1820, the *Baltimore Patriot* encouraged the city's idled workers to tramp into rural Pennsylvania, where "a thousand men would find EMPLOYMENT in cutting down . . . the present most abundant harvest."[45]

In the aftermath of the panic, private charity and public relief offered some limited assistance to suffering workers, but these resources were soon exhausted by the calamity. In Frederick and Montgomery Counties, the depression forced many "who have never before [known] what it was to want bread" to seek aid from "wealthy neighbors who can no longer provide relief." Diminished revenues and citizens' demands for retrenchment forced county governments to trim expenditures. In 1820, the directors of the poor in Lancaster, Pennsylvania, cited "the present reduced prices of agricultural produce" when they slashed payments to the county's needy. The following year, the Frederick County commissioners railed against the soaring medical bills and "superfluous luxuries" charged to the poorhouse. "We earnestly admonish the trustees, in these times of general pressure, to turn their attention to reform and prudent retrenchment, for which we think there is abundant room." Trimming expenses proved difficult. In 1823, the county's overseers of the poor requested an additional three thousand dollars because the "pressure of the time" had doubled the almshouse population during the previous year.[46]

Amid the maelstrom of the 1820s, the enslaved suffered most. The onset of Maryland's economic woes coincided with slavery's expansion into the Lower South, a development that tempted many of the state's slaveholders to balance their accounts with the flesh of their bondsmen and -women. The scale of the devastation was staggering (see figure 4). Between 1818 and 1829, slaveholders in Frederick County sold at least 952 people to speculators or planters from the Deep South. During the 1820s, the county's slave population stood somewhere between 6,370 and 6,685, so Frederick County lost at least 12 percent of its slave population to the interstate traffic in a single decade. The land records of neighboring Washington County suggest that the trade also cut a broad swath there, with the county's masters and mistresses consigning at least 209 people to traders' coffles between 1819 and 1826. Once sold, these men, women, and children were scattered throughout the South, with 244 going to Louisiana, 224 to Kentucky, 195 to Tennessee, 106 to Mississippi, 100 to Georgia, 49 to North Carolina, 34 to Alabama, 31 to Virginia, 27 to South Carolina, 10 to Missouri, and 1 to East Florida. Traders in Baltimore and the District of Columbia purchased the remaining 140 people.[47]

The tremendous sums that traders and planters from the Deep South offered for slaves spawned a bifurcated market in northern Maryland, with anemic local demand standing in stark contrast to vibrant southern markets. As early as 1818, Frederick businessman Andrew Turner wrote that "the Georgia people . . . always give better prices than the regular purchaser, who buys for his own use."[48] Despite having been offered $350 by a "western man" for a slave, Charles, Hagerstown master Otho Lawrence was determined "not to

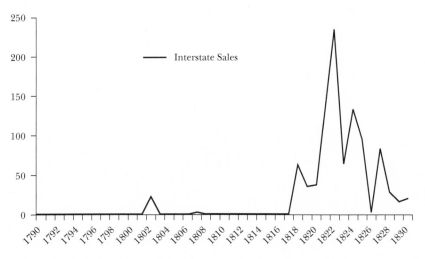

Figure 4. Documented Interstate Slave Sales, Frederick County, Md., 1790–1830. Source: Frederick County Court, Land Records, 1790–1830, Maryland Hall of Records, Annapolis.

sell him out of the state." But selling the bondsman to Sharpsburg physician John Hays meant accepting a lower price ($300) and taking a note instead of cash.[49] Maryland's courts strengthened the wall separating the local and interstate slave markets. In 1828, the Court of Appeals upheld the conviction for fraud of a man who had purchased and then sold a young woman outside Maryland despite promising her erstwhile master that she would "not be removed out of this state, nor sold to any person living out of this state, but that [she] should live as a slave in this state, so as to be near and convenient to her friends and relatives."[50]

The number of people jettisoned southward portended both slavery's vigorous expansion on the cotton frontier and its bleak prospects along Mason and Dixon's Line. The economic prospects of slaveholders in northern Maryland seemed to have been especially dimmed in the financial catastrophe of the 1820s. Indeed, Gregory believed that the economic "derangement" was most profound among slave owners. In the earliest stages of the Panic of 1819, Gregory informed his fiancée that "hundreds who a few months ago stood aloof from want and looked down with contempt on their slaves and subjects are today sinking into poverty and ruin!"[51] He had not exaggerated. The pressures on slave owners are revealed in the dramatic upswing in the number of slaves mortgaged during the 1820s (see figure 5). Slaveholders were feeling the effects of hard times, and they were not above mortgaging their bondspeople to save themselves.

The severity of the economic downturn caused some slaveholders to question their commitment to slavery. This erosion of confidence in the peculiar

Figure 5. Number of Slaves Mortgaged, Frederick County, Md., 1800–1830. Source: Frederick County Court, Land Records, 1800–1830, Maryland Hall of Records, Annapolis.

institution was apparent on Frisby Tilghman's Rockland plantation. In 1819, Tilghman had described his plantation as a model of Washington County's enterprising and improving spirit. He and his twenty-nine slaves had inaugurated a range of agricultural reforms: They practiced crop rotation, fertilized the fields with manure and plaster, and experimented with the latest implements. The results were impressive. Tilghman boasted that his estate's 260 acres of improved land yielded 1,100 bushels each of corn and wheat, 400 bushels of oats, and 300 bushels of rye. The plantation's pastures and woodlots were home to extensive livestock herds, including 200 to 300 sheep, 40 to 60 cattle, and 100 hogs.[52]

The robust agricultural economy of the late eighteenth and early nineteenth centuries had made Tilghman's large slaveholding profitable, but during the 1810s and 1820s, his large, unwieldy force became increasingly burdensome. Even before the economic collapse, Tilghman had made repeated efforts to hire out or sell unneeded slaves.[53] Former bondsman James W. C. Pennington, whose family belonged to Tilghman, remembered the planter grumbling about owning too many slaves. "I shall have to sell some of you," Tilghman once told Pennington's father, "and then the rest of you will have enough to do; I have not work enough to keep you all tightly employed."[54] Tilghman struck similar chords in his personal correspondence. In 1826, he lamented that farming had become unprofitable when "grain only brings 62¢ per bushel." Still, if wheat prices rebounded and stabilized, Tilghman believed he would "feel perfectly satisfied, provided we could get rid of the blacks."[55] Reducing the size of the plantation's enslaved workforce became the cornerstone of Tilghman's efforts to revive his fortunes. In 1827, he proposed to "curtail my farming and go more extensively into the graising system, which would enable me to curtail my number of hands."[56]

As commodity markets sputtered and crops failed, slaveholders began to falter under the weight of mounting debts. Even those who sold their bondspeople to the Deep South sometimes found it difficult to salvage their finances. In 1821, Montgomery County farmer William Darne pleaded for an extension from his creditor, Charles Carroll of Carrollton, claiming that a series of "unfortunate" events—the Hessian fly, a disease that killed his tobacco, and scarce currency—had left his finances in a shambles. Hoping to raise cash, Darne had offered two slaves to a trader, who balked at purchasing them because they were "rather above the age that Negro traders approve of, say about forty." Sensing that their master might make another attempt to sell them, the men ran away. Although he recaptured them, Darne could not find a purchaser for the aging fugitives and was "obliged to be at the expense of sending them to Alabama," where he hoped they might find a buyer.[57] Darne's woes continued unabated during the following years. By 1827, he had concluded that his tattered fortunes could not be mended in Maryland. In a final appeal for forbearance, Darne informed Carroll that his family and "a very few Negroes" were planning to settle near Tallahassee, Florida, where he would work as a merchant "while my negroes are getting the plantation open." "If I can make arrangements to go to Florida," he concluded, "I indulge a hope that I may be able to recover my losses."[58]

The economic crisis of the 1820s not only had shaken slaveholders' confidence in slavery but had sapped the institution's foundations by removing those slaves whose labor—both productive and reproductive—would ensure its future. The interstate trade ripped gashes through northern Maryland's slave population that boded ill for the institution's survival. Slave traders and southern planters seem to have been unconcerned about the sex of their quarry but remained interested in their ages. While men and women were sold in roughly equal numbers, the traffic bore heaviest on those adolescents and young adults whose children would soon perpetuate slavery.[59] Masters hoping to expand slavery's domain needed men who could hack plantations out of the canebrake and timber as well as women who would expand slaveholdings. The need for youthful servants was underscored by the average ages of those sold away from northern Maryland: 17.2 years (male) and 16.9 years (female).[60] These young men and women would build an empire for slavery but would not do so in northern Maryland.

The interstate traffic may have strengthened slavery by raising slave prices, but it also destabilized the institution by highlighting the dehumanizing violence that lay at its heart. The interstate trade seared itself into the memories of the enslaved. Decades after escaping from bondage in Frederick County, Lewis Charlton was haunted by the coffle he witnessed in the 1820s. "The slave owners bought up all the slaves they could," he remembered, "and had them all brought to the jail and handcuffed together with an iron collar around their necks." The bondsmen and -women were then marched 150 miles and crowded aboard a ship bound for South Carolina. Another slave recalled that George Kephart, an agent of the notorious trading firm Franklin and Armfield, struck fear into the slave community. "Ever'body in Frederick knowed Kephart, an' was *afeerd* of 'im, to," remembered Fred Fowler. "When it was reported that he was about, they trembled." So profound was the terror that gripped slaves at the approach of a soul driver that they sometimes mutilated themselves. When strangers approached a farm in Washington County, a young slave mistook them for traders and severed her hand with an axe, thus rendering herself worthless on the market. Fearing sale, a slave confined in the Hagerstown jail took similar action, smashing his hands and head against the prison walls. For some, the prospect of sale was unbearable. In 1859, a slave in Sharpsburg hanged himself after his wife was sold south.[61]

The enslaved had good reason to fear sale to the Deep South's cotton and sugar plantations. Not only were the bondsmen and -women being wrenched from their families and friends, they were being sent to states where manumissions were uncommon or unlawful. They were, moreover, being plunged into states whose climates, disease pools, and unrelenting work routines bore little resemblance to those of northern Maryland. After purchasing a plantation in Tensas Parish, Louisiana, Natchez merchant John Knight flirted with the idea of buying slaves from Maryland's Eastern Shore because "negroes from that quarter are more valuable for the swamps of Louisiana, being more easily acclimated, and with less sickness and danger, than from the more healthy regions of Maryland and Virginia." Knight seems to have abandoned this plan, for in the summer of 1844 he purchased forty-five people in Frederick County, Maryland, and had them shipped to his plantation. Because the slaves were "unacclimated," Knight deemed it essential that they be "gently dealt with, moderately worked, and well taken care of particularly for the first and second summer." Many slaves were stricken with illnesses during their first months in the Deep South, but Knight believed that they had been spared the worst. "I have lost *only four negroes* in all," he reported that fall. Adjusting to new crops was another matter. Knight sent his Marylanders into the cotton fields in 1845, a move that put them "to the full test of their skill, strength and willingness and ability to bear fatigue & labor, which they have before probably never experienced." Knight correctly anticipated that they would chafe under the heavy burdens and that some might "fly the track." Two of the men from Frederick County did escape, but Knight predicted that their absences would be brief: "I presume they will go not far, perhaps tarry about the plan' for a few days & then go in, if they have not already done so."[62]

Knight's slaves had been torn from their families and sent to a bewildering and terrifying environment, but they were fortunate compared to other Marylanders sent to the Deep South. Of the forty-eight slaves John Lee transported from Frederick County to Louisiana beginning in 1828, only thirty-three survived until the plantation failed in 1836. Those who remained on the plantation were in a sorry state. In 1835, Lee informed his partner that their "diminished and exhausted force" could not make a crop. Indeed, a neighbor had informed him that it was "probable we sh'd lose several of the hands in the course of the summer—& certainly unless they were much indulged—that when overworked & severely treated for one or two years, they were apt to die off in the hot weather."[63]

While the enormous power slaveholders wielded made it impossible for most slaves to thwart their owners' designs, the enslaved took desperate measures to avoid sale. The most widespread response to the threat of sale was flight. Frederick County slave Israel Todd escaped "to save his wife . . . and her brother from being sold south," while another man fled because "he felt that his owner was in the notion of trading him off."[64] In the 1820s, Rutlinger recounted the tale of a local slave who discovered that his wife and children had been sold to a trader and then "took the first opportunity to escape at night," pursuing his family to Pittsburgh, where he made an unsuccessful attempt to rescue them.[65] Resistance to the interstate trade could also turn violent. In 1822, a Washington County man ambushed the party that had purchased his family and "lodged the contents of a musket into the side" of a trader.[66] Those who escaped from traders' coffles sometimes returned to their old neighborhoods and waged a guerrilla war against slavery, attempting to liberate relatives. During the 1820s, an unnamed slave "who was sold three or four years ago to a soul driver" returned to Frederick County, passed as a freedman, and guided a fellow slave into Ohio.[67] After being sold to a trader, "Negro George" escaped and lurked outside Liberty-Town in Frederick County. There, he committed a series of "depredations" before being cornered by a white posse in the workshop of a free blacksmith. When called on to surrender, George emerged from the smithy wielding two axes and vowing to "kill or be killed." The stunned posse answered George's challenge with a deadly hail of gunfire.[68]

Hard times, the interstate slave trade, slave resistance, and slaveholders' growing displeasure with slavery soon manifested themselves in census returns. The slave population of northern Maryland declined precipitously between 1820 and 1860 (see table 1 in chapter 1). Slavery's expansion into the Deep South had arrested its development in northern Maryland; unwanted slaves would henceforth be sold south, not north. Other masters and mistresses chose to rid themselves of unwanted slaves through manumission. In the immediate aftermath of the Panic of 1819, the increasingly tenuous authority by which slaveholders held their chattels dovetailed with the worsening economic situation to drive the number of manumissions upward. Between 1790 and 1819, Frederick County's slave owners had manumitted a total of 629 slaves. That number spiked to 807 in the lean decade following the Panic of 1819, with most of the manumissions occurring during the worst years of the depression in the early 1820s (see figure 6 and table 2).

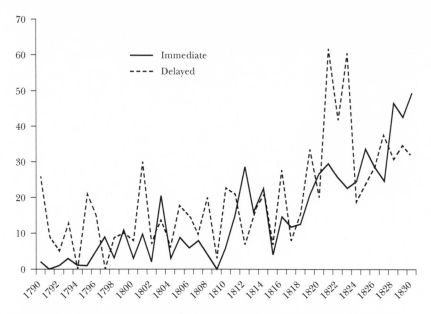

Figure 6. Number of Slaves Manumitted, Frederick County, Md., 1790–1830.
Source: Frederick County Court, Land Records, 1790–1830, Frederick County
Register of Wills, Wills, 1790–1830, both in Maryland Hall of Records, Annapolis.

Table 2. Number of Slaves Manumitted, Frederick County, Md.

Type of Manumission	1790–1818	1819–1830	1840–1848	1853–1860
Immediate				
Deed	221	289	113	180
Will	13	91	31	45
Total Immediate	**234**	**380**	**144**	**225**
	(37%)	(47%)	(47%)	(42%)
Delayed				
Deed	352	211	83	186
Will	43	216	78	125
Total Delayed	**395**	**427**	**161**	**311**
	(63%)	(53%)	(53%)	(58%)
Total Manumissions	**629**	**807**	**305**	**536**

Source: Frederick County Court, Land Records, 1790–1830 and 1840–1848, Frederick
County Circuit Court, Land Records, 1853–1860, Frederick County Register of Wills,
Wills, 1790–1830, 1840–1848, 1853–1860, all in Maryland Hall of Records, Annapolis.

Table 3. Sex of Slaves Manumitted, Frederick County, Md.

Sex of Slave (Type of Manumission)	1790–1818	1819–1830	1840–1848	1853–1860	Total
Male					
(Immediate)	107	177	60	117	461
(Delayed)	203	229	75	143	650
Total Male	**310**	**406**	**135**	**260**	**1111**
	(49%)	(50%)	(45%)	(49%)	(49%)
Female					
(Immediate)	127	202	81	107	517
(Delayed)	192	197	86	168	643
Total Female	**319**	**399**	**167**	**275**	**1160**
	(51%)	(50%)	(55%)	(51%)	(51%)

Source: Frederick County Court, Land Records, 1790–1830, 1840–1848, Frederick County Circuit Court, Land Records, 1853–1860, Frederick County Register of Wills, Wills, 1790–1830, 1840–1848, 1853–1860, all in Maryland Hall of Records, Annapolis.

"Dissipation and Riot": Policing the Rural Workforce

In December 1825, Maryland Governor Samuel Stevens Jr. issued a dire warning to the state legislature. African Americans were meeting "at public places for the purposes of dissipation and riot" and "in the woods for pretended worship." Without swift action from Maryland's authorities, these assemblies would undermine slavery and leave the state "seriously disturbed." Indeed, Stevens claimed that the social fabric had already begun to unravel. "The pernicious effects of their meetings at small villages and other places where plans of iniquity and vice are engendered and mature, are but too well known," he declared. The dangers were most acute for slaveholders, as "it is at these haunts . . . where [the slaves] so frequently perfect their plans for escape." While the defense of slavery figured prominently in the governor's address, his concerns about "the peace, the order, and the safety of society" encompassed a broader range of issues, most notably the proliferation of unlicensed taverns. No sooner had Stevens urged legislators to suppress the riotous meetings of free blacks and slaves than he launched into a discourse on "the evils emanating from the numerous tippling shops, which are now opened in every section of the state."[69]

The governor's decision to link the preservation of a labor system to fears about public morality was neither novel nor unique. In the same month that Stevens addressed the legislature on the need to strengthen slavery, the Frederick County Agricultural Society announced a series of contests that tied the county's emerging free labor regime to its nascent temperance movement. In addition to awarding silver cups to the author of the best essay "on the

comparative advantages of *free* or *slave* labor" and to the farmer "who cultivates
the most land with free white labor," the society offered a premium to "the
farmer who cultivates the most land without the use of ardent spirits, except
when used as a medicine." In the minds of the society's members, an economy
founded on free labor required a workforce that had internalized the values
of industry, temperance, and thrift. James Raymond, who penned the society's winning essay on the advantages of free labor, imagined that economic
pressures would discipline free workers and inculcate in them the values of
a market society. Raymond opined that "a man constantly stimulated by the
considerations that his character, his wages, in short, his living depends upon
the industry and fidelity with which he labors, is much more active than . . .
if he was put in motion by no other stimulant than fear of punishment." The
truth was more complicated.[70]

While the governor and the farmers of Frederick County were bemoaning
the pernicious effects of demon rum on the state's free and enslaved workers,
George Wills, an impoverished laborer, was languishing in the Frederick jail.
In 1824, Wills had knocked together a booth at a militia muster and peddled
whiskey to the soldiers without obtaining the necessary license, a crime that
carried a fifty-dollar fine. Unable to pay the fine, Wills was imprisoned for
eleven months. Those who fretted about unlicensed taverns might have
applauded the workman's arrest, but the circumstances that landed Wills
in the county jail should have given them pause. Wills had committed the
crime because he was "in very needy circumstances, with a family to support."
Like many of northern Maryland's poor laborers, Wills sometimes sought
his living on the shadowy margins of the economy. The behaviors that vexed
employers and masters—gambling, theft, and operating grogshops—were
difficult to uproot because petty crimes were a necessary part of poor workers' economic strategies.

Beginning in the 1820s, a growing chorus of agricultural reformers, evangelicals, and industrialists argued that all workers—black and white, free and
enslaved—must be broken of their intemperate habits. In 1822, the Frederick
County Trustees of the Poor asked that the almshouse be moved from town,
where "facilities of intemperance and mischief are continually offered to the
poor." If the almshouse were moved to the country, the poor could be weaned
off spirits and taught to labor steadily. "There such of the poor as could labor
would be profitably employed," they argued, "which would be conducive to
their health and the comfort of the rest."[71] The linkages among drinking, gambling, petty theft, and a poor work ethic were apparent to both employers and
slaveholders, who were convinced that workers' dissipated habits led inexorably
to rebelliousness. It was therefore not surprising that Mayor George Baer's

complaints about Frederick's growing number of brothels and unlicensed taverns included a reference to their "destructive and demoralizing" effects on apprentices. In addition to spreading disease and encouraging "gambling, intoxication and every description of vice," disorderly houses created spaces "where masters and servants are upon equal terms." Such concerns were not confined to public officials. In 1821, Hagerstown tailor G. C. Hamilton reported that one of his employees, Daniel Matzenbaugh, had broken his contract and fled town "indebted to a number of persons." Moreover, according to Hamilton, Matzenbaugh "is a drunkard, a great braggadocio, a foot racer, jumper, wrestler, cocker, swearer, and liar." The tailor's failings were reflected in the workshop, where, Hamilton sneered, "he cuts too deep, stitches himself into debt, and cabbages equal to any tailor." Farmer John Irvin observed similar character flaws in Daniel Knight, an itinerant laborer whom Irvin suspected of stealing from his farm near Gettysburg, Pennsylvania. Knight had no trade, but "road [in] races, and [was] fond of talking racing and gambling." Indeed, Knight preferred crime and gambling to regular employment and boasted to his erstwhile employer that "he will never make his living by working." Complaints about drunken workers were echoed by slaveholders, whose descriptions of unmanageable slaves bore a striking resemblance to those uttered by employers of free workers: "He is fair of speech, plausible and artful; fond of dress, drink, and gambling, of cock fighting and of women, but not of work," observed the master of a fugitive slave.[72]

Beginning in the 1810s and 1820s, northern Maryland's civil authorities, landowners, and merchants evinced heightened anxiety over the growing population of "vagrant, loose, and disorderly persons."[73] In many cases, these fears stemmed from the worsening economy, the expansion of the region's transportation networks, and a growing population of outsiders, including canal and road workers, wagoners, and peddlers. It is not surprising that the earliest and most persistent complaints about the rising tide of intemperance and disorder emerged from the towns and rural neighborhoods along major commercial arteries. By 1817, Washington County merchant Samuel Gregory, whose store was located along the National Road, lamented that "distilleries are daily increasing & more & more of that deadly poison is poured down the throats of unthinking, deluded mortals!"[74] Two years later, Bartgis echoed these complaints from Middletown, "which lies on the great western turnpike," noting that it had become a "place of considerable notoriety" because of the "many persons traveling through it."[75]

Whiskey flowed along the railroads, canals, and turnpikes. The managers of the Baltimore and Ohio (B & O) Railroad fought a determined, if futile, campaign against "ardent spirits" as construction snaked through northern

Maryland. In 1829, the B & O prohibited workers from drinking, a measure deemed necessary because the company's transient, often unstable workforce included "all descriptions of persons, the disorderly and intemperate, as well as the sober and correct." The railroad's fears of "disorder and riot" were not groundless, but keeping the workmen sober proved difficult. In 1831, the superintendent of construction in Frederick County complained that "licenses for retailing spirituous liquors are . . . obtained with so much facility and at so moderate a charge . . . and the cupidity of many is so great, that shops have been opened in many places contiguous to and along the line." The railroad echoed this lament in 1832, noting that "licenses are so cheaply and so easily obtained . . . that grog shops became very numerous in the immediate vicinity of the line, and were highly prejudicial to the labourers."[76]

Although public anxiety about disorder and intemperance first surfaced along canals, railroads, and turnpikes, it soon radiated outward to encompass the crossroads taverns, racetracks, and revivals where farmworkers congregated. In 1820, a resident of Washington County complained that the rural village of Orr's Gap was "becoming a far-famed Sunday theatre of every species of drunken riot, of profane swearing and obscene jest . . . and every sort of low jollity that would disgrace a savage tribe." The writer urged the sheriff to arrest the "wretched publican who presided as high priest over [these] horrid youth" before he further corrupted the community's morals.[77] Sharpsburg and other villages became scenes of brawls. In 1819, the townsfolk complained that the owner of a tippling house was leading people "into a vortex of death and destruction" by peddling whiskey.[78] They cited a recent "quarrel" among black men that left one slave "stabbed and severely wounded in several parts of the body." Camp meetings were another source of disorder. Despite their ostensibly religious purpose, these tumultuous gatherings sometimes degenerated into mayhem. In 1819, Bartgis stumbled across a revival near the Potomac River whose attendees were "guilty of every despicable act . . . roaring, ranting, ripping, tearing, cursing, and swearing." The meeting might not have netted any souls, Bartgis noted, but it did yield a stolen horse, two dead dogs, and eight "stark raving and mad" men who were maimed in fights.[79] County authorities made a concerted effort to enforce order at revivals and imposed fines on people caught peddling whiskey at these events, but these efforts had little effect.[80]

Stemming the torrent of whiskey that was flowing through the Middle Atlantic and bringing drunken workers to heel was a daunting challenge, but many reformers predicted that temperance would bring order and prosperity to the countryside. Having endured the "wasteful manner in which . . . work was done (particularly in harvest)" and suffered his workers' "improper and offensive conduct," a farmer in Lancaster County, Pennsylvania, offered "perquisites to such as observe abstinence from Rum." Slave owners quickly embraced the temperance cause. The wife of a slaveholder in Albemarle County, Virginia, was delighted when her husband banished whiskey from his fields. The workers harvested grain more efficiently and the cradlers, who had previously been "so broken down, that it was almost a week before they could do any other work," were "as fresh, and ready for other work, as if they had only been planting peas, or pulling fodder." Moreover, the family's slaves were more manageable: They "don't now drink half so much whiskey of their own getting . . . don't go to the groceries a fourth as often, and don't do a tenth of the stealing."[81]

Just as employers worried about bringing free, white laborers to heel, whites sensed that enslaved and free blacks were slipping out of their control. The tumultuous gatherings of whites at taverns, militia musters, and races had a rough analogy in the throngs of African Americans who flocked to towns on holidays and weekends to escape the isolation of rural life. Seated at the center of the region's transportation network, Hagerstown and Frederick emerged as hubs of the black community. As early as 1779, residents of Frederick were concerned that the abandoned military barracks on the town's outskirts were becoming a "rendezvous for Negroes in the night."[82] In 1798, the grand jury commissioned several constables to disperse the "disorderly meetings of Negroes and other ill-disposed persons, [who] frequently collect in numbers on Sundays and Holy Days in Frederick and other towns."[83] The constables seemed unequal to the challenge. In 1807, a visitor observed that Frederick's blacks spent Sundays "in noise and riot."[84] By 1818, the mayor conceded that efforts to "suppress the tumultuous meetings of Negroes . . . on Sabbath days" had failed and that "the evil, instead of being removed, has actually increased."[85] Hagerstown's constables and magistrates grappled with similar problems. In 1815, the constable of Hagerstown promised to eliminate the "dangerous, odious, and abominable concourses" of blacks who "frequently infest the public square, especially on the Sabbath day."[86] Despite these assurances, the problem continued unabated. In 1818, the councilmen complained that "numbers of people of color, are in the habit of collecting in groups, in the public square, in the streets and alleys, in stables, hay lofts, and other places, for the purpose of gambling." To combat this evil, they imposed a one-dollar fine on black men and women caught gambling or disturbing the peace.[87] Within two years, the councilmen were lamenting that blacks still gathered "in large assemblages at night and particularly on holidays . . . to play at cards and other unlawful games, tippling, riots, etc." The council subsequently strengthened the ordinance, declaring that those who "shall get drunk and become riotous" would receive "fifteen lashes on their bare back at the public whipping post."[88]

When blacks gathered at crossroads villages and towns, they gained something more important than time with family and friends: intelligence about pathways to freedom. These lessons were valuable to "Negro Harrison." Despite being "ignorant of the country" beyond his owner's farm in Frederick County, Harrison had befriended blacks in nearby Taneytown, who provided him with an education in local geography and assisted him when he escaped.[89] By 1828, concern about the weekend gatherings of slaves drove slaveholders in Frederick County to present the General Assembly with what must have been a familiar litany of complaints: "The frequent and illegal assemblages of Negroes, on holy days, week days, and the Sabbath allows them to array their plans, indulge in drinking, fighting, and carousing."[90]

Whites also complained about black religious gatherings, which drew large crowds and more than a little scrutiny from suspicious whites. The blacks who were uprooted from the Chesapeake and strewn across the farms, shops, and plantations of northern Maryland sought ways to create new communities. Funerals seemed to knit together the scattered, often isolated strands of the black communities. Pennington remembered that funerals brought together people from neighboring estates and served as catalysts for new communities. In defiance of slave owners, who often interred their chattels with little ceremony, an enslaved preacher would "send notice from plantation to plantation, calling the slaves together at the grave on the Sabbath, where he would sing, pray and exhort."[91] Small holdings, combined with the lack of independent black churches before the 1820s or 1830s, meant that most of these unauthorized interments occurred on marginal, unoccupied lands, much to the chagrin of angry landowners, who complained that their property sustained "much injury" from the "burying of persons of color."[92]

As the economy worsened and blacks slipped from their owners' control and the community's supervision, fears about crime and disorder began to escalate. In 1821, for example, a Frederick newspaper complained about growing numbers of beggars. The ranks of the criminals sometimes included both poor whites and blacks.[93] In 1823, a biracial gang attacked the Frederick County farm of Worthington Johnson and attempted to steal some turkeys. Johnson's overseer and slaves met these "plunderers" and engaged them in a battle of "stones and curses" along the banks of the Monocacy. In the aftermath of the battle, a paper reported with some satisfaction that "a daring worthless negro fellow" was believed to have drowned during the fight but that the neighborhood nevertheless remained "infested" with such criminals.[94]

In the midst of this maelstrom of "riot and dissipation," employers began to search for new, more effective means of controlling their workforces.

Slave owners conjured the specter of sale to the Deep South to cudgel disobedient slaves into submission. "It is a frequent custom in the District of Columbia, Maryland, and Delaware, for masters to endeavor to reform their bad slaves, by terrifying them with threats of selling for the Georgia market," wrote abolitionist Jesse Torrey Jr. in 1817. So vital was the threat of sale to preserving discipline that slaveholders were loath to surrender it. We glimpse the linkages between sale and slave discipline in the negotiations between Frederick County farmer Clotworthy Birnie and Montgomery County artisan Robert Lyles. In 1818, worsening commodity markets and personal reverses compelled Birnie to sell an entire slave family, but he refused to sell them to anyone involved in the domestic trade. Lyles's associates assured Birnie that "we have . . . never heard of his trafficking in slaves," but Birnie remained skeptical. He insisted on a bond and a personal pledge that the slaves would never be sold beyond Maryland.[95] The frustrated purchaser balked at these demands. Lyles offered to post a "good security that I will not sell them out of the state" and swore that "I am no speculator" but refused to guarantee that they would never be sold outside the state. "In doing so, I would be at once binding myself never to sell them, let their conduct be what it might."[96] For Lyles, relinquishing the authority to sell the slaves south was tantamount to surrendering his mastery and accepting their behavior, "be what it might."

Other slaveholders also grasped this lesson, which soon worked its way into Maryland law. Masters and mistresses throughout the state recognized that sale provided the surest guarantee that troublesome bondspeople would no longer challenge slavery in Maryland. Anne Arundel County slaveholder Luther Martin believed that the state would be better served by sending his slave "Negro Jacob" to Louisiana instead of the penitentiary for receiving stolen goods. In Louisiana, he argued, the slave "would be more effectually prevented from inflicting further injury to the state than by a short confinement . . . after which he would be again let loose upon society."[97] In 1819, the General Assembly embraced this logic. In a move designed to trim expenditures and strengthen slavery's ramparts, the legislature ruled that free blacks and slaves would no longer be received into the penitentiary. Blacks convicted of noncapital offenses would henceforth face flogging, banishment, and sale beyond Maryland and the District of Columbia.[98] In 1839, the legislature broadened its authority over slaves, making escape beyond the borders of Maryland a felony punishable by sale at public auction and permanent removal from the state.[99]

The Long Road from Slavery to Free Labor

In the wake of the financial crisis of the 1820s, slaveholders began grappling with challenges to slavery. The Panic of 1819 and the ensuing economic downturn shook slaveholders' confidence in the peculiar institution. Moreover, the looming presence of Pennsylvania sapped the foundations of slavery by encouraging Marylanders to question the economic and social value of bound labor. Unlike their brethren further south, masters on the Mason-Dixon Line had little difficulty imagining a society without slavery. Across the border and sometimes within their own neighborhoods, masters saw farmers growing the same crops with free laborers. Comparisons were inevitable, and slavery often fared poorly. After touring Harford County in 1831, Eli Ayers of the Maryland State Colonization Society noted that farmers on the sectional border were "favorably circumstanced for deciding upon the relative value of free and slave" labor. Looking across the Mason-Dixon Line, they bore "constant witness to the rapid increase of population, improvement of soil, [and] accumulation of wealth" in Pennsylvania, a sharp contrast to the depleted soil and declining population of Harford, "where slavery abounds." Advocates of free labor delighted in recounting stories of thrifty Pennsylvanians who purchased land from bankrupt slaveholders, cultivated that land with free laborers, and "made a fortune, on the same place, and at the same business, that a Marylander spent one."[100]

In the hands of free labor advocates, the relationship between slavery and wage labor was recrafted into a stark dichotomy that left little room for either coexistence or compromise between these labor regimes. Slavery may have worked in tandem with other labor regimes when commodity prices were high, but the stagnating economy of the 1820s and 1830s forced some employers to choose between free and unfree labor. In 1827, an agricultural reformer mocked slaveholders who complained about the Hessian fly and sighed "vainly for another Napoleon to restore us by his wars." The source of their woes, he insisted, was "that the maintenance of his negroes runs away with his crops, and brings him debt besides." Unless landowners abandoned slavery, their farms and plantations would be overrun by the "hardy sons of Pennsylvania, who are already settling on our upper county lands." Such arguments reverberated along the Mason-Dixon Line. "Whenever white labor competes with slavery, it undersells it, and drives it out in all temperate climes," declared a Baltimore County farmer in 1826. Five years later, Baltimore editor Hezekiah Niles thundered, "Free labor and slave labor cannot abide together, as the one becomes stronger and stronger . . . the other becomes weaker and weaker."[101] Ideologically, slavery and free labor were locked in an almost Manichaean struggle for survival.

For some free labor advocates, immigration was the key to economic recovery, but they believed that immigrants would not come unless slavery—and black people—vanished. From Hagerstown, colonization agent Ayers described how whites would fill the void created by the destruction of slavery and the removal of blacks. "All classes of blacks in this county are diminishing in number," he enthused, "and their place is filling up with an industrious white population." Eager to assure prospective immigrants that living and working in a slave state would neither undercut their racial prerogatives nor limit their economic prospects, writers proclaimed that "the slaves are gradually vanishing away, and free labor is becoming both productive and honorable."[102]

Agricultural reformers compared the northern and southern counties of Maryland to prove the superiority of free labor. "What counties have increased in population in the ten years between the two last censuses?" asked a Frederick County farmer in 1823. His answer: "Frederick, Washington, and Alleghany, where there are but few slaves." As to why these counties boasted growing white populations, the farmer explained that a small slave population translated into increased employment options for whites. Moreover, the absence of slaves created a setting where "labour is not servile and considered degrading."[103] This interpretation gained momentum over the following decades. Northern Maryland gradually became a powerful counterpoint to the state's southern, slaveholding counties. "It is a well authenticated fact," asserted the *American Farmer* in 1846, that Maryland's most prosperous farmers were to be found in the northern counties, where "the free labor system has obtained to a considerable extent."[104]

The colonization movement captured whites' growing doubts about the economic benefits of slavery and unease regarding the free black population. In May 1831, leading residents of Frederick County established an auxiliary of the new Maryland Colonization Society. Ayers believed that the county offered fertile soil for the movement: "The inhabitants of this county appear generally to have reflected upon the relative value of free & slave labour. Many Farmers have tried the experiment of manumitting their slaves, & hiring whites, to their entire satisfaction. The experiment has been so frequently tried that the result has become familiar through the county & has produced a general conviction of the superior economy of the latter over the former species of labor. The free blacks have, in consequence of the frequent manumissions, become a public burden."[105]

Interest in colonization ran high in neighboring Washington County. In 1833, William McKinney reported the formation of a Williamsport society whose ranks included "some of the wealthiest & most influential citizens." Even the black community was supportive, evidencing an "excitement" that was "one hundred per cent *more favorable* than I had calculated on being able to procure." McKinney may have exaggerated, for other agents noted that the initial enthusiasm for colonization had fizzled. By 1833, a dispirited Frederick County agent reported that his efforts to organize new auxiliaries had stalled "in consequence of the great indifference manifested on the part of its friends." Although he found that many whites were sympathetic to the cause, there was "such an apathy . . . amongst the friends of colonization that I fear but time alone can awaken them." In 1835, another agent reported that the societies in Frederick County are "all coming to nothing & at best have only a formal existence. They have no stamina."[106]

Northern Maryland's Quakers added their voices to the growing chorus challenging slavery. In December 1826, members of the Pipe Creek Meeting in Frederick County organized an antislavery society. By 1829, they felt confident enough to submit a petition to the General Assembly "praying that a law may be passed, declaring all children born of slaves, after a certain period shall be free." After their county's delegation to the General Assembly tabled an 1830 antislavery petition, the society's officers began querying politicians about their opinions on slavery. In a letter to one representative, the society demanded to know "your opinion in regard to slavery" and "your reason for joining . . . a conspiracy to smother a petition with one hundred or more names attached."[107]

Slavery's opponents remained a minority in the white community, but they seemed to have made strides. In 1839, an anonymous writer from Frederick County declared that the "anti-slavery cause is rapidly gaining ground." "Three years ago an abolitionist and amalgamationist fanatic and insurrectionist were interchangeable terms," he continued, but "now anti-slavery papers are read by our most respectable citizens."[108] Whether measured by the size of the slave population or its value, slavery seemed to be in a death spiral. In 1853, the *Hagerstown News* reported that "the slaves, since 1841, have decreased one-half in number and in value." The county's 1,788 slaves were valued at a mere $317,000, which translated to an average price of $177.50.[109] The steady erosion of slavery convinced some observers that Pennsylvania's free labor regime was making deep inroads into the Upper South. While traveling through Frederick County, Maryland, in 1828, Virginian J. H. Cocke Jr. declared that "the spirit of Yankeydom is coming south. I hope much is to be seen on the northern borders of the ancient dominion."[110] Landowners attempted to lure nonslaveholders to the Upper South by reassuring them that slavery was in retreat. "Northern farmers . . . are supposed to entertain certain objections to a residence in Virginia, on account of its slave labor," announced an 1832 advertisement for farmland near the Chesapeake and

Ohio Canal, "but there is little reason for this in Loudoun, or the country contiguous to the upper Potomac."[111]

Perhaps nothing signified slavery's dwindling importance in the minds of white Marylanders than their anemic response to the 1859 conventions called by masters from the Eastern Shore and southern Maryland to strengthen slavery's edifice. The meeting called in Hagerstown fizzled "owing to a misunderstanding as to the day, or lack of interest in the matter"; "but six or seven people attended." When a Frederick master threatened to burn "a brand that he will find difficult to remove" into anyone who opposed that county's meeting, a fellow slave owner derided the entire "laughable convention." "In Catoctin District there is only one slaveholder," he mocked, "and if he should ever take up the notion to brand every man who refuses to act with him, he would no doubt have to call . . . for a mite of assistance."[112] Northern Marylanders may have been indifferent to the conventions but took a definite interest in their fruits. In March 1860, the General Assembly made a last, desperate effort to buttress slavery by outlawing manumission and creating mechanisms for blacks to renounce their freedom. While the proposed legislation snaked its way through county conventions and into the legislature, citizens from the northern counties denounced it as an unnecessary and futile effort to resuscitate a dying institution. "It is seriously doubted if there be a demand for more slave labor in Maryland," opined a Frederick newspaper, for "machinery is rapidly superseding manual labor in grain growing districts." Even if the law shored slavery's foundations, the editor suspected that most slaves would find their way to cotton plantations. Nevertheless, the law passed and manumissions became illegal after June 1860.

As that deadline approached, slaveholders in northern Maryland flocked to courthouses to liberate their slaves. In Washington County, a newspaper reported that "quite a large number of persons . . . set their negroes free," while their neighbors in Frederick County manumitted an "unprecedented" number of slaves in the three months before the law took effect. This apparent rejection of slavery represented the culmination of trends inaugurated in the 1820s, when northern Marylanders began remaking their region into a bastion of free labor. By 1860, it seemed that the triumph of free labor was almost complete. Slaves constituted a mere 5 percent of the region's population, and slaveholders had shown themselves either unwilling or unable to take decisive action to check the institution's decline. Masters and mistresses may have recognized that slavery was stricken, but they remained determined to extend its life. Of the 129 slaves from Frederick County who were manumitted in the spring of 1860, only 33 were freed outright. While the remaining 96 would receive their freedom when Maryland abolished slavery in 1864, many of their owners envisioned slavery surviving into the 1880s, if not longer. Slaveholders imagined a long, protracted transition from slavery to freedom. The peculiar institution may have become untenable along the sectional border, but this realization did not spark a hasty, pell-mell retreat from slavery. Pressed by a flagging commodity markets and outflanked by their slaves, masters and mistresses fought a stubborn rearguard action to preserve slavery as long as they could.[113]

3. "There Are Objections to Black and White, but One Must Be Chosen"

Managing Farms and Farmhands in Antebellum Maryland

Between 1845 and 1847, Arthur W. Machen, a slaveholder in Fairfax County, Virginia, peppered his father with questions about the composition of his workforce. Like other landowners in this northern Virginia county, Machen was reeling from economic reverses. Soil exhaustion, languishing commodity markets, and increased competition from western wheat producers had reduced many area farmers to a hardscrabble existence. Amid these catastrophes, Machen attempted to salvage his fortunes by restructuring his labor force. His growing family and five slaves could handle some of the routine chores, he reckoned, but he worried about the additional hands that would be needed over the course of the year. "What can be done?" Machen asked his father. He knew that it was imperative to "*reduce* my force, *change* its description, or to *divide* the profit of the farm with someone who, under a prescribed system, would defray the entire cost of cultivation," but the choice among slaves, tenant farmers, and free laborers proved vexatious. Hired slaves were an option, but he feared that they would "ruin" his slaves' morale. Tenants or sharecroppers could be engaged, but Machen believed that the depressed market would make such arrangements unprofitable. White farmhands were available, but "the universal testimony of farmers is that a white hand worth having is the rarest of characters." Moreover, his father feared that whites—especially Irishmen—might refuse to work alongside blacks. Exasperated, Machen concluded, "There are objections to black and white, but one must be chosen."[1]

In theory, the decision should have been straightforward. While Machen pondered the composition of his workforce, a steady drumbeat of agricultural reformers and political economists was declaring that slavery was incompatible with the diversified agriculture practiced on the farms and small plantations of the Upper South. "There is but one element in the agriculture of Maryland to which slavery is attached with any affinity, and that is tobacco culture," proclaimed antislavery writer John L. Carey in 1845. "The rude hands of servile labor" could wield hoes on tobacco plantations, but they could not plow the wheat fields, tend the livestock, or operate the machinery on farms like Machen's.[2] Unlike free laborers, slaves lacked the "delicacy of touch" necessary for more complicated operations. "In grain growing districts, counties where a scientific agriculture prevails, where the mind of man as well as the hands of labor find employment in the culture of the ground, the rearing of trees, the improvement of breeds of cattle, horses, and swine," Carey contended, "there slavery cannot dwell. It is not compatible with such scenes."[3]

Many historians have echoed this argument, maintaining that slavery and wheat production were an imperfect fit. "The economically rational antebellum wheat farmer almost always employed wage labor," concludes historical geographer Carville V. Earle, because the crop's seasonal labor requirements made hired farmhands "decidedly cheaper and more efficient than slaves."[4] Still, Machen's dilemma should give us pause. Although he had declared that one system of labor discipline "must be chosen," Machen was in fact promiscuous when it came to constructing his force. Between 1843 and 1850, he employed hired slaves, free black and white farmhands who labored under annual and short-term contracts, and a welter of day laborers.[5] Each system of labor discipline had its flaws, but like an alchemist, Machen struggled to fuse them into an efficient, productive whole.

Machen's was not the only dissenting voice against the emerging free labor orthodoxy. Washington County planter John Blackford was disillusioned with workers of all stripes. Having dealt with drunken farmhands, both free and enslaved, and witnessed their shoddy work, he condemned both in the same breath, blasting his "lazy worthless negroes" and his hired hands, whom he called "inattentive disinterested characters."[6] Some farmers expressed a strong preference for bound labor. James P. Machen, who managed the family farm during the 1850s, made extensive use of hired slaves. He grumbled about the "exorbitantly high" wages they commanded but hastened to add that "labor of some kind must be had, and can any better and cheaper than slave be obtained?"[7] Others steered a middle course between slavery and free labor, creating modified forms of slavery that were more responsive to the region's changeable labor needs. Harford County farmer Ramsey McHenry proposed purchasing an "estate of large extent in the northern part of Maryland" and working it on a hybrid system, whereby the lands would be "parceled out among the servants on shares."[8]

This chapter examines farmers' and planters' protracted struggle to bend the ostensibly antithetical systems of slavery and wage labor to the seasonal routines of diversified agriculture. The task was daunting, for wheat was a temperamental staple: It required little attention for long stretches and then demanded the strenuous exertions of dozens of farmhands during the summer harvest. Although the composition of individual crews varied, employers' objectives remained constant: to maintain a small workforce during dull seasons, to mobilize a large number of laborers for the harvest, and, whenever possible, to winnow out laborers perceived as unnecessary or unproductive. Farmers developed numerous strategies to balance these competing imperatives. They infused their workforces with the necessary measures of flexibility and stability by amalgamating workers from different labor regimes into motley crews of slaves, contract workers, day laborers, and a smattering of tenants. To guarantee that the tenuous purchase on free and enslaved farmhands did not slip at harvest, employers wielded a combination of debt, restrictive contracts, and incentives to command workers' presence.

Managing laborers involved more than their recruitment. Farmers needed workers who were biddable and, perhaps more important, sober. The chapter concludes by examining efforts to discipline the rural workforce, focusing primarily on the temperance movement. Farmers' persistent yet often frustrating efforts to discipline their workers offer a powerful rejoinder to the free labor ideologues who imagined that an industrious, orderly workforce would spring from slavery's ashes. Slavery may have been on the wane, but employers could not rely solely on the workings of the labor market to discipline their laborers; rather, they needed to construct new economic, legal, and social controls to guarantee the survival of the nascent free labor regime.[9]

"The Changes of the Seasons": The Routines of Farmwork

"Nothing is more variable than the quantity of labour which the farmer has occasion to employ . . . at different times and under different circumstances," wrote Frederick County agriculturalist James Raymond. "The changes of the seasons, as they severally occur" necessitated "corresponding changes in the quantity of his labor."[10] Former slave George Jones concurred. His master's farm was "like all other farms in Frederick County, raising grains, such as corn, wheat and fruit, and on which work was seasonable, depending upon the weather, some producing more and some less."[11] The "seasonable" routines

of agricultural production exercised a powerful influence on farm management, affecting the number and kind of farmhands employed and the terms
under which they labored. The regimens of individual farms varied with their
acreage, crop mixtures, and workforce, but the fitful nature of rural work
remained a constant throughout the antebellum period.[12]

In northern Maryland, farmers began working their fields in March. As
winter faded to spring, workers trudged into the muddy, stubble-ridden fields
and busied themselves clearing debris, stones, and weeds, a disagreeable chore
called "grubbing." After the fields were cleaned, farmers commenced plowing,
harrowing, spreading fertilizers (manure, guano, or plaster), and sowing clover, corn, and oats. In April, they turned their attention to planting cabbage,
carrots, potatoes, tomatoes, and other garden crops for home consumption.
Farmers continued gardening in May, when they also sheared their sheep
and began hoeing corn.

The pace of labor quickened as the weather warmed. In June, the smell of
ripening sweet clover announced the beginning of hay-making season. This
flurry of activity continued without interruption for several weeks. The climax
of the growing season came in July, when farmers harvested the wheat sown
during the previous fall. Typically, they employed gangs of between fifteen and
thirty laborers to gather the grain. Harvesters were divided into squads of five
or six, with a man swinging a cradle or scythe in the lead, followed by a man
or woman who raked the cuttings into small piles. A binder (often a younger
worker or a woman) tied these bundles into shocks. The grain was then allowed to dry for a few days before wagoners hauled the sheaves into barns and
granaries. Depending on the weather, the size of the crop, and the number of
workers employed, the entire process took about three or four weeks.

With their wheat secured, farmers turned to harvesting their oats, which
likewise required a number of cradlers, rakers, and binders. When the summer
grain harvests were completed, farmers began making preparations for the
next year. In September and October, they dressed and fertilized their fields
before sowing them with wheat. At the same time, they harvested their corn
and potatoes, cut fodder, and hauled their produce to markets and mills.

Work slowed during the winter, but farmers and laborers were not idle.
Agricultural writers implored farmers "not to throw away in winter the hard
earned and precious products of the summer's labor" but rather to spend
the season "feeding and taking care of stock, [and] laying in a good supply
of wood."[13] Many farmers heeded this advice: Account books and diaries
reveal that they spent the season repairing fences, stocking icehouses, and
slaughtering livestock. Growers also turned their hands to trades during these
dull months. "My father was a farmer and made flour barrels in the winter,"

recalled a blacksmith, who added that it was not unusual for men "to farm in the summer and follow a trade in the winter."[14]

The seasonality that characterized men's working lives was largely absent from those of their wives and daughters.[15] Women may have experienced an intensification of work during the harvest, but many of their chores required steady attention throughout the year. Moreover, with the exception of occasional forays into the field, women's tasks seldom intersected with those of their menfolk. While men busied themselves with small grains, hogs, and cattle, women managed the dairy, tended the poultry, and oversaw a range of domestic manufactures. The sharpness of this division of labor shocked one immigrant, who exclaimed, "Sometimes you would think that they didn't know each other. . . . The wife is as little concerned over the good or bad farming of her husband as I care about the harem of the sultan of Turkey!"[16] Because many of women's responsibilities required attention throughout the year, and others, like spinning and sewing, could be completed regardless of the season, women's lives were marked by unrelenting toil. If anything, winter heralded an intensification of their domestic chores. A Frederick County farm boy remembered that his mother and sisters spent the "entire winter spinning [flax] from four o'clock A.M. to nine A.M. with the only abatement of time to do the cooking & milking, etc."[17]

Mechanization began altering the patterns of rural work in the 1830s. In the late eighteenth and early nineteenth centuries, farmers spent much of the winter processing the grains harvested during the previous summer, but the introduction of threshing machines during the 1820s allowed crops to be cleaned in a fraction of the previous time and with fewer hands. "Every farmer who has a crop, which would require the labor of five or six hands [in] the winter season, in getting it out the ordinary way, now has a machine, which gets out his crop in a few days," noted a Hagerstown paper. "This seriously affects the labouring part of the community."[18]

Hay making and grain harvesting underwent dramatic changes in the 1850s with the introduction of mechanical mowers and reapers. In some neighborhoods, broken and rocky fields prevented farmers from employing these machines. In 1854, a Frederick County newspaper complained that landowners had purchased a "good many self-raking reapers," but they "don't answer the farmers' purpose, consequently they have been thrown aside, and the old-fashioned cradle again resorted to."[19] Still, most farmers welcomed the new machinery. That same year, one man boasted that the McCormick reapers had "maintained their high reputation": "It is now no longer a question whether they can be used as an implement of economy in Washington County."[20] The savings farmers achieved with these machines were often quite impressive:

One man claimed that his Buckeye mower spared him the expense of hiring additional laborers during hay making and that his McCormick reaper cut his wheat for a mere twenty-two dollars.[21] In 1859, Jacob Miller, who farmed near Sharpsburg, reported that "farmers are using the reaper more and more every year" and predicted that "before many years the wheat, rye, oats, and barley will all be cut with reapers."[22]

The seasonal nature of agricultural production left a distinct imprint on the size and structure of rural workforces, which expanded and contracted with the changing labor demands. On Columbus Shipley's farm, the number of farmhands peaked at fourteen during the July wheat harvest before dwindling to two in January. Between these extremes, Shipley's crew ranged from six to eight laborers. A single month could witness dramatic fluctuations in the size of a workforce. In January 1852, Richard Gittings's Baltimore County farm employed between one and five workmen, while in June it employed between three and eight. Striking a balance between the harvest's heavy and urgent labor demands and the lighter but still important needs of the slower seasons presented a persistent challenge to farmers.[23]

The most effective strategy for weathering the seasonal swings in labor demands was to construct multitiered workforces.[24] A handful of domestics and farmhands laboring under annual or quarterly contracts formed the nucleus of the crew. This nucleus need not consist of hired laborers but could be assembled from a farmer's kin, his slaves, or a combination of both. An English traveler described the workforce of one farm as "five male negroes, all the year round, and in harvest five extra hands."[25] It was not unusual for farmers to create workforces that were an amalgam of slaves, free blacks, and whites. In 1857, Gittings described his "regular standing force" as "Black Man Jim, hired at $10 per annum and found [provided with food and lodging], Irishman Patrick hired by the month at $19.00 he finding himself, and a boy named Billy, about 16 years old, a servant of my own. Independent of the above force there is now hired at 75 cents per day and found (except when engaged in cradling wheat when the price is $1.25 per day), a black man, free, named Addison, Mr. Wilson's black man John, and Mr. Mansfield's black man Johnson."[26] As Gittings's case illustrates, the seasonal fluctuations in northern Maryland's labor markets yielded kaleidoscopic workforces whose contours and colors shifted with the seasons.

Around the nucleus of the workforce swirled an unstable cloud of seasonal workers and day laborers who assisted with such massive undertakings as harvesting, hay making, slaughtering livestock, and gathering ice. Landowners imbued their workforces with an additional measure of flexibility by engaging workers under seasonal contracts that extended from spring to fall. These agreements guaranteed farmers sufficient labor to tackle the summer harvests but allowed them to trim their payrolls during the dull season. When contracting with such farmhands, Arthur W. Machen believed that it "would probably be advisable to hire one or two for 8 or 9 months only, as fewer hands are needed in winter."[27] Beneath the regular workforce and the contract laborers stood a diverse collection of day laborers employed for specific tasks. In December 1839, for example, Harford County farmer and physician Robert H. Archer added ten casual laborers, including several free blacks and hired slaves, to his rolls. These workers spent several days butchering hogs alongside his permanent crew of three slaves and a free black contract laborer.[28]

Slavery and free labor may have been interwoven in the fabric of northern Maryland's workforce, but they remained distinct strands; the labor market neither blurred nor obscured the boundaries between these regimes. Seasonal demands tugged at both slavery and free labor, but they responded differently. Farmers' strategies for managing these regimes therefore differed as well.

Making Slavery and Free Labor Work

To agricultural reformer James Raymond, the variability of farmers' labor needs was the most compelling argument against slavery. "The inconvenience of making frequent changes in the quantity of slave labor . . . must present itself to anyone who reflects on the subject," he wrote. "But where labor is free, and therefore the subject of contract between employer and laborer, these changes are frequently taking place," and a farmer could purchase labor like "any other commodity, in such quantities, and at such times, as he wants it."[29] But how would these laborers be recruited and disciplined? Raymond never raised these thorny questions, but they were inescapable to farmers and planters struggling to assemble workforces that were both flexible and tractable.

The gritty, messy chore of managing the Upper South's workforces emerged in sharp focus during the wheat harvest. After their wheat ripened, growers needed to cut, shock, and store it quickly, for overripe grain might shatter or become lodged, and shocked wheat was vulnerable to smut.[30] Ever mindful of the adage that "a crop is never safe until it is in your pocket," anxious farmers recruited large workforces and drove them at a frenetic pace.[31] Jakob Rutlinger observed that small farmers often cultivated their lands with a few children and a slave but that during harvest "they hire day labor, as much as they can get, so that everything is quickly completed." Harvest crews were immense, sometimes swelling to forty hands "mowing, cutting, tying, shocking, everything all at once, as though it were a matter of life and death."[32]

Agriculturalists encouraged farmers to "lose no time in securing the services of such hands in your neighborhood as can be relied upon" and reminded them that it was "more economical to have too many, than to have too few hands."[33] The advice was sound. Many farmers mortgaged their wheat to merchants and millers in the months preceding harvest, thus risking severe losses if workers could not be secured and crops suffered.[34] Farmers who dallied might find themselves in a terrible bind. Such was the fate of Franklin Blackford. In 1839, the Sharpsburg farmer scoured the neighborhood for hands but found only one unemployed worker. Blackford must not have learned his lesson, because he found himself in similar straits in 1846. After a fruitless search for harvesters, he returned home lamenting that he "could find none."[35]

The harvest season's pressing labor demands created opportunities for farmhands to renege on their contracts or demand higher wages and bonuses. Midway through the 1830 harvest, free black Levy Austin capitalized on John Blackford's need for laborers to demand a bonus. The planter reluctantly complied but grumbled that "Austin, not satisfied with his wages, filched me out of $1.50."[36] Laborers sometimes banded together in small groups to demand more pay. In 1861, harvesters on Henry Massey's Harford County farm "struck for higher wages & struck off."[37]

Labor militancy might also be more organized and widespread. In 1853, farmhands carrying cradles, rakes, scythes, and other "emblems of their calling" rallied in Berks County, Pennsylvania, to demand the prompt payment of their wages, a twenty-five-cent increase in daily wages, and complimentary food and lodging.[38] Although the workers did not achieve their objectives, harvesters along the Mason-Dixon Line continued to press their demands. The following year, delegates to a "workingmen's meeting" held at Shippensburg, Pennsylvania, complained that the "present prices of grain, produce, &c., are such as to place them almost beyond the reach of those who are dependent upon their daily toil." Contending that "the fluctuations in the prices of breadstuffs . . . should be attended by corresponding changes in the price of labor," the assembled workers established wage scales for the upcoming harvest, which they pledged not to violate. For cradling, workers were to receive $2.25 a day; for binding, $1.50; for raking, $1.00; for mowing hay, $1.25; and for hauling, $1.00.[39] These calls reverberated across the Mason-Dixon Line into Frederick County, where "it was pretty well understood" that wages would be similar to those in Pennsylvania, and into neighboring Washington County, where farmers were astonished when "$2 a day and roast beef, including trimmings and side dishes, [were] freely offered and refused."[40]

In addition to demanding higher wages, harvesters insisted on immediate cash payments for their laborers. Explaining why he needed additional money for the harvest, Arthur Machen noted that "some of the hands . . . will expect payment at the close or during the course of their work."[41] Frederick County farmer Chester Coleman made a similar appeal, asking for $125 for "additional labor in securing our harvest, which is always a cash consideration among farmers here."[42] "To obtain a day's labor I must either pay in advance or as soon as the day is closed," he explained, because hands were "very scarce and difficult to obtain and consequently high in price."[43]

The desperate need for labor forced employers to tolerate undisciplined workers and to accept shoddy, hurried work. In the 1820s, Rutlinger found that the harvest was "very superficially and sketchily done. It is a grubby mess whereby a shocking amount of fruit is lost."[44] Another Frederick County resident was appalled by the liberties taken by the free black harvesters on a relative's farm. "They would cut through and then shoulder their cradles and walk back to the starting place and whet, and this they did in no hurry either." When asked why he tolerated such lackadaisical work, the farmer revealed the power laborers wielded at harvest: "He said this was the custom of the whole country; and if he made his blacks do it they would talk about him over the neighborhood for a hard master."[45]

To safeguard themselves against shoddy work and to prevent workers from bolting either for freedom or for better wages, employers dangled numerous incentives before their enslaved and free harvesters. Washington County farmer George F. Heyser rewarded his slaves' efforts during harvest with the same wages paid his free workers, while Lewis Machen allowed his bondsmen to earn "extras" during hay making and harvesting. Slave owners also granted their slaves holidays at the end of harvest, and many slaves used the time to earn extra wages. In 1854, James L. Hooff marked the end of harvest on his plantation in Jefferson County, Virginia, by throwing a "frolic" and letting "my boys go until Friday night." The next morning, he found only one slave on the plantation: The "balance of [the] hands are harvesting." In 1839, Baltimore County farmer Thomas Johnson allowed "Negro Marlborough" to seek outside employment after he finished harvesting Johnson's wheat.[46]

Farmers developed others strategies to bring their truculent free laborers to heel at harvest. To deter labor protests, they demanded that their hands sign "entire" contracts (also known as special contracts), which stipulated that a worker who quit before harvest or the completion of his contract would forfeit all accrued wages.[47] It remains unclear how extensively these devices were used, but scattered evidence reveals that workers paid a heavy price for abandoning their bosses at harvest. In 1841, Harford County farmer Ramsey McHenry fined Elijah Oliver and Elijah Kell two months' wages "for damages in consequence of . . . absconding just before harvest, contrary to agreement." The following year, McHenry fined John Barnes, who "quit just before harvest, in violation of his contract."[48] Frederick County farmer Charles H. Lighter took similar action in 1852, discharging farmhand Henry Hett without his previous three months' wages after he missed 19½ days during the wheat harvest.[49]

Landowners who combined farming with another business—a profession, a country store, or a mill—used the debts accrued through these operations to recruit harvesters. Such arrangements could benefit both employers and workers: Debts could be used to push workers into participating in the harvest, while the increased wages offered during the harvest allowed laborers quickly to retire their debts. Perhaps for this reason, a writer in Gettysburg, Pennsylvania, waxed poetic when describing the harvest, boasting that it united "Rich and Poor, the Landlord and the Tenant" in "joyous though heavy labor, blessed with a mutual contentment and happiness."[50] What Milly Ingram thought about the "joyous though heavy labor" remains a mystery, but she benefited from the opportunities created by the harvest. In 1836, she repaid Frederick County farmer and physician George Hughes for several bleedings and purges by working as a binder.[51] Many customers at George Feaga's grist- and sawmills, also in Frederick County, settled their accounts by laboring during the harvest.[52] Jacob Reichard pursued a similar strategy, using his general store and rental properties near Hagerstown to recruit harvesters. In 1851 and 1852, Reichard provided Benjamin Howl with a house, cash advances, and store credit, for which he received small cash payments and periodic labor. The vast majority of this labor, which comprised the bulk of Howl's payments, was done at harvest.[53]

Farmers further augmented their harvest crews by demanding that the families of their farmhands and tenants join the menfolk during the busiest seasons. Agricultural reformer Chauncey P. Holcomb reckoned that the chief advantage of employing cottagers and tenant farmers was that "their families are there, and . . . the wife, or junior members of the family . . . can be called on in the hurry and press of the harvest."[54] Another agriculturalist praised those Frederick County farmers who employed laborers and their families under twelve-month contracts, noting that "this system obviates much of the difficulty so often experienced by frequent change of hands at a time when field work is most pressing" and that farmhands employed by the year "will be less likely to be tempted away by the offer of a dollar or two higher wages during seed time or harvest."[55]

Continuing a practice that emerged during the early national period, landowners employed entire households to tap the labor power of their farmhands' wives and children. Landowners expected that their laborers' families would form an auxiliary workforce. In 1834, for example, Baltimore County farmer Philip R. J. Friese struck such a bargain with Daniel McKarran and his wife, Mary. Friese's contract specified that "the man [is] to operate as a farmhand generally and to take charge of the farm house [and] the woman to have the control of the dairy, attend to the cooking and other matters connected to the domestic management of the farm house."[56] In most cases, employers subsumed the earnings of women and children under a family wage. The 1852 contract between John Einholdt and his wife, Katherine, and a Baltimore County farmer named Preston stipulated that the couple would serve "as gardener, farmhand, and general servant for the time of one year . . . for the compensation of one year . . . for the compensation of $120 . . . said Preston also to provide us with boarding and room."[57]

Employers' desire to harness the labor of a free worker's family did not translate into a tolerance of nonworking women or children who were deemed unproductive. Whether they employed bound or free labor, landowners aggressively sought to winnow women, the young, and the aged from their rolls. "Every farmer should himself take special care that . . . he is not encumbered with a single idle mouth—of man, woman, child, or beast—with not one consuming non-producer on his estate," chided agricultural reformer John S. Skinner. The advice does not seem to have fallen on deaf ears. Friese found "reason to rejoice" when a manager and his "troublesome family" sought greener pastures." "There are few things less desirable on a farm, than a large family of small, idle, mischievous, ill-disposed, children whose parent prefers seeing them running about in filth and laziness than . . . giving them employment." Harford County landowner Sophia McHenry was even more callous. She had allowed a ditchdigger and farmhand named Brown to settle his wife and newborn child in an outbuilding but soon concluded that "both mother and child are encumbrances on my hands." She sent the family away, advising them to look for work on her cousin's farm, where they could be lodged in a ramshackle building being used as a stable.[58]

Those who owned their laborers would have nodded with approval. While numerous historians have demonstrated that slave owners' complaints about idle, unproductive women and children belied and belittled these workers' economic contributions, many masters and mistresses in northern Maryland seemed convinced that women and children were nuisances. Slave owners complained that their farming operations were hobbled by dependent slaves and that "slaves must all—big and little, young and old—be maintained throughout the year," while wheat "demands their labor not more than one aggregate month in the year." This arithmetic made some farmers wary of keeping bound women and children. Northern Virginian J. H. Turner made dispensing with "breeding women and young children" the cornerstone of his strategy for lopping off all "useless expenditures" and eliminating "everything that does not contribute . . . to our immediate comfort or profit." Believing it was "cheaper to buy than to raise," Turner owned none but adults, which resulted in everyone having "full employment" without "noisy groups of mischievous young negroes to raise." These words echoed along the Mason-Dixon Line. Mary C. Spence wanted to sell her late husband's slaveholdings because they included many "very young" people and others who were "getting old." An executor in Washington County explained that slaves under his care garnered little income because "many of said Negroes [are] women and children incapable of generating income." So strong were these prejudices that slaveholders sometimes balked at purchasing people encumbered with too many dependents. Lewis H. Machen refused to buy a woman who was "dogged with the disagreeable appendage of a young child and a bad husband," while a slaveholder in Jefferson County, Virginia, grumbled that a nursing mother and some of her five children would "have to be supported." For those seeking laborers along the Mason-Dixon Line, a worker's family might be a valuable resource, provided it did not become a drag on operations.[59]

Landowners may at times have hired married men with an eye toward gaining access to the labor of their wives and working-age children but were unwilling to employ single women burdened with dependent children. Because farmers believed that women were incapable of the heavy branches of agricultural labor and because child-rearing responsibilities might interfere with an employer's domestic and farm routines, single mothers were virtually unemployable. Rachel R. Dell and her toddler and infant found themselves in dire straits after being abandoned by their drunken husband and father. Describing her desperate scramble for work and her urgent need for public assistance, Dell wrote to the Carroll County court that "I have heard it has been communicated to you that I would not work, which is all false." "I would be very glad to get a situation," she continued, "but that is very hard to get as they are so small, one of them is only five months old and the other 18 months." The stigma attached to abandoned or unmarried mothers persisted after the Civil War. In 1865, a Freedmen's Bureau agent stationed in Winchester, Virginia, reported that "demand exceeds supply" for male farmhands but that women, especially those with young children, "find it difficult to obtain employment."[60]

The same pressures that drove single free mothers to the edges of the labor market also bore on their enslaved counterparts. Slave women and their offspring added to the financial value of their owners' estates, but because their labor was of little immediate worth, most slaveholders along the Mason-Dixon Line treated women and children as burdens. The Old South's traditional plantation staples—cotton, rice, sugar, and tobacco—generated numerous chores that could be performed by women and children wielding light hoes, but grain cultivation required workers with considerable chest and arm strength. The limits of women's employability were apparent on John Blackford's plantation. Between 1836 and 1838, Blackford's two adult women, Caroline and Daphney, performed a combined forty days of farmwork, the bulk of which were spent in the vegetable garden and orchard. With the exception of fruit picking, the plantation's children performed little agricultural labor. When women and children entered the fields, they were subject to strict gender and age hierarchies that relegated them to the least demanding positions. Only men drove the heavy cultivators, drills, and double-shovel plows used during planting season and swung the cumbersome cradles and scythes used in hay making and harvesting. Describing the gender and age divisions on a Virginia plantation, a former slave recalled that "de men would scythe and cradle, while de women folks would rake and bind. Den us chillum, boys and girls, would come along an' stack."[61]

We should not underestimate the value of the work performed by female slaves, for the gendered division of labor that kept women from performing certain tasks was sometimes murky. Women could be forced to perform a wide variety of agricultural and domestic chores. Slave owners attempting to sell women often boasted of their proficiency at "house and out work." In 1824, for example, a Frederick County master claimed that in addition to being a "good cook, [who] can sew, knit, wash, and iron," his female chattel could do "any kind of work" and was "famous in the harvest field or tobacco ground." Indeed, women's adaptability sometimes made them invaluable to their owners. When Rachel Teger died, her mistress, Martha Ogle Forman, recalled her many contributions to the plantation. Teger "was a field hand when I came here, but I soon discovered that she had a great deal of intelligence and industry." Teger ultimately became an indispensable worker, sewing clothing for her fellow slaves, whitewashing, mending rugs, making candles, spinning, and serving as a dairymaid, in which capacity she earned for her owners "thousands in butter." Still, women's contributions were usually undervalued by the region's farmers, who often wanted to limit the number of female slaves on their properties. Thus, a Frederick County master explained that he was selling a "a Negro Woman . . . accustomed to all kinds of work" because he had "too many women," a concern shared by a farm manager in Shepherdstown, Virginia, who believed that his employer should buy a man "as we have now . . . to many women who work in the field."[62]

Farmers also struggled to find suitable work for enslaved children. Landowners often hired free children to perform light chores, but they were not responsible for anything beyond their meager wages; the cost of young hirelings' maintenance remained squarely with their parents. The same was not true for slave children. Unwilling to support enslaved children during the years when their labor was of little or no value, some masters pressed children into the workforce at tender ages. Lewis Charlton remembered that his owner, a tanner, "imposed many laborious duties upon me, such as no child could possibly do." When he could not handle the heavy hides, his incensed master flogged him "so badly that I could not lay down for weeks." Those who possessed larger slaveholdings might ease their young slaves into the workforce more gradually. Baltimore County slave James Watkins did not work until he turned six, when his master assigned him "to attend the cows, and keep them off the corn." After performing light chores for three years, he began clearing stones, shearing sheep, and "making myself generally useful." Within three years, he was "employed in the general work of the farm."[63]

Impatient slaveholders concocted various schemes to avoid, defray, or eliminate the expense of raising enslaved children. Some owners hired slave children to white artisans, "not only because they save themselves the expense of taking care of them, but in this way they get among their slaves useful trades." These arrangements seldom generated much income, for, as one mistress found, "no one will take them to raise unless they can have their services until they are—girl 18 years and boy 20 years—of age for nothing. . . . [U]p to that time they are of no value to you and you run the risk of their life." Thus, it was not surprising that a Washington County master should offer to "put out" several children for "victuals and clothes."[64]

Landowners' disdain for unproductive workers extended to the aged. Employers were reluctant to hire men and women whose age prevented them from performing heavy manual labor. When they did make such hires, they did so only for brief periods and token wages. In 1838, John Blackford hired "Old Jim Adley," agreeing to "give him what I may think he, or what he may do, is worth." Over the coming months, Adley cleaned the stables, mended fences, and did other "piddling work," for which he received a pittance in cash, tobacco, and lodging. Slaveholders were less charitable. The commentaries sometimes scrawled alongside aged slaves' names in inventories reveal masters' lack of gratitude for a lifetime's labor: "nuisance," "not worth anything," "worse than nothing."[65]

While hirers could simply turn away old workmen, masters and mistresses needed to devise schemes to disencumber themselves of aged slaves. A 1790 Maryland law prohibited the freeing of slaves incapable of supporting themselves and required slave owners to support those who had "grown old in service." The General Assembly even lifted some of the burden from the shoulders of struggling masters in 1824, when it ordered counties to make "such suitable provision for all old and infirm . . . slaves belonging to insolvent estates . . . as may be necessary for their support and maintenance." Ignoring their legal duties as well as their moral obligations, slave owners remained eager to rid themselves of aged slaves. Although the 1790 statute fined masters and mistresses who permitted elderly slaves to "wander or remain at large, begging or becoming burdensome," some owners simply turned their slaves loose. David Richardson apparently took this tack with his "old servant woman," for his will indicated that she "has been at large for some years past." Others smuggled unwanted slaves across the Mason-Dixon Line and granted them de facto freedom. A Pennsylvanian recalled that when Maryland's laws prevented a legal manumission, "it was the custom of . . . people who wanted to get rid of their negroes to bring them across the line . . . and set them free." A few even shifted the expense of supporting aged servants onto younger slaves. Believing that slaves "too old or helpless to be manumitted" were "entitled to some consideration," David Shriver willed that some of his slaves be "bound out" and their wages applied to the "comfort and support" of their elders.[66]

Whether they bought or hired their laborers, employers along the Mason-Dixon Line were constantly calibrating their workforces. It was a delicate task, requiring equal measures of coercion and co-optation. Special contracts, debt, and the hiring of workmen's families as adjunct workforces made wage labor respond to the seasonal demands of wheat cultivation, while a combination of hiring and incentives did the same for slavery. Controlling the cost of their workers' maintenance and reproduction was another matter. Neither slave owners nor non-slave-owners had much interest in supporting dependent workers. These concerns may have been more acute among slaveholders. Pinched by a stagnating economy and nagged by fears that their bondsmen and -women might flee, they saw little reward in shouldering the cost associated with slavery's long-term survival. But where an employer could turn away a worker's family, slave owners would have to free or sell their unwanted laborers, a difficult task in a state whose slave owners saw little value in women's and children's labor and whose laws prohibited the manumission of slaves incapable of supporting themselves.

"He Will Never Make His Living by Working": Disciplining Rural Workers

In 1823, Rutlinger complained that farmhands in Frederick County wanted "big wages and little work." Even though Maryland was in the midst of a depression, laborers were pocketing their harvest wages and withdrawing from the workforce. "Most of them, when they are not employed, spend their time in the taverns," Rutlinger lamented. "A great many dissolute fellows are hatched out in this way."[67] The complaint was neither novel nor unique. However, a special urgency became attached to complaints about workers' morale and morality beginning in the 1820s. As northern Maryland became more dependent on wage labor, and as the region became more thoroughly enmeshed in wider markets and transportation networks, many residents sought to regulate the growing population of itinerant laborers and peddlers who traversed the area's canals and turnpikes.

The newly ascendant free labor ideology lent itself to the creation of personal and social restraints that many people believed were necessary to a market economy.[68] Beginning in the 1820s, agricultural reformers, evangelicals, and industrialists began a steady cant demanding that workers be broken of their intemperate habits. These leaders perceived clear connections between drinking, gambling, petty theft, and a poor work ethic.

Exorcising demon rum would be a difficult task, for the patterns of rural work and camaraderie—to say nothing of the commodity markets—were awash in alcohol. Apples, corn, and rye were less cumbersome and fetched higher prices when marketed as cider and whiskey, and the distilleries along the Mason-Dixon Line bought large quantities of these products from neighborhood farmers. So important was alcohol to the local economy that farmers sometimes scoffed at the temperance movement. "We would live happier lives were there more drunkards among us, because we would be wealthier," wrote one farmer, for the drunkard "swills down [our] corn and rye and thus makes markets for these articles." Farmhands certainly did their part to keep up demand for the region's liquid commodities. Workers demanded drams when working in inclement weather or when performing disagreeable chores, such as clearing land, digging ditches, or cleaning millraces. In 1855, the Hering family assembled fifty-seven farmhands, including many free blacks, to clean a millrace. "All their cry was for plenty of whiskey, until they drank better than eight gallons," wrote an amused observer, "and the result was a good many drunk niggers." Farmers fortified their harvesters with liberal doses of rotgut. Whiskey was a "necessary adjunct" to the harvest, recalled a Frederick County farm boy. "They had the erroneous notion, that men could endure more, who would moderately use stimulants, and that they were not so likely to be overcome in the harvest field." The fields were not the only places where alcohol flowed freely. The proceedings at country stores and taverns were often lubricated with whiskey. Describing a store in Emmitsburg, Frederick Stokes remembered that "there was always a bottle of whiskey on the shelf behind the counter and everybody who came in could have a drink free if he wanted to."[69]

Farmers were concerned that the disorder brewing at taverns would seep into their fields. As his workers began distilling cider and whiskey, Baltimore County farmer Philip R. J. Friese expressed "serious apprehensions" that the "ardent spirits" would "disturb all order and involve our little community in disgraceful confusion." Faced with the prospect of drunken workers, Friese considered "totally prohibiting the distribution of the least quantity of alcohol." His anxieties were not groundless. The previous week, a hand had "evinced a disposition to be troublesome by getting drunk and taking liberties incompatible with the situation he fills."[70] Excessive drinking not only disrupted farming operations but also wreaked havoc within workers' households. "Samuel Devilbliss yesterday and to day for the first time since he has been living here seems perfectly sober," wrote a relieved Anna Maria Shriver. During the previous two months, the Frederick County farmhand had been on "frolics" and was "crazy" with drink, which "gave his wife a great deal of trouble."[71] Such disturbances irked landowners, who were drawn into their employees' domestic squabbles. John Blackford was forced to provide separate quarters for a female worker after her husband "abused and threatened her in such a manner . . . that she had him taken before a magistrate."[72] When a farmhand's drinking spawned domestic violence and shattered his household, an employer risked losing the labor of an entire family. In 1833, Friese complained that farmhand James Hughes, "a victim of insatiable thirsts for ardent spirits," had gone into "such a frenzy that he destroyed nearly all his furniture and frightened his poor wife and children almost out of their senses." Hughes's family abandoned the abusive farmhand, depriving Friese of their services. Friese attempted to broker a reconciliation, but Hughes's wife "would not consent to return and live with him, as he uses malt liquor to keep him excited."[73]

The extent to which drunken slaves could disrupt a farm's operations and the near impossibility of preventing bondspeople from obtaining alcohol are illustrated by John Blackford's protracted struggle to keep the slaves on his Ferry Hill plantation sober. Because his property was adjacent to an important ferry and the Chesapeake and Ohio Canal, Blackford's slaves had constant interaction with boatmen, canal workers, and travelers, who provided the bondspeople with alcohol. In April 1837, Blackford complained that "Murf has been hanging about the packet boat all day [and] has obtained liquor sufficient to make him a fool." The following September, Blackford lamented that "there has been much disorder and intoxication about the ferry. Julius drunk. Murf not sober." Adding to Blackford's difficulties were his free black and white laborers, who shared the slaves' fondness for whiskey. Martin Shellman, a poor white farmhand and woodcutter, was often drunk, while farmhand James Moore stashed a bottle in an outbuilding and spent an evening drinking with Blackford's slave, Murphy. Drinking not only disrupted the work routine but also spawned disorder and strife in the quarters. During one binge, Murphy quarreled with slave women and thrashed a slave child. Drunken white workers also wreaked havoc among the slaves. In 1837, Shellman stormed into the plantation's kitchen "pretty well corned" and "made a fuss . . . with the negroes."[74]

Employers attempted to reform dissipated farmhands through a combination of admonitions, firing, and incentives. In 1831, Blackford caught one of his white farmhands, "Dutch John," stealing jugs of whiskey from Blackford's cellar and burying them in the garden. Outraged, Blackford "drove him off." In August 1838, he gave Shellman "a lecture on whiskey drinking," after which he promised to "quit and drink no more." Blackford's lecture proved ineffective and Shellman's vow worthless. The following March, Blackford scrawled in his diary, "Martin Shellman drunk. I gave him a *severe* lecture."[75] Baltimore County farmer William P. Preston adopted more stringent measures with farmhand George Einhous. In 1856, after enduring several years of the laborer's chronic drinking, Preston drafted a stringent contract requiring Einhous to remain on the farm, to abstain from alcohol, and in the event of a breach or violation of the agreement to surrender his wages "as an indemnity to [Preston] for the injury he has already sustained." Preston's demands were not unreasonable. In the contract's preamble, he noted that Einhous had "frequently become inebriated and at such times [had] gone off and remained away days or several weeks, greatly to [the] detriment of Wm. P. Preston's farm work." Einhous evidently managed to remain sober for more than a year before again yielding to temptation. On 29 April 1858, he scratched his signature under an entry in Preston's ledger: "In leaving your service without notice and unfortunately falling into my old habit of drinking, I have forfeited the wages due me."[76]

Slaveholders blustered about tavern keepers who sold "ardent spirits" to slaves. In 1830, an overseer on a farm near Williamsport threatened to prosecute those suspected of "dealing in any manner, especially in the articles of whiskey and other liquors, with the slaves of Mrs. Williams," while a slaveholder cautioned the town's merchants against "selling or bartering, to my servants, liquor of any description or quantity."[77] When threats against individual merchants failed, masters wielded their political power to convince municipal governments to enact ordinances that penalized merchants who catered to African Americans. In 1838, Frederick's aldermen decreed that "no person shall sell any distilled liquor to any free negro or slave, or suffer them to collect on [their] premises on the Sabbath" and imposed a ten-dollar fine on offenders.[78] Slaveholders made certain that these statutes were vigorously, if somewhat sporadically and unevenly, enforced. In 1856, Howard County masters organized a petition campaign against the pardon of a man convicted of operating an unlicensed tavern, complaining that he was in "the habitual habit of selling to blacks, bond and free, and also desecrating the Sabbath . . . to the great annoyance of our order loving and church going community."[79] Although most merchants and barkeepers probably continued to sell whiskey to slaves, a handful buckled under pressure from slaveholders. In 1840, the proprietor of a Washington County tavern announced that he would not allow "children, apprentices, or slaves" into his establishment "for the purpose of obtaining liquor, or of loitering about the room and smoking tobys."[80]

The danger that drunken farmhands would disrupt work routines loomed largest at harvest. In July 1837, John Blackford complained that his harvesters were "pretty hot with liquor" and that "Caroline, the black girl, was alarmingly drunk and not able to walk or stand."[81] Before he banished whiskey from his fields, Washington County farmer Paul Summers confessed, "I experienced much trouble, and indeed often dreaded the approach of Harvest, from the many unpleasant occurrences which were likely to take place among my hands," while another farmer bewailed the "noise, and bustle, and profanity, and contention" that excessive drinking spawned at harvest.[82]

The need to discipline harvesters stemmed not only from the season's pressing labor demands but also from the significance attached to harvesting. For both landowners and laborers, the wheat harvest represented the culmination of the agricultural year and was cause for celebration. Workers had good reason to greet harvest as a holiday; it brought together large numbers of men, women, and children, who rejoiced in the generous wages, ample whiskey, and bountiful meals proffered by landowners. "The fields were vast, wages good, and the people happy," recalled one farm boy. "When the harvest was over, [we had] such a feast. Tubs of lemonade and tables loaded with ginger bread and other good things."[83] For employers and those concerned with the community's morals, the festivities that accompanied harvest were laced with ambiguity. Because harvest blurred the distinction between recreation and work, the preindustrial traditions that flourished in and around harvest fields—feats of strength, drinking, courting, and fighting—were both reflections of workers' enthusiasm and potential sources of disorder.

Despite or perhaps because of the breakneck pace set by landowners, harvesters imbued their labors with an element of play.[84] After watching a gang of harvesters sweep across a field, a visitor to Frederick County noted that "their labor seemed turned to a sport, and ready hands and joyous hearts were making a short job of the task before them."[85] For men, harvest also offered an opportunity to demonstrate their physical prowess. Here again, we see the seamless blending of labor and leisure: A reaper who outdid his fellows not only earned bragging rights but also served his employer's interests. This conjuncture was apparent to Baltimore County slave James Watkins, whose overseer once came into the harvest field and, "thinking that the slaves had not worked hard enough," seized a cradle and set a blistering pace for the workers. When the slaves overtook him, the overseer's pride trumped his judgment: "He was determined not to be beaten, so [he] kept going at a furious rate till he was quite exhausted. He was almost immediately taken ill . . . and died the next day."[86]

The festive elements of the harvest season were not confined to the fields. As workers tramped the countryside seeking employment, morals sometimes slipped their moorings. Workers' mobility, combined with their anonymity, created innumerable opportunities for casual sexual relations. Farmhand Basil Evens of Frederick County suspected that his wife had spent the 1853 harvest "whoring across the mountains."[87] In 1848, an itinerant workman recalled that Susannah Stilley had "loose conversation" with harvesters on her husband's farm, "holding out inducements to him or others to have criminal conversations with her." At least some yielded to temptation. Another laborer saw "Susannah and a man in the act of copulation, in a barn. . . . They were at it a good while."[88]

Their spirits buoyed by harvest wages and liberal doses of whiskey, workers descended on the region's towns and villages to continue their revelries. While storekeepers welcomed the business, others worried about the disorder spawned by these celebrations. After the 1858 harvest, Shepherdstown was infested with "numbers of rowdies, drinking, hurrahing in our streets, to the annoyance of all peaceful citizens."[89] The following year, a newspaper in Chambersburg, Pennsylvania, complained that a massive brawl among the town's black residents had punctuated the harvest. "Harvest ended and Whisky plenty—courage up to fighting point, at it they went," the paper reported, "and for two days and nights the combat raged."[90]

Policing the roaming bands of harvesters was a difficult task, for the itinerant laborers were often unknown to their employers. On 20 June 1830, Blackford noted that four workmen, identified only by their first names, had arrived on his plantation seeking work as harvesters.[91] The harvest rolls of Washington County farmer George F. Heyser suggest that some of his harvesters were also complete strangers: "German Women," "Six Irish," "Black Woman," "Big Pennsylvanian," "Little Pennsylvanian."[92] Adding to employers' difficulties was the tremendous turnover from harvest to harvest. Between 1825 and 1841, Heyser employed a total of 164 harvesters, 117 of whom labored in only a single harvest. Only 7 workers assisted with five or more harvests.[93] Farmers thus confronted a nameless, constantly shifting workforce at the season when a breakdown of discipline could undo an entire year's labor. Because community restraints had been loosened and because many harvesters were unknown to their employers, personal appeals were ineffective tools for disciplining workers.

Beginning in the 1820s, temperance societies sprouted up along the Mason-Dixon Line, although it is unclear whether these organizations made significant inroads among Marylanders. The societies' few surviving records suggest that they had more widespread support from prosperous farmers, merchants, professionals, and tradesmen than from landless workers. In Frederick County, the Union Temperance Society of Middletown Valley enlisted some laborers, including a few African Americans, but enjoyed greater success among landowning farmers. Between 1843 and 1846, the society registered 170 men and 160 women. Of the 106 male society members whose occupations were recorded in the 1850 federal census, 32 (30 percent) were farmhands or laborers. Twenty-three of these laborers headed independent households, and 15 of them had accrued small amounts of real property. The temperance society also attracted some laborers' wives and daughters, who made up 25 percent of its female membership. By contrast, landowning farmers constituted 39 percent of the society's male members, and their wives and daughters represented 41 percent of its female members. The most striking feature of the society's members was their wealth. Although only one member was a slaveholder, a significant number were either landowners or members of landowning families. Indeed, 133 of the men and women identified in the census (73 percent) came from landowning families. The average value of these members' real estate was an impressive $3,525, with eighty-five members owning land valued above $1,000 and forty-eight owning property whose value exceeded $3,000.[94]

In neighboring Carroll County, the Sons of Temperance gained little support from landless workers. Located in the prosperous village of Westminster, the society attracted 232 members, most of them artisans, landowning farmers, and professionals. Of the 150 members located in the 1850 census, 55 (37 percent) were tradesmen, 41 (27 percent) were landowning farmers, and 33 (22 percent) were either merchants or professionals. Twenty-one laborers joined the society, including 9 who resided in artisans' households, suggesting that they were apprentices or journeymen. Thus, only 12 of the society's members appear to have been career laborers. As was the case with the Union Temperance Society, the Sons of Temperance drew significant support from landowning households: Seventy-four (50 percent) of the society's members were either landowners or the adolescent children of landowners. The average value of the members' real property was $3,757, with 27 members—mostly farmers—owning land valued at more than $3,000.[95]

Gauging the impact of the temperance movement in northern Maryland is difficult because antidrinking societies reported a mixture of successes and failures, together with a good deal of backsliding. In 1833, the Union Temperance Society of Middletown Valley boasted that "four of the more respectable stores of the valley, if not more," had stopped peddling whiskey. By 1841, however, these gains had been reversed and "the small stores in our neighborhood that had . . . stopped selling whiskey have again commenced." Worse, the society found that two large distilleries were under construction.[96] The situation was not as bleak in neighboring Frederick, where, a temperance advocate noted in 1841, "It is now a somewhat rare sight to see men reeling and staggering through our streets in a state of intoxication."[97]

Given the importance of the harvest, it is not surprising that the fledgling temperance movement chose harvest drinking as its first target. Indeed, interest in eliminating harvest drinking had preceded the establishment of local antidrinking societies.[98] In 1828, the Washington County Temperance Society included a stricture against harvest drink in its articles of incorporation. Brushing aside concerns that "it will be difficult to procure laborers without whiskey, especially during the busy season of haymaking and harvesting," the society proclaimed that "laborers enough can be found who will cheerfully dispense with whiskey."[99] Antidrink reformers evangelized throughout the county, sponsoring meetings at which farmers discussed "the propriety and expediency of excluding the use of ardent spirits from their meadows."[100]

Although farmers were divided about the economic benefits of temperance, something approaching a general consensus soon emerged about the advantages of employing sober farmhands. Indeed, farmers who sang the praise of the temperance movement emphasized its commendable effects on workplace discipline. A Washington County farmer boasted of the "harmony and good will . . . together with a readiness and promptness to obey command, formerly unknown," that prevailed among his harvesters. Another reported that "time is not wasted in foolish talking and wrangling . . . and the employer is saved the disagreeable duty of discharging hands for drunkenness, or the misconduct produced by it, at the time he has need of their help."[101]

Temperance societies reported impressive gains in their campaign against harvest drinking. In 1831, the Union Temperance Society of Harford County boasted of the "considerable number of farms, on which no ardent spirits were used during the last harvest." Within two years, the number of farmers in the county who had "banished ardent spirits" from their harvest fields had increased from 68 to 130, with "many others having partially discontinued its use." By 1836, about 160 of Harford's farmers had prohibited their harvesters from drinking.[102] From Frederick County came the encouraging news that 250 members of the St. John's Temperance Society had reaped three successive harvests "without consuming a drop of ardent spirits."[103] Reformers also trumpeted important strides in northern Virginia, where a Charlestown newspaper reported "with pleasure, that many farmers cut their last crop of grain without using a drop of spirituous liquors in their fields."[104]

Temperance reformers also achieved victories against the frolics that marked the conclusion of the harvest season. "We have no more 'harvest homes' in this section of the country," lamented an 1853 editorial in Hagerstown newspaper. Remembering the days before progress "swept all the customs of our forefathers," the nostalgic writer recalled that "many years ago, our country people . . . used to flock to town in large numbers, thronging its sidewalks and overrunning its stores, making purchases, and participating in the pleasures of what was termed a 'harvest frolic.'"[105] A few years later, the county's rural folk experienced "a sort of harvest frolic" when a circus visited Hagerstown following the harvest. Although the event drew "large numbers of persons, male and female, white and black," this pale imitation of earlier celebrations "passed off without much drunkenness or anything else of an unpleasant character."[106]

Temperance advocates achieved only an incomplete victory, however. Despite their proclamations, employers and reformers learned that the footloose and often besotted rural workforce was difficult to tame. Farmers who harvested their wheat without whiskey sometimes drew the ire of their workers. In 1854, teetotaler William Smith McPherson of Frederick County scribbled that "Ben Slater quit on acct. of whiskey."[107] These workers were, moreover, determined to celebrate at harvest. As late as 1859, a Hagerstown paper lamented that the Pennsylvanians who followed the wheat harvest "squander the fruits of such toil . . . in a twinkling of an eye!" "After their labor is over," the editor sniffed, "a large proportion of them take their harvest in town, spending in a very few hours at these revels all their hard earnings" and returning home with nothing but "reeling heads and sick stomachs."[108]

The attempts to root out harvest drinking were part of a larger campaign to strip farmwork of its disruptive, premodern features and to discipline both free and enslaved workers in a setting where employers' and slaveholders' authority was often compromised. Slaveholders and nonslaveholders alike joined in these battles, which were but one manifestation of the larger currents that cut across all segments of the rural workforce. Both employers and slaveholders felt the seasonal pressures of wheat production, and both groped for the levers that would allow them to manipulate farmhands. In the end, however, slavery proved less supple than free, wage labor. For slaveholders, side employments and incentives offered solutions to the intertwined problems of underemployment and harvest discipline, but there was no escaping the threat—or reality—that unsupervised slave wagoners and harvesters could dash into Pennsylvania. Moreover, slaveholders butted against the obdurate problem of finding employment for their enslaved women, children, and the elderly. Owners who were unwilling to either manumit or sell unwanted bondspeople faced a quandary. To preserve slavery along the sectional border, masters and mistresses needed to keep their bondspeople from absconding and to find more effective means of defraying the cost of their workforce's reproduction. Meeting these intertwined challenges required a renegotiation of slavery.

4. "... How Much of Oursels We Owned"

Finding Freedom along the Mason-Dixon Line

The image still haunted her. In the spring of 1820, Eliza Thomas had witnessed her master, Colonel James Samuel Hook, being "caught in a sawmill, and drawn out like a plank. . . . [Y]ou could n't tell he'd ever been a man." Decades later, she remembered that the colonel's death was the beginning of "awful times" for his enslaved men and women. All slaves dreaded their owners' deaths, which often heralded the dissolution of the estate and the destruction of fragile slave communities. Hook's unexpected demise must have been especially bitter for Thomas and many others on his Frederick County plantation, for they had been promised their freedom. Hook died intestate and never made formal, written arrangements to manumit his chattels, but many of his people believed that freedom was tantalizingly close. They "did not know how much of oursels we owned," Thomas poignantly recalled, but she insisted that many of her fellow slaves "ought to have gone free." Hook had purchased Thomas days before his death with the understanding that he would set her free. "My time was not quite out," Thomas recalled, "and massa made [Hook] promise that he would free me, just as soon as ever it was." Thomas's husband, an enslaved carpenter, Josh Gowins, had also expected to be manumitted, "but he was sold at the block, jis like the cattle, and stript half naked so they might see he was strong." Whatever promises or understandings Hook had made with his slaves were brushed aside by his executors, who moved quickly to sell his "45 Valuable Negroes, consisting of men, women, and children." Thomas, her husband, and their five children were sold as slaves for life to planter Samuel Ringgold.[1]

Eliza Thomas and her family were not alone in the treacherous terrain between slavery and freedom. In 1847, J. E. Snodgrass recounted the story of an African American woman in Williamsport who "regarded herself as a 'free woman'—free as the air of the surrounding hills." Despite having enjoyed her freedom "for some time," and despite being acknowledged as free by "all who knew her," the woman was in a precarious situation because she had not been legally manumitted. "She had no free papers," Snodgrass wrote, "having omitted to secure them, it was said, through over-confidence in . . . a verbal promise of freedom. Fatal omission, too frequently made by the virtually freed." The woman's illusion of freedom was shattered when men seized her and her baby and dragged them to Hagerstown, "there to await the highest bidder for [their] blood and bones." The woman's ordeal was made more agonizing by her master's decision to separate mother and child because the infant was "deemed an encumbrance . . . in the slave mart."[2]

The promise of freedom through either immediate or delayed manumission and the threat of sale loomed large in the minds of Eliza Thomas, the unnamed slave woman, and their enslaved brethren and sisters along the Mason-Dixon Line. While some waited anxiously for their freedom, others forced slave owners' hands by striking northward for freedom. The connections among manumission, slave discipline, and the domestic trade appeared in stark relief during a series of 1849 incidents that unfolded on a plantation owned by William Henry Warfield and his sister, Susanna. In January of that year, a Quaker had purchased the son of "Little Sam," for the ostensible purpose of manumitting him but instead sold him to a trader. Sam's resentment over the betrayal simmered until May, when he and his father, "Big Sam," headed for Pennsylvania. Discovering the escape, William Henry Warfield fumed that he would "sell them and whip them," which prompted a quick reproach from his sister, who warned that "if they hear that they will not return." Within days, the fugitives were captured and imprisoned. Warfield "spoke kindly" to the fugitives and "asked them if they were willing to go back, to which they said No!" He then transferred them to the pen of notorious slave dealer Joseph S. Donovan. Warfield subsequently sold the fugitives to Donovan for $850 but reserved the right to void the transaction within five days. While he haggled with Donovan, Big Sam's mother (and Little Sam's grandmother) pled with Susanna to spare the fugitives from being sold to the Deep South, where she feared "they would be cut up so." Susanna Warfield soon joined her brother in Baltimore, where they "agreed that if they would take an oath on the Bible that Big Sam would serve five years, and Sambo [Little Sam] fifteen, that he, William Henry, would take them back." After mulling the proposal, the slaves responded, "Yes, Master William, we will serve you [on] those terms, better than ever."[3]

Bargains like these were not uncommon. As the antebellum decades progressed, growing numbers of African Americans found themselves laboring under a diverse array of agreements, some verbal and unenforceable, others written and binding, that moved them toward freedom. Far from being a barometer of masters' and mistresses' unease over slavery, delayed manumission was both a measure of their determination to preserve the peculiar institution and a recognition that their authority was eroding. As their slaves slipped from their clutches, masters grasped for instruments that would give them a new purchase on their bondsmen and -women. Some seized on slave owners' traditional weapons, the whip and the sale. "For a trifling offence we send them to the whipping-post," declared one mistress, "and for anything which is very bad we sell them for the south, which is as dreadful to them as death."[4] Former slave George Ross remembered slaveholders making desperate pleas to keep their bondsmen and -women from escaping. "Often the argument is used . . . that they have been treated well, and it would not be fair for them to go away." Ross's master made a similar pitch before Ross escaped from Hagerstown: "You are a good boy, and we will give you enough to eat and drink & clothe you pretty well, & pay your doctor's bills . . . & you should make yourself satisfied."[5]

Floggings, sales, and paternalistic appeals were clumsy tools. Beaten slaves might retaliate by running into Pennsylvania, while the faintest whiff of sale might also provoke slaves to bolt, and promises of good treatment would have rung hollow. In the eyes of some observers, slavery's visage along the Mason-Dixon Line bore little resemblance to the face it showed on the Deep South's cotton, rice, and sugar plantations; the routines of work on wheat-producing farms and plantations, combined with Maryland's liberal manumission laws, granted enslaved workers more independence and cracked open the door to freedom. Still, the institution retained much of its terrible vigor in the Upper South. "I was born and raised in Hagerstown . . . where slavery is perhaps milder than in any other part of the slave states," declared George P. C. Hussey, who hastened to add that he had "seen *hundreds* of colored men and women chained together, two by two, and driven to the south" and "tied up and lashed till the blood ran down to their heels."[6] The ravages of the interstate trade reminded the enslaved of the precariousness of their situation and the shallowness of their owners' paternalism, while the steady stream of runaways fleeing across the Mason-Dixon Line underscored for slaveholders that their human chattels were anything but content.

The Old South may have schooled slaveholders in the art of delusion and made dissimulation a virtue for their bondsmen and -women, but some masters and slaves along the Mason-Dixon Line displayed a remarkable frankness. Here on slavery's tattered margins, the institution's thin paternalistic facade was scoured away, and the property relations that lay at the heart of the institution were laid bare by flight and sale. Washington County planter John Thomson

Mason thought his slaves were contented until they escaped to New York. In a letter dictated to abolitionist Gerrit Smith, they explained to their former master that although they "had been very kindly used," the threat of impending sale spurred them northward. "Nothing but the threat of sale prompted them to run away," Smith continued, adding that the fugitives had heard rumors that their master was "laboring under great pecuniary embarrassment & that his slaves & other property would soon be sold by the sheriff."[7] Under such circumstances, slaveholders quickly learned that their chattels yearned for freedom. When asked whether slaves "who are well used, were tolerably contended in their servitude," a Hagerstown mistress replied that "they were not, that the most fervent, unwavering, undying wish of their hearts, was to be free."[8]

Abolitionist James W. C. Pennington was equally blunt about the master-slave relationship. "The being of slavery, its soul and body, lives and moves in the chattel principle, the property principle, the bill of sale principle," he declared. "The mildest form of slavery . . . is comparatively the worst form," Pennington continued, for "it only keeps the slave in the most unpleasant apprehension" and "trains him under the most favorable circumstance the system admits of, and then plunges him into the worst of which it is capable." Pennington knew that of which he spoke. He was raised on a plantation outside Hagerstown and had known "the mildest form of slavery," but he had experienced the anguish of having his friends and family sold to the plantations of the Deep South.[9] Pennington's observations were echoed by Ross, who likewise remembered that slavery near Hagerstown was in some ways more benign than slavery further south. "Slavery is harder down there [Virginia] than in Maryland," he remembered, adding that "down in Prince George's County, Md., they are a little harder than they are in the upper part of the State." He was, however, adamant that slavery had lost none of its malignancy, for the interstate trade cut swaths through the black community. "I have seen hundreds of cases where families were separated. . . . I have seen this many & many a time, and heard them cry fit to break their hearts."[10] Both masters and slaves understood that they were tied together by nothing more than a property relationship, and both understood that northern Maryland was embedded in a vast plantation complex that extended from their wheat fields to the cotton and sugar fields of the Deep South. It was therefore not surprising that Louisiana planter J. H. Shepherd should respond to news that his family's slaves in Shepherdstown, Virginia, were growing restless by making an ominous suggestion. "I should like very much to have [your] Negroes on one of our places for twelve months; they would receive a lesson in obedience that they would not get over for some years."[11]

The paradoxical adaptations, compromises, and negotiations that extended slavery's moribund existence along the sectional border are the focus of this chapter. During the years immediately following the American Revolution, landowners had grafted slavery onto northern Maryland's agricultural economy, but the changes they implemented proved unsustainable. Slave owners soon found themselves grappling with a host of unanticipated discipline problems. Harvesters ran away. Wagoners drove their teams into Pennsylvania. Slaves sent jobbing refused to surrender their earnings, much less themselves, to owners entitled to neither. This breakdown unfolded against the background of slavery's expansion into the Deep South. Hoping to salvage something from the wreckage of slavery, northern Marylanders consigned hundreds, perhaps thousands, of people to the South's cotton and sugar plantations, but their participation in the interstate trade merely hastened the collapse of their rickety authority. In a desperate attempt to shore the institution's foundations, growing numbers of slave owners dangled the promise of freedom before their remaining chattels. By proffering freedom through postdated manumissions, they found a measure of control of their slaves, whose freedom was conditional on their continued good behavior, and found another means of extracting labor from disaffected servants. For their part, the enslaved received not only their freedom but legal protection against sale beyond Maryland before their terms expired. Fraught with mistrust, dishonesty, and outright fraud, the negotiations between masters and slaves created one of the Old South's most peculiar slave societies.

The Contours of Black Life

Slavery wore many masks along the Mason-Dixon Line. The institution might wear the disguise of a humane counterpoint to the nightmarish conditions in the Deep South or reveal its monstrous nature. Stephen Pembroke spent fifty years in bondage around Sharpsburg and never flinched at describing slavery's brutality. Having lost kin to the interstate trade and witnessed people "working all day . . . with iron collars on their necks," Pembroke swore that he "would rather die the death of the righteous than be a slave, always under dread and never getting a good word." Yet even he conceded that slavery had "many degrees," with some masters being "moderate" and others being "rigid and wicked."[12] If the physical treatment and work routines of slaves in northern Maryland defy easy categorization, slaves' lives had one constant: loneliness. Because slaveholders had difficulty finding steady employment for large standing workforces, most bondspeople found themselves living in units comprising nine or fewer slaves. Throughout the antebellum period, more than half of the masters in these counties possessed just one or two slaves.[13] Their isolation became more pronounced as the antebellum decades progressed. In 1820, 60 percent of the enslaved people in Frederick County and 65 percent of those in Washington County lived in homes that contained nine or fewer slaves. By 1850, these figures had increased to 74 and 70 percent, respectively. The small scale of slaveholdings was one of the defining characteristics of slavery in antebellum Maryland and was, as historian Barbara Jeanne Fields observes, the "cause of much of the suffering incidental to slavery."[14]

While separation from families and friends caused anguish and loneliness for the enslaved, it also created consternation among slave owners.[15] In 1826, owner John Goldsborough complained that the sale of one man's wife had made the man "so restless and so anxious" that Goldsborough "would now rather have another hand on his farm." As long as the separation continued, Goldsborough believed that the slave would "probably never be satisfied."[16] Slaves' persistent demands to be reunited with their kin compelled some owners to yield. Explaining his decision to sell a "valuable farmhand," a Washington County farmer noted that the slave was "sold for no fault, but having a wife in Hagerstown makes him dissatisfied with me."[17] Masters could, of course, ignore their slaves' protests and erect additional barriers between the slaves and the families from whom they were separated. Pennington remembered that his owner became "greatly irritated" when two slave men returned late from family visits and thundered that there would be "a general whipping-match among them."[18] Another master presented his slave, Perry, with a terrible choice when the bondsman was late returning from his wife's home. Perry could "relinquish his visits to Mary," who lived more than twenty miles away, in Hagerstown, or "receive a certain number of stripes the morning after his return." His answer was terse: "I will choose to take the stripes massa."[19] Still, limiting slaves' contact with their families could backfire: Disgruntled bondsmen or -women might express their outrage by overstaying their passes or by running into Pennsylvania. A Frederick County master learned this lesson when Francis Hill escaped. Speculating on what caused Hill's flight, the slave owner mused that Hill had "always been anxious to live in town" with his family.[20]

The simmering resentments and running battles caused by fragmented slave families were further inflamed by the scattered nature of slave communities along the Mason-Dixon Line. Small slaveholdings meant that neighborhoods, not plantations, would be the building blocks of the slave community.[21] Living in an oppressive isolation, the enslaved sought fellowship whenever the opportunity arose. They gathered at the husking frolics that punctuated the calendar and transformed camp meetings, funerals, and Sunday services into social gatherings. On holidays and weekends, throngs of blacks descended on the region's towns and milled about country stores and taverns. While these boisterous gatherings were by-products of an agricultural economy that dictated small holdings, they alarmed slaveholders, who rightly sensed the get-togethers' subversive potential.

To a certain extent, slaves' desire for companionship could be made to serve the interests of slaveholders and the white community.[22] Farmers looking to muster large numbers of laborers to husk corn, to slaughter livestock, or for other projects could depend on the eager participation of African Americans. Joshua Hering, whose family farmed in Carroll County, recalled that his neighbors "would always count, with absolute certainty, upon every Darkey who was within reach" when they organized husking bees. "There was scarcely a night in the late fall that you could not hear, from some part of the neighborhood, the corn husking songs of the Negroes."[23]

Funerals remained a cornerstone of black communities as they matured during the antebellum decades. In Frederick, Jesuit priest John McElroy observed that black funerals drew large numbers of mourners during the 1820s and 1840s.[24] The eagerness with which African Americans attended funerals also struck others, who saw in such occasions the ligaments of northern Maryland's black communities. "The colored people love to congregate, and these occasions gave them an opportunity to get together," observed a Frederick County master. Explaining why his bondspeople attended funerals "nearly every week," he noted that "it was customary, when one of the colored people would die, to have the funeral service performed in all the colored churches, far and near. So that, the death of one darkey, would furnish material for a number of funeral services; and they always used every such occurrence, for all that was in it."[25] Susanna Warfield concurred that "the darkies will preach a funeral over two or three times for a frolic," adding that black funerals would cause the roads to become "lined with darkies . . . all out in their best."[26]

Like funerals, camp meetings provided relief from the isolation of rural life and muddied the distinction between religious services and social gatherings. When a clerk at a Frederick County store asked a field hand why he wanted to purchase hair tonic, the slave explained that he was going to "a woods meeting" and planned "to take my gal down dare."[27] Blacks tramped considerable distances to these services. African Methodist Episcopal minister Thomas W. Henry recalled that his Christmas and Easter sermons in Washington County drew people "from every direction." "They came from the lower part of the Maryland tract and up the Potomac on the Maryland side, from Harper's Ferry, and a great many a considerable distance in Virginia."[28] Despite or perhaps because of the small size of the black population, camp meetings attracted considerable numbers of African Americans. In 1818, a revival near Sharpsburg drew "about three thousand whites, and from three to five hundred blacks."[29] In 1854, "a large number of darkies" celebrated Whitsunday along Antietam Creek, where "they conducted themselves with propriety and enjoyed themselves very much."[30] Four years later, a Middletown newspaper reported that "quite a large number of 'wooly heads' . . . passed through our town on Sunday last to attend a wood's meeting about five miles east of this place."[31]

Not surprisingly, black religious services aroused slaveholders' fears. Masters and mistresses worried that black preachers or white abolitionists would sow discontent among the enslaved. When two of her family's slaves escaped, Warfield's suspicions turned immediately to the funeral they had attended the previous week. "They may have been decoyed away by some abolitionist who may have been at the great funeral sermon," she mused, for "a strange preacher preached it."[32] The anxiety aroused by "strange" preachers was not confined to funerals. The motley crowds that assembled at camp meetings unsettled slaveholders, who feared that the revivals would spawn disorder and undermine slaves' morale. James Lawrence Hooff may have captured the prevailing attitude among slave owners when he sneered, "There is a bush meeting now being held in the woods . . . for loafers and servants."[33] Despite the presence of white constables and the strict propriety of the attendees, a Frederick County newspaper sensed menace in the eight hundred blacks who spent Whitsunday 1854 "feasting and dancing along the Monocacy River." "We are not prepared to sanction these occasions," the editor noted, for "the mischief that may come of such assemblies is not to be prevented by one or two police officers."[34] Whites expressed similar concerns about independent black congregations. In 1854, a slaveholder in rural Frederick County complained about a new black church, where the "young fellows congregate . . . to arrange plans for mischief and rascality, drinking, eating and gambling all hours of the night, robbing hen-roosts and piggeries and disturbing the neighborhood by their yells going home."[35]

Religious services were vital to the creation of the black communities, but African Americans along the Mason-Dixon Line found other, more mundane, opportunities to forge bonds of family and friendship. On weekends and holidays, the crossroads and country stores that dotted northern Maryland became gathering points for enslaved and free blacks, who, like the area's whites, flocked to these destinations seeking amusement and fellowship. Located at the intersection of several transportation arteries, John Blackford's Ferry Hill plantation typified the crossroads where rural blacks congregated. These gatherings were a recurring nuisance to Blackford, whose journals contain numerous references to rowdy black crowds. On 15 November 1835, for example, he complained that "a number of negroes collected on this side of the river—twenty or more—and [were] quite noisy and annoying." He recorded a similar meeting on 28 May 1837 and another on the following 17 September, when he grumbled that "a number of Negroes came over . . . apparently drunk and making much noise and quarreling, etc."[36]

When slaves descended on these intersections, they often gathered at country stores. "There were a good many Negro slaves in the neighborhood," recalled a former clerk from rural Frederick County. "They would come to the village nearly every Saturday night to make their little purchases of tobacco, etc." Although the slaves were "polite, well behaved, and gave us no trouble," many masters worried that such gatherings would erode slave discipline.[37] When interacting with merchants, slaves shed their deference and learned to deal with whites on terms of relative equality. A Scotsman visiting a country store in Frederick County was struck by how "familiar with white men" slaves were when peddling their homemade brooms.[38] Describing one merchant's business with his slaves, a Frederick County master grumbled that "he is on the most intimate terms with them all, he has a sum of money on lone of my Bill, and holds conversation with them most familiarly, and solicits their custom to his store."[39] Masters were quick to sense the danger arising from these transactions.

Convinced that merchants were receiving stolen livestock and produce, slaveholders mounted a vigorous assault on those suspected of doing business with slaves. Newspapers printed ominous warnings, threatening disreputable storekeepers with "the lash of the law." "It is high time to put an end to the infamous practice of dealing with the Negroes," fumed one master, "which practice has, for a long time, flourished with impunity, not only with my negroes, but negroes belonging to others."[40] Slaveholders lobbied for harsh punishment of merchants convicted of receiving stolen merchandise. When a tanner convicted of purchasing two stolen hides petitioned the governor for a pardon, angry masters rallied against his release from the state penitentiary. "I believe him to be a very bad citizen," stated one. "He has been . . . of great disadvantage to my slaves, and those of many others, by dealing and trading with them in a private way." Another threatened that "to pardon him would be productive of a very great dissatisfaction amongst all the slaveowners about Westminster to whom he has been a great annoyance—they would complain bitterly."[41]

Much to the chagrin of their owners and of municipal authorities, free blacks and slaves continued flocking to towns and villages during the late antebellum decades. In 1835, Frederick's aldermen attempted to curb this long-standing problem by approving harsher punishments for blacks caught roaming the streets after ten o'clock: Slaves violating the curfew might receive thirty-nine lashes, while free blacks faced twenty-dollar fines or thirty days in the county prison.[42] Three years later, city officials increased the fines levied against those who sold "any distilled liquor to any free negro or negro slave, or suffered them to collect on his or her premises on the Sabbath day."[43] Despite these ordinances, authorities continued to wrestle with the disorder created by illegal, unruly assemblies of poor whites, free blacks, and slaves. In 1851, in 1854, and again in 1858, Frederick's aldermen strengthened the ordinances against the "noisy and rude crowds of boys, negroes or other persons."[44] Hagerstown's aldermen had enacted similar ordinances, but they proved a poor deterrent. In 1849, a constable stumbled across some "twenty or more colored gentlemen" who had gathered to "raffle, with cards and dice, for turkeys, geese, chickens, and whiskey." The men scattered at the constable's approach, and through "some amusing specimens of 'Tall Walking,'" most escaped arrest.[45] Frustrated by the persistence of such assemblies, another constable prowled the streets with a cowhide, snapping it at "all the colored boys, whom he could catch in any kind of mischief."[46]

Slaveholders' anxieties about the deterioration of slave discipline became more pronounced as the antebellum decades progressed. The counties along the Mason-Dixon Line were thoroughly enmeshed in a transportation network that brought slaves into routine contact with transient poor whites and free blacks whose commitment to the peculiar institution was at best suspect. The canals, railroads, and turnpikes that traversed the region rendered it difficult, if not impossible, for slaveholders to police the borders of their estates. The intensification of commercial activity broadened slaves' horizons by granting them greater mobility and bringing them into more frequent contact with free blacks and nonslaveholding whites. In 1848, for example, New Englanders Robert and Sarah Davis assisted a runaway slave named Sam, whom they had encountered while traveling on the National Road. Although Sam admitted that there was a fifty-dollar reward for his capture, the passengers on the stagecoach assured the fugitive that he was safe and took up a collection for him.[47] Slave boatmen and wagoners wove webs of familial and personal connections that extended across the state and facilitated escapes. Montgomery County mistress Eleanor Brooks highlighted the corrosive effects of the Chesapeake and Ohio (C & O) Canal on slave morale when she described the suspected route of her runaway slave Charles Ringgold. "He was hired on the C & O Canal," she noted, "and has probably made his way up it to Mr. Abraham Barnes's in Washington Co., where he pretends to have a wife, and thence to Pennsylvania."[48] In 1860, slave owners living along the C & O protested the General Assembly's decision to lease the state's interest in the canal to northerners, warning that slaves would be "persuaded and aided away, by the lowbred set of abolitionists that now traverse said canal." In a petition laced with xenophobia, they argued that leasing the canal to northern interests would open the floodgates to abolitionists and foreigners, who already "tamper with our Negroes in every possible way."[49] Railroads presented another challenge to slave owners along the Mason-Dixon Line. In 1842, the loss of twelve slaves prompted a sharp complaint from Congressman John Thomson Mason of Washington County, who claimed that railroad employees were involved in a "well concerted scheme for the escape of slaves from this neighborhood." After fugitives "crossed the Maryland line on foot," Mason alleged that "a car takes up the slaves at or near Chambersburg. . . . This gives them a start upon their pursuers, difficult to overcome, and thus the losses are fast becoming very numerous."[50]

Adding to slave owners' worries were the peddlers who trawled the countryside receiving produce and dispensing alcohol, often with few questions asked. In the 1830s, northern Virginians complained that trading carts "generally owned and managed by Free Negroes (and sometimes by white men, of no higher growth of character)" were conducting a brisk and illegal trade with slaves. This commerce, the Virginians argued, had encouraged "innumerable depredations by the slaves of the neighborhood, who always find . . . ready purchasers."[51] Slave owners sometimes directed their wrath against immigrants in particular. In 1841, residents of Jefferson County, Virginia, lamented that peddlers, "many of whom are foreigners," were prowling the quarters and conducting a "highly injurious" traffic.[52] These concerns were echoed by Maryland's slaveholders. In 1820, a Washington County master railed against the peddlers who were trespassing on his farm and "dealing with his servants for produce" and "furnishing them with liquor."[53] The General Assembly recommended legislation for "the suppression of stragglers and venders of small wares and notions, of no use, but of great injury to our people." In particular, they suggested the "exclusion of all foreigners from the right to peddle anything" and the limiting of peddling licenses to "our people alone."[54]

Slavery's decay in the counties south of the Mason-Dixon Line was accelerated by developments in Pennsylvania. Slaveholders soon discovered that the Mason-Dixon Line was becoming a trip wire, which, when sprung, would break their hold on their human chattels. During the early national period, some Marylanders and Pennsylvanians conspired to cheat the enslaved out of their freedom by smuggling them across state lines. This shadowy traffic continued over the following decades, but it gradually became a pathway to freedom through which Marylanders manumitted their slaves, bound them as apprentices or servants, and sent them into Pennsylvania to work off the price of their freedom. Although the trade in indentured freedpeople had the potential to undercut the Gradual Emancipation Act, northern courts generally approved of the practice because the unfree blacks carried into Pennsylvania were moving toward freedom. In 1828, for example, Jonas Owens of Cecil County, Maryland, sold his slaves, sixteen-year-old William Taylor and eleven-year-old Harriet Wilson to James Hasson of Cumberland County, Pennsylvania. As part of the agreement, Owens filed a deed of manumission declaring that his chattels would receive their freedom when they turned twenty-eight. Taylor protested the arrangement and sued for his and Wilson's freedom, but a Pennsylvania court ruled that their manumission and subsequent sale complied with the state's Gradual Emancipation Act. "If Taylor was not a slave in Maryland, but quasi a servant for years, there is no law to prohibit his being held in the same condition in Pennsylvania," the court ruled, adding that the "transfer was not against the right and interest of Taylor but in favor of both; for after twenty-eight years of age he becomes free."[55]

Pennsylvania's courts were less supportive of slaveholders whose intention was to defraud the enslaved or of those who actions ran counter to the letter and spirit of the emancipation law. In 1821, James M. Russell purchased an enslaved Marylander, Charity, and simultaneously executed a deed of manumission and an indenture. Under the agreement, Charity, who was then forty, promised serve Russell "in the state of Pennsylvania . . . for ten years" in exchange for "sufficient meat, drinking, clothing, washing and lodging, &c., and one dollar when free." After serving for five years, Charity sued for her freedom because her age, combined with the length of her term, violated a provision of the 1780 statute that declared "no covenant of personal servitude . . . shall be valid or binding on a negro . . . for a term longer than seven years" unless the servant was younger than twenty-one when the agreement was made. The state supreme court upheld Charity's suit because holding her "would be contrary to the spirit of the laws of Pennsylvania, for the gradual abolition of slavery."[56] Spiriting term slaves and indentured free blacks across the Mason-Dixon Line became so commonplace during the 1820s that Pennsylvania's slave population increased from 211 to 386 during the decade. In 1833, a senate committee in Pennsylvania reported that "Negroes of all ages are brought in considerable numbers . . . and emancipated on serving a certain number of years, seldom exceeding seven, unless they happen to be mere children." Far from decrying the practice, the committee discouraged the state from denying the "unhappy bondsman . . . a chance of obtaining his liberty, by a commutation of his personal services during a brief period in this commonwealth, for those of perpetual bondage elsewhere."[57] In 1847, the Pennsylvania legislature declared that slaves carried across the Mason-Dixon Line were entitled to immediate freedom and could seek redress in the state's courts.[58]

The corrosive effects of Pennsylvania's free soil on the property rights of Maryland slave owners grew more apparent as the antebellum decades progressed. Indeed, the simmering conflict caused by Pennsylvanians' interference with the recovery of fugitive slaves intensified as the sectional crisis gained momentum. In the 1842 case of *Prigg v. Pennsylvania*, the U.S. Supreme Court declared the commonwealth's 1826 personal liberty law unconstitutional. The decision maintained slave owners' right to recover fugitive slaves but also declared that state governments were under no compulsion to assist in the recovery of fugitive slaves.[59]

In response to *Prigg*, Pennsylvania enacted an even more stringent personal liberty law in March 1847. This sweeping statute littered barricades, snares, and traps before the southerners who prowled north of Mason and Dixon's Line in pursuit of quarry: It stiffened the penalties imposed on kidnappers, hobbled slave catchers, and prohibited state and local authorities from assisting in the recovery of runaway slaves. Its opening section declared that people convicted of abducting free blacks would face fines of between five hundred and twelve hundred dollars and would "undergo a punishment, by solitary confinement . . . at hard labor" for five to twelve years. The law also attempted to defang or at least muzzle slave catchers by criminalizing the violence that often accompanied the capture of fugitive slaves. It stipulated that anyone who seized an alleged runaway in a "riotous, violent, tumultuous, and unreasonable manner" could be prosecuted for a misdemeanor. Anyone convicted could be fined between one hundred and one thousand dollars and imprisoned in a county jail for three months. Not only would slave catchers have to carry out their nefarious business in a manner that did not "disturb or endanger the public peace," they would have to do so without the assistance of public officials. Seizing on Supreme Court justice Joseph Story's opinion that states were not required to assist in the recovery of runaway slaves, the legislature declared that Pennsylvania's judges, justices of the peace, and aldermen had no jurisdiction in cases arising from "persons escaping from the service of their masters," nor were they allowed to grant certificates or warrants for the removal of suspected slaves. Judges did, however, retain the power to "inquire into the causes and legality of the arrest or imprisonment of any human being" and to issue writs of habeas corpus when necessary. The law extended downward to local jailers, who were barred from lodging "any person claimed as a fugitive from servitude or labor" unless ordered to do so by a judge—an impossibility under the new statute.[60]

Marylanders bewailed the law's pernicious effects on slave discipline. A lawmaker from Washington County complained that his constituents lived "within arm's reach of [the] boundary line" and were "more exposed in the loss of [their] slave property" than were other slave owners. Describing the erosion of slave prices and morale, he claimed that "since the passage of that law, our slave property has depreciated to more than half its real and actual value; our slaves have absconded by scores." The rising tide of slave resistance compelled some masters and mistresses to sell their human chattels southward, a move that locked flight and sale in an upward spiral. A Hagerstown editor made these connections explicit, declaring that the Pennsylvania law had made property in slaves "insecure in Maryland, and its value greatly diminished here, while in other regions it is increasing." By undermining slave discipline, the "lovers of blacks" had forced slave owners to either lose their chattels through escape or sell them away from "mild discipline of Maryland to the far South." "Thousands and tens of thousands from the cotton and rice fields there, might justly accuse of their fate, the false and misguided philosophy of their too busy friends." The editorial would have resonated with slaveholders along the sectional border. In July 1847, a mistress near Martinsburg, Virginia, wrote that her husband was considering taking their slaves "to the south" after several of them made an unsuccessful bid for freedom. "It is very evident we cannot keep them in these border counties," she explained, "they are going off all around us. The abolitionists and Pennsylvania have destroyed the tie between master and slave."[61]

The enslaved were eager to sunder the ties (chains) between themselves and their owners. Emboldened by *Prigg* and the 1847 personal liberty law and terrified that their nervous masters and mistresses might sell them South, bondspeople marshaled themselves into bands before striking for the Mason-Dixon Line. Indeed, the 1840s witnessed a steady drumbeat of such mass escapes. In July 1846, for example, the *Herald of Freedom* reported that eight slaves, including two men, two women, and four children, had "decamped in a body . . . for Pennsylvania." That September, the headlines "Oceans of Runaway Negroes" and "Something Wrong" trumpeted the escape of fifteen slaves from Washington County, who had "absconded in a body" and had managed to reach Chambersburg, Pennsylvania, before nine of them were arrested. October 1847 brought news that seven slaves who had "started for the Democratic soil of Pennsylvania" had been captured near Chambersburg. A month later, a "batch of six or eight slaves" from Funkstown made "for the old Democratic Land of Pennsylvania."[62] The sight of slaves fleeing en masse taught masters and mistresses that slaves were becoming dangerous investments. The border skirmishes that erupted from the 1830s through the 1850s would teach slave owners just how dangerous their human chattels were.

Mass escapes not only revealed slaves' determination to preserve families and communities but also signaled their willingness to resist capture by force. We glimpse these intertwined motives at work among brothers John, Jerry, and Wesley Sinclair and their "trusted friend" Anderson, who fled from slavery near Harper's Ferry, Virginia, in 1826. Before fleeing, these men "placed their heads together . . . and swore a solemn oath that they would not surrender to any eight men or less." The same steely resolve characterized the slaves who escaped during the 1840s. In 1845, a constable stumbled across ten runaway slaves near Smithburg, Maryland. A posse of eight townspeople confronted the fugitives, but "the negroes being armed with hatchets, clubs, and pistols, refused to be taken peaceable." When the dust settled and the smoke cleared, a newspaper reported that "several of the white men" and about half of the slaves were "severely wounded" but that only one of the fugitives had been taken into custody. Another pitched battle erupted on the night of 9 September 1849, when a gang overtook eight runaways near Boonsboro. "An attempt was made to arrest them," noted one newspaper, "which proved unsuccessful and resulted in three of the whites receiving severe stabs." Later that week, six enslaved people from southern Frederick County struck "a straight course for the Pennsylvania line" but were caught by a "strong force" near the village of Wolfsville, Maryland. The slaves were armed with "bowie knives [and] dirks," and they made a "desperate resistance" that left two of their pursuers "dreadfully lacerated." Capture did not equal surrender. African American mobs sometimes descended on county jails to spring runaways. In 1847, for example, an armed body attacked the Hagerstown prison in an unsuccessful attempt to liberate fugitives.[63]

The courage and defiance of the fugitives was matched by that of northern free blacks. In an apt analogy, historians Ira Berlin and Steven Hahn have likened northern free black communities to the maroon settlements of the Americas and Caribbean. Like the maroons, who lurked on the fringes of plantation societies, northern free blacks knew that they were enmeshed in a slave system that was difficult to escape. The Fugitive Slave Law of 1793 and the more virulent statute of 1850 allowed slave owners to reclaim their chattels anywhere in the United States. Many runaways who had spent years on free soil, as well as some free blacks who had never been on slave soil, lived under the constant threat of being dragged south.[64]

Because the peculiar institution had a national reach, African Americans north of the Mason-Dixon Line fought a spirited resistance against kidnappers and slave catchers. Black Pennsylvanians created organizations to assist runaways. In 1841, for example, Gettysburg's African American community established the Slave's Refuge Society to "assist such of our brethren as shall come among us for the purpose of liberating themselves, and to raise all the means in our power . . . to give liberty to our brethren groaning under the tyrannical yoke of oppression." As the sectional crisis intensified, Marylanders who ventured north in pursuit of runaway slaves often found themselves in hostile territory. In 1841, "eight or ten" free blacks in Lancaster, Pennsylvania, unleashed a "shower of stones" on a Maryland master who, in company with the town's police, had arrested a female slave. An officer shot and mortally wounded one of the free blacks, but not before the slave was rescued. Such attacks were not unusual. In March 1845, slave catcher Thomas Finnegan was attacked by what one paper called "a horde of free negroes, perhaps a hundred," during a foray into Chambersburg. After unleashing volleys of "stones and other missiles," the mob rushed Finnegan, whose pistols misfired, and would have inflicted "such punishment as they thought proper" had not a few whites intervened to save him from "Judge Lynch." Later that year, blacks in Lancaster attempted to rescue fugitive Asa Stanton, who had been remanded to his master by a local court. Those African Americans who assisted Finnegan and his ilk also received their comeuppances. An early historian of the Underground Railroad recounted the story of a black Chester County man who not only kept slave owners apprised of fugitives moving through his neighborhood but sometimes captured and sold runaways. When local blacks discovered his dealings, "a number of people assembled and gave him a terrible beating, from the effects of which he never recovered."[65]

The violence subsequently intensified. In 1847, slaveholders from Hagerstown ventured into Pennsylvania to recapture a dozen runaways. Having recovered some of the fugitives outside Shippensburg, the slaveholders hauled them to Carlisle for examination. When the judge acceded to their request, a "large crowd of infuriated colored men and women" assaulted the posse with clubs and paving stones. The ensuing melee freed two slaves and left prominent Hagerstown citizen James H. Kennedy mortally wounded. Although several members of the mob were arrested and convicted, the riot outraged white Marylanders. "If they continue to perpetrate these outrages," bellowed a Hagerstown editor, "they must expect that [we] will take measures, by way of retaliation." Even whites who owned no slaves found common cause with slaveholders in the aftermath of the riot. Among those signing a petition condemning the attack were many "who do not own slaves on principle" but who would not "violate, or . . . see violated, the chartered rights of his fellow citizens."[66]

The bloodiest skirmish on this fractious borderland erupted in 1851 at Christiana, Pennsylvania. There, Baltimore County slave owner Edward Gorsuch and a federal posse attempted to capture two fugitives who had escaped in 1849. On 11 September, Gorsuch and his party surrounded the bondsmen and their free black allies at the home of William Parker, himself a runaway slave from Anne Arundel County. Reinforced by upward of a hundred black and white allies, the people inside Parker's house unleashed a hail of gunfire that left Gorsuch dead and his son wounded. In the aftermath of the fight, the fugitives eluded their captors and fled north to Canada.[67]

Faced with a stagnating economy and the steady erosion of slave discipline, some northern Marylanders chose to disentangle themselves from the peculiar institution. Those determined to wash their hands of slavery had two options: manumit their slaves, or shovel them into the churning interstate slave trade. At first blush, the decision appeared to involve polar opposites, but the two options were in fact inseparable. Sale inside northern Maryland had, of course, long been integral to preserving the master-slave relationship. Owners unwilling to manumit truculent slaves might dispose of them on the local market, while bondspeople unable to secure their freedom might clamor for more agreeable masters.[68] But as the domestic traffic accelerated and as masters and mistresses grew more apprehensive about the security of their slave property, both slaves and owners realized that the threat of sale and the promise of freedom were in fact different sides of the same coin. This harsh reality was made apparent to Sharpsburg slave Stephen Pembroke when he broached the subject of manumission. When Pembroke told his master, "I am getting old, and ought to have some rest," the angry slaveholder snapped, "No, sir; if you speak about freedom, I will sell you further South."[69]

Manumission, the Interstate Slave Trade, and Slave Discipline

It is difficult to determine the precise dimensions of the interstate slave trade for the remainder of the antebellum decades. The land records of Frederick County for 1840–48 and 1853–60 include only thirty-two slaves sold to speculators or nonresident planters. This low figure is doubtless illusory. Northern Maryland stood at the crossroads of the Upper South's most important slave trading routes, and abundant anecdotal evidence indicates that the domestic trade retained its virulence throughout the antebellum decades.[70] Coffles were not unusual sights in northern Maryland during the 1840s and 1850s. Hagerstown slave Charles Watts offered a bleak portrait of the slave trade in a letter he penned to abolitionist Gerrit Smith. "I most tel you of the Slave trade is now gone onn in part of the county," he began. "A few weeks ago [there] have been twenty five taken from here some of them taken from their wife and children and some children taken from their mother . . . eleven of them was my cusins."[71] Frederick County farmer Allen Sparrow remembered that the interstate trade was commonplace in the antebellum decades. "I have seen

from 20 to 30 Negros cuft together one on each side to a long chain," with
Georgia traders driving them with whips. The traders roamed the countryside
purchasing their victims "as a man would horses and cows," sometimes offering twelve hundred dollars for a "good looking" slave.[72]

As enslaved people fled before the slave traders, speculators sensed new
opportunities to profit from the chaos unleashed by the interstate traffic.
Traders began forging alliances with slave catchers, hoping either to capture
runaways and carry them to the Deep South or to buy them "as they ran"
from slave owners who wanted to recoup some of their investment. In 1831,
Reuben Carlley, an agent of the notorious soul driver George Kephart, outlined such a scheme to an associate in Chester County, Pennsylvania. "I will,
in all cases, as soon as a negro runs off, send you a handbill immediately," he
promised, asking only that his partner "inform me of any negro you think has
run away—no matter where you think he has come from, nor how far—and I
will try to find out his master." Giddy with excitement, the trader added that
"Kephart and myself are determined to go the whole hog for any negro you
can find. . . . I have plenty of money if you can find plenty of negroes."[73]

The connections among manumission, flight, and forced relocation surfaced often along the Mason-Dixon Line. While making preparations to transport his slaves from Frederick County to a sugar plantation in Lafourche
Parish, Louisiana, in 1828, John Lee claimed that he had mulled a scheme
to manumit his slaves "as an inducement to good conduct on the part of the
slaves, and in recompense for their greater services to be performed in the
South." In the bitter legal dispute that followed the failure of the Louisiana
plantation, Lee testified that he had wished to "liberate them all after service
for a certain term," but his partner and brother-in-law, Outerbridge Horsey,
had "utterly refused." Horsey averred that he had no knowledge of the scheme.
"But if true," he testified, he "would have declined the proposal as insincere
& deceptive & only calculated to awaken false hopes in the servants, for the
selfish purpose of reconciling them to go & preventing escape."[74] Regardless
of the truth behind Lee's and Horsey's testimonies, the motives they ascribed
to their actions are revealing. Both men recognized that manumission, slave
discipline, and forced relocation to the Deep South were inextricably linked.
For Lee, the promise of freedom was an inducement to guarantee his slaves'
cooperation in his southern venture, while his partner believed that any such
offer was merely a scheme to prevent them from escaping before they were
shipped to Louisiana. The connections between the interstate trade, which
eroded the bonds linking master and slave, and manumission would be a recurring theme in slavery's history in northern Maryland. Slaveholders could

decide the fate of their chattels but could not discount their agency. Flight was a powerful weapon for the enslaved, and it guaranteed that slaves' fears and yearnings would figure into the brutal arithmetic that consigned some to freedom and others to Louisiana.

Northern Maryland's slaveholders had an ambivalent relationship with the interstate slave trade. Some owned plantations on the cotton frontier and were actively involved in the domestic trade. Frederick County master William M. Beall owned land in Louisiana, Arkansas, and Mississippi, and his son-in-law, John Knight, of Natchez, Mississippi, routinely purchased bondspeople for shipment to the Southwest.[75] Other slave owners were more conflicted about the interstate traffic. For some, the trade's innumerable cruelties and the terrible conditions on the Deep South's cotton and sugar plantations provided a foil against which they forged an identity as benevolent, paternalistic masters. Marylanders knew better than to trust the likes of trader Austin Woolfolk, who assured a Baltimore County farmer that "9 times out of 10, negroes are better off in Louisiana than in Maryland."[76] Northern Maryland slaveholders understood that local conditions differed radically from those in the Deep South. The news that his daughter, Mittie, had accepted a marriage proposal from a Louisiana planter caused great anguish for Harford County farmer John Anthony Munnikhuysen, who worried that the cruel regime on a sugar plantation would crush her spirit. "I don't see how I can object but I don't think I will ever consent to her going out there," he wrote to his son in 1860. "Mit has never been used to seeing negroes flayed alive and it would kill her."[77]

For some northern Marylanders, the need to shield their bondspeople from the auction block became a justification for slavery. To the extent that the region's slave owners constructed a paternalistic ethos, it involved an unequal bargain whereby the enslaved offered labor and obedience and their owners sheltered them from the domestic traffic. Sharpsburg farmer Jacob Miller articulated this bargain in 1859, when he described how the county sheriff had confiscated several of his slaves for debt. Although the sheriff attempted to console Miller by noting that the bondspeople would settle his accounts, the distraught slaveholder felt a profound sense of guilt. "Now I would almost as soon he would have my life as to have taken them three boys from me, and I believe they would have risked their lives for me," he wrote to a relative, adding that "if those boys had been bad fellows as some are I would [not] have said a word, but they were . . . always willing to do my bidding." The cause of Miller's anguish seems to have been his deficiencies as a master. Despite having no qualms about selling "bad fellows," Miller believed that his slaves' good conduct had entitled them to his protection. Owing to his financial failure, the slaves had been ripped "from their home of which they were well contented" and sent "to the South, where they will run the risk [of] not getting a good home."[78]

Slaveholders who participated in the interstate trade attempted to distance themselves from the anguish they were causing in the quarters. White Marylanders relocating to the Deep South might spare a favored few to appease their slaves and assuage their consciences. Explaining why he had not taken his slave, Beck, to his new plantation in Louisiana, John Lee noted that "her mother (an old and faithful servant) begged so earnestly that this, her youngest child, might not be separated from her, that this respondent could not permit himself to send her away." Lee's benevolence did not extend to Beck's four siblings, who were sent to Louisiana, but did secure the grudging consent of Beck's mother, who was willing "to acquiesce in the separation from all the rest, if only Beck should be spared."[79] Other slaveholders expressed their misgivings about the traffic by attempting to recover slaves that their families had previously consigned to the Deep South. In 1842, Baltimore County farmer William Fell Johnson made inquiries about two slaves, Reuben and Duke, whom his father had sold to a trader in 1826 or 1827. Johnson hoped to secure their "redemption" and send them to Liberia, provided that doing so was "not attended with too great a pecuniary sacrifice."[80]

Slaveholders' ambivalence about the interstate traffic may have been a tacit acknowledgment of its corrosive effects on slave discipline. Masters and mistresses were mindful of the possibility that their chattels might respond to an approaching sale by escaping and thereby inflict a severe financial wound. In 1848, the enslaved workers of the Antietam Ironworks grew apprehensive and dissatisfied with their bankrupt owner, John McPherson Brien. "Many of them came to me & expressed their unwillingness to remain with me, to my great astonishment, for I have always treated them most kindly," the disgruntled slave owner wrote. Although outraged by his chattels' "gross ingratitude," Brien could not discount their concerns, for "it will be a serious loss to me if they would leave this place for Pennsylvania."[81] The executor appointed to handle the dissolution of Brien's property shared these fears, noting that the bondspeople were "apprehensive of being sold away" and might "run away and escape in the non-slaveholding States, which their proximity to the State of Pennsylvania will enable them readily to accomplish." In the end, the slaves were sold, but the threat of escape had figured into the calculations of both their master and his executor.[82]

Slaveholders and county authorities continued to wave the threat of sale outside over the heads of unruly slaves. Sale proved a potent but unwieldy weapon, for punishments designed to bolster slavery were prejudicial to the interests of individual slaveholders. Maryland's slaveholders bristled at the statutes that sacrificed their property at reduced prices. Henry Ankeny of Washington County insisted that his "rights as a master" had been compromised by the "extreme sentence" imposed on his slave, George Barnes, who had been convicted of forgery. Ankeny railed against the unfairness of the law demanding his slave's sale outside Maryland, complaining that he would be denied his slave's services and, perhaps more important, that Barnes would fetch only a fraction of his actual value if sold as a convict.[83] Frederick County mistress Mary Hall voiced similar concerns when two of her slaves were indicted for petty larceny. Worried that a conviction and scourging would diminish their value, she petitioned the governor for permission to sell them outright, thus sparing the state—and herself—the costs of a trial.[84]

In addition to reducing a slave's value, the laws requiring the sale of convicts outside Maryland jeopardized slaveholders' control over their remaining slaves, who might protest the court's ruling by escaping into Pennsylvania. In 1838, Frederick County master Frederick Schley petitioned the governor to pardon his slave, Tom, who had been convicted of petty larceny and sentenced to be sold outside Maryland. Schley's son, who managed the family's farm, was confident that a sale would result in "many, if not all of my other servants, mak[ing] their escape into Pennsylvania," which was only ten miles away. Indeed, Schley predicted that within a week of the sale, he "would not have a negro on the farm." His slaves, he explained, were convinced that Tom's arrest was a "a mere trick and contrivance, for the purpose of selling Tom, *for a good price,* to a slave trader." "These poor creatures have been so often tricked in this way," Schley continued, that "they would run off, under the full conviction, that they would soon be the next victim of the trader."[85]

The officials responsible for selling slave convicts encountered legal barriers that undercut the slaves' value on the otherwise buoyant interstate market. Several states prohibited the importation of slave criminals, and buyers were understandably wary of purchasing convicts. The case of Washington County constable William Freaner and slave William Gross illustrate the dangers and difficulties that attended the sale of slave convicts. Described by a friend as "a poor man" with a "very large family," Freaner made himself indispensable to the slaveholders of Washington County during the 1830s and 1840s. Indeed, his neighbors declared him "a valuable & meritorious police officer & particularly so in a community possessing slaves." Transactions involving enslaved and free blacks seem to have been a routine part of Freaner's duties. He sometimes served as the middleman for those trafficking slaves. In 1842, for example, Freaner advertised for "ten or fifteen likely young negroes of either sex, for which the highest price IN CASH will be given." The advertisement smacks of one posted by a trader, but Freaner offered assurances that "the gentleman desirous of purchasing them intends them for his own use." Some of the deals that Freaner brokered may not have been aboveboard. At least one kidnapper thought that the constable might be willing to traffic in stolen people. In 1839, a young Marylander, John P. May, approached Freaner and offered to sell him free blacks from Pennsylvania. Freaner seemed interested and agreed to meet May at a prearranged location. When May brought a teenaged black from Mifflin County, Pennsylvania, to the rendezvous, he was greeted by Freaner and several officers, who dragged the kidnapper to the county gaol.[86] For Freaner, the trade in African American bodies was an inescapable part of life along the Mason-Dixon Line, a market that he not only participated in but also policed.

The chain of events that brought Freaner and Gross together began in September 1845 at a revival near Hagerstown. Like many camp meetings, this one seems to have been a raucous affair that drew slaves, free blacks, and poor whites looking to catch the spirit (or to drink some spirits). At some point, four African Americans, including Gross, ordered cakes from one of the peddlers whose booths and tables dotted the grounds. When they refused to pay, the incensed baker called on several bystanders for assistance. In the ensuing melee, the blacks beat one of these men "so badly that he died from the wounds."[87] That December, the Washington County court convicted Gross of murder in the second degree and sentenced him to receive thirty-nine lashes and to be sold outside Maryland, a sentence that the sheriff charged Freaner with executing.

No sooner had the gavel sounded than slave trader Elijah McDowell intervened in the proceedings. McDowell and Freaner were more than passing acquaintances. In his petition for a pardon, Freaner claimed that McDowell worked for Hope H. Slatter, a "well known . . . large negro buyer for the Southern market & often concerned by his agents in purchasing slaves in the said County." McDowell encouraged the judge and sheriff to spare the lash, as the "young strong & good looking" convict might fetch six hundred dollars if he was unscarred. McDowell's argument convinced the court officials, who ordered Freaner to transport Gross to Richmond via Baltimore and "there to sell him, as his own property, without disclosing the fact of his conviction." The constable knew that it was illegal to smuggle slave convicts into many states of the Deep South, but he insisted that such transactions occurred "every day." Moreover, he argued that the state's laws had placed him in an impossible position. Maryland required that many slave "criminals be sold out of the state," but "every state at the south prohibits their introduction, so that this law of this state is impossible to be executed, unless the fact of conviction is suppressed."[88]

The scheme soon unraveled. When Freaner arrived in Baltimore, he heard that Slatter was preparing a shipment of slaves for New Orleans. Instead of traveling to Richmond, Freaner chose to discharge his duties at Baltimore. Freaner claimed that he never intended to cheat the trader. Slatter never asked if the slave was a criminal, and Freaner never volunteered the information. When Slatter inquired if Gross was "all right," Freaner interpreted the question as pertaining to "soundness of body" and answered, "Yes, he is all right." Slatter paid Freaner $620 for the slave, a sum that Freaner reckoned would have netted the trader a "fair & liberal profit." The boat carrying Slatter's human cargo arrived in New Orleans in January 1846. Upon learning that the shipment included a convict, local authorities seized Gross and auctioned him for the state's benefit. Slatter turned his wrath on Freaner, from whom Slatter received a "considerable judgment" for fraud.[89]

The interstate traffic both upheld and undermined slave owners' authority. The threat of sale might intimidate an individual slave, but the destructive energies unleashed by the domestic trade strained the bonds connecting masters and slaves and clouded slavery's future in northern Maryland.

Term Slavery

The tension between the interstate trade and manumission compelled northern Maryland's slaves and slave owners to navigate a treacherous course between Scylla and Charybdis. The Deep South's insatiable demand for bound laborers gave masters and mistresses along the sectional border a vested interest in the survival of slavery, but the promise of freedom beckoning from across the Mason-Dixon Line rendered its future uncertain. For many slave owners, the prospects of manumitting their chattels, selling them southward, or watching them escape were equally unpalatable. Those seeking a path between these stark yet intertwined alternatives turned to delayed manumission or term slavery, which promised to ease the pressures that were crushing the peculiar institution. Whether executed through a will or postdated deed of manumission, term slavery agreements differed from simple promises of freedom. While both deferred a slave's freedom and made manumission conditional on a slave's good behavior, term slavery hemmed the master-slave relationship with a series of legal safeguards. The enslaved received guarantees, albeit imperfect, that their day of liberation would come and that they would not be sold south before the completion of their terms.

Although it is difficult to determine how many bondsmen and -women labored under delayed manumission agreements, evidence suggests that term slaves constituted a significant minority of the region's slave population. On

Table 4. Slave Sales, Frederick County, Md.

Description of Slave (Type of Transaction)	1790–1818 N (%)	1819–1830 N (%)	1840–1848 N (%)	1853–1860 N (%)
Slaves for Life (Local Sale)*	463 (77.9)	371 (27.2)	142 (33.1)	38 (9.7)
Slaves for Life (Interstate Sale)†	88 (14.8)	888 (65.1)	23 (5.3)	9 (2.3)
Term Slaves (Local Sale)	43 (7.2)	105 (7.7)	265 (61.6)	344 (88.0)

Source: Frederick County Court, Land Records, 1799–1830, 1840–1848, Frederick County
   Circuit Court, Land Records, 1853–1860, both in Maryland Hall of Records, Annapolis.
* Excludes slaves who were mortgaged and redeemed by their owners.
† Includes sales to nonresidents and to agents of slave traders in Baltimore and the
   District of Columbia.

the eve of the Civil War, anywhere from 10 to 30 percent of Frederick County's slaves had delayed manumission or term slavery agreements.[90] By the 1850s, these temporary servants had become the mainstay of the local market, accounting for 88 percent of documented slave sales (see table 4). Indeed, local demand for lifelong slaves seems to have slackened in the waning years of the antebellum period. J. W. Dixon, whose family had owned slaves in Frederick County, remembered that few people were willing to purchase slaves for life. "So far as I could ever ascertain," he wrote, "very few . . . had come into their owner's possession through purchase, but in nearly every case by inheritance alone."[91] Delayed manumissions also left an indelible mark in the census returns from Frederick County, whose black population grew freer as it grew older. Not only were most slaves children or adolescents, but the ratio of blacks to slaves increased steadily among those in their thirties, forties, and fifties.[92] In many ways, slavery in Frederick County had come to resemble its counterpart in Baltimore, where historian T. Stephen Whitman has trenchantly observed that delayed manumission created a "transmuted form of slavery as a stage of life rather than as a lifelong institution."[93]

Several circumstances contributed to make term slaves attractive to local purchasers. On the most basic level, they were less expensive than slaves for life. The 1855 inventory of Frederick County slaveholder Thomas Warfield illustrates the relative value of lifelong slaves and term slaves. When appraised as slaves for life, Warfield's adolescent slaves Alfred, Ann Maria, and Gusty were valued, at $500, $375, and $400, respectively. Because the slaves were to be manumitted at age twenty, however, their values were $140, $100, and $75.[94] These values seem consistent with the prices that term slaves commanded. In Frederick County, the average price of term slaves varied depending on the slave's sex and the length of remaining service, with men fetching between

$168 and $325 and women bringing between $103 and $301. Such prices represented an impressive bargain for buyers. Those who purchased adolescents or young adults would receive from six to fifteen years of service for an average annual cost of between $16 and $27.[95]

Term slaves' appeal to prospective purchasers was enhanced by the additional leverage their owners gained over them. In drafting delayed manumission agreements, slaveholders drew explicit connections between slaves' eventual freedom and their conduct. In 1857, Albert Ritchie stipulated that Margaret Bacon would receive her freedom on 1 January 1868, "if her deportment shall be good."[96] Once proffered, the promise of freedom could be dangled before recalcitrant slaves and used to cudgel them into submission. When one of her family's term slaves refused to keep flies off the table, Susanna Warfield's father barked, "You have forfeited your freedom!"[97]

Slaveholders' control over term slaves was strengthened by a series of statutes that allowed greater disciplinary latitude. In 1805, the legislature declared that fugitive term slaves could have their terms extended "for such length of time . . . as justice may require," provided that "no negro or mulatto so adjudged shall be liable to be sold or assigned to any person residing out of this state."[98] In 1834, the assembly amended portions of this law. Noting that term slaves "frequently abscond" and that captured fugitives "have little difficulty in continuing to abscond until the authority of the master is put at complete defiance, and the value of their service completely lost," the legislature authorized county courts to extend the terms of "notoriously vicious and turbulent" slaves and, more important, to sell them beyond the state's borders.[99]

Recognizing that successful implementation of the delayed manumission laws was predicated on slaves' continued confidence that freedom would be received, the Maryland General Assembly enacted several pieces of legislation to prevent fraud. In 1810, it imposed a five-hundred-dollar fine on slaveholders convicted of selling term slaves to nonresidents or of selling "such servant or slave for a term of years longer than he or she is bound to serve."[100] In 1818, the assembly admitted that this law "had been found insufficient to restrain the commission of such crimes and misdemeanors" and created additional penalties, including prison sentences, for slaveholders convicted of selling term slaves to nonresidents and for nonresidents who smuggled term slaves beyond the state's borders.[101] In 1835, the law's provisions were extended to include Marylanders who "shall purchase or receive . . . any servant or slave, who is, or may be entitled to freedom after a term of years . . . with an intention to transport such servant or slave out of the State."[102]

The effect of these statutes remains unclear. The trial of Frederick County master Abram Warfield demonstrates the ease with which slaveholders and their associates might defraud slaves of their promised freedom. In 1843, Warfield, who was staggering under a series of financial reverses, sold a term slave, Samuel, to a Baltimore trader. Warfield never mentioned that Samuel was entitled to his freedom, and the merchant subsequently resold him to the Deep South. Samuel's previous owner, Dr. B. E. Hughes, caught wind of the transaction and brought charges against Warfield. At the trial, Hughes's testimony was refuted by David Hargate, who testified that Hughes, not Warfield, had perpetrated a fraud. According to Hargate, Hughes had confessed that he "was sorry that he had sold the said Negro Sam for life . . . as he was entitled to freedom after a term of years." Because the prosecution could not produce any written evidence (a deed of manumission or a receipt), Hargate's statements were sufficient to create reasonable doubt and acquit Warfield. Over the ensuing weeks, suspicions were raised about Hargate's testimony. Witnesses testified that Warfield had been heavily indebted to Hargate, who had learned about Warfield's surreptitious visit to Baltimore. Hargate used this information to blackmail Warfield, threatening to "reveal something that would put him . . . in a worse situation than his debts, unless he settled like a gentleman." Thus, Warfield squared his accounts with Samuel's purchase money, and Hargate gratefully perjured himself. Hargate's eventual conviction and imprisonment for perjury offered Samuel little comfort: There is no evidence that the court attempted to redeem him.[103]

Still, the statutes outlawing the exportation of term slaves were not toothless. State officials seemed determined to safeguard term slaves' promised freedom. In 1818, the Harford County court convicted John Ritchie of selling "Negro Poll" outside Maryland despite knowing that she was "entitled to her freedom." Governor Charles Ridgely of Hampton pardoned Ritchie but stipulated that he must execute a bond guaranteeing that he would purchase Poll and any children she may have had and return them to Maryland.[104] In May 1830, the Frederick County court sentenced David Bennett, an agent of slave trader John Derrick, to two years in the Maryland penitentiary for purchasing and exporting a young woman entitled to her freedom at age twenty-one.[105] Later that year, the court brought similar charges against Bennett's employer, who had apparently left the state.[106] In 1835, the court responded to a complaint lodged by five men and indicted John Hartzock Jr. for selling a term slave to a nonresident.[107] So real was the threat of prosecution that Joseph Geasey of Frederick County fled the state after discovering that he had inadvertently sold a term slave to a nonresident.[108] Blacks who were being defrauded of their freedom could call on the assistance of white allies, who might bring the slaves' complaints before county authorities.[109] After soul drivers spirited her to Martinsburg, Virginia, Betty Toogood contacted white friends in Frederick, who "strongly corroborated" her claims before a local magistrate. "If she is entitled to freedom," warned a newspaper, "we trust the indignation of the offended laws will demand justice from those who attempted to enslave her."[110]

The case of "Negro Charles" offers insight into both slaves' treacherous path toward freedom and the workings of the laws protecting term slaves. Charles's mother, Maria, had been promised her freedom at age thirty-one by Anne Arundel County slaveholder Susanna Pitts. Under the terms of her manumission, Maria's children were also entitled to their freedom when they reached their thirty-first birthdays. Charles was subsequently sold to Frederick County resident Philemon Smith, who resold him to John H. Harding of Montgomery County. On 4 October 1833, Harding sold Charles "as a slave for life to Henry Kidwell . . . a person engaged in the business of buying slaves for the purpose of transporting them out of the state." While in Kidwell's custody, Charles successfully petitioned the Frederick County court for his freedom.[111]

Although it is impossible to determine how many masters and speculators evaded the ordinances against exporting term slaves, the laws gave some slaveholders pause. In 1825, Frederick County resident Upton Wager purchased Cass and subsequently resold her to Kentucky trader Samuel J. Dawson. At the time, Wager "was totally ignorant of the condition of said girl," who was entitled to freedom in 1836. Soon after the sale, however, Wager had a conversation with Cass's previous owner that caused "considerable doubt with me respecting the time of her service." Worried that he had inadvertently violated Maryland law, Wager approached Dawson and voided the transaction. By that time, rumors of the illegal sale had reached county officials, and Wager was soon convicted and imprisoned for the offense. Cass's reputation seems to have had little bearing on the proceedings. Despite protests from several citizens that she was "vicious, ill-disposed, and of bad habits" and that it "would have been a relief to the neighborhood and the county had she been driven from it," Cass received her freedom because of her master's criminal dealings.[112]

Delayed manumission agreements neither slaked slaves' thirst for freedom nor guaranteed their pliability. Indeed, a Baltimore County judge believed that delayed manumission rendered slaves "wholly unfit to enjoy the benefits designed for them, as they thereby become a sort of middle class, neither slaves nor free; exempted from many of the motives for obedience which influence slaves, and possessed of some rights in common with free men, which encourage them in acts of insubordination."[113] The enslaved continued to bargain with their owners and to search for opportunities to improve their lot. Mary Jones insisted that she had not absconded from her master "with the intention of robbing him or stealing her time" but rather had "left his premises for a time to hunt for another and more congenial master."[114] The reduced prices of term slaves may have encouraged such negotiations, for it allowed masters to sell dissatisfied bondsmen and -women at a lower cost. While attempting to broker the sale of a "negro girl," William Grammer insisted that she was "a good girl, but being corrected a few weeks since desires to leave and get another master." Grammer offered the remaining eleven years of her term for $230 but added, "I suppose she could be bought for $200 cash."[115]

When a new owner would not make enslavement more palatable, term slaves expressed their dissatisfaction through flight and violent resistance. Frederick County master Roderick Dorsey discovered the extent of one term slave's anger during the winter of 1840–41. In November, Dorsey apprehended his slave, Samuel, who had fled into Pennsylvania. Dorsey confronted Samuel in prison, and the bondsman offered the "most earnest" assurances that he would remain on the farm. Within a month, however, Samuel was arrested at "the house of a free Negro in the neighborhood . . . with some 15 or 20 other Negroes, who had by previous arrangement met there for the purpose of running off in a body." Dorsey offered Samuel another opportunity to reform but warned that he might be sold to a trader. Samuel was unimpressed. According to Dorsey, the slave threatened "that if he ever escaped from jail, he would 'put it out of the power of your petitioner to ever sell a Negro.'"[116]

The rebelliousness manifested by term slaves was in some cases driven by lingering suspicion about their owners' integrity. Despite assurances that he would receive his freedom in five years, Harford County bondsman Samuel Archer fled into Pennsylvania. Archer feared having his term extended and being sold south because he "had seen too many . . . held over their time, or cheated out of their freedom." Indeed, his mother had been "kept over her time, simply that her master might get all her children. Two boys and girls were thus gained, and were slaves for life."[117]

While parents neared freedom, their children lingered in bondage and remained susceptible to abuse and sale. The desire to preserve their families and protect their children compelled some term slaves to stake everything in desperate attempts to free their offspring. In 1858, Frederick County slaves Rezin and Emeline Martin, who were approaching the dates of their manumissions, escaped with their daughter, Elizabeth, who had also been promised her freedom. Having heard rumors that their daughter's master was straining under financial burdens, the Martins became fearful that she might be sold outside the area. Hoping to secure Elizabeth's freedom or hasten their own manumissions, the Martins scoured the neighborhood for loans or prospective purchasers. Emeline twice begged a neighbor, John Strausburger, for money "to buy themselves." When Strausburger rebuffed her, Emeline turned to another neighbor, who refused to purchase their daughter but agreed to "give her money toward buying herself." The family ultimately decided that the surest path to freedom led to Pennsylvania, but their attempted escape was unsuccessful.[118]

For those tarrying in bondage, term slavery was a galling condition. Not only did the enslaved surrender years of labor, they often witnessed their children and grandchildren being born into slavery. The chains of term slavery chafed, but the institution was, in many ways, preferable to the alternatives. People seeking their freedom might settle for their owner's verbal pledge or begin the laborious process of purchasing themselves, but these agreements were fraught with difficulties. Bondsmen and -women who received postdated deeds of manumission had legal protections that slaves with simple promises of freedom lacked.

A promise to manumit a slave could be ignored, retracted, or simply misinterpreted. Even when verbal promises were unambiguous, their execution sometimes depended on the assertiveness of the enslaved. Soon after he purchased Nelson Williams, John Crumbaugh of Frederick County made the following proposition: "I have a little son, two years and some months old. Now if you are a good boy, when he is twenty-one, I'll give you your freedom." After working as a teamster and foreman on Crumbaugh's farm for nineteen years, Williams walked into his owner's office and declared, "Well, boss, you always said you were a man of your word. . . . I guess I'm my own master." Crumbaugh waffled. "I don't know about that," he replied, "I can get a thousand dollars for you tonight." Undaunted by Crumbaugh's thinly veiled threat, Williams replied, "I know that, boss. You can. But you promised me my freedom when he was twenty-one . . . if I was a good boy. Now, have I not been a faithful servant?" Crumbaugh reluctantly agreed but now stipulated that Williams must leave Maryland and settle in Liberia. "You colored people get so trifling when you go free," Crumbaugh declared, explaining the fresh demand. "I am afraid I'll get into trouble, because Maryland law makes me go your security for your good behavior." Williams remained unbending. "If you are to make [the] choice for me where I shall make my living after I am my own master, I might as well remain your servant," he replied. In a masterful stroke, Williams then called his master's bluff and volunteered to remove to Pennsylvania. Chilled by the prospect of losing a valuable farmhand, Crumbaugh relented and freed Williams, who remained in the neighborhood for a few years before departing for Pennsylvania.[119]

Unless backed by a will or postdated deed of manumission, there was no guarantee that slaveholders would honor promises to free their slaves. In 1836, a traveler in Virginia encountered a coffle that included a slave from Frederick County whose hopes for freedom had been dashed. The former owner of the young slave had "all along been promising to give him his liberty at his death; but alas! He had recently died in a fit of insanity, and had left no will." Unswayed by the slave's protests, the administrator auctioned the young man to a trader bound for Mississippi.[120] Even slaves of well-intended owners might find the path to freedom blocked or at least lengthened by the confusion that often swirled around such informal agreements. When Frederick County master Patrick Quinn found himself "getting very weak," he directed that his slave, Maria, be freed after a certain period. However, after Quinn's death, those in attendance could not agree on the length of the term he had specified. The minister, whose hearing was "somewhat impaired," confessed that he "did not hear the time at which Negro Maria was to be free, the deceased having spoken in an undertone," while the executor remembered Quinn mumbling five years and another witness heard three years.[121]

For slave owners and their chattels, postdated deeds of manumission were safer than self-purchase agreements. If the enslaved were to raise the often considerable sums needed to ransom themselves, masters and mistresses would have to surrender a measure of control over their slaves and allow them to seek outside employment, a dangerous prospect for those living near free soil. With equal measures of naïveté and trust, the owner of R. S. W. Sorrick gave his bondsman a pass to travel from Hagerstown to southern Pennsylvania, where he promised to earn four hundred dollars for his freedom. "I remitted him a portion of the money," Sorrick recalled after he escaped to Canada; "the balance I have never paid."[122]

Sorrick was fortunate. Most slaves who attempted to buy themselves found that the road to freedom was long, winding, and fraught with dangers. Scraping together the hundreds of dollars needed to ransom an enslaved spouse or child might take years. Washington County slave Hercules Turner, for example, spent years earning the three hundred dollars needed to free himself, a feat that he accomplished at age thirty. He then spent five years saving one hundred dollars to buy his wife from a neighboring planter, but the young woman died within a few years of receiving her freedom. Turner then "put his shoulder to the wheel" for six years to save three hundred dollars and free his second wife.[123] The informal agreements that slaves struck with their masters and mistresses carried no legal weight and could be undone on a mere whim. In 1837, the Maryland Court of Appeals heard the case of Beverly Downing, an enslaved man who had entered into an agreement to purchase himself from his mistress, Sophia Bland. Between 1833 and 1835, Downing "went at large and acted as a free man, by keeping an oyster house, and boot-black shop, and otherwise acting as his own master." Downing's labors took him from Baltimore to New York, where he served as waiter on a steamboat on the North River. Downing earned the two hundred dollars demanded by his mistress, but her agents had him arrested as a fugitive slave and ordered him sold. Downing appealed for his freedom, but the court ruled that "we cannot maintain the principle that a slave can enter into any binding contract with his master, or . . . appear as a suitor in any of our courts . . . to enforce any alleged contract."[124]

Invested with few legal rights, free and enslaved blacks scrimping and saving toward freedom were easy prey for criminals, dishonest slave owners, and slave traders. Such was the fate of Anne Keyte. After completing her term, the young freedwoman began working for the twelve hundred dollars needed to purchase her husband. Keyte had raised four hundred dollars when she had "every cent stolen" and had to begin from scratch.[125] The threat of robbery paled in comparison to the specter of being spirited to the Deep South before the transaction could be completed. Faced with the choice of accepting a trader's immediate and often generous cash payment or waiting for a slave's intermittent and meager installments, many slave owners chose the soul drivers. When Washington County freedman Thomas W. Henry learned that the children born during his wife's unexpired term would spend their entire lives in bondage, he saved nine hundred dollars to hasten her manumission and buy their two youngest children outright, but a sudden upsurge in slave prices foiled Henry's plans to save his entire family. "About the time that I had finished paying for these three of my family," he wrote, "it seems that the price of poor colored people had increased, and . . . two of my children (who were yet slaves) were sold."[126]

Until they registered a deed of manumission, masters and mistresses were under no legal compulsion and few moral compunctions to honor their agreements with slaves laboring toward freedom. Some owners reneged on their agreements, pocketed the payments, and sold the unfortunate bondsman or -woman to a trader.[127] One man, "Big Bob," had almost finished paying the two thousand dollars his master demanded for Bob and his wife when a Georgia trader passed through Hagerstown and offered to purchase the enslaved blacksmith. "No," his master said, "I can't sell. I have promised him his freedom and he has nearly paid for himself now." "Oh that's nothing," the trader breezily replied, "I buy lots of 'em just that way, don't you see, the price is all clear profit to the owner." Bob's master continued to waffle, but the trader's persistence—and his fifteen hundred dollars—soon softened the master's resolve. After all, breaking an agreement with a slave was not a crime. "Bob can't help himself," the trader argued, "he has no papers." Bob was outraged when he discovered that his master had sold him and demanded an explanation, but the duplicitous slave owner could not muster the courage to face Bob. The man locked himself away and shouted, "I couldn't help it, I couldn't help it." After the trader dragged Bob to Georgia, his former master tried to "get rid of the unpleasantness" by selling Bob's wife, Cassie, into the next coffle marching through town.[128]

Northern Marylanders were caught in the pull of slavery's expansion to the Deep South, but the institution's gradual disappearance north of the Mason-Dixon Line also exercised a powerful influence on the region's free and enslaved residents. Bob, Cassie, and hundreds of their enslaved brethren were sold south, while hundreds of slaveholders sacrificed humanity for quick profits. The "middle ground" between slavery and freedom was, as Barbara Jeanne Fields observes, a treacherous place. It was, however, a place where masters and their chattels could negotiate paths out of slavery. Such agreements were never bargains between equals. Flight was the best card in a slave's hand, but it was a dangerous card and could be trumped by an owner's title, the workings of federal and state laws, and sale. The enslaved played their hands with courage and skill, and some managed to wrest freedom from their owners, but freedom would come on their masters' terms and work for their benefit.

The Trials of Emily and John Webb

Emily Webb spent years hunched over a washboard in Berryville, Virginia, scouring and scrubbing her way to freedom. Her master, Dr. Samuel Rench of Williamsport, Maryland, had "given me my time, in consideration of my bearing and maintaining my children till they are arrived at an age profitable to him." Both the enslaved laundress and the doctor stuck to the bargain. Despite having no legal claim to her offspring, Webb "fed, nursed, and clothed them, and paid their doctor's bills" until Rench swept in and carried his chattels "away to Maryland as fast as they arrived at ten years of age." While she toiled over her laundry, her enslaved husband, John Webb, was adding to the family's coffers by hiring himself to shoemakers, tanners, and farmers in northern Virginia. By 1835, the couple had saved the $150 needed to purchase Emily, but they could not muster the additional $150 to ransom their two youngest children. Undaunted, they continued scrimping.[129]

In 1838, Emily and John Webb's labors suffered a crushing setback when two of their sons escaped to Canada. Rench immediately struck back against the Webb family by selling their youngest sons, John and William, to Newton Boley and William Crow, who operated a slave trading business in Charlestown, Virginia. Ever resourceful, the Webbs answered with a freedom suit. Maryland law required slave owners to register slaves brought into the state within thirty days, a technicality that Rench had ignored when carrying his chattels across the Potomac. Emily Webb searched the county records in Hagerstown to confirm that "the names of my sons had been omitted to be registered" and obtained a certificate from the clerk, who opined that Rench could not have sold John and William because "my sons were free by reason of the omission."[130] The case rested on sound legal footing, but as Webb soon discovered, southern courts were unsympathetic toward those seeking their freedom.

After having her petition rebuffed by two Virginia courts, Emily and John took more drastic measures to secure their children's freedom. They concocted a scheme to steal their children and take them to Maryland, where they hoped their case would receive a more sympathetic hearing. John presented their plan to his master, Bushrod Taylor, who gave the bondsman his blessings. Under cover of a pass provided by Taylor, John snuck into Boley and Crow's pens and managed to squeeze the younger child through a window grate, but the older child would not fit through the narrow opening. John implored his younger son to "fly with him," but the boy steadfastly refused to abandon his sibling, declaring that "he would go back and die, rather than leave his brother to be driven alone to the south." John later made another unsuccessful attempt to free the children, but the couple never pried the boys from Boley and Crow's clutches. The traders retaliated by smuggling the brothers to the Deep South, selling John in Augusta, Georgia, and William in New Orleans. They later croaked to Emily that her "sons, being fine, intelligent boys, sold higher than any they had ever sold of their age."[131]

While Emily and John were fighting a series of pitched battles for their youngest sons, they were engaged in another struggle for the freedom of their remaining children. In 1838, Taylor bought George, Martha, and Mary Webb from Rench with the express understanding that he would sell them to their parents. Taylor's asking price of seven hundred dollars was more than the couple's strained finances could bear, but the clever and increasingly desperate parents scraped together the money by leveraging the only resource at their disposal: their children. They borrowed several hundred dollars from various sources and secured these debts with liens on their enslaved children. Emily raised hogs, made soap, and made an unsuccessful foray into the grocery business to service these debts, but the Webbs soon staggered under the weight of the interest payments. Taylor became increasingly abusive toward the family, and it seems probable that the family would have remained in bondage were it not for the intervention of abolitionist Charles T. Torrey, who spirited them to freedom in 1842.

Torrey's death in the Maryland penitentiary transformed him into an antislavery martyr and catapulted the members of the Webb family to a fleeting national celebrity. While the specifics of their arduous journey from slavery to freedom were unusual, the family's plight was in many ways emblematic of how emancipation unfolded along the Mason-Dixon Line. Freedom did not come suddenly, nor did it arrive through a mandated program of delayed manumission. Instead, it arrived fitfully amid countless escapes, skirmishes, sales, and unequal bargains. There was, of course, a moment when slavery finally died, and at that moment northern Maryland's slaveholders, like their brethren further south, behaved badly. One master greeted the news that Maryland had abolished slavery by demanding that his former bondsman strip naked or continue working until the clothes were paid for.[132] Most slaveholders had, however, recognized that the institution was fatally stricken decades before its final demise. Like their counterparts in other societies where slavery's collapse preceded general emancipation, northern Maryland's masters reconfigured a dying institution to suit their labor requirements.[133] They clung to their human chattels, who might still fetch a tidy sum, and found ways to splice the most attractive elements of the emerging free labor regime onto slavery's withering body.

While their authority might have been compromised during the early national and antebellum decades, slaveholders could dictate the pace of its collapse because their property rights were safeguarded by state and federal authorities. Maryland's slaves faced better odds than did their counterparts in the Deep South when attempting to escape from bondage, but flight remained a desperate gamble. The immediate and delayed manumission agreements that masters and slaves forged on this uneven battlefield reflected their relative power. Masters would relinquish their property, and slaves would receive their freedom, but not before slave owners extracted several years of labor and not before slaves enlarged their owners' estates by bearing children.

The machinations of delayed manumission often caused the slave/free axis to fall along generational lines. A purchaser bought only a fixed amount of a term slave's life, but any children born during that time would be permanent additions to the owner's estate. Unless the owner specified otherwise, children born to term slaves were slaves for life. Most slaveholders seemed content with this arrangement. Of the 508 women freed in Frederick County through delayed manumissions, 146 (29 percent) had specific provisions made for children born while they remained in bondage. Of these, only 18 were manumitted with the promise that their children would be freeborn or liberated with their mother. The remaining 128 were manumitted under agreements stating that any additional offspring would receive their freedom anywhere between the ages of eleven and forty, with most being freed in their twenties or thirties. A few masters fixed the number of generations that would be born in bondage. When Robert Dodds manumitted Hester in 1832, he specified that her sons would remain slaves until age twenty-one and her daughters would remain enslaved until they were twenty but that her grandchildren would be freeborn.[134] Most slave owners were less generous. Some ensured that the cycle of delayed manumission would continue in perpetuity. In 1830, for example, Daniel Boyle freed his slaves at age twenty-eight but stipulated that "their children forever" must serve the same terms.[135] A few even demanded longer terms from subsequent generations. When Jacob Lewis manumitted Savilla, he demanded that any sons born during her servitude would remain in slavery until age thirty, while daughters would remain in bondage until twenty-five; freedom would not accrue to her grandsons until they reached thirty-five and to her granddaughters until they reached thirty.[136]

The fracturing of families along the slave/free axis often redounded to slaveholders' benefit. Some masters dodged laws forbidding the manumission of young children by selling them to their free parents.[137] Others leveraged the authority they wielded over their slaves to gain access to the labor of the slaves' free relatives. On Susanna Warfield's plantation, a free black washerwoman lived with her enslaved husband, who helped support his free kinfolk by raising garden crops.[138] Likewise, a slaveholder living near Sharpsburg confessed that he "did not wish any of [his slaves] to marry slave women," preferring that "they should marry free women and bring them to that place." Despite professions of altruistic motives, labor concerns were never far from his mind. He considered his slaves' wives necessary adjuncts to the workforce and paid them for cleaning, cooking, and mending for his white laborers.[139]

The generational division of black families between slavery and freedom allowed many masters to graft the most attractive elements of free labor onto the peculiar institution. In particular, this division created opportunities to transfer the expense of child rearing onto free blacks without surrendering ownership of their young slaves. Not every slave owner who concocted such a scheme was attempting to dodge his or her responsibilities. A few subsidized the households that contained their dependent slaves, but their motives were not necessarily altruistic. Indeed, providing occasional support to these semi-independent households may have been less expensive and less troublesome than raising slave children in masters' households. Such arrangements also allowed slaveholders to maintain their connections with the children's parents, who formed an auxiliary workforce. Howard County master Thomas Anderson may have weighed these considerations after determining that he could not provide "constant employment" for his slave, Rebecca Garrett. To ease his financial burden, Anderson leased Garrett to her free husband, William, reserving to himself the "right, at any time, to take and remove her, or any child or children, she might afterwards have." Rebecca subsequently bore five enslaved children, who placed a tremendous strain on the family's resources and prevented William from reimbursing Anderson for his wife's hire. Still, Anderson permitted Rebecca and the children to remain with William and never balked at providing them with cash and food.[140]

Some slaveholders had no compunction about shirking their responsibilities and compelling free blacks to support their young slaves. In some cases, owners simply dispatched children on extended stays to their free parents. An Alleghany County master pursued this strategy, sending a young slave on a yearlong visit to his father, a free black carpenter and preacher.[141] Such arrangements were often informal and without legal standing, amounting to little more than abandonment. Even before he freed teenage slave Jane Addison, a Frederick County slaveholder had "long since given up any claim in the girl to her mother," whom he had liberated fourteen years earlier.[142] As this case suggests, sending children to their parents could be a precursor to legal manumission. When John Andrews manumitted his slaves William and Eleanor, he specified that their infant daughter, Mary, was to remain under "his direction and control, until she shall have attained the age of eighteen years, claiming no other authority over her than as guardian to an infant or master of an apprentice."[143]

Free black parents might shoulder the expense of their enslaved children's upbringing, but slaveholders did not believe that doing so entitled these parents to their offspring's labor. In 1830, Mrs. Francis Warfield freed Rachel Jason but stipulated that her free husband, Aaron, must "support and bring up" their enslaved sons. Aaron raised the boys for several years, occasionally hiring them out for "victuals and clothes" to defray the cost. Warfield never filed a deed of manumission, however, and her heirs swooped in and claimed the children when they were capable of working.[144] Other slave owners made no pretense of freeing their young chattels. In the 1840s, a Frederick County master sent "Negro Dick" to be raised by his free mother, an "aged woman," until he was "large enough to be taken," when his master planned to "hire him for wages."[145] Elias Ramsburg concocted a similar scheme when he manumitted Caroline Tyler. Although Tyler received her freedom outright, the slaveholder charged her with raising her three- and four-year-old children until they were seven.[146]

Eager to disencumber themselves of older slaves, slave owners also foisted the expense of maintaining such people onto their free relatives, who were forced to shoulder the additional weight to prevent their elders from being abandoned and maltreated. In 1844, free black David Gray negotiated an agreement with his mother's master, Paul Summers, whereby Gray agreed to provide a "valuable consideration" and the slave owner promised to "maintain his aged mother, Martha Barns, a slave, for and during her life." To further indemnify Summers, Gray posted a two-hundred-dollar security, which would be forfeited if he defaulted.[147] David Bryan became a millstone around his family's neck when financial reverses left his master bankrupt and incapable of supporting Bryan. Over sixty years old and "unable to walk or help himself," Bryan became the responsibility of his free son, who was "hardly able to keep his own family by working [as] a day laborer when he can get work."[148] In some cases, slaveholders liberated slaves with the express condition that they would be responsible for supporting unproductive relatives who could not be manumitted because of age or disability. Frederick County mistress Mary Brengle freed her unnamed "Negro Man" and granted him one hundred dollars but specified that he must support his aged mother.[149] George Lands faced an even more daunting challenge when he was freed "for the purpose of supporting his aged Mother . . . and several small children, one of which is nearly quite blind."[150]

The agreements that resulted in growing numbers of African Americans receiving their freedom and bearing the economic burden of supporting their enslaved children and aging kinfolk were part of slaveholders' efforts to meld what they perceived to be the most attractive elements of free labor with slavery. The dictates of wheat production had compelled masters to imbue slavery with a flexibility usually associated with free labor: Slaveholders sought additional chores to keep workers employed, offered incentives and relaxed discipline during harvest, and pruned unneeded hands from their workforces. They even found ways to make slaves marketable within Maryland's border counties. In the end, however, their greatest success came not through alterations in work routines but by exchanging deferred freedom for years of labor, ownership of their former slaves' children, and the prospect of having their erstwhile slaves remain tethered to their enslaved kin and their erstwhile masters' and mistresses' farms and plantations.

5. "Chased Out on the Slippery Ice"

Rural Wage Laborers in Antebellum Maryland

In July 1861, a white farmhand identified only as Grimes and several free black harvesters left the Carroll County store of C. S. Snouffer, where they had spent the evening drinking. As they milled outside the store "talking about the nearest road to the place they were at work," a Mr. Drum "took the idea that it was a squad of Negroes" and accosted the farmworkers. A local newspaper reported that "the darkies left (being afraid)" but that Grimes, who carried a pistol, took umbrage and challenged Drum. Outraged at the "black" man's impudence, Drum sprinted across the road and "struck him over the head two or three times with a cane, and tore his clothing very much, and also took [the] pistol out of Grimes's pocket." Grimes sought refuge inside the store, where he begged a young clerk for assistance. The clerk confronted Drum, who promptly threatened to "put the contents of his own pistol into him, which he immediately did." Having worked himself into a frenzy, Drum barged into the building and shot Grimes, inflicting a severe wound in his thigh.[1]

This violent encounter was, to a large extent, fueled by mistaken identities. In the dark, Drum assumed that all of the farmhands were African Americans, which made Grimes's resistance an unbearable insult and a challenge to the racial order. Grimes was not, however, confused about his racial identity. Poverty might have compelled him to work alongside black men, but he must have felt it unnecessary, even degrading, to suffer abuse from a white man. For their part, the black harvesters had no illusions about their position in the racial hierarchy. Aware of their vulnerability and possessed of good sense, they scattered before the armed, drunk, and belligerent whites. Amid the gunshots we snatch glimpses of how class and race operated in northern Maryland.

Blacks and whites might find themselves in the same economic straits, working together in harvest fields or mingling in grogshops, but these encounters occurred within the context of a slaveholding state, thereby guaranteeing that racial boundaries would retain much of their strength.

Northern Maryland's volatile agricultural economy narrowed the distance between free black and white farmhands. The lives of all farmworkers were defined by uncertainty: A catastrophic crop failure, a misstep near a threshing machine, or the mundane pattern of seasonal unemployment offered no quarter and cared little about race. Possessed of few skills and scant property, white farmhands could neither drive their black counterparts from the fields nor demand special treatment from employers. Blacks and whites often received identical wages, and landowners seemed indifferent to the racial composition of their workforces.[2] This rough equality fostered fleeting moments of affection, friendship, and respect among the poor. In 1855, for example, Nace Dorsey, a free black farmhand, lived with slaves in a house owned by their master and passed his evenings at a Sharpsburg tavern with white laborers and other "plain people," many of whom rallied to his defense when he was imprisoned for stealing a mackerel.[3] Blacks and whites sometimes mingled during the holidays that punctuated the growing season. To wealthier whites, these motley bands of workers were objects of derision and fear. In 1854, a young woman sneered at the mixed crowd that attended Barnum's traveling exhibition in Frederick. "Twas a perfect crowd of Negroes and people of the lowest order, with a few of the better class," she confided in her diary. "I was scarcely in the tent before I wanted to come out."[4] Her contempt for the racially mixed underclass was echoed by other middle- and upper-class whites. In 1856, a newspaper editor blasted the "drunken rowdies, black and white, principally from the country," who marked Whitsunday by swarming into Rockville and shattering "the quiet of our usually peaceable town."[5] The rural underclass may have seemed like an undifferentiated mass, but race and gender exerted a powerful influence on its members.

This chapter reconstructs the lives of landless workers—blacks and whites, men and women. Where previous chapters focused on employers' efforts to tame these footloose workers, this chapter examines how workers navigated the treacherous shoals of the rural economy. It begins with a broad overview of the forces that shaped the experiences of all rural laborers, then considers how race and gender operated in their lives. The portrait that emerges is grim. The machinations of Maryland's economy might have brought together free blacks and poor whites, but they seldom found common cause. Indeed, their lives offer a counterpoint to the narratives of class formation and collective resistance spun by historians focusing on artisans and factory operatives. Northern Maryland's rural laborers were engaged in a relentless struggle, one made all the more difficult by the fissures dividing the rural proletariat.

Seasons of Work, Seasons of Want

The rural workforce was an unstable concoction. Its contours and composition were constantly in motion, shifting with the seasons and with the varied fortunes of the economy. The ranks of this protean workforce were filled by landless rural residents, members of families that owned small amounts of land, canal and railroad workers, displaced factory operatives and dockworkers, and under- or unemployed craftsmen and apprentices. It was, moreover, a mobile force. When winter brought work on the farms to a grinding halt, many laborers tramped into crossroads villages, river towns, and seaport cities, where they subsisted on intermittent employment and poor relief. As winter yielded to spring, small troops of farmhands drifted back into the countryside. This trickle became a torrent during the wheat harvest, when thousands followed the ripening grain north from Virginia into Pennsylvania. Not surprisingly, the workforce created by these accretions was a motley assemblage, riven along overlapping lines of age, ethnicity, gender, and race.

The churning waters of the agricultural workforce crested during the wheat harvest, when, as one newspaper noted, "every sickle is busy . . . and every idler capable of handling one has been pressed into service."[6] Even those on the fringes of the economy—beggars, drunkards, and petty criminals—trudged into the fields when the grain was ripe.[7] It is, therefore, fitting that a discussion of rural workers begins at the harvest, for the roaming gangs of harvesters embodied the diversity, mobility, and instability that were the hallmarks of the rural proletariat. Moreover, the harvest season provides a counterpoint to the remainder of the year, when unemployment thinned workers' ranks and sent desperate laborers scrambling for a living. Farmhands' prospects shone brightest at harvest, when work abounded, wages were comparatively generous, and otherwise powerless workers could wrest concessions from employers.

The wheat harvest spawned a massive labor mobilization that blurred distinctions between rural and urban workforces. From the countryside, newspapers trumpeted the "great demand and uncommonly high wages" being offered to harvesters, enticing townsfolk "who are laboring for low wages, or even high wages at ordinary work, to come on and assist our farmers. A rich reward awaits them."[8] Urban workingmen answered with enthusiasm. Indeed, the exodus of workers from Hagerstown startled one editor, who lamented the "general dullness and desertion of our streets during harvest," while a

Washington County farm boy recalled that the wheat harvest "caused such a demand for labor that it depopulated the towns of all able-bodied men and boys."[9] This pattern persisted after the Civil War. In 1866, the Freedmen's Bureau assistant superintendent at Harpers Ferry, West Virginia, reported that "the time for Harvest being near at hand, those who have heretofore been laying about the Towns preferring a small ten cent job to going into the country at steady work, have left, unable to resist the offers of big wages tendered them."[10]

Common laborers from internal improvement projects, along with artisans and their apprentices, were swept along in the stampede. Just as harvest exposed the fundamental unity of the rural and urban workforces, it also laid bare the ties among factories, workshops, and fields. These linkages were apparent when the Chesapeake and Ohio Canal suspended operations for the 1829 harvest. The "hands are very plenty," observed Frederick tailor Jacob Englebrecht, "owing, I suppose, to the . . . Canal's stopping during the harvest to give the farmers a chance to have the grain cut." Likewise, artisans abandoned their regular pursuits during harvest. The harvest crew on Joseph M. Wolf's Washington County farm included a saddler, two shoemakers, and a wagon maker. Apprentices, too, joined in the movement from workshop to harvest field. Foregoing harvest earnings or surrendering them to a master craftsman was unpalatable to many apprentices, who negotiated indentures that preserved their freedom to labor independently at harvest. When apprenticing himself to a rough carpenter, Joel Stimmel demanded "four weeks in harvest for his use," while Peter Powell stipulated that his son receive the equivalent of eight days' harvest wages if he was needed in his master's smithy during harvest.[11]

The surge of harvest workers spilled across state borders, creating a migrant force that spanned the Mason-Dixon Line. Among those toiling in the harvest fields were residents of the mountainous regions of Maryland, southern Pennsylvania, and northwest Virginia, who poured into the fertile valleys and followed the harvest's northerly march. "The grain in our section ripened some weeks before the Pennsylvania fields," recalled one Marylander, "and many persons journeyed from that state to our valley to help harvest the crop. In squads, many came from the mountainous portions of Huntington and Bedford counties, and were called 'backwoodsmen.'"[12] These migrations must have been regular occurrences. In 1856, a Hagerstown paper announced, "As usual, quite a large influx of harvest hands from the mountains of Pennsylvania has taken place, and these with the aid of reapers, will speedily disrobe the fields of their mantles of waving grain."[13] Farther south, the migration drew the attention of a newspaper editor in Charlestown, Virginia, who found "upon our streets quite a number of harvest hands . . . from the more mountainous counties, seeking employment in harvesting our grain."[14] Although the composition of this migrant workforce remains unclear, some were impoverished laborers or farmers who possessed marginal lands. Among the Pennsylvanians who followed the 1846 harvest into Washington County was Amok Hauck, whose family lived near Shippensburg. Accompanied by his eldest son, Hauck had hoped to "make a little money to procure necessaries" for his wife and fourteen children. He harvested near Hagerstown and earned $12.50 before succumbing to a lethal combination of alcohol and exhaustion and collapsing in a meadow.[15]

The eagerness with which workers followed the harvest bespoke the importance of harvest wages, the loss of which could spell catastrophe for working families. Because they seldom found steady employment during the winter, farmhands deprived of harvest earnings might face severe privation. Elias Kroft made this connection explicit when he demanded additional daily wages of between seventy-five cents and one dollar during the harvest, as "the support of his wife and children during the winter chiefly depended on what he earned during Harvest time."[16] Hagerstown attorney Thomas Kennedy underscored the importance of harvest wages when he petitioned Governor Samuel Sprigg to pardon Samuel Riley, a free black man who had been convicted of assisting fugitive slaves. Noting that the jury had been sharply divided and that Riley's family had suffered during his fourteen-month imprisonment, Kennedy urged the governor to release Riley before the wheat ripened. "Harvest is now at hand," Kennedy wrote, "and if released [Riley] will be able to do something to help himself and wife."[17] The friends and neighbors of white farmhand John Buchart echoed this argument when petitioning for his release from the penitentiary. Buchart had completed his six-month prison sentence for assault, but his "very poor" family was unable to pay the fifty-dollar fine imposed by the court, which meant that he would have to serve an additional thirty days.[18] Worried that Buchart would not receive his freedom until "the harvest is over and labor [is] not much in demand," the petitioners begged the governor's mercy so that their friend might "realize the fruits of his labor during the approaching harvest."[19]

Uncertainty about finding regular employment and steady wages gnawed at farmhands. The seasonal fluctuations in the agricultural labor market may have borne heavily on Harry Luckett, a free black farmhand employed on Richard Vansant's Baltimore County farm from 1855 to 1859. During his forty-month tenure with Vansant, Luckett was seldom fully employed. On average, he worked about fifteen days per month. During the slowest seasons, Luckett was often entirely unemployed. He found steadier work during the summer, but even hay making and harvesting could not guarantee full employment. Indeed, Luckett worked more than twenty days in only thirteen of forty months. The irregularity of employment was matched by seasonal fluctuations in wages. Luckett's winter earnings were often paltry, sometimes dwindling to nothing. The irregularity of employment left him to garner a disproportionate share of his annual earnings—between 20 and 25 percent—during the harvest.[20] The same seasonality marked the incomes of other agricultural workers. For example, white farmhand John Stockman's daily wages ranged from $1.25 during the wheat harvest to a mere 50¢ in the winter.[21] Likewise, "Negro Abraham Cooper" spent the winter and spring of 1840 mending fences, cutting firewood, and tending livestock, for which he received 40¢ per day. As the weather warmed and tasks became more demanding (grubbing, harrowing, and planting), Cooper's daily wages increased to 75¢. His earnings peaked during June (hay making) and July (wheat harvest), when they climbed to between $1.00 and $1.25 per day.[22]

For free labor ideologues, seasonal fluctuations in the agricultural labor market were a decided advantage to the region's overall economic development. In a society where free labor predominated, unemployed farmhands could work at commercial or industrial employments during dull seasons. "Hireling laborers upon a farm are not necessarily confined to that occupation," observed Frederick attorney and agricultural reformer James Raymond. "They often unite some mechanical art . . . to that of laboring on the farm in the summer months," so that they are "in one shape or another . . . constantly promoting the tri-fold interests of himself, his employer, and his country."[23] The laboring poor were less sanguine. For them, unemployment—whether occasioned by changing seasons, crop failures, or economic downturns—translated into an unending and sometimes desperate search for work. Immigrant Jakob Rutlinger likened the plight of landless workers to that of "someone who can't skate and is chased out on the slippery ice." "If they are careful and capable of much work they can make a living," Rutlinger observed, "but it must be sought ceaselessly and anxiously." Workers might find steady employment during the summer, but their livelihoods became "uncertain and subject to capricious change" in the colder months. Rutlinger's family members had experienced many of these trials firsthand: They survived their first winter in Maryland by binding books, making hatboxes, weaving straw hats, operating a singing school, and peddling firewood.[24]

To cope with the seasonal swings in the labor markets, rural workers often danced between agricultural and nonagricultural employments. The confession of Amos Green, a free black executed for raping a German woman, offers a rare glimpse into the migratory lives of rural laborers. When Green met his alleged victim, he was working at the flour mills near Ellicott City, Maryland. The mills suspended operations in the spring, and Green tramped through nearby Howard and Prince George's Counties, where he found intermittent work as a farmhand. With the onset of winter, he turned his hand to the copper deposits in the Little Patuxent River. Despite its tragic ending, Green's career was not unusual: Rural laborers needed to cobble together livelihoods from a sometimes dizzying array of chores. African Methodist Episcopal minister Thomas W. Henry recalled that his parishioners' poverty required him to stitch together a livelihood from a variety of employments. "Whenever I found myself pushed, I would turn to anything that I could get to do. Sometimes I was called upon to go to quarry rock—sometimes to the harvest field; and in this way I supported myself and family."[25] John Dougherty's career was also a patchwork affair. After emigrating in 1825, the Irishman labored for three years in Philadelphia before moving to Reading, where he "worked at different places wherever I could find employment but did not work one whole year for any one person." Dougherty subsequently moved to the Great Valley and labored "on the Columbia Railroad and sometimes with the farmers and sometimes followed ditching." Even members of landowning families shuffled from farms to industrial employments. David Heim not only managed his father's Frederick County farm but also labored on neighboring farms, collected produce for urban merchants, followed the wheat harvest into Pennsylvania, and spent several months as a boatman on the Chesapeake and Ohio Canal.[26]

The seasonality that characterized agricultural labor may have been less pronounced in the mills, factories, and internal improvement projects that dotted the countryside, but these industries, too, experienced seasonal downturns. Frozen creeks and millponds forced grist- and sawmills to suspend operations during the coldest months. Likewise, the pace of work on railroads and turnpikes slackened during winter. Although contractors on the Baltimore and Ohio (B & O) Railroad retained a "large number of workmen" during the winter of 1828–29, the "excessive severity" of the weather forced them to winnow their workforce to about one thousand, approximately half the number employed during spring and summer.[27] Turnpike construction also suffered from seasonal downturns. Contractor John Piper employed a modest workforce on the National Road near Cumberland during the warmer seasons but discharged the entire crew at the onset of winter.[28] The tightening of labor markets during the winter could have dire consequences for manual laborers. In 1849, Susanna Warfield discovered that an Irish family had squatted in a dilapidated shanty on a neighboring plantation. Although the structure's door and floorboards had been stripped by previous occupants, the family, which included a pregnant woman, spent several weeks in the shack, subsisting on charity from local families. "They are fresh immigrants," Warfield lamented, "and all work being suspended on the road the man cannot get work."[29]

As winter brought the rural economy to a standstill, unemployed workers who remained in the country drifted into an underworld of shooting matches, gambling houses, and grogshops. There, they filled their idle hours and empty pockets by engaging in activities that roused magistrates' suspicions but were nevertheless thoroughly ingrained in the rural economy. Indeed, for many poor whites, operating an unlicensed gambling house or selling whiskey was a necessary adjunct to seasonal labor. James Brightwell, a Frederick County farmhand and woodcutter, sold "a small quantity of liquor" at a backwoods shooting match that he organized during the winter of 1820–21. Arrested and fined, the illiterate Brightwell called on his friends, who petitioned the governor on his behalf. The shooting match, they argued, had been held "according to the customary practice of his neighborhood." Moreover, Brightwell's motive for hosting the event was to provide for his "wife and four small children," who were "altogether dependent upon his labor, [as] he has no property whatsoever."[30] By emphasizing that the shooting match transpired in accordance with "the customary practice of the neighborhood," Brightwell's supporters underscored how such unlawful activities were woven into the area's social fabric. The boundaries among legal business, sociability, and criminal activity became muddled. This ambiguity seems to have been the undoing of Isaac Mons, a small farmer of "very moderate circumstances with a large family," who was convicted of keeping a gambling house during the winter of 1856–57. To supplement his income, Mons constructed a shed on his farm in which operated a blacksmith shop and a "very small country store." There was, however, slight distinction between these businesses and a gambling house, for Mons's "neighbors and customers proved to be in the habit, during the winter months, of using a room adjoining his store . . . to amuse themselves at cards, and sometimes to play for money."[31]

Those without the resources to engage in petty production scraped through the winter months by resorting to scavenging and theft. The desperation felt by poor people is revealed in the trifling articles stolen: a single board or a handful of shavings that might keep a hearth burning through a cold night. Dire poverty probably drove both former slave "Negro Jim," who stole a single stick of firewood from the Frederick courthouse, and free black Prosper Jackson, who was arrested in November 1832 for stealing two fence rails valued at twelve cents.[32] Despite the small amount of property involved, such offenses could lead to significant fines or imprisonment. In 1835, for example, free black Jane Williams was sentenced to two years in prison for stealing wood chips from a construction site on the outskirts of Frederick. Two years later, another free black, Nelson Carter, received the same sentence for stealing a board from the Chesapeake and Ohio Canal on a "cold and snowy night." While not condoning these crimes, many citizens were sympathetic toward the perpetrators. Seventy-six residents of Williamsport petitioned the governor to pardon Carter, praising him for supporting his wife and children "in an unusually creditable manner for a colored man" and noting that his crime was born of desperation, not dishonesty.[33] Williams's attorney made a similar appeal, praising his client's solid reputation and noting that she had stolen only a handful of shavings. Moreover, he added, such crimes were ubiquitous during winter: "The season of the year at which the chips were taken was cold . . . and numerous others besides this woman had gone to the place and taken away the hewings of the lumber."[34]

Petty crime was a dangerous undertaking. In addition to serving time in county jails, those convicted of trifling offenses were burdened with court and prison fees that often kept them languishing in prison. In 1841, for example, the Frederick County Court received petitions from three people who had completed their sentences but remained imprisoned because they could not pay the small fines. Because he was unable to pay the five-dollar fine for larceny, free black Thomas Airs "has now been in jail for four months and from his utter poverty is likely to remain there unless your honors release." Betsey Greenwood was also convicted of larceny in October 1840 and sentenced to thirty days' confinement, a five-dollar fine, and a bevy of court expenses. The following March, her supporters reported that she "remains confined and is utter insolvent and unable to pay said fee." After completing a nine-month prison sentence, George Hartman spent several months in prison because "he is poor and utterly destitute and not worth a penny."[35] While these people languished in prison, they and their dependents had no income, a frightening prospect for those who lived on the cusp of poverty.

Recognizing the desperate plight of the poor during the winter months, prominent citizens and municipal governments provided assistance by distributing firewood to suffering families. In 1839, judge and politician John Buchanan donated a large quantity of firewood to Williamsport's municipal government, which appointed a committee to distribute the firewood "to all families who most need wood at this time."[36] During the harsh winter of 1845, residents of Hagerstown worried that the public relief budget might be overwhelmed by the growing numbers of "poor and destitute, by whom we are surrounded." To keep "the purse strings of the rich from continuing undrawn," concerned townspeople organized a bazaar and donated the proceeds to the poor relief fund.[37] But private charity and public assistance were unequal to the need. Municipal governments often burned through the funds allocated for poor relief, forcing the appropriation of additional funds or the curtailing of programs. In February 1849, Frederick's aldermen discovered that their winter relief funds were already exhausted and scrambled to find an additional one hundred dollars "for the purchase of wood for gratuitous distribution among the poor."[38]

When their earnings were exhausted and outdoor relief failed, those who could not or would not turn to crime, petty production, or independent marketing sought refuge in the county almshouse. Not surprisingly, almshouse admissions followed a seasonal pattern. In January 1855, the Frederick County almshouse sheltered 100 people. A month later, the population had increased to 102. By late April, warming weather and an improved job market had whittled the figure to 85. This trend continued through June, when the number of inmates dwindled to 77.[39]

Seasonal downturns were, to a large extent, predictable and manageable: Harvest wages, casual employment in cities, and the underground economy sustained workers during the winter, and public and private charity caught those who stumbled. More threatening were the innumerable tremors that threatened workers' finances. The countryside was fraught with dangers; disease and injury struck suddenly and left workers' lives in shambles.

Manual labor placed tremendous strains on workers' bodies and endangered their health. Rutlinger believed that working on farms entailed "ruining all your strength as well as digging yourself an early grave if you are not accustomed to such hard work." He was not exaggerating. Rural laborers ran a gauntlet of dangers that might leave them disabled and dependent on charity. The introduction of horse-powered threshing machines and mowers presented a special danger to farmhands. White farmhand Harrison McGinnis made a "foolish attempt" to walk across the top of a threshing machine and "had his leg caught in the breakers, and the foot, ankle, and leg, horribly mutilated." Free black George Harrison was tending a threshing machine when he caught his sleeve in an exposed gear, which "drew his arm in between the cylinder [and] crushed and tore it a shocking manner."[40]

The cessation or slowing of agricultural labor during the autumn, winter, and early spring offered little respite from occupational dangers. The chores performed during these seasons—lumbering, working in distilleries or mills, and quarrying—maimed or killed numerous workers. While cutting wood outside Frederick, white laborer John Finch had "his leg crushed by the falling of a tree, which remained upon the mangled limb for nearly two hours," leaving him, his wife, and their six children dependent on charity.[41] Those who ventured into distilleries, mills, and quarries faced additional dangers: Bubbling stills, spinning gears, whirling belts, and explosions inflicted grievous injuries on unsuspecting workers. Such was the fate of George King, who was crippled by "severe burns and scalds" sustained at a Carroll County distillery.[42] Workers who lowered their guard even momentarily exposed themselves to great peril. Edward Coyle was greasing a sawmill on Antietam Creek when the machine lurched, ensnaring his forearm in the gears, pulling him through the machinery, and crushing him to death.[43] Limestone quarrying presented its own dangers. The workers who blasted limestone from northern Maryland's hills ran a gauntlet of flying debris, falling rocks, and unstable explosives that maimed many workers. In November 1839, for example, Jacob and George Miller were employed at a limestone quarry near Uniontown, Maryland, when an accidental blast left them blind and "very much injured."[44]

Exposure, overwork, and the innumerable dangers that lurked in rural workplaces exacted a heavy toll. When calamity struck, afflicted workers sought shelter in the poorhouse. "This fall we all know has been an extremely sickly one," reported Frederick County's trustees of the poor in 1821. Although an "immense number of sick have consequently flocked to the Alms-house for maintenance," the trustees noted that many had been "discharged well, and but comparatively few have died." The movement of people through the Frederick County almshouse would not have struck rural laborers as unusual. Indeed, the transitory lives of unskilled workers were often punctuated with stints in the almshouse. Irish immigrant John Dougherty first entered the Chester County almshouse in 1836, when he was stricken with the ague. After recuperating, Dougherty reentered the workforce and supported himself until October 1840, when he maimed his hand at a stone quarry. By January 1841, the combined effects of his injury and the seasonal downturn in the economy left Dougherty "not able to get a living." Once again, the Irishman turned to the Chester County almshouse. Pennsylvanian George Eckart also made frequent trips to the almshouse. After having "his hand hurt by a thrashing machine," Eckart entered the Lancaster County almshouse and "staid for two or three months." The workman's wounds may not have fully healed, for he returned to the almshouse three times between 1838 and 1841. Eckart left the institution in March 1841 to "drive cattle to Philadelphia" but was soon "taken sick" and forced to seek refuge in the Chester County almshouse.[45]

For the poor, the almshouse was an integral component of their strategy for economic survival. Most of the laborers who appeared on the almshouse steps were seeking medical care, shelter from the biting cold, or a temporary reprieve from the capricious economy. Few workers lingered in almshouses. In 1856, the director of the Frederick County almshouse reported that most inmates stayed "but for a few days, some of them merely for rest, and others for medical treatment; a majority of them do not stay over a week." Only the "deranged, crippled, or superannuated" remained for longer periods. Published reports from almshouse directors confirm that these institutions' populations were transitory. Between May 1846 and May 1847, the Hagerstown almshouse admitted seventy-five people, sixty-two of whom were discharged within a year. The story was much the same in Frederick County. Of the 312 people admitted in the year ending in January 1858, 203 were discharged, and 19 died.[46] When bodies gave out, the almshouse offered a last resort.

Other struggling workers sought refuge with their families. Surviving the rural economy required equal measures of flexibility and tenacity mixed with a generous pinch of luck. Most workers chose to meet this challenge with their families. Spouses and children might become encumbrances, but the laboring poor reckoned that a family could draw more wages than a single, isolated worker. When disaster struck, members of working families could lean on their kin. For those possessed of neither property nor a trade, earning one's daily bread was a family undertaking.

Working Families

In 1848, shoemaker Alexander Redman led one of his children to a thicket outside their home in rural Washington County. There, Redman took a razor and slashed the child's throat "so effectually as almost to have severed the head from the body." After committing the murder, the dazed shoemaker wandered to a neighbor's house and confessed to murdering the child "because he was afraid it would come to want." He then returned to his own home and killed himself, leaving behind his wife, four dependent children, and "some little property." In the aftermath of these tragic events, Redman's friends testified that he suffered from "temporary fits of madness" caused by "excessive dissipation" but insisted that he had been sober for several months. Echoing the shoemaker's confession, they affirmed that he had for some time been languishing under a "depression of spirit, caused by fear of coming to poverty and want."[47]

It is unwise to attach undue significance to the gruesome drama that unfolded at Redman's home; his periodic bouts with alcoholism and "fits of madness" suggest a disturbed individual, not a social critique. We might, however, imagine others sharing the nightmares that haunted Redman, for workers' families teetered between ruin and bare subsistence. Plagued by difficulties, they survived by forging strong bonds of mutual dependence. Young, childless couples were often able to weather economic storms, as were families with healthy children old enough to work. Broken families or those saddled with infant or sick children labored under a heavier load. Disease, injuries, and the burden of caring for aged relatives added to the strain. When working families collapsed or faltered, the results were often catastrophic.

Most studies of unskilled laborers have depicted them as rootless, unattached men and have thus devoted little attention to workers' families.[48] Indeed, the notions that agricultural wage laborers were scarce throughout much of the antebellum period and that they were, for the most part, young men waiting to climb the agricultural ladder to landownership have blinded scholars to the struggles of rural wage laborers and their families.

The argument that most antebellum farmworkers were the adolescent or adult children of landowning farmers is not groundless. Of the 2,892 workingmen enumerated in the 1850 federal census of Washington County, 1,831 (63 percent) were not heads of households.[49] But only 510 of these men were the children of landowning farmers, artisans, or professionals who might expect to inherit property, receive an education or craft training, or assume control of their fathers' businesses. Many workingmen reached adulthood and established independent households without accumulating significant amounts of real property or becoming artisans, farmers, or professionals. Washington County contained 1,061 landless male workers who were heads of households. Most of these men were married. Of the 870 whites, only 16 were single, while all but 6 of the 191 African American laborers who headed households were married. The vast majority of married laborers had children. Indeed, only 103 (12 percent) of the white families and 24 (13 percent) of the black families were childless. Workers' families tended to be young. Among those considered, 551 (63 percent) of the white families and 115 (60 percent) of the black families consisted of married couples and children under the age of fifteen. An additional 149 white families and 27 black families included both dependent and adult children, raising the overall share of laboring families with dependent children to about three-quarters.

The rural labor market encouraged interdependence within workers' families. Despite being the titular heads of their households, workingmen could not survive without the assistance of their wives and children, who performed unpaid household labor, engaged in domestic manufacturing or outwork, and made occasional forays into the ranks of wage laborers. Conversely, prevailing ideas about gender norms, which emphasized female dependency, dovetailed with women's domestic responsibilities and limited employment opportunities to undermine their ability to maintain independent households or support families without a husband's earnings.[50]

The bonds of interdependence within workers' households were a by-product of the labor market. So strong was employers' preference for married men as farm managers and overseers that single men sometimes found it difficult to secure such positions. Perhaps for this reason, an unemployed overseer boasted that his wife previously "had charge of a Dairy of ten well fed cows, from which she generally made 50 lbs of excellent butter per week."[51] Those less fortunate found their opportunities restricted. Among the reasons a Baltimore County farmer cited for refusing to hire Joseph Pickering as an overseer was his "not having a wife to look after the dairy."[52] Employers' preference for married men extended downward to common farmhands. Basil Evens and his wife, Sarah, were promptly discharged when he demanded that she be exempted from fieldwork.[53] Unmarried farmhand Philip Lester found it difficult to obtain employment from Cecil County farmer Sidney George Fisher. Fisher initially had been reluctant to hire Lester but relented after discovering that he "expects soon to be made happy and . . . that his intended is a good housekeeper and competent to manage a dairy." But Lester's wife proved to be a disappointment, and Fisher's relationship with the farmhand soured. Fisher complained that Lester's wife suffered from a weak constitution and was "too delicate for life on a farm" and that her frequent illnesses "affect my comfort somewhat, as things do not go on so well." Not surprisingly, Fisher soon dismissed the couple.[54]

In addition to making their husbands more attractive to prospective employers, wives made important contributions to their families' incomes. Although farm ledgers seldom contain separate entries for laborers' and overseers' wives, their presence often determined whether the family had access to housing, firewood, and pasturage. The importance of women's unpaid farmwork is revealed in the accounts of Thomas, a black farmhand who worked in Baltimore County. Between 3 August and 16 September 1828, Thomas labored for daily wages of fifty cents and provided his own food and lodging. When his wife, Betty, began working as a laundress and dairymaid, the couple received housing, firewood, and access to the vegetable garden. The value of Betty's labor was also reflected in her husband's wages; instead of receiving a daily wage, Thomas now received a monthly salary of fifteen dollars.[55]

Although men's wages were the mainstay of workers' households, women's unpaid domestic chores were crucial to families' survival. Indeed, the loss of a mother might cripple a family with dependent children, for it shifted domestic burdens unto the husband, limited his mobility, and curtailed his earnings. Such was the fate of black laborer Lewis Jackson, who petitioned for outdoor relief soon after his wife's death. Explaining why he and his newborn daughter were "without visible means of support," Jackson stated that he had been forced to raise the child "without any assistance."[56] Still, the most eloquent testimony to women's importance to poorer families is the fact that few laboring men attempted to raise children on their own: Of the 1,061 households headed by free black and white laborers in the 1850 Washington County census, only 6 consisted of single men and dependent children.

The bonds of interdependence that bound together working couples radiated outward to encompass their families and households. Jacob Reichard's accounts with tenant farmer John McFerren illuminate the tangled skein of dependency that united rural households. Having fallen into Reichard's debt, McFerren mustered the labor of his entire family in an unsuccessful attempt to square their accounts. He contributed corn, firewood, and staves, while his wife and daughters added butter, eggs, and rags. The family dog even lent a hand, adding "two puppies" to the McFerrens' credits.[57] Jeremiah Harlan's accounts with his tenants in Harford County further underscore the importance of women's and children's labor to a household's survival. In 1823, Harlan leased a cottage and provision grounds to "Negro Anthony Smith" and his family. Harlan retained them as tenants for several years despite the Smiths' continued inability to settle debts for housing, bacon, cider, cornmeal, and beef. Smith's entire family contributed to the struggle to extricate themselves from debt: His daughter worked in wheat harvests; his wife earned $2.34 by spinning and washing; and he sold a cow, valued at $12, that had probably been cared for by his daughter or wife. The family's efforts proved futile. On 26 April 1826, Harlan sued them for their outstanding debts and evicted them from his property.[58]

The webs of dependency that enabled workers' families to survive were also a potential liability. The contributions of both spouses were essential, an arrangement that placed additional strain on marriages and exacerbated family tensions. The divorce proceedings of Otho and Margaret Snyder illuminate the friction caused by a spouse's unwillingness to contribute to the family's finances. In 1848, Otho, a wagoner, petitioned for a divorce from his wife, a laundress, claiming that her "vicious conduct" was responsible for their frequent quarrels. Neighbor Thomas Henry supported this contention, describing Margaret as "a very quarrelsome kind of woman" who had accused her husband of adultery with four different women and "provoked him so much as to make him strike her." Merchant John Lashbaugh, who sometimes employed Otho, was unaware of Margaret's suspicions but insisted that her overbearing attitude had wrecked the marriage. According to Lashbaugh, Margaret often interrupted Otho's discussions with his employers, an irksome habit that once led Otho to "threaten to take the wagon whip to her."[59]

Other witnesses described the marriage differently. Free black James Gruber conceded that Margaret's accusations sometimes sparked violent arguments but insisted that she was "good tempered and works hard." Gruber's sympathetic testimony was echoed and amplified by female witnesses who portrayed Margaret Snyder as a diligent, dutiful woman saddled with a worthless husband. Sarah Kelley conceded that her neighbor was "very passionate" but swore that she was an "industrious woman who works at her washing every day, while her husband does not." Mary Brown was more adamant: Margaret Snyder "is hard working and a good enough wife, except when she gets mad—and there is cause for her to get mad. Sometimes Otho gets things for the house and sometimes he does not, sometimes he provides for them and when he does not she does."[60]

The testimony in Otho and Margaret Snyder's divorce proceedings illuminates a critical fault line in working families: Spouses had little tolerance for partners who did not fulfill their obligations. Margaret Snyder was a hellcat. Even sympathetic witnesses noted that she threw stones at her husband and forced him to spend many nights sleeping in the stables. Still, the testimony suggests that her suspicions and violent temper were born of frustration. There was universal agreement among the witnesses that she was an industrious, frugal woman who shouldered her share of the family's financial burdens. Her husband was less dependable. Indeed, Lashbaugh's testimony demonstrates that Margaret had little confidence in her husband's business acumen, while Kelley's and Brown's statements reveal that Otho's shortcomings forced his wife to become the family's primary provider. Regardless of Margaret's temper and Otho's dalliances, it seems that a breakdown of gendered financial roles was, to a large extent, responsible for the foundering of their marriage.[61]

Because the survival of a poor household hinged on all members' contributions, the disability of a husband, wife, or working child might plunge the family into ruin. After having "the bones of his arm dreadfully shattered" in an accident, Baltimore County farmhand Solomon Osburn saw "the savings of some years of industry" evaporate. His family became dependent on handouts and the earnings of his wife, whose health deteriorated from exposure and overwork. Within two years, the combined pressure of his "melancholy affliction," mounting medical bills, and the unpredictability of private charity forced Osburn to seek public relief.[62] Women's wages might have softened the impact of a husband's incapacitation, but women's domestic responsibilities kept them tethered to their households and narrowed their employment prospects. When black laborer Hilleary Hillman became "seriously afflicted with a cancer" that left him bedridden, his wife tried to provide for their family. Despite making a determined effort, she soon discovered that her wages were "greatly inadequate for their support."[63]

An excessive number of dependent children might also upset the delicate equilibrium of a working family. James Spencer cited rheumatism and a "painful excrescence on one of his hands" as the causes of his family's financial woes, but even a healthy worker would have been hard-pressed to support his wife and seven children, the youngest of whom was a newborn and the three oldest of whom were "able to do little [other] than earn their victuals and clothes."[64] A disabled or sick child might also wreak havoc on a poor household. Laborer Peter Snavely augmented his earnings by hawking and peddling because of his blind daughter, "the support of whom would in any situation be a burden, but to a poor man is particularly so."[65] Similarly, Mary Kelly began selling liquor to ease the "great mental and pecuniary embarrassment" occasioned by the "severe illness" of her daughter.[66]

Inadequate housing, poor nutrition, and exposure made impoverished families more susceptible to disease, which added to their financial hardships. When illness struck, many working families compensated by resorting to the small crimes and petty marketing that allowed the poor to survive economic downturns. After the Washington County court fined laborer George Rudy $37.80 for selling liquor, he protested that he was "extremely indigent [with] a wife to support by his individual exertions" and that he could not find regular employment because he and his family "had for a considerable time been afflicted with a lung disease."[67] The burden of supporting ailing relatives drove some able-bodied workers to commit petty crimes. James Wilson of Harford County explained that he stole firewood worth two dollars because his mother was "lying ill with an abscess of the liver and cannot recover and my sister is also ill with an inflammation of the lungs."[68]

With luck, a family might be spared disease or injury, but there was no escaping the ravages of time. As their strength ebbed, aging workers were cast adrift in a labor market that valued power and stamina. Those lucky enough to find work received meager wages. John H. Miller found that his wages on a dairy farm were insufficient to support himself and his "aged and decrepit wife." Miller compensated by stealing a small pot of cream and "other trifling articles," an act that earned him a sentence in the penitentiary and caused his wife to become "utterly destitute."[69] When employment proved unobtainable, some older poor people turned to domestic manufacturing and petty marketing. Thomas Nixon, whom his attorney described as a "poor man, old and infirm," supported himself by working as an unlicensed hawker and peddler because he was "unable to procure a living through his labour" and wanted to "avoid the almshouse."[70]

Most superannuated workers lost the struggle to keep poverty at bay; relief rolls and almshouse registers are littered with those who succumbed to the pressures of the rural economy. Of the 226 petitions for outdoor relief received by the Carroll County levy court between 1837 and 1851, 103 (46 percent) cited advanced age or a combination of age and illness as the cause of their poverty.[71] Almshouses were also crowded with the elderly. In 1850, for example, the average age of inmates in the Washington County almshouse was 57.8 (male) and 42.3 (female). Those confined to Frederick County's poorhouse were somewhat younger, but their overall cast remained elderly.[72]

Aging workers' inability to support themselves may explain why few households headed by laborers contained elderly relatives. Landowners might wield the promise of land or productive property to guarantee their children's support of themselves or their widows, but the poor had little leverage over their children. Some working families sought to disencumber themselves of aged relatives or to at least convince county governments to share the expense. In 1846, free black Matilda Brown complained that she was "getting weary" of her "very aged and blind" mother and petitioned Carroll County's levy court to grant a small pension.[73] Brown's petition was not unique: Many poorer families saddled with aged relatives sought relief. "We have at considerable expense, more than we are able to bear, been keeping old Grandmother Bowers for the last nine months," explained one petitioner, reminding the court that "you are aware of the expense it is upon a poor man that depends upon his labor for a living."[74]

The apparent callousness that working families evinced toward their aged kin was a product of the tremendous pressures households faced. When a poor household faltered or collapsed, the repercussions rippled outward with devastating consequences for extended family members. Abandoned or widowed women and their children often sought refuge with the women's elderly parents, who lacked the resources to support dependents. After leaving her husband, who had "frequently beat her inhumanly" and subjected her "to the extreme want for the ordinary necessaries of life," Rebecca Haggerty was forced to live with her father, "an aged and extremely poor man." Haggerty remained with her father until she heard rumors that her husband had died in Pennsylvania, rumors she believed because of his "vagrant and drunken" lifestyle. Hoping to relieve her father of "the burthen of supporting herself and child" and to secure "sustenance for herself," Haggerty chose one of the few options available to single women—remarriage.[75] The expense of supporting the illegitimate or orphaned children of a relative might also strain a family's resources to the breaking point. Such was the fate that befell Barney Ohlwine when his deceased son's fiancée, Sarah Turner, left the couple's illegitimate child at his doorstep. Ohlwine, who described himself as "almost blind and past labor," depended on his daughter's earnings and could not afford the expense "of supporting other people's children." Rather than leave the child "friendless and unprotected," he begged the Washington County court to apprentice it to another family.[76]

Tossed about in the tumultuous rural economy, common laborers clung together in fragile households. The workingmen who headed these households belie the traditional image of agricultural laborers. They were not single or unattached. They were not poised to become landowners. And they often leaned heavily on their families' exertions. Workers' families could provide refuge in an otherwise unforgiving environment, but they were continually besieged by difficulties. Too many children, the burden of supporting an elderly relative, or the sudden loss of a breadwinner through death, disease, or injury might shatter a household and send its surviving members scurrying for shelter with their relatives or in the almshouse.

Single Women in the Rural Economy

In 1886, Civil War correspondent and novelist George Alfred Townsend released *Katy of Catoctin; or, The Chain-Breakers,* a piece of historical fiction set among the rolling hills of northern Maryland. The work was ambitious. Townsend attempted to capture the excitement and fear that gripped Marylanders as the country spiraled toward secession and war. He peopled his landscape with runaway bondsmen and -women, slave catchers, and some of the generation's most prominent figures, including John Brown and John Wilkes Booth. Although the narrative sometimes strains credulity and is brimming with the sentimental conventions of Victorian fiction, *Katy of Catoctin* contains flashes of insight about life along the Mason-Dixon Line. Townsend had settled in Frederick County's Catoctin Mountains in the 1880s and seems to have immersed himself in local history. Perhaps the most perceptive moment in the novel occurs when the dashing Booth is flirting with a beautiful but humble farm girl, Nelly Harbaugh. In the course of their conversation, the young woman confides that it took her "six whole months to make five dollars, when I wanted to buy a pair of shoes!" "Oh shame!" the actor retorted, "and I was making my three dollars a day as second walking-gentleman." Feeling a "cold blush of modesty" and a twinge of defiance, Harbaugh describes the broken, sometimes dangerous path trod by laboring women. "I could only make thirty cents a day, and could only find work at seeding and harvest, hardly four weeks in all; and rain, or too many laborers, or woman's ailing, would throw me out a day here and a day there, so it was winter before I had my shoes."[77]

Harbaugh's description of her travails would have rung true with her nonfictional sisters, who eked out precarious livings on the margins of the economy. In a society that was structured around households and that had a labor market dominated by single men or male-headed families, single women had few opportunities, and unwed mothers had fewer still. The wages of women employed on the region's farms averaged between a quarter and a third of men's wages, making it difficult for women to support themselves and their children in the absence of men.[78] Free women might have felt the pressure of slavery more acutely than their male counterparts. A farmwife in northern Virginia confessed that she preferred enslaved domestics because they were more tractable than free women. "If you hire an Irish girl, if she don't like you, she will leave sometimes in less than a month, or stay all winter and leave in the spring, just as your busy time is about commencing."[79]

There was a market for women's labor, but farmers were not indiscriminate hirers. Those seeking dairymaids and domestic servants often bemoaned the scarcity and poor quality of women available for such positions. In 1837, Chester Coleman complained that he had been unable to secure "good and efficient female help" and that "the help we generally get is not worth the having, either that of black or white, and this for half the time is not to be had at all."[80] Employers wanted help, but they preferred single, childless women. The lone woman hired by farmer and merchant Stephen P. Grove was young and unencumbered by family obligations. Mary Benner, the daughter of a local laborer, was nine years old when she began sewing, cooking, harvesting, and tending livestock on Grove's farm outside Sharpsburg.[81] Of the ten women employed by Washington County farmer Joseph M. Wolf between 1848 and 1859, only four can be identified in the 1850 or 1860 census, suggesting that they might have married and changed their surnames soon after leaving his employ. Among those located in the census records were two single women, Lucinda Thomas (age twenty-four) and Eve Dephenbaugh (age sixteen), both of whom lived with their mothers and dependent siblings. Another of these women, Susan Bowers, was a single mother who lived near Wolf's farm. The only married woman employed in Wolf's household was free black Susan Diggs, who lived with her husband and four children. Unlike the other women, who were employed as dairymaids or domestic servants and who lived with Wolf, Diggs worked as a laundress, a job that did not require her to reside in Wolf's house.[82]

The harvest season offered women greater opportunities to enter the agricultural workforce. Farm ledgers reveal that women constituted a significant and underpaid minority of the harvest workforce. Of the 164 harvesters employed by Washington County farmer George F. Heyser between 1825 and 1841, 18 (11 percent) were women.[83] In Baltimore County, the Virdin family employed a slightly higher percentage of female hands in their harvest fields: Of the 49 workers involved in gathering the 1839 harvest, 9 (18 percent) were women.[84] On both farms, women were confined to lighter chores (raking, binding, cooking), guaranteeing that their wages would lag behind those of male harvesters. This disparity is apparent in the wages earned by carpenter Peter Fogle and his wife, Sarah, during the 1852 harvest. Although both toiled for nine days, Peter earned $9.50 for cradling, while Sarah received a meager 50¢ for "cuking."[85]

Although paltry, harvest wages were important to women, who sometimes joined the roaming bands of harvesters. In 1842, Sevilla Moonshour left her home in Frederick County and traveled to Carroll County, where she found employment with a farmer near Taneytown. She continued with that farmer from 30 June through 3 July, when another farmer, Henry Hess, hired her to rake. Moonshour remained with Hess through 9 July. The following day, she "was engaged in carrying water for some hands cutting grain" on yet another farm. By 12 July, Moonshour had again changed employers.[86] The wages women garnered at harvest may have remained in their pockets and granted them a small measure of independence. In 1844, Mormon missionary Jacob Hamblin encountered a woman in rural Washington County who "offered me some money that she had earned in the harvest field."[87]

The freedom to seek employment in a farmer's household or to become a migrant harvester was predicated on being unencumbered by domestic obligations. A married woman could not enter the workforce without her husband's approval, which was sometimes withheld. This requirement could have a disastrous impact on women trapped in abusive marriages. Amanda Double's husband, Martin, was an abusive and drunken lout who threatened to "beat her brains out," laced her food with arsenic, committed adultery, denied her the "necessaries of life," and forced her "to go out in all kinds of weather to sweep and do outwork." Short of divorce, there was little she could do to improve her situation, for her "very jealous" husband "refused to let her do any work for any person for the purpose of providing for herself."[88]

Women abandoned by their husbands occupied a nebulous and vulnerable legal status. Under Maryland law, an abandoned woman could not petition for a divorce unless "such abandonment has continued uninterruptedly for at least three years, and is deliberate and final."[89] Until the divorce was finalized, women had no legal right to their property or wages, and they could not enter into contracts. Worse, they remained subject to their husbands, who might return, bringing chaos. Soon after her 1833 marriage to Henry Eaton, Mary discovered that he had a "wayward disposition and a strong propensity towards dissipation." He abandoned his family for extended periods and spent his time "in the society of the dissolute." In 1836, Henry enlisted in the army, leaving his family destitute. Undaunted, Mary began sewing women's clothing and seems to have prospered. Not only was she "nothing of an encumbrance to the county," but she had "for years supported herself by her individual exertions," employed apprentices in her business, and "realized a little money [that] she has been anxious for some time to invest in a home for herself and children." Despite her achievements, Mary's position remained vulnerable. After an absence of several years, Henry Eaton returned and threw Mary's household into disarray. She was forced to discharge her apprentices because her husband "indulges in language in their presence of the grossest character and repugnant to female modesty." He had, moreover, begun beating her. One "sally of rage" left her bedridden for days and "unable to attend to her daily vocations." In 1846, Mary petitioned for a divorce, but the case was dismissed.[90]

Given the legal and social impediments strewn in their paths, it is not surprising that single mothers clung to the lowest rung of the rural economy. Shorn of male support, abandoned or unwed mothers walked a treacherous path through pregnancy and childbirth. For some, finding shelter or securing medical attention proved impossible. In 1859, a German immigrant gave birth in a stable after being abandoned by her "worthless husband," who was later discovered "drunk and oblivious to her condition."[91] While the unnamed German woman's plight was desperate enough, other single mothers and their children were even less fortunate. Julian Bost, whom the coroner described as "a single woman," died alongside her child "through want of the necessary assistance in the delivery—no person being present at the time."[92] Complications and illnesses arising from pregnancy prevented some single mothers from rejoining the workforce. After being abandoned by her husband, free black Julia Patrick tried to support herself and her newborn, but "being weak and feeble and unable to do any kind of work through sickness," she soon found herself "entirely destitute of support."[93]

Women might brighten their employment prospects and ease the strain on their family's resources by apprenticing their adolescent children through the county orphans court, but this option was not available to those with infants. In her petition for outdoor relief, widow Eliza Koon pleaded that she had "two small children entirely two young to bind out and depending upon her for the necessarys of life," leaving her family "entirely dependent upon the charitableness of the people of the neighborhood."[94] In 1844, Catherine Taylor, a widow with three children, found herself in similar straits, claiming that she had "made some effort to put her children out, but in consequence of their being too small no person wanted them and they have to remain on her hands."[95]

Many single mothers became objects of charity. Free black Betsey Reister depended on the support of a neighboring family after giving birth, but because she was "incapable of compensating them in any way," she soon became a burden to her caretakers, who grumbled that they "are not in a condition to keep her free of charge" and warned that "had it not been for them she must be exposed to increased suffering."[96] When private charity failed, single mothers turned to public relief, becoming a disproportionate share of the young women on relief rolls. Of the nine female paupers of childbearing age in the Frederick County almshouse in 1850, seven were mothers with infants. A similar pattern prevailed in the Washington County almshouse, where all five of the female paupers of childbearing age had babies. Single mothers also constituted a significant share of the women receiving outdoor relief. Of the twenty-two women of childbearing age listed as paupers in the 1850 census of Frederick County, sixteen (73 percent) were single mothers.[97]

The path leading single mothers to the almshouse was well trodden, but many found the means to survive and preserve their families. Households headed by single women with dependent children may have constituted only a small fraction of the households enumerated in the 1850 Washington County census, but they represented a considerable minority of the female-headed households. Of the 549 households headed by white women, 59 (11 percent) comprised single women and dependent children, while another 48 (9 percent) consisted of single women, young children, and adults with different surnames. Given the pressures that slavery placed on black families, it is not surprising that a higher percentage of households headed by free black women consisted of mothers and their dependent children. Of the 76 households headed by black women, 24 (32 percent) consisted of women and dependent children. Another 11 (15 percent) included single women, dependent children, and adults with different surnames. Despite these racial disparities, certain similarities between black and white female-headed households reveal much about single mothers' economic strategies. That many women with dependent children (42 percent) expanded their households to include adults with different surnames—often other single mothers—suggests that they either leased rooms to boarders or pooled their meager resources with women in similar situations.

Single women with adolescent or adult children fared better, as employers and landlords were willing to engage these women to gain access to their children's labor. An employer, landlord, or merchant might extend credit to an unwed or widowed mother if he believed that her children's services might offset the expense. For example, Elizabeth Ware, a woman in her sixties, rented a house from Franklin Osburn, a farmer and merchant in Jefferson County, Virginia. In 1860, Ware headed a household that included herself, her son, Richard, who was twenty-one years old; a daughter or daughter-in-law, Susan, age twenty-four; and three children who were eight years old, two years old, and two months old, respectively.[98] Between 1855 and 1861, Ware's family accumulated debts totaling $187.97 for rent, food, firewood, and credit at their landlord's store. Elizabeth settled a small part of her family's debt by working as a farmhand, but her age and sex prevented her from working routinely. In 1856, for example, she worked in the wheat harvest for four days. The following year, she spent thirteen days harvesting and another four days hoeing and cutting corn. Her wages for this work were but $8.74. Elizabeth and Susan further contributed to the family's income by sewing clothing for Osburn's household and for sale in his store. Still, their income from seamstress work was meager, amounting to only $22 over the course of six years. Richard earned the bulk of the family's income by working as a field hand. During his family's tenure at Osburn's farm, Richard earned $80.98, more than three-quarters of which ($61.12) was earned harvesting wheat.[99] Although the Wares never settled their accounts, Richard's work at critical junctions of the growing season seems to have been crucial to the family's continued presence on Osburn's property.

Given the importance of children's wages to their families' economic survival, single mothers strove to secure the greatest possible returns for the labor of their offspring. In 1840, the promise of higher wages led free black Fanny Baptist to remove her son, Tom, from Robert Archer's farm, where he had been working for food, clothing, and an annual wage of forty dollars. "I kept this boy all winter and clothed him for twelve months," the angry farmer scrawled in his account book, "now he went off with his mother who said she could hire him for $6 pr. month."[100]

Small amounts of personal or real property allowed some single women to keep their footing in the rural economy. We catch a glimpse of one such woman in the account books of Joseph M. Wolf, a Washington County farmer. Between 1848 and 1854, Wolf recorded numerous transactions with Sarah Bowers and her son, George.[101] During those years, Sarah accumulated debts totaling $77.80 for flour, a few hogs, pasturing her cow and other livestock, and renting Wolf's plow. She settled a significant portion of her debt ($23.01) through sewing and light agricultural labor such as gardening, pulling blades from corn stalks, and assisting with the threshing machine. George made a similar contribution, adding $22.42 to his family's account by planting corn, cutting firewood, and harvesting. Wolf's ledgers do not encompass all of her family's economic activities, for Sarah settled the remainder of her debts and moved $8.91 into the black with cash payments.[102] Although it is unclear how she earned the money, it is likely that her real property, worth $250, combined with her access to Wolf's pastures, allowed her to raise garden crops, sell hogs or poultry, and market dairy products. Moreover, she had reduced her

expenses by sharing her household with Mary Bowersmith, a single woman
with three dependent children and $300 worth of personal property. Such
an arrangement would have allowed the women to pool their resources, reduce their expenses, and avoid the almshouse. Still, theirs would have been
a precarious existence, for even a slight reversal of fortune could wreck their
finances. In 1832, Eliza Mercer, a widow with six small children, was pushed to
the brink of ruin when a B & O train struck and killed her cow. "I am in great
need of another cow," Miller pleaded in a letter to the railroad's president.
The cow, she explained, had been the family's only productive property and
their principal source of both income and food.[103]

Because the rural economy afforded single women few opportunities, many
sought their livelihoods on its shadowy fringes: They turned to petty production or operating unlicensed boardinghouses, grogshops, and restaurants.[104]
The marginality or downright illegality of these operations is suggested by
the small number of female proprietors who purchased licenses from the
county courts. In 1850, for example, Frederick County granted sixty-six tavern
licenses to men and only nine to women. The gender imbalance was even
more skewed among merchants. Only 15 women received merchant licenses,
compared to 266 men. Moreover, the average value of women's stock ($259)
lagged far behind that of men ($930).[105]

The centrality of petty marketing to single women's economic strategies
surfaced when the Maryland General Assembly imposed license fees on a range
of small-scale economic activities. Beginning in 1820, the assembly enacted
a series of license laws to regulate the sale of manufactured goods, produce,
and spirits.[106] In 1828, the legislature passed its most stringent—and contro-
versial—measure. Whereas previous laws had targeted wholesale merchants
and exempted petty marketers, the new statute required any person "other
than the grower, maker, or manufacturer" to obtain a twelve-dollar license
before selling any "goods, wares or merchandize, foreign or domestic." The law
extended to other small businesses as well; brewers and distillers were prohibited from selling alcohol in quantities of less than a pint without a license, as
were the owners of "cook shops" and oyster houses. Violations were adjudged
misdemeanors and carried the penalty of fines, imprisonment, or both.[107]

The 1828 statute unleashed a torrent of criticism from those who objected
to its perceived inequity and the burdens it imposed on the poorest free
people. "I know not what justice is," fumed Washington County legislator
Thomas Kennedy, when "the richest merchant and the poorest milliner, the
keeper of an oyster house, a booth, or a stall . . . are all put upon an equality,
each hav[ing] to pay twelve dollars a year license."[108] A Hagerstown editor
urged the legislature to create exceptions for single women and widows who

peddled butter, milk, or domestic manufactures, arguing that it would "be a considerable relief to many females, whose stock in trade is small."[109] When the legislature revisited the issue in 1832, Kennedy demanded concessions for female milliners and peddlers. In a scathing indictment of the 1828 statute, he painted a bleak portrait of single women's plight and underscored the importance of petty marketing to their welfare: "I have known many a worthy lady who had been raised in affluence, who had been taught by smiling hope to look for happiness, but who was reduced to poverty by the changes of the time or by the loss of a beloved partner, or by the cruel neglect of a worthless or dissipated husband . . . who toiled day and night to support themselves and their suffering children, and sometimes supported by the aid of kind friends would be enabled to lay in a small stock, and were thus prevented from soliciting alms from the cold hand of charity, and nobly support themselves."[110]

Kennedy's impassioned speech resonated with his fellow legislators. The debates culminated with the General Assembly rescinding the most offensive elements of the 1828 law. Under the modified statute, retail licenses would cost between $50 and $120, depending on the value of an applicant's "stock of goods, wares or merchandize generally on hand, at the principal season of sale." The law stipulated that female milliners and retailers of "other small articles of merchandize" would "pay six dollars for a license," provided that their stock did not exceed five hundred dollars and that they refrained from selling spirituous liquors.[111]

The constraints of the rural economy forced some single women to combine their marketing with illegal activities, such as peddling alcohol. Proprietors of small groceries, cookeries, and taverns tiptoed along and across the boundary separating legal and illegal pursuits. Women who sold alcohol roused the anger of local authorities, who believed that such businesses were a public nuisance and arrested or fined proprietors. In 1828, for example, the Allegany County sheriff fined Anne Hosford for selling liquor without a license. Petitioning the governor for a pardon, Hosford's attorney described his client's plight. "Your petitioner is a widow with a family," he declared, who "keeps an ordinary house for the purpose of supporting herself and family [and] has no means of subsistence." Although the fine was small, Hosford had few resources and could not pay "without jeopardizing the support of herself and children."[112]

When women could not muster the resources for a grogshop or petty marketing, they sometimes turned to selling themselves. Women's marginal position within the rural economy dovetailed with the expansion of Maryland's network of canals, railroads, and turnpikes to make prostitution a viable if not lucrative option. The pressures that drove women to prostitution are well illustrated by the experiences of Matilda Green. In January 1854, Matilda's alcoholic husband, Edward, went on a tremendous bender that culminated in his enlisting in the U.S. Army. The bedraggled Edward promptly escaped from the recruiting depot and returned home, where he remained for three months before being recaptured. Edward begged his wife to accompany him to Baltimore "to assist in getting his discharge," which she did. While awaiting his discharge, Edward was stunned to learn that Matilda had resorted to prostitution after he enlisted and, moreover, had recently been arrested in a Baltimore brothel. After his "expulsion" from the military, a dismayed Edward learned that his wife had gone to Frederick, where she had begun "residing at houses of prostitution and unlawfully cohabiting with other men." In the three years following their separation, Matilda moved among brothels in Baltimore, Frederick, and Hagerstown. Matilda's disapproving sister, Elizabeth Springer, testified that in these years, Matilda "has been living in a bawdy house, has contracted a venereal disease . . . and has not been doing anything for a living."[113]

The survival of working families hinged on women's contributions, but the codependency that characterized laboring families did not alter their fundamental gendered inequalities. The relative weakness and vulnerability that defined married women's lives elsewhere were also present in the northern Maryland countryside. Still, male-headed households may have been havens for poor rural women, whose dismal employment prospects and miniscule earnings could not sustain independent homes. A childless woman might muddle through without male support, but those with dependent children faced a dire situation. When abandonment, death, or divorce stripped a woman of her husband's support, she had little recourse but to seek public assistance or scrape out a living on the margins of the economy through petty marketing, operating unlicensed groceries or grogshops, or prostitution.

Suspended between Slavery and Freedom:
Rural Free Blacks

Buffeted by tempestuous agricultural economy and by white authorities who viewed them with suspicion, northern Maryland's free blacks walked a tightrope. Doing so required dexterity and nimbleness; even poor whites, who labored under few legal restraints, could easily lose their footing. The additional burdens heaped on blacks made the task especially daunting.

The households of free black and white laborers were similarly structured. Regardless of race, most workers' families consisted of married couples with dependent children. Other striking similarities existed between the households of black and white workers. Their average sizes were nearly identical—5.09 for blacks and 5.12 for whites. Workers' households also tended to be racially homogenous. Of the households headed by free blacks, 187 (98 percent) consisted entirely of African Americans, while only 11 white laborers' households (1 percent) were multiracial. Rates of property ownership did not differ markedly. About 15 percent of white workingmen owned real property, with an average value around $335. A slightly larger 16 percent of the black laborers who were heads of households owned property, but its average value ($223) lagged that of whites.

The structural similarities between black and white households should not, however, distract attention from the special challenges confronting African Americans. Families making the transition from slavery to freedom often found themselves in limbo: They could neither cast off the shackles of bondage nor enjoy the benefits of free labor. Free black Anne Briscoe was "much crippled by an affliction of the spine" and was, along with her children, maintained by an enslaved relative, Abraham Ireland. This Herculean task might have strained any laborer, but it was insurmountable to Ireland, who could support his kindred only by "his labour at night, by sawing wood, after he has served his master through the day."[114] To survive in the tempestuous economy, laborers needed to muster the resources of their entire family, a feat that slavery often precluded.

African Americans strove to ransom their enslaved kin and disentangle their families from white masters. The most pressing concern for many blacks was to liberate their enslaved wives, for doing so would limit the number of children born into slavery. Of the 114 slaves purchased by free blacks, the largest number (41) were wives being ransomed by their husbands. Because of women's limited earnings and because men commanded higher prices, only three women scraped together enough money to ransom their husbands. After reclaiming their spouses, African Americans moved to liberate their children. Twenty-eight of the recorded transactions involved parents purchasing their offspring, and another forty-two were parents manumitting their children. Most of the children were quite young: The average age of the twenty-five children whose ages were recorded was 11.2 years. Similarly, the average age of the twenty-eight children manumitted outright was 8.4, while the average age of those whose parents entered them into term slavery agreements was 11.8. Not all parents who bought their children manumitted them immediately. Perhaps because of their age, only ten of the children purchased by their parents were immediately freed. Another two received their freedom through delayed manumission agreements.

Blacks who refrained from liberating their children may have been deterred by state laws that forbade the manumission of slaves incapable of supporting themselves. In addition, a desire to retain possession of their children—and of those children's labor—and to safeguard them against white interlopers may have led black parents to purchase their children and keep them in bondage. Although Thomas Denby manumitted his ten-year-old son, Thomas, and six-year-old daughter, Catherine, he "reserved their services . . . for my own use and benefit" until they reached the ages of twenty-one and eighteen, respectively.[115] A few blacks made the difficult decision to sell their enslaved children. In 1847, for example, Malinda Howard filed a delayed manumission for her twelve-year-old son, Lloyd, and then sold the remaining nine years of his term to a white farmer for $150.[116] Washington Mitchell sold the unexpired term of his eight-year-old daughter, Ruth, to a Frederick merchant for $50 and agreed that any children born during her servitude would become her master's property. In exchange for her service, Ruth would receive freedom dues of $20.[117]

African Americans had good reason to keep their children in bondage. Over the course of the antebellum decades, Maryland's General Assembly enacted a series of increasingly harsh apprenticeship laws that undermined black parents' authority over their free children. The emerging legal regime vested control of black children in the hands of county authorities, who exercised great latitude in wrenching young African Americans from their families and binding them to white masters. Although Maryland's original apprenticeship law had been race neutral, in 1808 the legislature authorized county courts to bind out "the child or children of any pauper or vagrant, or the child of lazy, indolent and worthless free negroes."[118] In 1819, that authority was broadened to include black children "not at service or learning a trade, or employed in the service of their parents." Thus, perceived parental turpitude or children's unemployment became causes for removing African American children from their families. Worse, the legislation extended black women's terms of service from sixteen to eighteen years and allowed masters to forgo educating black apprentices in exchange for small cash payments.[119]

The grounds for binding out black children became even more nebulous in 1840, when the assembly enacted the state's most draconian apprenticeship code. Under the new statute, county officials could apprentice young blacks "to some white person" if they believed that such an arrangement "would be better for the habits and comfort" of the children. In a significant departure from previous laws, which required local officials to "gratify the inclinations" of the child's parents respecting the choice of a master or mistress, the 1840 statute contained no such provisions. To guarantee that its provisions would be aggressively enforced, the law provided cash incentives to county officials who bound out black children. Moreover, "any negro or other person" who abducted or enticed a black apprentice would face a prison sentence between one and four years. The legislature further diminished black parents' authority in 1845, when it authorized the masters of African American apprentices to sell their unexpired terms to persons within the same county.[120]

Despite the legal apparatus arrayed against African American families, relatively few black children were apprenticed. Between 1837 and 1860, only 465 blacks were apprenticed in Carroll, Frederick, Howard, and Washington Counties.[121] Blacks did, however, constitute a disproportionate percentage of those bound out. Most of these apprenticeships (375) were compulsory, triggered by a child's being impoverished, orphaned, or judged to be the offspring of "lazy and worthless negroes." The masters of these children were concerned with securing laborers for their farms, a fact reflected in the large number of adolescent male apprentices. Some 221 (48 percent) of the black apprentices were males between the ages of ten and twenty-one, and the majority of them were to learn farming, labor, or "usefulness." Black children bound under these circumstances had few opportunities to acquire skills: Only 10 of the African Americans bound out by county authorities were placed with tradesmen. Black parents fared little better in securing craft training for their children: Of the 90 black children who were voluntarily apprenticed by their parents, only 4 were bound to craftsmen.

The fierce resistance mounted by African American families might explain the small number of black apprentices. Abduction was the most direct strategy for thwarting their children's indenture. In 1829, for example, free black Adam Shorter was indicted for "stealing and carrying away three indented Negro children."[122] The struggle to free black children from the clutches of a white master sometimes mobilized entire families. When free black Priscilla Dorsey died, leaving behind five dependent children, her brothers and sisters "agreed to divide the children amongst them, as nearest of kin." As the children's father, a slave, had been sold outside Maryland, Samuel Dorsey took possession of his eight-year-old niece, Lucy Powell. Dorsey supported her by hiring her to different families for her clothing, food, and small cash payments. He continued this arrangement until one of his niece's employers claimed that he was "better able to care for her" and had Powell bound to him for three years. Samuel Dorsey and his siblings appealed the indenture, and it was annulled on the grounds that it had been made without their consent.[123]

The preponderance of economic and legal authority confronting African American families forced some to concede the battle over their children. Instead of resisting county authorities, they sought to negotiate the most advantageous contracts for their offspring and to guarantee that their households would continue to benefit from the children's labor. In some cases, black parents arranged contracts that protected their sons and daughters from the apprenticeship system's worst abuses. When free black William Riggs apprenticed his daughter, Lucretia, to learn housekeeping, he specified that her master must "enter into a recognizance with security to be forfeited in case he should remove or carry [her] out of the state." After his daughter's master refused to post the required security, Riggs successfully petitioned to have the apprenticeship agreement voided.[124] Others challenged the legitimacy of their children's indentures and demanded that they be bound to different masters. Free black Sophia Johnson conceded that she could not support her son, John Hammond, but insisted that his current master, Amos Welsh, held him "against his will and without authority." Citing irregularities in her son's indenture, she asked that John be bound to a master of her choosing.[125]

Another strategy employed by black parents to avoid the involuntary and uncompensated apprenticing of their children was to bind them to a white master in exchange for cash payments. Of the ninety black children apprenticed by their parents, thirty-two (36 percent) were bound for monetary considerations. Such transactions reflected antebellum Maryland's changing legal climate, which was reducing black apprentices to chattel. Changes in the state's apprenticeship laws allowed masters to sell the unexpired terms of their black apprentices, an opportunity that many of them seized.[126] Recognizing that their hold on children was tenuous and that their children were a valuable financial resource, some black parents preempted whites and sold their offspring into temporary servitude.

Blacks who decided to apprentice their children found numerous ways to leverage their labor. In some cases, they bound out their children as collateral. In 1841, for example, Absalom Reed apprenticed his son to Frederick County farmer James Nickum to secure a one-hundred-dollar loan.[127] More commonly, blacks bound out their children for a single payment or for annual wages. When Jane Dunn bound her teenage children, John and Mary Bryan, to a Washington County farmer, their indentures stipulated that Dunn was to receive annual payments of thirty-five dollars and twenty-five dollars, respectively, for their labor.[128] The indentures that Dunn negotiated were quite advantageous, for the wages her children garnered would have matched her earnings as a domestic servant or dairymaid. Most agreements were less remunerative. In 1853, for example, Nelly Fisher bound her eleven-year-old son, Robert Stewart, to farmer Martin Emmett in return for annual payments of four dollars.[129]

In apprenticing their children to white masters, some black parents were simply adding another component to their multifaceted relationships with employers or landlords. Between 1829 and 1833, for example, the family of

Nat Cooper, a black tenant on Robert Archer's Harford County farm, earned $220.98. Of that amount, $164.64 was earned by Cooper's children, Nat, Jane, and Jim. The younger Nat collected $34.25 by laboring in wheat harvests, while Jane earned $8.75 by working as a domestic servant and seamstress during the winter. Jim, however, made the largest contributions to the family's coffers, first by earning $40.46 through an annual contract and then by apprenticing himself until the age of twenty-one, for which he received $80.[130]

The legal strictures on their families were but one of the impediments hobbling African Americans. Slaveholders had crafted the state's legal apparatus, which guaranteed that blacks seldom received a fair shake in the county courts. Free blacks may have been more vulnerable to the frauds landowners perpetrated on other workers as well. Lewis Charlton remembered that a Harford County farmer once refused to pay his wages of $235 "but said he would compromise by giving me three cents and calling it square." Charlton fought a protracted and ultimately futile legal battle to recover his wages. The "court was a mockery," he later fumed. "There was no such thing as justice. . . . [T]he law protected the white man and trampled upon black men."[131]

As the antebellum decades progressed, Maryland lawmakers tightened the legal strictures that circumscribed black workers' mobility. Fearful that free blacks would smuggle slaves into Pennsylvania or that outsiders would spread the contagion of abolitionism among bondspeople, Maryland slaveholders clamored for tighter restrictions on blacks' interstate mobility. In 1832, the General Assembly responded by prohibiting free blacks from entering the state and staying longer than ten successive days. Violations were punishable by a fifty-dollar fine for each week that the free black remained in Maryland. Those unable to pay this onerous fine and the attendant court expanses and prison fees would be sold at public auction. The statute also restrained Maryland free blacks from traveling outside the state. Free blacks leaving the state for periods longer than thirty days were required to file papers with their county courts lest they be considered nonresidents upon their return. Finally, the law imposed a twenty-dollar daily fine for whites who hired nonresident blacks for longer than four days.[132]

Despite its severity, the 1832 statute did not satisfy Maryland's slaveholders, who particularly objected to the loopholes that allowed blacks to make brief forays across the Mason-Dixon Line. Over the following decade, slave owners and those dependent on free black laborers became increasingly shrill in demanding laws that would limit African Americans' movements. An anonymous contributor to the *American Farmer* argued that blacks would receive better food and wages were they "compelled to hire by the year in the county where they reside." "And where would be the great hardship of restraining them from going to and fro between Maryland . . . and Pennsylvania, Delaware and New Jersey," he continued, "or, if they do go there, compelling them to remain among those who are so ready to receive our slaves?"[133] After a black wagoner assisted several fugitive slaves, a slave owner condemned the existing statute as inadequate to "prevent this, or any free negro fellow, from going into Pennsylvania, making the necessary arrangements, coming back, and carrying off as many as choose to go."[134] In 1840, the General Assembly yielded to slaveholders' demands and enacted an even harsher law that completely prohibited free blacks from entering Maryland. Regardless of the duration of their visit, free blacks who ventured into the state faced a twenty-five-dollar fine for the first offense and a five-hundred-dollar penalty for subsequent violations. Again, those who could not discharge their fines and legal expenses were to be auctioned into slavery.[135]

The statutes had a chilling effect on free blacks' mobility and by extension their employability. Farmers and merchants were enmeshed in commodity markets and transportation networks that spanned the sectional border, but Maryland's laws made the Mason-Dixon Line an impenetrable barrier for black laborers. Although there is no evidence that employers were fined for violating Maryland's laws, the statutes proved a severe hindrance to black workers. A Pennsylvanian whose farm was four miles north of the Mason-Dixon Line recalled that "the colored men employed as farmhands could not be sent across the line, even with a team, lest they would be claimed as slaves." Such was the fate of a free black from Frederick County who "went into Pennsylvania with a drove and cattle and was gone more than the legal twenty days." After he returned to Maryland, "two miscreants, utterly worthless in purse and character," had him arrested. Saddled with more than seventy dollars in fines and court costs, he was auctioned and "sent to the far South."[136]

Itinerant laborers in the Middle Atlantic needed the freedom to roam the countryside seeking employment: Harvesters followed the ripening wheat from Virginia to Pennsylvania, while boatmen, drovers, and wagoners crossed and recrossed the sectional border en route to commercial entrepôts. But with the enactment of Maryland's 1832 and 1840 statutes, black Pennsylvanians who tramped into Maryland ran the risk of enslavement. In 1851, for example, Philadelphian Edward Davis went "to the country in quest of the means of subsistence." Although Davis originally planned to find work in southeast Pennsylvania, he abandoned this plan, crossed the Susquehanna, and went to Havre de Grace, where "he sought for, and obtained employment." Arrested and fined twenty dollars, Davis languished in prison for two months before being sold to traders and sent to Georgia. There, he toiled for several years on cotton plantations and railroads before escaping to Pennsylvania on a steamship.[137]

Compared to their white counterparts, free black farmhands moved in narrow orbits. Dependent on white patrons and unwilling to abandon enslaved relatives, free blacks remained tethered to particular neighborhoods. Because free blacks were vulnerable to kidnapping or legal harassment, they chose to remain in districts where they were known. Thus, farmhand Sam Walker never bothered to obtain his freedom papers while laboring near his deceased master's plantation. Only after discovering that "farmers in our part had . . . slaves or hands of their own" and concluding to "try some other parts" did he secure his papers. Despite having lost his freedom papers, free black Damon Brown remained undisturbed until he moved outside his neighborhood, when he was beset by "frequent and very unpleasant interruptions." The presence of enslaved kin tightened the hobbles on free blacks. In the 1820s, freewoman Monica Weller accompanied her husband, William, from his home in southern Frederick County to the plantation of his new master, John Gleason, near Liberty-Town. Although her husband died soon after he was sold, Monica remained on the plantation for about eleven years, possibly because her freeborn son had been apprenticed to Gleason.[138]

Dovetailing with the legal and social constraints on free blacks' mobility was a series of ordinances and statutes that circumscribed African Americans' economic activities. Driven by fears that free blacks would fence property stolen by slaves, authorities erected legal barriers to prevent blacks from engaging in the petty production and proprietorship that were often essential to the working poor's economic survival. In 1827, authorities in Hagerstown directed constables to "disperse and prevent idle and disorderly persons, rude and noisy boys and persons of colour from frequenting the market-house."[139] In 1832, the Maryland General Assembly prohibited blacks from selling "bacon, pork, beef, mutton, corn, wheat, tobacco, rye, or oats" without first obtaining written permission from their employer, a justice of the peace, or "three respectable persons." The legislation also made it difficult for free blacks to obtain liquor licenses by stipulating that they must undergo additional examinations by a county court.[140]

The Maryland legislature also limited blacks' freedom to contract and change employers. In 1854, responding to concerns from farmers and planters on the Eastern Shore, who perceived a growing assertiveness among free blacks, the General Assembly imposed penalties on blacks who abandoned their employers before completing their contracts. Those convicted under this statute could be arrested, returned to their employers, and held financially responsible for lost time and court expenses. Repeat offenders faced arrest, brief prison sentences, financial penalties, and reduction to the status of a "free negro apprentice." The legislature also limited blacks' ability to entertain offers from competing employers. Any white person who knowingly contracted with a black man or woman who had already hired him- or herself to another employer could be fined an amount equivalent to two-fifths of the worker's wages and be compelled to return the employee to the original hirer.[141]

Making a living in the countryside along the Mason-Dixon Line was not for the fainthearted. Under the best of circumstances, working families had to harness the labor of men, women, and children while drawing on reserves of ingenuity, perseverance, and luck. The burden shouldered by free blacks was, however, even more onerous. Living in slavery's long shadow, they were forced to support kin who remained in bondage while being denied the fruits of their relatives' labor. The constraints that slavery imposed on free blacks' inter- and intrastate movements added to their woes. Free blacks lacked the mobility, the nimbleness, that laborers needed to survive in the unstable rural economy because they were often shackled to a neighborhood and dependent on white protectors.

"A Valuable Colored Man": Race, Class, and the Rural Workforce

On 6 February 1847, a crowd gathered for an auction at a country store on the banks of Sam's Creek. There, a white man named John B. West stabbed "a valuable colored man, who belonged to Mr. Evan L. Crawford" of Carroll County. The cause of the affray remains a mystery. A local newspaper reported that the unnamed slave had given "a slight provocation" but added that West was "intoxicated at the time." The slave succumbed to his wounds the following day. While he suffered, West fled the state, leaving behind a wife and several "helpless children."[142] With the exception of the snippet in the paper, much of this episode has been lost to history. It is, for example, unclear whether the bondsman was among the pieces of property being auctioned that day. Likewise, the relationship between the enslaved man and West remains shrouded in unanswerable questions. Had they once passed the bottle in a harvest field, were they nursing grudges, or was the deadly melee a chance encounter between strangers, one free and white, the other bound and black?

Despite these unknowns, this passage offers vital lessons. We may not know the victim's name, but his description as "a valuable colored man" illustrates how slavery and its handmaiden, the interstate trade, created an environment in which most whites viewed free blacks and slaves as commodities. The editors recorded West's name and family ties, but it was his victim's value that struck them and presumably their readers as important. African Americans and poor whites may have stood in the same position relative to capital, but only the latter could be and often were reduced to capital. All too often, white laborers threw their muscle behind this process. By becoming kidnappers, slave catchers, and agents of soul drivers, poor whites drove deep wedges into the ranks of the rural proletariat and revealed how pervasive, even hegemonic, the chattel principle was on the Mason-Dixon Line. Fragile moments of solidarity occurred among rural workers, including a few episodes of interracial cooperation, but these stirrings of class consciousness were undercut by laborers' other identities. Race and slavery conspired with the grinding poverty that was the common lot of farmhands to leave the rural workforce in shambles.[143]

Poor whites seldom found common cause with the enslaved. Whites may have been willing to undermine the authority of slaveholders and enrich themselves by fencing stolen goods or selling the occasional dram to a bondsman, but few were willing to assist runaway slaves. Maryland imposed stiff penalties on those who aided fugitives. Under an 1819 statute, anyone convicted of "having enticed, persuaded, or assisted any slave or servant . . . to run away from his lawful owner" faced six years in the penitentiary. Perhaps this measure explains why there are only a few examples of whites accompanying fugitive slaves during the antebellum period and why those partnerships were fraught with ambiguity and danger. Runaways rightly feared that their white companions might betray them to reap the rewards offered by masters or slave dealers. Slave owner George Littleford had "strong reason to believe" that his slave, Harry Warren, had been lured away by an Irishman who would "probably pass as Harry's master [and] will no doubt sell him at the first opportunity." Littleford's suspicions may not have been groundless, for evidence indicates that fugitives were wary of their white accomplices. In 1846, for example, a "colored man" parted company with his white companion out of fears that he "wished to sell him." Whites had few compunctions about selling suspected runaways. While riding across northern Frederick County, William Otter came across a stranger with a black man in tow. The stranger claimed that he "believed [the black man] to be runaway" but was uncertain of or indifferent to his legal status. Eager to disencumber himself of the black man, the stranger eagerly asked Otter "what I would give for him haphazard."[144]

Working alongside slaves caused some poor whites to empathize with African Americans' plight, but such feelings seldom emboldened challenges to the peculiar institution. When Otter overtook a runaway named Congo near Hanover, Pennsylvania, the bondsman's coworkers expressed some outrage at the slave's treatment and made a slight show of resistance, but they did not prevent his capture. As Otter approached the sleeping Congo, his foreman protested that "the negro was very tired, that he had worked hard that day," and that Otter had "no business with the negro." Congo's employer proved less sympathetic. He washed his hands of the fugitive and told Otter that he "might do with him as [he] pleased." Unable to prevent Congo from being dragged away in chains and unwilling to intervene more forcefully on his behalf, the foreman begged Otter "not to abuse the negro."[145] Compared to most laboring whites, this foreman was an abolitionist. Many white laborers followed Otter's example and treated runaway slaves as valuable commodities. In 1850, for example, seven workmen on the Baltimore and Susquehanna Railroad captured a group of slaves near the Pennsylvania line. The laborers brought the fugitives to their masters and "promptly divided the $300 reward." Those who caught fugitives were eager to maximize their gains. After returning a slave to his master in Frederick County, Otter attempted to increase his bounty by claiming that he had captured the bondsman in Pennsylvania. When the slave owner reneged and offered only half of the promised twenty-dollar reward, Otter snapped, "I felt no disposition to take any man's negro for that sum." After several weeks of haggling, Otter hauled the master before a magistrate and won a judgment for the remaining sum.[146]

The meager wages paid to common laborers sometimes paled in comparison to the windfalls that came from capturing a fugitive, a calculation the led some poor whites to make slave catching one of their many lines of work. On 26 March 1851, for example, William Callender purchased a five-thousand-dollar life insurance policy from the Keystone Insurance Company of Harrisburg. He also purchased a large quantity of arsenic, which he used to commit suicide the following day. Keystone refused to honor the policy on two grounds: Callender had killed himself, and he had "misrepresented his occupation, stating that he was *a farmer.*" The company argued that Callender was actually a slave catcher. In the course of suit initiated by Callender's executor, witnesses testified that both statements contained kernels of truth. One claimed that Callender had been raised as a farmer, that he had farmed in 1843 or 1844, that he had rented "some land on shares" in the spring of 1850, and that he had hired a plowboy in the spring of 1851. The same witness averred that Callender had worked as a brick maker in 1850. Another swore that Callender had been "running a railroad market car" in 1850 but that he abandoned that business four months before his death. Still, the evidence that Callender was "in the still more perilous business of *slave-catching*" voided the policy. Callender's winding career path was not exceptional. After deserting the Royal Navy, Otter worked numerous jobs: He ran a tavern and oyster stand, worked as a master plasterer, sold horses, and, when the opportunity presented itself, caught slaves. So seamlessly were these jobs intertwined that Otter once suspended the hunt for a runaway from Frederick County to plaster a house.[147]

Hounding fugitive slaves was not the only measure of poor whites' contempt for enslaved and free blacks. Driven by equal measures of greed and racism, whites abducted an untold number of people from the growing ranks of the Middle Atlantic's free black community and sold them to the Deep South. The kidnappers were a motley crew: A few were black, some were petty criminals and common laborers looking for a quick buck, and others were professionals. John Wooford epitomized this hard-bitten set. In 1822, William Humbere, a free black laborer at the Catoctin Furnace, claimed that Wooford was the "inhuman wretch" who had stolen his son, Solomon. According to Humbere, Wooford had served time in the Maryland Penitentiary, was "a great fighter and much inclined to stealing," and had a terrible visage that was "pock-marked [with] a part of his nose bitten off." Another kidnapper, Frederick A. Klause, admitted that he was once "a pirate on the high seas." In 1830, Klause received a ten-year prison sentence for spiriting a black man from Maryland to Louisville, Kentucky, and selling him "to some negro trader from Louisiana." In light of their hardscrabble lives, we should not be shocked that some blacks entered into criminal enterprises with white kidnappers. In 1836, a "negro man" persuaded a slave woman to "elope with him and go to Pennsylvania, with the promise that he would there marry her & that she would there be free." Unknown to her, the man was working in collusion with William McKee, who planned to capture her at Emmitsburg and take her south.[148] Wooford, Klause, McKee, and their confederates were probably as economically marginal as their victims, yet their survival and that of many poor whites and a few blacks hinged on their ability to exploit the enslaved and free blacks in their midst.

Whites evinced a callous disregard for blacks. In their eyes, blacks were objects of sport, in every sense of the word. Blacks were not only valuable quarry but also the butts of cruel jokes that mocked the plight of runaway slaves and kidnapping victims. Roderick Dorsey, a free black with a reputation for assisting fugitives and for being "very loud in denouncing the negro catchers," was the victim of an embarrassing scheme concocted by James McCullough, who lived down the street from Dorsey. McCullough blackened his face, donned tattered clothes, and recruited young men to chase him through Emmitsburg. With the gang on his heels, McCullough ran to Dorsey's doorstep and pleaded for assistance. Eager to help the "fugitive," Dorsey secreted him under a bed. The mob soon gathered outside Dorsey's home and began shouting for him to surrender the runaway. At this point, McCullough leapt up, overturned the bed, and scrambled through a back window. Assorted toughs then smashed down the front door and sprinted through the house in pursuit. While a local historian drolly noted that "this raised Roderick's wrath," the prank underscores the lack of empathy between whites and free blacks.[149]

Poor whites and blacks were buffeted by crosscurrents. The routines of farm work and rural life brought them together, but the dangerous undertow of the interstate trade pulled them apart. Slavery and the domestic traffic created a yawning chasm between black and white workers and made moments of interracial understanding, much less cooperation, distressingly rare. The rough equality that employers imposed on their workers neither obscured nor undermined the distinctions of race. Indeed, racial animosities reared their heads whenever whites mustered the strength to kick against their black co-workers. In 1831, for example, "an altercation of a very serious nature" transpired between black and white workmen on the Baltimore and Ohio Railroad near New Market, Maryland. Although the causes of the riot remain unclear, it may have been triggered by the introduction of black workers or by whites attempting to defend skilled or supervisory positions. Evidence from other industries suggests that whites expected blacks to occupy the least desirable, lowest-paying positions. When a manager at Antietam Woolen Manufacturing complained that "it is hard to get white [workers] in attending the carding machines on account of the dirtiness of the work and the wages [being] so low," he proposed solving the problem by hiring "some little Negro Boys."[150]

Blacks who overstepped the boundaries established by their white coworkers risked intimidation and violence. The Reverend Thomas W. Henry, who ministered to the enslaved workers at the Antietam Iron Works, recalled that "the white help had a spirit of animosity against [the] servants because of their being so well treated." The ironmaster not only allowed the slaves to gather refuse fuel and earn overtime wages (privileges denied the white workers), he also appointed slaves as foremen and managers. The white ironworkers' resentment simmered until 1835 or 1836, when, during the owner's absence, they attempted to flog several of the slave workers. The enslaved workmen mounted a spirited resistance and forced the whites to retreat to Sharpsburg, where they summoned the militia. When the company arrived at the furnace, the soldiers found that the slaves had scattered into the hills and woods.[151]

While rural industries provided settings for racial conflict, they could, on rare occasions, foster fleeting alliances between blacks and whites. In 1838, a resident of Mechanicstown reported that about twelve hands from the nearby Catoctin Furnace, "having indulged too freely in their libation at the race course, came into town, accompanied by two stout negroes, for the purpose, as one of them afterwards expressed himself, of 'using up the people.'" A group of townsfolk confronted the ironworkers, who became belligerent and refused to disperse. The constable soon arrested the black ironworkers, whom the correspondent identified as slaves, but "their white associates rescued them from the officer." The ensuing brawl turned against the ironworkers, who beat a hasty retreat to the furnace. "It was a fortunate circumstance that the two negroes left the town a few moments before the fight commenced," the correspondent concluded, "for such was the excitement that I have no doubt, had they remained they would have been killed on the spot."[152] It is not clear that the white ironworkers were moved by a sense of brotherhood with their enslaved counterparts; their decision to rescue the slaves may have been spurred by whiskey rather than by a budding interracial camaraderie. Moreover, the claim that the residents of Mechanicstown would have murdered the blacks but not the whites suggests that whites considered the acts of hooliganism committed by African Americans more dangerous than those perpetrated by whites.

There was nothing unique about the rabble that descended on Mechanicstown. The historical record is peppered with nervous, sometimes frightened complaints about gangs of black and white workmen. While it may be tempting to view these crowds as something akin to the many-headed hydra of sailors and slaves who prowled the revolutionary Atlantic, such an interpretation may be too romantic.

Poor whites turned against blacks and each other with a frequency and a ferocity that left the rural workforce bloodied and divided. Indeed, violence was endemic in the masculine world of farmhands. In 1827, for example, a husking match in Frederick County descended into bedlam when a white worker, identified only as Davis, assaulted Sam, a free black farmhand, for reasons that have been lost to history. In the ensuing melee, Davis brandished a knife and stabbed Sam, killing him immediately. Another bloody and pointless fight occurred in 1860, when a drunken white, Jacob Funk, accosted free black woodcutter Robert Bush and "made certain inquiries about a hog and woman." Bush, who was resting on a fence, replied that he "attended his own business and knew nothing about the hog or the woman." Funk snapped that "he would make Bush know something about it" and knocked the woodcutter off the fence. The men were soon throwing punches, knives, and axes at other. Funk's blade found its mark and inflicted a mortal wound "about four inches long, from which [Bush's] bowels protruded."[153] While fights between blacks and whites were common, they often stemmed from the nature of agricultural labor, not simmering racial hatred. Muddled by whiskey and exhaustion, farmworkers developed quick, violent tempers. During the winter of 1833, an argument between two drunken workers culminated in one of the men having "a piece of his ear bitten off."[154] Such episodes were common. In June 1844, farmhand Valentine Mumell thrashed fellow laborer Joshua Wilson so severely that he was bedridden for two days and required a doctor's attention. Mumell must have been a brawler: Later that year, he left another coworker, Fritz Keating, incapacitated for four days after a "serious affray."[155] Far from being evidence of a rough culture that united farmhands, these outbreaks of violence were symptomatic of a deeper, more profound atomization of the rural workforce.

The Maryland countryside offered poor, thin soil in which alliances between black and white farmworkers could take root. The state's legal terrain was uneven; slaves, free blacks, and whites trod different legal landscapes. Maryland's court system was geared for the defense of slavery, and the faintest hint that rowdies might threaten either the peculiar institution or white supremacy brought a swift, often brutal response. When a slave assaulted a white man at Burkitsville in 1858, an angry crowd seized the young man, dragged him before an impromptu court, and "sentenced to him to receive forty lashes well laid on." The same year, a Westminster newspaper reported that "some seven Etheopean bloods" had made "proposals of an unnamed nature" to a young white woman. Six of the men were arrested, convicted, and sentenced to receive anywhere from five to twenty lashes, which were administered by the sheriff "with a degree of strength that will make the boys remember him to the end of their days."[156] Acts of intimacy between slaves and whites drew harsh reprisals. In 1861, for example, the Carroll County Court sentenced a white woman, Emeline Haines, to an eighteen-month stint in the penitentiary. The father of her child, a slave, Matthew Ward, received an even harsher sentence: He was sold outside Maryland.[157]

Poor whites were opportunists. They sniffed about the countryside for chances to profit from the slaves' dreams of freedom or at least a better lot in bondage but never flinched from reaping a quick windfall from anxious slave owners. Poor whites turned against their black coworkers and against the region's slave owners. In 1854, for example, authorities arrested three men in Frederick County for "enticing negro slaves to abscond from their masters." They planned to encourage the fugitives to "take a direction so as to be caught by these parties, who would either secure the reward, or take them off and sell them to the Southern traders." Others preyed on the cupidity of masters and mistresses.[158] In 1861, James Liggett of Washington County, Maryland, notified John A. Gordon of Spotsylvania, Virginia, that had he tracked down Gordon's runaway slave in Pennsylvania and offered to capture the fugitive and secure him in the Hagerstown jail for seven hundred dollars. Unknown to Gordon, Liggett had already captured the bondsman and lodged him in the prison when he negotiated for the slave's return. Liggett was convicted of obtaining money under false pretenses and was sentenced to serve six months in the penitentiary, to pay a fifty-dollar fine, and to make five hundred dollars restitution.[159] The mercenary outlook that drove poor whites appeared in sharp relief in a telling story recounted by Otter, in which a slave owner identified only as "an old gentleman" grew suspicious that two of his slaves were stealing bacon from his farm. One day, Otter and the unnamed master followed the young men and a parcel of stolen bacon to a "widow woman's house, a tenant of his, who had a daughter whose name was Elizabeth." Otter and the slave owner crept alongside the house and began peering through cracks in the wall. Inside, they glimpsed the tenants and slaves celebrating over their loot. While the old woman sat in a corner "singing for life," Elizabeth danced back and forth between her "sooty companions," who hooted, "Dance to me, Miss Betsey." The next morning, the irate master summoned the slaves to his barn and began lashing them with a cowhide. Between cuts, he mocked the bondsmen by shouting, "Dance to me, Miss Betsey."[160]

CONCLUSION
Sharpsburg, Maryland, 1862

The fires that engulfed the barns and stables of George Carey and the Mumma family were distant memories on 17 September 1862, when once again the farms outside Sharpsburg were embroiled in fire and smoke. Most people in the neighborhood had forgotten "Negro Anthony" and his desperate flights to avoid being sold south for conspiring to torch Carey's outbuildings. Harry, the slave who stood trial for setting fire to the Mumma barn in 1822, probably did not live to see soldiers of the Third North Carolina infantry finish his work by torching the Mumma house and outbuildings during the battle.[1] Much had changed in the decades since these men struck their blows against slavery. Slavery had marched across the Deep South, an expansion made possible in part by the sweat and tears of northern Marylanders. Slavery's growth in northern Maryland had been arrested, and the area's slave population had been whittled down by flight, manumissions, and sales. Term slavery had become commonplace, and many African Americans were experiencing bondage as a temporary yet brutal and unjust passage. By 1860, the workings of delayed and immediate manumissions had resulted in Sharpsburg having a free black population of 203, easily surpassing the village's 150 slaves.

The lives of the free and enslaved blacks who witnessed the Battle of Antietam open a window into the transformations that had remade slavery along the sectional border. Among those living near the battlefield was Nancy Miller. She had been manumitted in June 1859 and remained in the neighborhood working as a domestic servant. Also on the battlefield was a man identified by an interviewer as "the slave foreman," who remembered that his master was a "good man to his black people." Like many slaves in northern Maryland, he had been given wages at harvest and had been allowed to seek outside employment during slack seasons. "When I worked in harvest all day cradling wheat I was paid as much as anybody else," he remembered, "and if I went with the horses to do teaming for a neighbor that money for what I had done was mine." So content was this man in his position that he rebuffed the recruiters seeking volunteers for the Union Army. The experiences of Miller and the slave foreman reveal how much slavery had been modified: Masters and mistresses used freedom, harvest wages, and the opportunity to earn money to gain leverage over their chattels.[2]

Other slaves from the neighborhood took a bold, decisive stand for freedom. They enlisted in what had become a crusade for freedom, but they did so far from their birthplaces. Louis Jourdan was born into bondage in 1840 near Boonsboro, a small town about a dozen miles from Sharpsburg. In 1859, Jourdan, his parents, and his nine siblings were sold to traders and scattered across the Deep South. Louis and two of his brothers were shipped to New Orleans and sold to a planter in Assumption Parish. In 1864, he enlisted in the Tenth U.S. Colored Heavy Artillery. Also in the fight was Fred Fowler, a fugitive from Frederick County. In 1858, Fowler caught wind that his master, a physician for a slave trader, planned on "selling him the following winter, probably because some other less valuable slave could do the work." A free black guided Fowler to an agent of the Underground Railroad in Gettysburg, whence he was smuggled to Canada. In 1863, Fowler returned to the United States and enlisted in the Twenty-ninth Regiment of Connecticut Colored Volunteers. The paths that led Jourdan and Fowler to regiments raised in Louisiana and Connecticut underscore the extent of slavery's reach. Slaves from northern Maryland might find themselves on a Louisiana plantation, while an enslaved man seeking his freedom could be safe only if he escaped to Canada.[3]

Given the marginal economic and political role that slavery played in northern Maryland, and considering the region's comparative insignificance within the plantation system, it may be tempting to dismiss this story as an interesting but ultimately trivial footnote in the history of slavery. Indeed, some historians have suggested that the recent outpouring of studies that treat slavery's peripheries—cities, industries, and rural areas with few plantations and slaves—has focused undue attention on these settings. Philip D. Morgan claims that these studies have unleashed a "centrifugal" tendency that has sent the historiography of slavery "spinning off in all directions." He suggests that slavery in "farms, shops, ships, and manufacturing enterprises may be likened to safety valves that helped keep the great engine running" but insists that plantations were the "engine that drove the Atlantic slave system."[4]

Morgan's lament is symptomatic of a larger ailment in the historiography of the Old South. Since the 1970s, scholars have expanded the study of slavery beyond the plantation districts. While this approach has broadened our understanding of geographic and temporal change in the South, it has also caused fragmentation. "Like blind men groping an elephant," observes Robert Tracy McKenzie, "scholars have begun to describe different parts of the whole but as yet have no systematic basis for comparing them."[5] Yet disarming the tensions between periphery and core and between local peculiarities and regional generalities requires something more than comparison: It requires an integrative framework that illuminates the connections among the Old South's numerous slave and slaveholding societies.[6]

Northern Maryland may have been a backwater in the sprawling plantation complex, but its history was inextricably linked to developments in the Deep South. The interstate trade was and remains the touchstone for interpreting slavery in northern Maryland, for it bound the fate of slavery in these counties to its strength on the South's cotton and sugar plantations. Slaves' financial value in northern Maryland was underwritten by the interstate trade, which simultaneously undercut slaves' value by driving frightened bondspeople into Pennsylvania.[7] On the national level, therefore, the distinctions between periphery and core collapsed under the weight of the interstate trade.

Although northern Maryland's slaves lived in the shadow of the auction block, the domestic traffic was not an all-encompassing reality. The circumstances of slavery along the Mason-Dixon Line differed markedly from those in the Deep South. In most of the categories of slave treatment sketched out by Eugene Genovese, bondspeople in northern Maryland fared better than their counterparts further south.[8] The enslaved may have had fewer opportunities for family and community life on their home places, but the bondspeople on wheat-producing farms and small plantations were seldom subjected to work routines as grueling as those of the Deep South's cotton and sugar estates. More important, slaves along the Mason-Dixon Line benefited from greater access to freedom than was available to their counterparts elsewhere. Maryland's manumission laws remained quite liberal through the 1850s, and in the decade preceding the Civil War, free blacks outnumbered slaves in all of the state's northern counties. Slaves whose owners refused to grant them legal manumission could steal their freedom by escaping into free territory, a task that, while dangerous, was easier for Marylanders than for Mississippians. The interstate trade may have loomed over these distinctions like the Sword of Damocles, threatening to obliterate them at any moment, but it never erased local variations within the peculiar institution.

The distinctions between national and local are, of course, somewhat artificial, for slaveholders and the enslaved understood their worlds in both contexts. Indeed, the contours of slavery in northern Maryland were formed

by crosscutting local and national currents. The combined effect of these influences was most visible in the working of delayed manumission agreements,
whereby slave owners and their chattels attempted to reconcile the tensions
that were destroying slavery along the border. In the hands of slaveholders, the
promise of freedom, however far removed, became a patch to prevent slavery
from unraveling altogether as a consequence of the destructive pull of the
interstate trade. Bondsmen and -women laboring under delayed manumission
agreements exchanged years of labor and risked having additional children
born into bondage for protection from the interstate trade. Term slaves who
struck for immediate freedom risked having their servitude extended and,
perhaps more threateningly, being sold away. Far from being removed from
the mainstream of historical scholarship, northern Maryland thus stands in
the vanguard of the emerging literature emphasizing the centrality of the
domestic trade to any understanding of slavery in the Old South.[9]

In a larger sense, northern Maryland offers an opportunity to plumb the
murky waters dividing slavery from free labor. Over the past decade, scholars
have attempted to bridge these straits, to reconfigure the dichotomous relationship between slavery and free labor into a more fluid, nuanced spectrum.[10]
If there was anyplace where different labor regimes could have existed along
a spectrum, it was northern Maryland. The imperatives of the agricultural
economy exerted their influence on both slavery and free labor, and landowners bent both regimes to their needs. The concerns voiced by employers
of free labor and owners of slaves were strikingly similar: Both worried about
the expense of seasonal underemployment, groused about drunken farmhands, and complained about women, children, and other undesirables. To
combat these problems, farmers concocted roughly analogous strategies for
disciplining enslaved and free workers. Whether they bought labor or laborers, farmers employed similar tactics to discipline their workforce. They used
bonuses and extras to induce workers to exert themselves at harvest. They
refused to hire sold or manumitted male workers' unwanted dependents.
And they combined lectures, fines, and (for slaves) the occasional flogging
to curb workers' excessive drinking.

Slavery could be hammered into something resembling free labor, but, as
former bondsman Stephen Pembroke observed, slavery "is a hard substance;
you cannot break it nor pull it apart, and the only way is to escape from it."
Having been threatened with sale to the Deep South after an unsuccessful
escape attempt and having witnessed the sale of several family members,
Pembroke understood that the interstate trade scoured away any superficial
similarities between slavery and free labor.[11] If the experiences of bound and
free laborers were fundamentally shaped by their respective statuses, the rough

contours of their lives were nevertheless hacked and hewed by their interactions with workers of different races and statuses. Nor were systems of labor discipline insulated from each other; slavery and the various manifestations of free labor may have remained distinct components of the workforce, but employers found innumerable ways of splicing them together on the region's farms and in its shops. Thus, the boundaries of labor regimes and the meanings of workers' statuses are best viewed through a shifting lens that is capable of viewing individual groups of workers in detail, of expanding outward to view the workforce as a whole, and of widening to encompass the larger national and international forces that interacted with local processes to shape the landscape of slavery and free labor.

Notes

Abbreviations

AF	*American Farmer* [Baltimore]
FTH	*Frederick-Town Herald*
HF	*Herald of Freedom* [Hagerstown]
HFT	*Herald of Freedom and Torchlight* [Hagerstown]
HM	*Hagerstown Mail*
HSFC	Historical Society of Frederick County, Frederick, Md.
MdHR	Maryland Hall of Records, Annapolis
MdHS	Maryland Historical Society, Baltimore
MH	*Maryland Herald* [Hagerstown]
MHETWA	*Maryland Herald and Elizabeth-Town Weekly Advertiser* [Hagerstown]
MHHWA	*Maryland Herald and Hagerstown Weekly Advertiser*
MSA	Maryland State Archives
NARA	National Archives and Records Administration, Washington, D.C.
RB	*Republican Banner* [Williamsport]
TPA	*Torchlight and Public Advertiser* [Hagerstown]
UMCP	Special Collections, University of Maryland, College Park

Introduction

1. William H. Seward, *The Irrepressible Conflict: A Speech by William H. Seward, Delivered at Rochester, Monday, Oct. 25, 1858* (Albany, N.Y.: Albany Evening Journal, 1858), 2.

2. On the historical significance of the Battle of Antietam, see James M. McPherson, *Crossroads of Freedom: Antietam* (New York: Oxford University Press, 2002).

3. *MHETWA*, 4 January, 11 January 1804; WASHINGTON COUNTY COURT (Dockets and Minutes) February 1804, MSA C3004-6, MdHR; MARYLAND GOVERNOR AND COUNCIL (Pardon Papers) Wm. Claggett and Robert Hughes to

Gov. Robt. Bowie, 29 February 1804, MSA S1061-11, MdHR 5401-11; MARYLAND GOVERNOR AND COUNCIL (Pardon Record) 1791–1806, MSA S1107-2, MdHR 1931; Nathaniel Rochester Jail Docket, 1804–06, Western Maryland Room, Washington County Free Library, Hagerstown, Md.; *MHHWA*, 15 August 1804, 1 March 1805. The judges ruled Anthony's testimony inadmissible in Ford's trial for arson, a capital offense, under a 1717 law that allowed slaves and free blacks to testify against slaves and free blacks, "provided such evidence or testimony do[es] not extend to the depriving them, or any of them, of Life or Member" ("A Supplementary Act Relating to Servants and Slaves," 8 June 1717, in *Laws of Maryland at Large*, comp. Thomas Bacon [Annapolis, Md.: Green, 1765]). The law remained in force until 1808, when the General Assembly declared that slaves and free blacks could testify "in all criminal prosecutions against any negro or mulatto or slave, or against any negro or mulatto free or freed" ("A Further Supplement to the Act, Entitled, An Act Relating to Servants and Slaves," 24 December 1808, in *Laws of Maryland, Made and Passed at a Session of Assembly, Begun and Held at the City of Annapolis, on Monday the Seventh of November, 1808* [Annapolis: Green, 1809]). An 1801 law declared, however, that slave testimony would be admissible in all cases in which free blacks stood accused of receiving stolen merchandise ("An Act Respecting Free Negroes," 31 December 1801, in *Laws of Maryland, Made and Passed at Session of Assembly, Begun and Held at the City of Annapolis, on the Second of November, 1801* [Annapolis: Green, 1802]). Speice purchased Anthony from Sharpsburg resident John Wade in March 1801 for $130 (WASHINGTON COUNTY COURT [Land Records] Purchase agreement between Ludwick Speice and John Wade, 18 March 1801, Liber N, ff. 376, MSA C1959-16, MdHR). Anthony's second escape may have been more successful than his first. There is no record of his being returned to the Washington County prison in either 1805 or 1806, and the sheriff continued to advertise for his return through late April 1805 (*MHHWA*, 26 April 1805).

4. Stephen W. Sears, *Landscape Turned Red: The Battle of Antietam* (New York: Ticknor and Fields, 1983), 182–85; *Federal Gazette and Baltimore Daily Advertiser*, 13 June 1799; *Alexandria Advertiser*, 31 March 1801; *MHHWA*, 13 June 1806, 3 April, 7 August 1807, 17 August 1814, 24 January 1822; WASHINGTON COUNTY CIRCUIT COURT (Docket and Minutes) March 1822, MSA T3063-42, MdHR. Census returns suggest that the Mumma family never owned more than four slaves. In 1800, the enumerator credited Jacob Mumma Sr. with two slaves. Two decades later, he owned a girl under fourteen, while his son, Jacob Mumma Jr., owned a man and a woman, both between the ages of twenty-six and forty-five, and a girl under fourteen (Manuscript Returns, 1800 U.S. Census, NARA; Manuscript Returns, 1820 U.S. Census, NARA). Sarah may have been a recent purchase at the time of her escape, for Mumma noted that she was "formerly the property of Jacob Schnebly, in Hagerstown" (*MHHWA*, 7 August 1807). Mumma apparently decided to sell the eighteen-year-old Tillman after his capture. In 1821, Washington County farmer John Davidberger advertised for the return of Samuel Tilghman, "a stout made" blacksmith then aged twenty-four (*TPA*, 24 June 1821). It is unclear whether the barn that burned in 1822 was the one torched by Confederate soldiers during the Battle of Antietam. A National Park Service report on the Mumma barn indicates

that it was built around 1790 and was still standing in 1862, but the document makes no mention of damage from earlier fires (Audrey T. Tepper, *Historic Structure Report: The Mumma Barn, Antietam National Battlefield* [Denver: U.S. Department of the Interior/National Park Service, 2000], 27).

5. Charles G. Steffen, *From Gentlemen to Townsmen: The Gentry of Baltimore County, Maryland, 1660–1776* (Lexington: University Press of Kentucky, 1993), 46–70. Although Steffen applied these analogies to colonial Baltimore County, they are applicable to the other counties of northern Maryland for most of the early national and antebellum decades.

6. John Mitchell Account Books, 1805–1840, UMCP. In 1810, Mitchell's household included eight free people and one enslaved black. By 1820, the number of free people had dropped to six, while the number of slaves had increased to two. One of the slaves was a male between the ages of fourteen and twenty-six, while the other was a young woman of approximately the same age. It is unclear if Mitchell owned these people or if they were some of his hired slaves (Manuscript Returns, 1810 U.S. Census, NARA; Manuscript Returns, 1820 U.S. Census, NARA). For a discussion of the importance of labor exchanges to farm households, see Michael Merrill, "Cash Is Good to Eat: Self-Sufficiency and Exchange in the Rural Economy of the United States," *Radical History Review* 3 (Fall 1976): 57–60.

7. *Maryland Commercial and Universal Advertiser*, 18 October 1786; FREDERICK COUNTY COURT (Judgment Record) 1801, MSA C810-18, MdHR 12,968; *Maryland Journal and Baltimore Advertiser*, 27 January 1778, quoted in Lathan A. Windley, comp., *Runaway Slave Advertisements: A Documentary History from the 1730s to 1790*, 4 vols. (Westport, Conn.: Greenwood, 1983), 2:202; *MHETWA*, 2 January 1800. On the importance of the underground economy to poor whites and slaves, see Charles C. Bolton, *Poor Whites of the Antebellum South: Tenants and Laborers in Central North Carolina and Northeast Mississippi* (Durham, N.C.: Duke University Press, 1994), 46–47; Timothy J. Lockley, *Lines in the Sand: Race and Class in Lowcountry Georgia, 1750–1860* (Athens: University of Georgia Press, 2001), 57–97; Jeff Forret, *Race Relations at the Margins: Slaves and Poor Whites in the Antebellum Southern Countryside* (Baton Rouge: Louisiana State University Press, 2006), 74–114; Wilma A. Dunaway, *Slavery in the American Mountain South* (New York: Cambridge University Press, 2003), 139–62.

8. On the growing tension between poor whites and slaves in the colonial Chesapeake, see T. H. Breen, "A Changing Labor Force and Race Relations in Virginia, 1660–1710," *Journal of Social History* 7 (Autumn 1973): 3–25.

9. Although her work does not specifically address convict laborers, historian Christine Daniels has found that indentured servants in colonial and early national Maryland enjoyed more rights than historians have previously thought. Servants routinely negotiated and renegotiated the terms of their service. Despite their low standing, servants could and did petition county courts for redress of any number of grievances, and justices often intervened on servants' behalf (Christine Daniels, "'Liberty to Complaine': Servant Petitions in Maryland, 1652–1797" in *The Many Legalities of Early America*, ed. Christopher Tomlins and Bruce H. Man [Chapel Hill: University of North Carolina Press, 2001], 18–49).

10. *Pennsylvania Packet*, 17 June 1778; *Bartgis's Federal Gazette* [Frederick, Md.], 27

October 1796; WASHINGTON COUNTY CIRCUIT COURT (Docket and Minutes) November 1819, MSA T3063-37, MdHR.

11. Karl Marx, *Capital: A Critique of Political Economy* (New York: Random House, 1906), 329.

12. Solomon Davis Account Book, 1810–1826, Special Collections, Duke University Libraries, Durham, N.C. On black family strategies for securing the freedom of their kin, see T. Stephen Whitman, *The Price of Freedom: Slavery and Manumission in Baltimore and Early National Maryland* (Lexington: University Press of Kentucky, 1997), 119–39; Christine Hünefeldt, *Paying the Price of Freedom: Family and Labor among Lima's Slaves, 1800–1854* (Berkeley: University of California Press, 1994).

13. See, for example, Peter Way, *Common Labor: Workers and the Digging of North American Canals, 1770–1810* (Baltimore: Johns Hopkins University Press, 1993); Mathew E. Mason, "'The Hands Here Are Disposed to Be Turbulent': Unrest among the Irish Trackmen of the Baltimore and Ohio Railroad, 1829–1851," *Labor History* 39 (August 1998): 253–72; Seth Rockman, *Scraping By: Wage Labor, Slavery, and Survival in Early Baltimore* (Baltimore: Johns Hopkins University Press, 2009); Christine Stansell, *City of Women: Sex and Class in New York, 1789–1860* (Urbana: University of Illinois Press, 1982).

14. Although Barbara Jeanne Fields offers a brief discussion of free blacks' daily lives, her work focuses primarily on the intellectual and disciplinary problems that Maryland's growing free black population created for slaveholders (*Slavery and Freedom on the Middle Ground: Maryland during the Nineteenth Century* [New Haven: Yale University Press, 1985], 63–89). Fields is not the only scholar to have overlooked rural free blacks. Indeed, most studies of southern free blacks have focused on cities. See, for example, Christopher Philips, *Freedom's Port: The African-American Community of Baltimore, 1790–1860* (Urbana: University of Illinois Press, 1997); James Sidbury, *Ploughshares into Swords: Race, Rebellion, and Identity in Gabriel's Virginia, 1730–1810* (Cambridge: Cambridge University Press, 1997), 169–231; Suzanne Lebsock, *The Free Women of Petersburg: Status and Culture in a Southern Town, 1784–1860* (New York: Norton, 1984), 87–110. To a certain extent, this bias seems justified, for urban blacks established more stable and visible communities and institutions. Still, studies of urban free blacks do not reflect the experience of most southern free blacks: As Ira Berlin has noted, "Most free Negroes, like most Southerners, lived in the countryside and earned their living working the land" (*Slaves without Masters: The Free Negro in the Antebellum South* [1975; New York: New Press, 1992], 218). Signs indicate that scholars are beginning to expand their focus beyond the cities. For recent studies discussing rural free blacks, see Melvin Patrick Ely, *Israel on the Appomattox: A Southern Experiment in Black Freedom from the 1790s through the Civil War* (New York: Knopf, 2004); Brenda E. Stevenson, *Life in Black and White: Family and Community in the Slave South* (New York: Oxford University Press, 1996), 259–313.

15. See David E. Schob, *Hired Hands and Ploughboys: Farm Labor in the Midwest, 1815–1860* (Urbana: University of Illinois Press, 1975); Richard D. Brown, "Farm Labor in Southern New England during the Agricultural-Industrial Transition," *Proceedings of the American Antiquarian Society* 99 (April 1989): 113–19; Ross W. Beales Jr., "The Reverend Ebenezer Parkman's Farm Workers, Westborough, Massachusetts, 1726–82," *Proceedings of the American Antiquarian Society* 99 (April 1989): 121–49.

Although not all poor whites worked in the fields, a spate of recent studies has focused on these landless laborers. See, for example, Bolton, *Poor Whites*; Wilma A. Dunaway, *Women, Work, and Family in the Antebellum Mountain South* (New York: Cambridge University Press, 2008); Forret, *Race Relations*; Lockley, *Lines*.

16. See, for example, Winifred Barr Rothenberg, *From Market Places to a Market Economy: The Transformation of Rural Massachusetts, 1775–1850* (Chicago: University of Chicago Press, 1992).

17. Sidney W. Mintz, *Caribbean Transformations* (Chicago: Aldine, 1974), 94. Mintz expanded this argument in subsequent works. In 1978, he suggested that the various labor systems that had coexisted throughout Caribbean history were implemented to serve the larger national and international economies in which they were embedded. It was, therefore, incumbent on scholars to neither define nor study labor systems in isolation, for all were "linked intimately by the world economy that had . . . given birth to them" (Sidney W. Mintz, "Was the Plantation Slave a Proletarian?" *Review* 2 [Summer 1978]: 81–98).

18. Mintz, "Was the Plantation Slave a Proletarian?" 86. These two examples are somewhat arbitrary, but they illustrate the larger point that employers have shown almost unbounded creativity when it comes to crafting workforces from distinct pools of laborers. In his study of agricultural slavery in ancient Rome, for example, Moses I. Finley concludes, "The coexistence of free and slave labor . . . was more than a coincidence in time and place; it was often a symbiosis . . . where an adequate supply of free, seasonal labor was a necessary condition for both the operation of the slave latifundia and the economic survival of the peasantry" (*Ancient Slavery and Modern Ideology* [New York: Vintage, 1980], 77). More recently, Julie Greene has shown how the U.S. government concocted various schemes to manage the racially diverse workforce of Americans, Europeans, and West Indians who built the Panama Canal (*The Canal Builders: Making America's Empire in the Panama Canal* [New York: Viking, 2009]).

19. John Bezís-Selfa, "Slavery and the Disciplining of Free Labor in the Colonial Mid-Atlantic Iron Industry," *Pennsylvania History* 64 (Summer 1994): 270–86.

20. Patricia A. Schechtner, "Free and Slave Labor in the Old South: The Tredegar Ironworkers' Strike of 1847," *Labor History* 35 (Spring 1994): 165–86.

21. Wayne K. Durrill, "Routine of Seasons: Labour Regimes and Social Ritual in an Antebellum Plantation Community," *Slavery and Abolition* 16 (August 1995): 161–87.

22. Edmund Ruffin, "Management of Wheat Harvests," Report of the Commissioner of Patents for 1850, pt. 2, Agriculture, *House Executive Documents*, 31st Cong., 2nd sess., no. 32, serial 601, p. 108.

23. FREDERICK COUNTY REGISTER OF WILLS (Wills) Will of Thomson Mason, 26 September 1784, Liber GM 2, ff. 404, MSA C898-3, MdHR 40,285-3.

24. Elie Williams to Otho Holland Williams, 17 March 1789, Otho Holland Williams Papers, MdHS.

25. John Blackford Journals, 26 June–4 July 1829, MS 1087, MdHS.

26. John Bezís-Selfa, "A Tale of Two Ironworks: Slavery, Free Labor, Work, and Resistance in the Early Republic," *William and Mary Quarterly*, 3rd ser., 56 (October 1999): 677.

27. O. Nigel Boland, "Proto-Proletarians? Slave Wages in the Americas," in *From*

Chattel Slaves to Wage Slaves: The Dynamics of Labour Bargaining in the Americas, ed. Mary Turner (Bloomington: Indiana University Press, 1995), 123–47. Loren Schweninger has documented a divergence between slaves' legal status and their daily lives, demonstrating that "a group of virtually free slaves" engaged in self-hire and independent production ("The Underside of Slavery: The Internal Economy, Self-Hire, and Quasi-Freedom in Virginia, 1780–1865," *Slavery and Abolition* 12 [September 1991]: 1–22). See also David E. Paterson, "Slavery, Slaves, and Cash in a Georgia Village, 1825–1865," *Journal of Southern History* 75 (November 2009): 879–930. On slaveholders' selective embrace of bourgeois values, see Mark M. Smith, "Time, Slavery, and Plantation Capitalism in the Ante-Bellum South," *Past and Present* 150 (February 1996): 142–68; Steven G. Collins, "System, Organization, and Agricultural Reform in the Antebellum South," *Agricultural History* 75 (Winter 2001): 1–27. For examples of slaveholders' attempts to imbue slavery with greater flexibility, to adapt the institution to employments usually dominated by wage labor, and to make the enslaved respond to incentives, see Keith C. Barton, "'Good Cooks and Washers': Slave Hiring, Domestic Labor, and the Market in Bourbon County, Kentucky," *Journal of American History* 84 (September 1997): 436–60; Charles B. Dew, *Bond of Iron: Master and Slave at Buffalo Forge* (New York: Norton, 1994).

28. Edmund S. Morgan, "Introduction to the Francis Parkman Prize Edition," in *American Slavery, American Freedom: The Ordeal of Colonial Virginia* (New York: History Book Club, 1995), xiv.

29. Tom Brass, introduction to *Free and Unfree Labour: The Debate Continues,* ed. Tom Brass and Marcel van der Linden (New York: Lang, 1997), 20. Brass was responding specifically to an argument advanced by Robert J. Steinfeld and Stanley L. Engerman, who suggest that the distinction between free and unfree labor was an "arbitrary not a natural classification" and was shaped by highly contingent and specific economic, legal, and political circumstances ("Labor—Free or Coerced? A Historical Reassessment of Differences and Similarities," in *Free and Unfree Labour,* ed. Brass and van der Linden, 107–26).

30. Peter Kolchin, "Variations of Slavery in the Atlantic World," *William and Mary Quarterly,* 3rd ser., 59 (July 2002): 551.

31. U.S. Census Office, *Census for 1820* (Washington, D.C.: Gales and Seaton, 1821), 21–28.

32. U.S. Census Office, *Sixth Census or Enumeration of the Inhabitants of the United States, as Corrected at the Department of State in 1840* (Washington, D.C.: Blair and Rives, 1841), 201.

33. Mary Fitzhugh Hitselberger and John Philip Dern, *Bridge in Time: The Complete 1850 Census of Frederick County, Maryland* (Redwood City, Calif.: Monocacy, 1978), xvi–xvii.

34. George Washington, *Letters on Agriculture from His Excellency George Washington, President of the United States, to Arthur Young, Esq., F.R.S., and Sir John Sinclair, Bart., M.P.,* ed. Franklin Knight (Washington, D.C.: the Editor, 1847), 34; John Palmer, *Journal of Travels in the United States of North America in Lower Canada, Performed in the Year 1817* (London: Sherwood, Neely, and Jones, 1818), 39–40.

35. FREDERICK COUNTY COMMISSIONERS OF THE TAX (Assessment Record), Real Property, 1835, MSA C755-5, MdHR 19,271.

36. U.S. Census Office, *Agriculture of the United States in 1860: Compiled from the Original Returns of the Eighth Census, under the Direction of the Secretary of the Interior* (Washington, D.C.: U.S. Government Printing Office, 1864), 203.

37. Ira Berlin, *Many Thousands Gone: The First Two Centuries of Slavery in North America* (Cambridge: Harvard University Press, 1998), 8.

38. Gary B. Nash and Jean R. Soderlund, *Freedom by Degrees: Emancipation in Pennsylvania and Its Aftermath* (New York: Oxford University Press, 1991), 5.

39. "From Luray to Philadelphia," *Friends' Intelligencer* 38 (July 1881), 380; Thomas J. C. Williams, *A History of Washington County, Maryland, from the Earliest Settlements to the Present Time, Including a History of Hagerstown* (Hagerstown, Md.: the Author, 1906), 250–51; James A. Helman, *History of Emmitsburg, Maryland* (Frederick, Md.: Citizen, 1906), 91.

40. Steven Deyle, "The Irony of Liberty: Origins of the Domestic Slave Trade," *Journal of the Early Republic* 12 (Spring 1992): 37–62.

41. T. Stephen Whitman, "'I Have Got the Gun and Will Do as I Please with Her': African-Americans and Violence in Maryland, 1782–1830," in *Over the Threshold: Intimate Violence in Early America*, ed. Christine Daniels and Michael V. Kennedy (New York: Routledge, 1999), 256–57.

42. *MHHWA*, 5 June 1807.

43. On resistance to the slave trade in the Chesapeake, see John Joseph Condon Jr., "Manumission, Slavery, and Family in the Post-Revolutionary Rural Chesapeake: Anne Arundel County, Maryland, 1781–1831 (Ph.D. diss., University of Minnesota, 2001), 146–48; *MHETWA*, 20 November 1800, 15 September 1802; *National Intelligencer and Weekly Advertiser* [Washington, D.C.], 13 November 1810.

44. Matthew Patton to Rev. Robert Green, 13 July 1802, Loose Correspondence, Incoming, 1796–1819, Papers of the Pennsylvania Abolition Society [microfilm edition], Historical Society of Pennsylvania, Philadelphia.

45. Grand Jury Report, Alexandria, Va., January Term 1802, enclosed in George Drinker to Joseph Bringhurst, 10 December 1804, Loose Correspondence, Incoming, 1796–1819, Papers of the Pennsylvania Abolition Society.

46. Ted Alexander, "A Regular Slave Hunt: The Army of Northern Virginia and Black Civilians in the Gettysburg Campaign," *North and South* 4 (September 2001): 82–89.

47. *MHETWA*, 9 January 1800; *FTH*, 6 August 1815.

48. FREDERICK COUNTY COURT (Land Records) Manumission of "Negro Cyrus," 12 May 1791, and Indenture of "Negro Cyrus," 12 May 1791, Liber WR 10, ff. 34–36, MSA C814-40, MdHR 40,341-2.

49. FREDERICK COUNTY COURT (Land Records) Purchase agreement between Philip Dietrich and Charles Baltzell Jr., 7 January 1804, Liber WR 25, ff. 291–92, MSA C814-55, MdHR 40,341-17.

50. FREDERICK COUNTY COURT (Land Records) Affidavit of Mary Brown, 13 April 1803, Liber WR 24, ff. 251–52, MSA C814-54, MdHR 40,341-16.

51. Petition of "Negro Diana," n.d., Maryland Manuscripts Collection, UMCP. For a similar complaint, see Petition of "Negro William," n.d., Maryland Manuscripts Collection, UMCP.

52. *MHHWA*, 24 July 1816.

53. *Votes and Proceedings of the Senate of the State of Maryland, November Session, 1796* (Annapolis: n.p., 1797), 37.

54. The cross currents of slavery and freedom along the sectional border are discussed in Julie Winch, "Philadelphia and the Other Underground Railroad," *Pennsylvania Magazine of History and Biography* 111 (January 1987): 3–25; T. Stephen Whitman, *Challenging Slavery in the Chesapeake: Black and White Resistance to Human Bondage, 1775–1864* (Baltimore: Maryland Historical Society Press, 2007); Stanley Harrold, *Border War: Fighting over Slavery before the Civil War* (Chapel Hill: University of North Carolina Press, 2010).

55. Frederick Douglass, *Life and Times of Frederick Douglass* (Boston: De Wolfe and Fisk, 1892), 198–99; R. C. Smedley, *History of the Underground Railroad in Chester and the Neighboring Counties of Pennsylvania* (Lancaster, Pa.: Heistand, 1883), 37; James W. C. Pennington, *The Fugitive Blacksmith; or, Events in the History of James W. C. Pennington, Pastor of the Presbyterian Church, New York, Formerly a Slave in the State of Maryland,* 3rd ed. (London: Gilpin, 1850), 22–23.

56. Isaac Weld, *Travels through the United States of North America and the Provinces of Upper Canada during the Years 1795, 1796, and 1797* (London: Stockdale, 1800), 133. The term *Chesapeake borderlands* is from Stanley Harrold: according to Harrold, in the Upper South, "traditional southern economies and values interacted with modernizing influences from the North. There was a tension between free and slave labor, between industry and agriculture, between conflicting moralities, and between hope and despair among black families as economic change led on the one hand to manumission and on the other to sale south" ("On the Borders of Slavery and Race: Charles T. Torrey and the Underground Railroad," *Journal of the Early Republic* 20 [Summer 2000]: 273–74).

57. For a discussion of the migration of Pennsylvania Germans into northern Maryland, see J. Thomas Scharf, *History of Western Maryland,* 2 vols. (1882; Baltimore: Regional, 1968), 1:58–74; Elizabeth Augusta Kessel, "Germans on the Maryland Frontier: A Social History of Frederick County, Maryland, 1730–1800" (Ph.D. diss., Rice University, 1981); Todd Harold Barnett, "The Evolution of 'North' and 'South': Settlement and Slavery on America's Sectional Border, 1650–1810" (Ph.D. diss., University of Pennsylvania, 1993); Robert D. Mitchell, "Agricultural Regionaliza-tion: Origins and Diffusion in the Upper South before 1860," *International Geography* 2 (1972): 740–42. The spread of farm design and folk architecture across the Maryland-Pennsylvania border is discussed in Henry Glassie, "Eighteenth-Century Cultural Process in Delaware Valley Folk Building," *Winterthur Portfolio* 7 (1972): 29–58; Paula Stoner, "Early Folk Architecture of Washington County," *Maryland Historical Magazine* 72 (Winter 1977): 512–22.

58. *AF*, 10 December 1819; Washington, *Letters on Agriculture,* 30–31.

59. James Weston Livingood, *The Philadelphia-Baltimore Trade Rivalry, 1789–1869* (Harrisburg: Pennsylvania Historical and Museum Commission, 1947); Jane N. Garret, "Philadelphia and Baltimore, 1790–1840: A Study of Intra-Regional Unity," *Maryland Historical Magazine* 55 (March 1960): 1–13; Jo N. Hays, "Overlapping Hin-terlands: York, Philadelphia, and Baltimore, 1800–1850," *Pennsylvania Magazine of History and Biography* 116 (July 1992): 295–321.

60. *Patriot and Commercial Advertiser* [Baltimore], 16 January 1823.

61. *Register of Pennsylvania*, 24 January 1829.

62. *RB*, 21 November 1835.

63. Manuscript Returns, 1820 U.S. Census, Frederick County and Washington County, Md., NARA.

64. U.S. Census Office, *Agriculture in the United States in 1860*, 231.

65. Fields, *Slavery and Freedom*, 84.

66. For discussions of how economists and antislavery ideologues crafted free labor against the foil of slavery, see David Brion Davis, *The Problem of Slavery in the Age of Revolution, 1770–1823* (New York: Oxford University Press, 1999); Seymour Drescher, *The Mighty Experiment: Free Labor versus Slavery in British Emancipation* (New York: Oxford University Press, 2002); Eric Foner, *Free Soil, Free Labor, Free Men: The Ideology of the Republican Party before the Civil War* (New York: Oxford University Press, 1970). The gulf between free labor ideology and the realities of wage labor is explored in Thomas C. Holt, *The Problem of Freedom: Race, Labor, and Politics in Jamaica and Britain, 1832–1938* (Baltimore: Johns Hopkins University Press, 1992).

Chapter 1. "The Land Flows with Milk and Honey": Agriculture and Labor in the Early Republic

1. John F. D. Smyth, *A Tour in the United States of America*, 2 vols. (Dublin: Perrin, 1784), 2:161; Julian Ursyn Niemcewicz, *Travels through America in 1797–1799, with Some Further Accounts of Life in New Jersey*, trans. Metchie J. E. Budka (Elizabeth, N.J.: Grassman, 1965), 110–13.

2. Brooke Hunter, "Wheat, War, and the American Economy during the Age of Revolution," *William and Mary Quarterly*, 3rd ser., 62 (July 2005): 505–26; George Terry Sharrer, "Flour Milling and the Growth of Baltimore, 1783–1830" (Ph.D. diss., University of Maryland, 1975), 90–135.

3. Despite an outpouring of works on unskilled workers in the young republic's cities and industries, little has been written on the nation's rural laborers. On unskilled urban workers, see Seth Rockman, *Scraping By: Wage Labor, Slavery, and Survival in Early Baltimore* (Baltimore: Johns Hopkins University Press, 2009); Billy G. Smith, *The "Lower Sort": Philadelphia's Laboring People, 1750–1800* (Ithaca: Cornell University Press, 1990); Peter Way, *Common Labor: Workers and the Digging of North American Canals, 1780–1860* (Baltimore: Johns Hopkins University Press, 1993).

4. Gideon Denison Account Book, 1796–1799, Hargrett Rare Book and Manuscript Library, University of Georgia Libraries, Athens.

5. Rockman, *Scraping By*, 38. For other studies emphasizing the interchangeability of laborers in the late colonial and early national Middle Atlantic, see Thomas M. Doerflinger, "Rural Capitalism in Iron Country: Staffing a Forest Factory, 1808–1815," *William and Mary Quarterly*, 3rd ser., 59 (January 2002): 3–38; Graham Russell Hodges, *Slavery and Freedom in the Rural North: African Americans in Monmouth County, New Jersey, 1665–1865* (Madison, Wis.: Madison House, 1997), 47–48; Gary B. Nash and Jean R. Soderlund, *Freedom by Degrees: Emancipation in Pennsylvania and its Aftermath* (New York: Oxford University Press, 1991), 33; Christopher M. Os-

borne, "Invisible Hands: Slaves, Bound Laborers, and the Development of Western Pennsylvania, 1780–1820," *Pennsylvania History: A Journal of Mid-Atlantic Studies* 72 (Winter 2005): 82–84; Steven Sarson, "'The Torment with Servants': Management and Labor in a Southern Maryland Household," *Maryland Historical Magazine* 102 (Fall 2007): 131–55.

6. O. H. Williams to Philip Thomas, 16 February 1791, David Bryan to O. H. Williams, 2 March 1792, both in Otho Holland Williams Papers, MdHS.

7. Dr. Philip Thomas to O. H. Williams, 9 April 1794, O. H. Williams to Benjamin Williams, 6 May 1794, both in Williams Papers.

8. "Interesting Travels in America, Translated from the German of Bulow," *The Port-Folio*, June 1802.

9. Richard Parkinson, *The Experienced Farmer's Tour of America: Exhibiting, in a Copious and Familiar View, the American System of Agriculture and Breeding of Cattle, with Its Recent Improvements* (London: Stockdale, 1805), 31–32.

10. Robert J. Steinfeld, *The Invention of Free Labor: The Employment Relation in English and American Law and Culture* (Chapel Hill: University of North Carolina Press, 1991), 123–72; Christopher Tomlins, *Law, Labor, and Ideology in the Early American Republic* (New York: Cambridge University Press, 1993).

11. James T. Lemon, *The Best Poor Man's Country: A Geographical Study of Early Southeastern Pennsylvania* (New York: Norton, 1976); Michael V. Kennedy, "'Cash for His Turnips': Agricultural Production for Local Markets in Colonial Pennsylvania, 1725–1783," *Agricultural History* 72 (Summer 2000): 587–608.

12. On the market orientation of the farmers and planters in northern Maryland, see Hunter, "Wheat,"; Kenneth E. Keller, "The Wheat Trade on the Upper Potomac, 1800–1860," in *After the Backcountry: Rural Life in the Great Valley of Virginia*, ed. Kenneth E. Koons and Warren R. Hofstra (Knoxville: University of Tennessee Press, 2000), 21–24; Elizabeth Augusta Kessel, "Germans on the Maryland Frontier: A Social History of Frederick County, Maryland, 1730–1800" (Ph.D. diss., Rice University, 1981), 97–99; John F. Kvach, "Wheat, Wealth, and Western Maryland: The Growth and Evolution of Flour Milling in Frederick County, Maryland, 1748–1789" (master's thesis, West Virginia University, 2002), 97–114; Sharrer, "Flour Milling."

13. Christian Boerstler, "The Journal of Doctor Christian Boerstler: Prominent Funkstown Resident, 1785–1866," trans. Jeffrey A. Wyand, 6 July 1787, MdHS.

14. *Bartgis's Maryland Gazette* [Frederick, Md.], 25 April 1793; David Shriver to Andrew Shriver, 1 May 1795, Shriver Family Papers, 1774–1894, MS 2085, MdHS.

15. George Washington, *Letters on Agriculture from His Excellency George Washington, President of the United States, to Arthur Young, Esq., F.R.S., and Sir John Sinclair, Bart., M.P.*, ed. Franklin Knight (Washington, D.C.: the Editor, 1847), 34–35; *The Key* [Frederick, Md.], 20 January 1798.

16. Joseph Scott, *A Geographical Description of the States of Maryland and Delaware; Also of the Counties, Towns, Rivers, Bays, and Islands, with a List of the Hundreds in Each County* (Philadelphia: Kimbee, Conrad, 1807), 148.

17. Tench Coxe, *A Statement of the Arts and Manufactures of the United States of America, for the Year 1810* (Philadelphia: Cornman, 1814), 87.

18. Washington, *Letters on Agriculture*, 34–35.

19. Scott, *Geographical Description*, 148; Coxe, *Statement*, 83.

20. In 1791, French traveler Ferdinand Marie Bayard noted that landowners in Frederick County "have been growing tobacco profitably for several years," but he was silent on its importance in relation to other crops. Tobacco was probably the principal staple of some of the larger planters who settled along the Potomac River in Frederick and Washington Counties. When an early frost struck southern Washington County in 1792, a local newspaper reported that the tobacco had been "totally destroyed" and that "the loss sustained . . . is very considerable in this part of the county, and will be severely felt by the suffering individuals, whose labor and expectations for the whole season have been blasted." See Ferdinand Marie Bayard, *Travels of a Frenchman in Maryland and Virginia with a Description of Philadelphia and Baltimore in 1791; or, Travels in the Interior of the United States, to Bath, Winchester, in the Valley of the Shenandoah, etc. etc.*, trans. Benjamin C. McCary (Ann Arbor, Mich.: Edward, 1950), 34; *Washington Spy* [Hagerstown, Md.], 26 September 1792.

21. Bayard, *Travels*, 34.

22. *Washington Spy* [Hagerstown, Md.], 7 September 1791.

23. *Pennsylvania Gazette*, 10 June 1789.

24. Tobias Lear, *Observations on the River Potomack, the Country Adjacent, and the City of Washington* (New York: Loudon, 1793), 9. For other descriptions of flourishing commerce on the Potomac River and its Maryland tributaries, see Dan Guzy, "Bateaux, Mills, and Fish Dams: Opening Navigation on the Monocacy River and the Conococheague and Antietam Creeks," *Maryland Historical Magazine* 98 (Fall 2003): 281–301; Niemcewicz, *Travels*, 161; *Maryland Chronicle and Universal Advertiser* [Frederick], 5 April 1786; *The Hornet* [Frederick, Md.], 20 March 1804; Edward Green Williams to William E. Williams, 10 October 1817, Williams Family Papers, MdHS.

25. John Thomson Mason Account Book, 1802–1835, Manuscripts Division, Library of Congress, Washington, D.C..

26. Horatio Ross to Major Henry Bedinger, 19 March 1796, Vertical File, MdHS.

27. Zephaniah Buffinton Papers, ca. 1813, MS 2852, MdHS.

28. Mark Pringle to Paca Smith, 28 October 1811, Mark Pringle Letterbooks, 1796–1798, 1811–1818, MS 680, MdHS.

29. Harry Dorsey Gough Ledger and Family Accounts, 1816–1826, in Harry Dorsey Gough Account Books, 1753–1852, MS 400, MdHS.

30. *Maryland Chronicle and Universal Advertiser* [Frederick], 8 February 1786.

31. Richard Lynn Bushman, "Markets and Composite Farms in Early America," *William and Mary Quarterly*, 3rd ser., 55 (July 1998): 351–74. Historian Michael V. Kennedy has reached similar conclusions in his study of colonial Pennsylvania, noting, "No simple dichotomy existed between farmers who produced goods for home consumption and those who produced for commercial sale" ("'Cash,'" 608).

32. Washington, *Letters on Agriculture*, 34–35.

33. W. Faux, *Memorable Days in America: Being a Journal of a Tour to the United States, Principally Undertaken to Ascertain, by Positive Evidence, the Condition and Probable Prospects of British Emigrants* (London: Simpkin and Marshall, 1823), 149–50.

34. *FTH*, 5 August 1809.

35. Ibid., 26 August 1806.

36. Joseph Austin Durrenberger, *Turnpikes: A Study of the Toll Road Movement in the Middle Atlantic States and Maryland* (Cos Cob, Conn.: Edwards, 1968), 37.

37. *FTH*, 28 August 1802.

38. *MHHWA*, 31 December 1817.

39. *Bartgis's Maryland Gazette* [Frederick], 25 April 1793.

40. *The Hornet* [Frederick, Md.], 10 January 1804.

41. *MHETWA*, 13 April 1803.

42. Durrenberger, *Turnpikes*, 65–68.

43. *The Hornet* [Frederick, Md.], 17 January 1804.

44. *MHETWA*, 13 April 1803.

45. *Maryland Chronicle and Universal Advertiser* [Frederick], 21 February 1787.

46. *FTH*, 22 June 1811, 24 October 1818.

47. Ibid., 9 February 1817.

48. Elie Williams to Otho Holland Williams, 21 October 1787, Williams Papers.

49. William Lee to Joseph Chapline, 23 April 1803, Joseph Chapline and Joseph C. Hayes Papers, 1741–1841, Special Collections, Duke University Libraries, Durham, N.C.

50. David Shriver to Andrew Shriver, 1 May 1795, [Buchard] Kohl to Andrew Shriver, 1 July 1795, Contract of Andrew Kenna, 15 March 1796, Agreement between Joseph Kork and Andrew Shriver, 2 February 1798, John Schley to Andrew Shriver, 27 November 1801, Abraham Shriver to Andrew Shriver, 21 April 1802, all in Shriver Family Papers.

51. SPECIAL COLLECTIONS (Annan Collection of Clotworthy Birnie Papers) Upton Scott to Clotworthy Birnie, 28 October 1806, MSA SC 725, MdHR.

52. SPECIAL COLLECTIONS (Annan Collection of Clotworthy Birnie Papers) Clotworthy Birnie Diary, 7 September 1810, MSA SC 725, MdHR.

53. Wm. Napier to C. Birnie, 10 July 1811, Osborne Sprigg to Clotworthy Birnie, 6 December 1810, Clotworthy Birnie Papers, 1799–1890, MS 2318, MdHS.

54. In his effort to purchase bondsmen and -women, Birnie attended a slave auction in Frederick, visited neighboring slaveholders, and traveled south to Prince George's County to inspect slaves. He also purchased slaves from his uncle's estate. See SPECIAL COLLECTIONS (Annan Collection of Clotworthy Birnie Papers) Clotworthy Birnie Diary, 17 October, 1, 2 December 1810, MSA SC 725, MdHR. For the purchase of slaves, see SPECIAL COLLECTIONS (Annan Collection of Clotworthy Birnie Papers) Clotworthy Birnie Ledger, 1810–1847, MSA SC 725, MdHR.

55. SPECIAL COLLECTIONS (Annan Collection of Clotworthy Birnie Papers) Upton Scott to Clotworthy Birnie, 8 March 1812, MSA SC 725, MdHR.

56. SPECIAL COLLECTIONS (Annan Collection of Clotworthy Birnie Papers) Clotworthy Birnie Ledger, 1810–1847, MSA SC 725, MdHR.

57. Manuscript Returns, 1820 U.S. Census, Frederick County, Md., NARA.

58. *FTH*, 9 June 1810.

59. *MHHWA*, 26 February, 2 April 1817.

60. On the use of slaves in the industries of the early republic, see John Bezís-Selfa, *Forging America: Ironworkers, Adventurers, and the Industrious Revolution* (Ithaca: Cornell University Press, 2004); Laura Croghan Kamoie, *Irons in the Fire: The Business*

History of the Tayloe Family and Virginia's Gentry, 1700–1860 (Charlottesville: University of Virginia Press, 2007); T. Stephen Whitman, *The Price of Freedom: Slavery and Manumission in Baltimore and Early National Maryland* (Lexington: University Press of Kentucky, 1997).

61. The shifting landscape of labor relations in the early national Middle Atlantic has received extensive commentary elsewhere. See, for example, Paul G. E. Clemens and Lucy Simler, "Rural Labor and the Farm Household in Chester County, Pennsylvania, 1750–1850," in *Work and Labor in the Early Republic*, ed. Stephen Innes (Chapel Hill: University of North Carolina Press, 1998), 144–88; Sharon Salinger, *"To Serve Well and Faithfully": Labor and Indentured Servants in Pennsylvania, 1682–1800* (New York: Cambridge University Press, 1987), 137–71; Nash and Soderlund, *Freedom by Degrees*; Rockman, *Scraping By*; Sarson, "'Torment with Servants.'"

62. For overviews of emancipation in New England and the Middle Atlantic, see Arthur Zilversmith, *The First Emancipation: The Abolition of Slavery in the North* (Chicago: University of Chicago Press, 1967); Joanne Pope Melish, *Disowning Slavery: Gradual Emancipation and "Race" in New England, 1780–1860* (Ithaca: Cornell University Press, 1998). On the enactment of gradual emancipation laws in the Middle Atlantic, see Hodges, *Slavery and Freedom*, 92–166; Nash and Soderlund, *Freedom by Degrees*; Shane White, *Somewhat More Independent: The End of Slavery in New York City, 1770–1810* (Athens: University of Georgia Press, 1991). On the process of manumission in the Upper South states where slavery remained legal, see Patience Essah, *A House Divided: Slavery and Emancipation in Delaware* (Charlottesville: University Press of Virginia, 1996), 36–107; Whitman, *Price of Freedom*; John Joseph Condon Jr., "Manumission, Slavery, and Family in the Post-Revolutionary Rural Chesapeake: Anne Arundel County, Maryland, 1781–1831" (Ph.D. diss., University of Minnesota, 2001); Eva Shepherd Wolf, *Race and Liberty in the New Nation: Emancipation in Virginia from the Revolution to Nat Turner's Rebellion* (Baton Rouge: Louisiana State University Press, 2006).

63. The discussion of slavery's decline in Harford County is drawn from Richard S. Dunn, "Black Society in the Chesapeake, 1776–1810," in *Slavery and Freedom in the Age of the American Revolution*, ed. Ira Berlin and Ronald Hoffman (Charlottesville: University Press of Virginia, 1983), 49–82.

64. Max L. Grivno, "'There Slavery Cannot Dwell': Agriculture and Labor in Northern Maryland, 1790–1860" (Ph.D. diss., University of Maryland, 2007), 75–76.

65. Although the migration of planters into western Maryland postdated the settlement of planters in the Virginia Piedmont, the movements were roughly analogous. For the movement of slavery into the Virginia Piedmont, see Philip D. Morgan and Michael L. Nichols, "Slaves in Piedmont Virginia," *William and Mary Quarterly*, 3rd ser., 46 (April 1989): 211–51; Michael L. Nichols, "Piedmont Plantations and Farms: Transplanting Tidewater Traditions?" *Magazine of Albemarle History* 49 (1991): 1–18.

66. The accounts of Barnes's estate are included in the Mason Account Book.

67. *MHHWA*, 20 November 1807.

68. See Paul G. E. Clemens, *The Atlantic Economy and Colonial Maryland's Eastern Shore: From Tobacco to Grain* (Ithaca: Cornell University Press, 1980); Lois Green Carr and Lorena S. Walsh, "Economic Diversification and Labor Organization in

the Chesapeake, 1650–1820," in *Work and Labor in Early America*, ed. Stephen Innes (Chapel Hill: University of North Carolina, 1988), 144–87.

69. The activities of Rochester and his associates were reconstructed from various documents in the Rochester Family Papers, 1780–1994, Rare Books and Special Collections Library, Rush Rhees Library, University of Rochester, Rochester, N.Y.

70. *MHHWA*, 26 August 1812, 24 October 1804; *MHETWA*, 8 May 1800. For similar examples, see *The Republican; or, Anti-Democrat* [Baltimore, Md.], 22 November 1802; *MHETWA*, 5 January 1805; *MHHWA*, 21 November 1810, 18 September 1811, 28 April 1813, 1 June 1814; *FTH*, 18 November 1820.

71. *MHETWA*, 8 May 1800; *MHHWA*, 31 October 1810, 16 January 1807. Similar examples abound in county records and newspapers. In 1798, the Washington County Court held an inquest for "Negro Mingo," who belonged to Calvert County slaveholder William Wells. Wells had hired Mingo to Washington County farmer Joseph Clark, who apparently allowed him to hire himself in the neighborhood. In 1812, the Washington County employer of "Negro Jim" reported that the bondsman had escaped and would likely return to the neighborhood of his master's plantation in St. Mary's County. See WASHINGTON COUNTY COURT (Judgment Record) Liber 1, ff. 16, MSA C1957-1, MdHR 11,898; *MHHWA*, 13 April 1812.

72. Petition of "Negro Rachel," 1792, Maryland Manuscripts Collection, UMCP. A notation on the reverse of Rachel's petition indicates that the county officials ordered her and Truman to appear in court, but the outcome of the case remains unclear.

73. Petition of Walter Butler, 24 November 1795, Maryland Manuscripts Collection, UMCP.

74. *MHHWA*, 21 August 1800.

75. Boerstler, "Journal," n.d. [1805].

76. George Buchanan, *An Oration upon the Moral and Political Evil of Slavery: Delivered at a Public Meeting of the Maryland Society for Promoting the Abolition of Slavery, and the Relief of Free Negroes, and Others Unlawfully Held in Bondage* (Baltimore: Edwards, 1793), 13, 16.

77. Bayard, *Travels*, 31–32.

78. On the antislavery activities of Methodists and Quakers in the early national Chesapeake, see Kenneth Carroll, "Religious Influences on the Manumission of Slaves in Caroline, Dorchester, and Talbot Counties," *Maryland Historical Magazine* 61 (June 1961): 176–97; Wolf, *Race and Liberty*, 7–16, 31–34, 51–54; Whitman, *Price of Freedom*, 96–97. FREDERICK COUNTY COURT (Land Records) Manumission of Elizabeth, Matilda, and Archibald, 1 January 1792, Liber WR 10, ff. 421, MSA C814-40, MdHR 40,341-2; [T. Alt] to Thos. Harrison, 21 May 1787, Loose Correspondence, Incoming, 1784–1795, Papers of the Pennsylvania Abolition Society, Historical Society of Pennsylvania, Philadelphia; Robert Emory, *History of the Discipline of the Methodist Episcopal Church* (New York: Lane and Tippett, 1845), 274–76, 277–78.

79. Minutes, Baltimore Circuit, 1794–1816, Minutes, Harford Quarterly Meeting, 1799–1830, both in Lovely Lane Museum and Archives (Methodist Historical Society), Baltimore.

80. Faux, *Memorable Days*, 142–43.

81. *The Port-Folio*, 26 December 1807.

82. In 1824, a resident of Washington County testified that John Berry had sold for about eight hundred dollars "as he was counted a valuable hand, being a good wagoner, and that other gentlemen had bid for him" (*Niles' Weekly Register* [Baltimore, Md.], 2 October 1824). Northern Maryland's newspapers abound with advertisements praising slaves' skills as wagoners. For examples, see *MHHWA*, 26 June 1807, 24 June 1808, 29 June 1814, 9 August 1815, 5 June 1816; *FTH*, 4 October 1823; *RB*, 18 December 1830.

83. *FTH*, 11 August 1807.

84. *Frederick Plain Dealer*, 19 August 1813.

85. *FTH*, 15 August 1815; *HM*, 29 June 1832.

86. *MH*,, 14 January 1818.

87. "An Act to Prevent the Inconveniences Arising from Slaves Being Permitted to Act as Free," 22 May 1787, in *Laws of Maryland, Made and Passed at a Session of Assembly, Begun and Held at the City of Annapolis on Tuesday the Tenth of April, in the Year of Our Lord One Thousand Seven Hundred and Eighty-seven* (Annapolis: Green, 1787).

88. "A Supplement to the Act, Entitled, An Act to Prevent the Inconveniences Arising from Slaves Being Permitted to Act as Free," 4 February 1818, in *Laws Made and Passed by the General Assembly of the State of Maryland, at a Session Begun and Held at the City of Annapolis, on Monday the First Day of December, Eighteen Hundred and Seventeen* (Annapolis: Green, 1818).

89. "Ten Dollars Reward" [broadside], 24 June 1793, Maryland Manuscripts Collection, UMCP.

90. *Potomack Guardian and Berkeley Advertiser* [Shepherdstown, Va.], 30 June 1796.

91. *Baltimore Telegraph and Daily Advertiser*, 10 August 1801.

92. Paul Finkelman, *An Imperfect Union: Slavery, Federalism, and Comity* (Chapel Hill: University of North Carolina Press, 1981), 47–49.

93. "The General Position of Lancaster County in Negro Slavery," *Papers Read before the Lancaster County Society* 15 (January 1911), 60. It is unclear whether Smith received her freedom.

94. Writ of Habeas Corpus, Republic v. John Roberts for Negro Hannah, 14 April 1787, Writ of Habeas Corpus, Republic v. John Roberts for Negroes George and Nancy, 14 April 1787, both in Writs of Habeas Corpus for Black Slaves and Indentured Servants, 1784–1787, Records of the Supreme Court of Pennsylvania, Eastern District (Record Group 33), Pennsylvania State Archives, Harrisburg.

95. *Negro David v. Porter* in Thomas Harris and John McHenry, comps., *Maryland Reports: Being a Series of the Most Important Law Cases Argued and Determined in the General Court and Court of Appeals of the State of Maryland, from May, 1797, to the End of 1799*, 5 vols. (Annapolis: Green, 1818), 4:418.

96. Lathan A. Windley, comp., *Runaway Slave Advertisements: A Documentary History from the 1730s to 1790*, 4 vols. (Westport, Conn.: Greenwood, 1983), 2:305–6, 326, 334.

97. *MHHWA*, 29 November 1815. The petitioners were probably protesting Pennsylvania's antikidnapping law, which was enacted in 1780 and strengthened in 1788. Under the revised law, anyone convicted of kidnapping a free black with the intention of selling him or her into slavery would face six months at hard labor and a one-

hundred-pound fine. See Thomas D. Morris, *Free Men All: The Personal Liberty Laws of the North, 1780–1861* (Baltimore: Johns Hopkins University Press, 1974), 25–27.

98. T. Stephen Whitman, *Challenging Slavery in the Chesapeake: Black and White Resistance to Human Bondage, 1775–1865* (Baltimore: Maryland Historical Society, 2007), 194.

99. Morris, *Free Men All*, 44–46, 49–53.

100. *FTH*, 7 June 1828.

101. Other historians of manumission in the early republic have reached similar conclusions. See Whitman, *Price of Freedom*; Wolf, *Race and Liberty*.

102. FREDERICK COUNTY COURT (Land Records) Manumission of Kate, Robert, and Sam, 11 April 1793, Liber WR 12, ff. 49, MSA C814-42, MdHR 40,341-4.

103. FREDERICK COUNTY COURT (Land Records) Manumission of Milly, Arch, Rachel, et al., 19 October 1795, Liber WR 13, ff. 584–85, MSA C814-43, MdHR 40,341-5.

104. FREDERICK COUNTY COURT (Land Records) Manumission of Sal and Silas, 12 August 1816, Liber JS 3, ff. 338, MSA C814-81, MdHR 40,341-43-1. Such agreements were not uncommon. In 1806, George Fryberger declared that his slave, Bill, would receive his freedom in 1813 unless he "become disobedient or abscond or absent himself at unreasonable times." Any such "turbulence or misbehavior" would result in Bill's manumission being delayed until 1818 (FREDERICK COUNTY COURT [Land Records] Manumission of Bill, 2 June 1806, Liber WR 29, ff. 94–95, MSA C814-59, MdHR 40,341-21).

105. FREDERICK COUNTY REGISTER OF WILLS (Wills) Will of Jacob Smith, 30 July 1817, Liber HS 2, ff. 98–99, MSA C898-9, MdHR 40,285-8.

106. FREDERICK, COUNTY COURT (Land Records) Manumission of Beck, Esther, Abraham, et al., 2 April 1793, Liber WR 11, ff. 461–62, MSA C814-41, MdHR 40,341-3.

107. FREDERICK COUNTY COURT (Land Records) Manumission of Jenny and Beck, 19 April 1813, Liber WR 44, ff. 185, MSA C814-74, MdHR 40,341-36.

108. FREDERICK COUNTY COURT (Land Records) Manumission of "Negro Kate," 1 January 1801, Liber WR 20, ff. 388–89, MSA C814-50, MdHR 40,341-12.

109. FREDERICK COUNTY COURT (Land Records) Purchase Agreement between Anthony Kimmell and Anna Israel, 27 August 1840, Liber HS 11, ff. 386–87, MSA C814-139, MdHR 40,341-101.

110. FREDERICK COUNTY COURT (Land Records) Purchase Agreement between John Walker and John Cregar, 29 December 1809, Liber WR 36, ff. 98–99, MSA C814-66, MdHR 40,341-28.

111. FREDERICK COUNTY COURT (Land Records) Agreement between Harry Peter and Roger B. Taney and Frederick Schley, 2 December 1817, Liber JS 5, ff. 850–51, MSA C814-83, MdHR 40,341-45.

112. FREDERICK COUNTY COURT (Land Records) Agreement between Ann Koon and Henry Keller, 19 June 1829, Liber JS 32, ff. 76–77, MSA C814-110, MdHR 40,341-72.

113. SPECIAL COLLECTIONS (Annan Collection of Clotworthy Birnie Papers) Upton Scott to Clotworthy Birnie, 18 January 1812; Clotworthy Birnie Diary, 25 January 1812; Upton Scott to C. Birnie, 8 March 1812, all in MSA SC 725, MdHR.

114. James A. Henretta has emphasized the powerful grip that independent, family-owned farms held on rural people's economic and social outlooks in "Families and Farms: *Mentalité* in Pre-Industrial America," *William and Mary Quarterly*, 3rd ser., 35 (January 1978): 3–32. Despite farmers' increased participation in commercial agriculture in the decades following the American Revolution, the household remained the basic unit of rural production well into the antebellum decades. See Christopher Clark, *The Roots of Rural Capitalism: Western Massachusetts, 1780–1860* (Ithaca: Cornell University Press, 1990), 59–117.

115. Drew R. McCoy, *The Elusive Republic: Political Economy in Jeffersonian America* (Chapel Hill: University of North Carolina Press, 1980), 13–17.

116. FREDERICK COUNTY COURT (Court Papers) Contract between George Dillenher and John Dillenher, 16 April 1770, MSA C773-15, MdHR 9723-1.

117. FREDERICK COUNTY REGISTER OF WILLS (Wills) Will of Peter Weedle, 27 October 1787, Liber GM3, ff. 455–56, MSA 898-4, MdHR 40,285-4.

118. HARFORD COUNTY REGISTER OF WILLS (Orphans Court Papers, Exhibits) Nathan Rigbie Ledger, 1772–1797, MSA C934-2, MdHR 17,109.

119. Washington, *Letters on Agriculture*, 75–76.

120. Martin Bruegel, *Farm, Shop, Landing: The Rise of a Market Society in the Hudson Valley, 1780–1860* (Durham, N.C.: Duke University Press, 2002), 20.

121. Benjamin Rush, *An Account of the Manners of the German Inhabitants of Pennsylvania, Written in 1798* (Philadelphia: Town, 1875), 24–25.

122. Governor Thomas Johnson to General George Washington, 21 September 1785, McPherson Family Papers, 1729–1842, MS 1714, MdHS.

123. Lorena S. Walsh, "Rural Africans in the Constitutional Era in Maryland, 1776–1810," *Maryland Historical Magazine* 84 (Winter 1989): 327–41.

124. Niemcewicz, *Travels*, 116; Boerstler, "Journal," 6 July 1785; *Washington Spy* [Hagerstown, Md.], 17 August 1796; *FTH*, 7 November 1807.

125. FREDERICK COUNTY CIRCUIT COURT (Miscellaneous Papers) Grand Jury Report, March 1798, MSA T189-2, MdHR.

126. For a discussion of Baltimore's almshouse, see Rockman, *Scraping By*, 194–230.

127. "An Act for the Relief of the Poor of Washington County," 30 December 1796, in *Votes and Proceedings of the Senate of the State of Maryland, November Session, 1796* (Annapolis: n.p., 1797).

128. "An Act to Incorporate Frederick-Town, in Frederick County," 14 January 1817, in *The Laws of Maryland from the End of the Year 1799*, ed. William Kilty et al., 5 vols. (Annapolis: Green, 1820).

129. "An Ordinance to Regulate the Police of Hagerstown and Its Additions," 29 May 1824, Mayor and Council Minutes, 1797–1827, Office of the City Clerk, Hagerstown, Md.

130. *MHHWA*, 13 August 1822.

131. Parkinson, *Experienced Farmer's Tour*, 27–32, 421–22.

132. Ibid., 172–74, 234, 422.

133. Ibid., i–ii.

134. Charles Brockden Brown, "An Account of Parkinson's Tour in America," *Literary Magazine and American Register* 5 (March 1806): 219–27.

135. John Beale Bordley, *Essays and Notes on Husbandry and Rural Affairs*, 2nd ed. (Philadelphia: Budd and Bartram, 1801), 387–91. For discussions of Bordley's writings and of cottagers in southern Pennsylvania, see Lucy Simler, "The Landless Worker: An Index of Economic and Social Change in Chester County, Pennsylvania, 1750–1820," *Pennsylvania Magazine of History and Biography* 109 (April 1990): 163–99; Lucy Simler, "Tenancy in Colonial Pennsylvania: The Case of Chester County," *William and Mary Quarterly*, 3rd ser., 41 (October 1986): 542–69. The relationship between emancipation in Pennsylvania and the growing number of cottagers is explored in Nash and Soderlund, *Freedom by Degrees*, 188–93. For a discussion of the connection between tenancy and slavery in the southern upcountry, see Wilma A. Dunaway, *Slavery in the American Mountain South* (New York: Cambridge University Press, 2003), 140–47.

136. Roger Johnson Account Books, 1806–1842, MS 496, MdHS.

137. Aquilla Hall Account Book, 1799–1812, Historical Society of Harford County, Bel Air, Md.

138. *FTH*, 6 March 1819.

139. Agreement between Robert N. Carman and Leven Hall, 20 March 1820, Robert N. Carman Memorandum Book, 1804–1836, Johnson Papers [unprocessed], MdHS.

140. Memorandum Book, 1827–1832, Mt. St. Mary's College and Seminary Archives, Emmitsburg, Md.

141. *FTH*, 22 August 1818.

142. Advertisements for farmhands or farm managers with wives were commonplace. See, for example, *Baltimore Patriot and Evening Advertiser*, 12 October 1813; *Baltimore Patriot and Mercantile Advertiser*, 25, 26 February 1819; *Baltimore Patriot*, 7 August 1820.

143. Seth Rockman, "Women's Labor, Gender Ideology, and Working-Class Households in Early Republic Baltimore," *Pennsylvania History* 66 (Supplemental Issue 1999): 174–200.

144. Petition of "Elizabeth," 1 February 1793, Frederick County Court Papers, Box 3, MdHR.

145. *FTH*, 11 June 1825, 5 October, 17 February 1816; *MHHWA*, 27 December 1817.

146. MARYLAND GOVERNOR AND COUNCIL RECORDS (Pardon Papers) Petition of John Woolford, n.d. [1812 or 1813], MSA S1061-16, MdHR 5401-16.

147. *Maryland Chronicle; or, The Universal Advertiser* [Frederick, Md.], 6 June 1787.

148. David Montgomery, *Citizen Worker: The Experience of Workers in the United States with Democracy and the Free Market during the Nineteenth Century* (New York: Cambridge University Press, 1993), 31–32; Cheesman A. Herrick, *White Servitude in Pennsylvania: Indentured and Redemption Labor in Colony and Commonwealth* (Philadelphia: McVey, 1926), 260–61; Eugene Irving McCormac, *White Servitude in Maryland, 1634–1820* (Baltimore: Johns Hopkins University Press, 1904), 221; *MHHWA*, 8 October 1817; *FTH*, 2 October 1819.

149. Fifteen of the estates belonged to slave owners (one of whom also owned an indentured servant) and included a total of 114 slaves. See FREDERICK COUNTY REGISTER OF WILLS (Inventories) Liber GM 2, MSA C807-5, MdHR 14,541.

150. McCormac, *White Servitude,* 219–24.

151. "An Act to Repeal Certain Parts of an Act, Entitled, An Act to Prevent Disabled and Superannuated Slaves Being Set Free . . . and for Certain Other Purposes," 14 December 1790, in *Laws of Maryland, Made and Passed at a Session of Assembly, Begun and Held at the City of Annapolis, on Monday the First of November, in the Year of Our Lord, 1790* (Annapolis: Green, 1791). The 1699 law this statute repealed had declared that "any white woman, either free or servant, that shall suffer herself to be begot with child by a negro or other slave or free negro . . . the issue or child or any such unnatural and inordinate copulations shall be servants until they arrive at the age of thirty one years" ("An Act Relating to Servants and Slaves," 22 July 1699, in *Archives of Maryland: Proceedings and Acts of the General Assembly of Maryland, March 1697/8–July 1699,* ed. William Hand Browne (Baltimore: Maryland Historical Society Press, 1902).

152. "An Act Relative to German and Swiss Redemptioners," 16 February 1818, in *Laws Made and Passed by the General Assembly . . . Eighteen Hundred and Seventeen.*

153. Steinfeld, *Invention,* 166–69.

154. SPECIAL COLLECTIONS (Annan Collection of Clotworthy Birnie Papers) Clotworthy Birnie Diary, 12 December 1811, 4 July, 9 August 1812, MSA SC 725, MdHR.

155. The court agreed that Boswell had been ill-used and ordered his former master to make additional compensation. See FREDERICK COUNTY COURT (Petitions) Petition of Wm. Boswell, n.d. [1788], MSA C847-1, MdHR 40,295-1/50; Susannah Warfield Diary, 4 January 1849, Warfield Family Diaries, 1845–1885, MS 760, MdHS; *Washington Spy* [Hagerstown, Md.], 26 September 1792. That year, Thomas Tyler brought his bound Irishwoman, Ann Dunn, into court with her "mulatto bastard child" (FREDERICK COUNTY COURT [Minutes] 1773–1775, MSA C831-8, MdHR 6832).

156. Thomas Cooper, *Some Information Respecting America* (London: Johnson, 1794), 20; Isaac Weld Jr., *Travels through the United States of North America and Canada, and the Provinces of Upper and Lower Canada, during the Years 1795, 1796, and 1797,* 2 vols. (London: Stockdale, 1807), 1:29; SPECIAL COLLECTIONS (Annan Collection of Clotworthy Birnie Papers) Clotworthy Birnie Jr. to Clotworthy Birnie, 26 August 1819, MSA SC 725, MdHR.

157. *MHETWA,* 31 August 1803; WASHINGTON COUNTY COURT (Dockets and Minutes), February 1804, MSA C3004-6, MdHR; *FTH,* 14 June 1817; *Baltimore Patriot and Mercantile Advertiser,* 8 March 1819.

158. Robert E. Cray Jr., "Remembering the USS *Chesapeake:* The Politics of Maritime Death and Impressment," *Journal of the Early Republic* 25 (Fall 2005): 445–74.

159. *State Papers and Publick Documents of the United States, from the Accession of George Washington to the Presidency, Exhibiting a Complete View of Our Foreign Relations since That Time* (Boston: Wait, 1819), 6:21–25; Cray, "Remembering the USS *Chesapeake,*" 465, 472–74.

160. *Butler and Others against Delaplaine,* in *Reports of Cases Adjudged in the Supreme Court of Pennsylvania,* comp. Thomas Sergeant and William Rawle Jr. (Philadelphia: Small, 1823), 7:378–86.

161. *FTH,* 13 August 1808.

162. Ibid., 20 August 1808.

163. Ibid., 2 October 1813.

Chapter 2. "A Strange Reverse of Fortune": Panic, Depression, and the Transformation of Labor

1. *FTH*, 2 July 1831.

2. Anne Royall, *The Black Book; or, A Continuation of Travels, in the United States*, 2 vols. (Washington, D.C.: the Author, 1828), 1:276.

3. Thomas Hamilton, *Men and Manners in America* (Philadelphia: Carey, Lea, and Blanchard, 1833), 288.

4. James W. C. Pennington, *The Fugitive Blacksmith; or, Events in the History of James W. C. Pennington, Pastor of a Presbyterian Church, New York, Formerly a Slave in the State of Maryland*, 3rd ed. (London: Gilpin, 1850), 70.

5. Mathias Bartgis Journal, 24 August 1819, HSFC.

6. Thomas Kennedy to Samuel Sprigg, 19 September 1822, Thomas Kennedy Papers, 1820–1826, MS 1337, MdHS.

7. George Terry Sharrer, "Flour Milling and the Growth of Baltimore" (Ph.D. diss., University of Maryland, 1975), 146–68.

8. *MHHWA*, 25 October 1815, 31 December 1817. On the actions of Baltimore's financial community during the 1810s, see Sharrer, "Flour Milling," 237–40.

9. Thos. S. Lee to Eliza Horsey, 24 October 1813, Outerbridge Horsey Collection of Lee, Horsey, and Carroll Family Papers, 1684–1843, MS 1974, MdHS; *Political Examiner* [Frederick, Md.], 1 November 1815; *Bartgis's Republican Gazette* [Frederick, Md.], 3 January 1818; *MHHWA*, 21 January 1818; *The Torch Light* [Hagerstown, Md.], 28 July 1818.

10. Sharrer, "Flour Milling," 239–40; Samuel Rezneck, "The Depression of 1819: A Social History," *American Historical Review* 39 (October 1933): 28–47; Gary L. Browne, "Baltimore and the Panic of 1819," in *Law, Society, and Politics in Early Maryland*, ed. Aubrey C. Land, Lois Green Carr, and Edward C. Papenfuse (Baltimore: Johns Hopkins University Press, 1977), 212–27; Samuel F. Gregory to Lavina Richmond, 1 January 1819, Gregory Family Papers, 1817–1833, MS 416, MdHS.

11. *AF*, 9 June 1819.

12. SPECIAL COLLECTIONS (Annan Collection of Clotworthy Birnie Papers) Clotworthy Birnie Jr. to Clotworthy Birnie, 28 June 1819, MSA SC 725, MdHR.

13. Sharrer, "Flour Milling," 326.

14. Return of Ignatius Davis (Frederick County, Md.), 1820 U.S. Census of Manufactures, NARA.

15. Return of Jno. Christian Hover (Frederick County, Md.) and Return of John Conch (Frederick County, Md.), both in 1820 U.S. Census of Manufactures, NARA.

16. Samuel F. Gregory to Lavina Richmond, 7 June 1819, Gregory Family Papers.

17. *TPA*, 18 January 1820.

18. J. Jakob Rutlinger, "Day Book on a Journey to North America in the Year 1823," in *The Old Land and the New: The Journals of Two Swiss Families in America in the 1820s*, ed. and trans. Robert H. Billigmeier and Fred A. Picard (Minneapolis: University of Minnesota Press, 1965), 228–29.

19. Bartgis Journal, 25 August 1819.

20. WASHINGTON COUNTY CIRCUIT COURT (Docket and Minutes), October 1810, MSA T3063-19, MdHR; WASHINGTON COUNTY CIRCUIT COURT (Docket and Minutes), October 1814, MSA T3063-27, MdHR; WASHINGTON COUNTY CIRCUIT COURT (Docket and Minutes), November 1819, MSA T3063-37, MdHR. The severity of the crisis confronting debtors in 1819 left a powerful impression on the region's residents. In 1829, a Hagerstown editor remembered that "ten years ago the number of actions [for debt] were at least 600." Having survived the "effects of speculation in land and the excessive emission of paper money," the farmers had now embraced a "more cautious and economic mode of living" (*Farmers' Register and Maryland Herald*, 17 November 1829).

21. Kennedy was one of the bill's chief supporters. In an attempt to garner the support of his colleagues from the state's tobacco counties, whose primary staple had not suffered such a dramatic drop, Kennedy conceded that many northern Marylanders had "speculated largely" but argued that "if the legislature did not interpose, things would find their level, but it would be such a level as an earthquake or a hurricane would produce on a large city" (*MHHWA*, 8 February 1820). For the act's provisions, see "An Additional Supplement to the Act, Entitled, An Act for Regulating the Mode of Staying Executions, and Repealing the Acts of Assembly Therein Mentioned," 12 February 1820, in *Laws Made and Passed by the General Assembly of the State of Maryland at a Session Begun and Held at the City of Annapolis on Monday the 6th Day of December 1819* (Annapolis: Green, 1820).

22. David Barclay to John Mantz, 22 April 1820, John Mantz Letterbook, 1811–1820, Quynn Family Collection, 1796–1899, MS 1033, MdHS.

23. Return of John Mantz (Frederick County, Md.), 1820 U.S. Census of Manufactures, NARA.

24. Bartgis Journal, 1 September 1819.

25. Return of John Mantz (Frederick County, Md.), 1820 U.S. Census of Manufactures, NARA.

26. *FTH*, 20 March 1819.

27. Ibid., 19 February 1820.

28. Jacob Englebrecht, *The Diary of Jacob Englebrecht, 1818–1882*, ed. William R. Quynn, trans. James Lowery, 2 vols. (Frederick, Md.: Historical Society of Frederick County, 2002), 1:40.

29. John Blackford to Uriah Blue, 2 December 1824, Papers of the Blackford, Grove, Mayer Family, 1767–1984, MS 1063, MdHS.

30. *Farmer's Repository* [Charlestown, Va.], 7 June 1820.

31. The impact of the Hessian fly on the nation's economy is discussed in Brooke Hunter, "Creative Destruction: The Forgotten Legacy of the Hessian Fly," in *The Economy of Early America: Historical Perspectives and New Directions*, ed. Cathy Matson (University Park: Pennsylvania State University Press, 2006), 236–62.

32. *RB*, 14 April 1832.

33. "Memorial of the Washington County Bank, at Williamsport, Maryland, in Favor of the Recharter of the Bank of the United States, March 21, 1834," *Senate Documents*, 23rd Cong., 1st sess., no. 195, serial 240.

34. *RB*, 18 June 1836.

35. On 1 July 1836, Englebrecht observed that "the crops will be very short generally in our neighborhood," in consequence of which many farmers had decided not to harvest their wheat. He recorded a conversation with one drover who said that "on his way down he had been offered several wheat fields to pasture his cattle in" (Englebrecht, *Diary*, 1:525; *RB*, 18 June 1836).

36. *RB*, 10, 14 September 1836.

37. Ibid., 15 April 1837.

38. George F. Heyser Harvest Rolls, 1783, 1822–1855, 1861–1865, MS 2191, MdHS.

39. *FTH*, 18 September 1819.

40. W. Faux, *Memorable Days in America: Being a Journal of a Tour to the United States* (London: Simpkin and Marshall, 1823), 159–60.

41. SPECIAL COLLECTIONS (Annan Collection of Clotworthy Birnie Papers) Clotworthy Birnie Diary, 4 March 1820, Andrew Thompson to Clotworthy Birnie, 25 May 1820, MSA SC 725, MdHR.

42. *MHHWA*, 13 June 1820.

43. *Niles' Weekly Register* [Baltimore, Md.], 24 July 1819.

44. Samuel F. Gregory to Lavina Richmond, 9 July 1819, Gregory Family Papers.

45. *Baltimore Patriot*, 13 July 1820.

46. Minutes, 5 January 1820, Lancaster Directors of the Poor and House of Employment, Lancaster County Historical Society, Lancaster, Pa.; Minutes, 26 May 1821, Board of Commissioners of Frederick County, Minute Book, 1803–1826, HSFC; FREDERICK COUNTY TRUSTEES OF THE POOR (Proceedings) 16 May 1823, MSA C854-1, MdHR 19,461-1.

47. FREDERICK COUNTY COURT (Land Records) Liber JS 10-33, MdHR; WASHINGTON COUNTY COURT (Land Records) Liber DD-HH, MdHR. Using land records to investigate the interstate slave trade is problematic, as many transactions involving slaves were never recorded in the county courts. For example, when several men accused of shooting a fugitive slave petitioned the governor for a pardon, their appeal stated that the victim, "Negro George," had been sold six times during the previous decade, but none of those transactions were recorded in the Frederick County land records. See MARYLAND GOVERNOR AND COUNCIL (Pardon Papers) Petition of John Smith, James Mumford, James Merryman, et al., 1818, MSA S1061-18, MdHR 5401-18. Thus, the number of slaves sold to the Deep South is almost certainly higher than these records indicate. For discussions of the problems inherent in using land records to study the domestic slave trade, see Herman Freudenberger and Jonathan B. Pritchett, "The Domestic United States Slave Trade: New Evidence," *Journal of Interdisciplinary History* 21 (Winter 1991): 447–77; Steven Deyle, *Carry Me Back: The Domestic Slave Trade in American Life* (New York: Oxford University Press, 2005), 283–96.

48. SPECIAL COLLECTIONS (Annan Collection of Clotworthy Birnie Papers) Andrew Thomas to Clotworthy Birnie, 12 October 1818, MSA SC 725, MdHR.

49. Otho Lawrence to Dr. John Hays, 12 September 1832, Joseph Chaplin and John C. Hays Papers, 1741–1891, Special Collections, Duke University Library, Durham, N.C.

50. *Price vs. Reid* (1828) in *Reports of Cases Argued and Determined in the Court of Appeals of Maryland in 1827, 1828, and 1829,* comp. Thomas Harris and Richard W. Gill (Annapolis: Green, 1829), 291–95.

51. Samuel Gregory to Lavina Richmond, 9 July 1819, Gregory Family Papers.

52. Tilghman described his farming operations in a letter dated 1 June 1819 (*AF,* 18 June 1819).

53. In 1816, Tilghman sought employers or purchasers for "several valuable Negro Men, Women, and Boys" (*MHHWA,* 4 December 1816). These efforts seem to have intensified as the economy worsened. In 1820, he offered to hire out "four Negro Men and Boys" and "two small Boys and three Girls" (*MH,* 9 May 1820). He posted a similar announcement two years later (*MH,* 8 January 1822). Tilghman also extended generous terms to those wishing to purchase his slaves. In 1817, he offered two years' credit to encourage anyone interested in purchasing "several young negro women" (*MHHWA,* 25 April 1817).

54. Pennington, *Fugitive Blacksmith,* 6.

55. Frisby Tilghman to James Hollyday, 4 November 1826, Hollyday Family Papers, 1711–1934, MS 1508, MdHS.

56. Frisby Tilghman to Susan Hollyday, 14 October 1827, Hollyday Family Papers.

57. Wm. Darne to Chas. Carroll of Carrollton, 26 October 1821, Charles Carroll of Carrollton Papers, MdHS.

58. Wm. Darne to Chas. Carroll of Carrollton, 16 March 1827, Wm. Darne to Chas. Carroll of Carrollton, 3 October 1827, both in Carroll-McTavish Papers, 1652–1867, MS 220, MdHS.

59. Of the 1,088 slaves sold from Frederick and Washington Counties whose sex can be determined, 560 (52 percent) were male and 528 (48 percent) were female.

60. FREDERICK COUNTY COURT (Land Records) Liber JS 10-33, MdHR; WASHINGTON COUNTY COURT (Land Records) Liber DD-HH, MdHR.

61. Lewis Charlton, *Sketch of the Life of Mr. Lewis Charlton, and Reminiscences of Slavery,* ed. Edward Everett Brown (Portland, Me.: Daily Press, n.d.), 5; Frederick Bancroft, *Slave Trading in the Old South* (1931; Columbia: University of South Carolina Press, 1996), 65; Thomas J. C. Williams, *The History of Washington County, Maryland, from the Earliest Settlements to the Present Time, including a History of Hagerstown,* 2 vols. (1906; Baltimore: Regional, 1968), 1:251. Incidents of self-mutilation and suicide were not uncommon. On 21 January 1836, Englebrecht noted that an imprisoned fugitive slave had severed four of his fingers while awaiting sale to the "Soul Drivers" (Englebrecht, *Diary,* 1:513). A similar case of self-mutilation was recorded in the *Banner of Liberty* [Liberty-Town, Md.], 13 June 1856. For the suicide in Sharpsburg, see *Baltimore Sun,* 10 October 1859.

62. John Knight to Wm. M. Beall, 27 January, 7 February, 10 November 1844, 7 May 1845, Wm. M. Beall to John Knight, 9 July 1844, all in John Knight Papers, 1784–1891, Special Collections, Duke University Library, Durham, N.C.

63. Answer of John Lee, 1 November 1837, John Lee to Outerbridge Horsey, 28 February 1835, both in Lee Family Papers, Special Collections, Duke University Library, Durham, N.C.

64. William Still, *The Underground Rail Road: A Record of Facts, Authentic Narratives,*

Letters, &c., Narrating the Hardships, Hair-Breadth Escapes, and Death Struggles of the Slaves in Their Efforts for Freedom, as Related by Themselves and Others or Witnessed by the Author: Together with Sketches of Some of the Largest Stockholders and Most Liberal Aiders and Advisers of the Road (Philadelphia: Still, 1883), 262, 396.

65. Rutlinger, "Day Book," 233.

66. *MH,* 5 November 1822.

67. Ibid., 22 January 1822.

68. MARYLAND GOVERNOR AND COUNCIL (Pardon Papers) Petition of John Smith, James Mumford, James Merryman, et al., 1818, MSA S1061-18, MdHR 5401-18.

69. Annual Message of Governor Samuel Stevens Jr. to the Legislature, December 1825, Maryland Governor and Council Letterbook, 1819–1834, MdHR.

70. *Genius of Universal Emancipation,* 21 January 1826; James Raymond, *Prize Essay on the Comparative Economy of Free and Slave Labor in Agriculture* (Frederick, Md.: Thomson, 1827), 12.

71. FREDERICK COUNTY TRUSTEES OF THE POOR (Proceedings) 1822–1838, MSA C854-1, MdHR 19,461-1.

72. *FTH,* 25 March 1820; *TPA,* 26 June, 31 July 1821.

73. In 1817, Frederick's municipal government enacted an ordinance against such people, declaring that anyone who lacked visible means of support was to be confined to the county workhouse for thirty days (*FTH,* 12 April 1817).

74. Samuel F. Gregory to Lavina Richmond, 3 May 1817, Gregory Family Papers.

75. Bartgis Journal, 2 September 1819. Later that year, an Englishman traveling along the National Road in Washington County was shocked to discover a "little tavern, where, though it is Sunday, all is smoke and fire, and Bacchus is the God" (Faux, *Memorable Days,* 163).

76. Violent strikes among the railroad's workmen were not unusual (Matthew E. Mason, "'The Hands Here Are Disposed to Be Turbulent': Unrest among the Irish Trackmen of the Baltimore and Ohio Railroad, 1829–1851," *Labor History* 39 [August 1998]: 253–72). On efforts to curb the workers' drinking, see *Fifth Annual Report of the President and Directors to the Stockholders of the Baltimore and Ohio Railroad Company* (Baltimore: Wooddy, 1831), 113–15; *Sixth Annual Report of the President and Directors to the Stockholders of the Baltimore and Ohio Railroad Company* (Baltimore: Wooddy, 1832), 73.

77. *MH,* 7 November 1820. Although concerns about such rural gatherings assumed a special urgency during the 1810s and 1820s, they were not necessarily new. In 1794, for example, the Frederick County Court had indicted several men for gathering at a rural blacksmith shop and spending six hours in a "riotous, tumultuous, and unlawful manner" (Indictment of Frederick Graff and "divers other persons," November 1794, Frederick County Court Papers, Box 60, MdHR). Five years later, the court indicted John Buckey for "selling liquor at races at Carroll's Manor . . . without a permit" (Indictment of John Buckey, November 1799, Frederick County Court Papers, Box 3).

78. *TPA,* 15 June 1819.

79. Bartgis Journal, 28 August 1819.

80. In Carroll County, revivals often resulted in indictments for selling liquor to

attendees. In September 1853, the county court indicted seven people for selling spirits at one revival. Despite the fifty-dollar fine imposed on each of the three people convicted of the offense, the court found itself grappling with the same problem in September 1858, when it indicted six people for peddling alcohol liquor at a camp meeting (Carroll County Circuit Court, Criminal Docket, 1856–1863, MdHR). The general reputation of camp meetings does not seem to have improved during the antebellum decades. When announcing a revival outside Hagerstown in 1847, an editor expressed his hope that the townsfolk "will not be annoyed, as has too often heretofore been the case, by the ill-behaviour of the large crowds which usually attend such gatherings" (*HF*, 25 August 1847).

81. "Temperance," *Evangelical Magazine and Gospel Advocate*, 18 May 1833, 160; "Harvest Drink," *Southern Planter*, October 1842, 234.

82. Council to Abraham Faw, 7 December 1779, Journal and Correspondence of the Council of Maryland, 1779–1780, Liber CC, ff. 45, MdHR. Blacks continued to congregate in the dilapidated barracks and powder magazine through the 1820s. In 1825, the General Assembly authorized the sale of the abandoned buildings, noting that they had "almost constantly been . . . occupied by free persons of color, which causes complaints by neighboring citizens" (Untitled Resolution, 25 January 1825, in *Laws Made and Passed by the General Assembly of the State of Maryland, at a Session Begun and Held at the City of Annapolis, on Monday the Sixth Day of December, Eighteen-Hundred and Twenty-four* [Annapolis: Hughes, 1825]).

83. FREDERICK COUNTY CIRCUIT COURT (Miscellaneous Papers) Grand Jury Report, March 1798, Box 2, MSA T-189-1, MdHR.

84. *The Port-Folio*, 19 December 1807.

85. *Bartgis's Republican Gazette* [Frederick, Md.], 13 June 1818.

86. *MHHWA*, 23 August 1815.

87. "An Ordinance for Preventing Immoral Practices and Disorderly Assemblages of People of Color within Hagerstown and Its Additions," 4 May 1818, Mayor and Council Minutes, Office of the City Clerk, Hagerstown, Md.

88. "A Supplement to an Ordinance for Preventing Immoral Practices and Disorderly Assemblages of People of Color within Hagerstown and Its Additions," 20 May 1820, Mayor and Council Minutes, Office of the City Clerk, Hagerstown, Md.

89. *FTH*, 1 September 1821.

90. Ibid., 7 June 1828.

91. Pennington, *Fugitive Blacksmith*, 67.

92. *MHHWA*, 23 March 1814.

93. *FTH*, 8 August 1818.

94. *Patriot and Commercial Advertiser* [Baltimore], 5 February 1823.

95. SPECIAL COLLECTIONS (Annan Collection of Clotworthy Birnie Papers) Geo. Baer to Clotworthy Birnie, 2 October 1818, Andrew Thomas to Clotworthy Birnie, 5 October 1818, MSA SC 725, MdHR.

96. SPECIAL COLLECTIONS (Annan Collection of Clotworthy Birnie Papers) Robert Lyles to Clotworthy Birnie, 10 November 1818, MSA SC 725, MdHR.

97. GOVERNOR AND COUNCIL (Pardon Record) Pardon of "Negro Jacob," 25 September 1818, MSA S1107-3, MdHR 1932.

98. The statute's provisions for conducting slave sales were confusing. The law stated that slaves would be sold "for the benefit of the state or county" and that they would "be valued and paid for, as is now or shall hereafter be directed by law." Yet the statute made no provisions for conducting these sales, nor did it say how the proceeds were to be divided ("An Act to Repeal All Such Parts of the Laws of This State as Authorize the Courts of Law to Sentence Negro or Mulatto Slaves, or Free Negroes or Mulattoes, to Undergo a Confinement in the Penitentiary," 18 February 1819, in *Laws Made and Passed by the General Assembly of the State of Maryland, at a Session Begun and Held at the City of Annapolis, on Monday the 17th Day of December, 1818* [Annapolis: Green, 1819]).

99. After deducting the necessary expenses, the proceeds of the sale would be paid to the slave's owner ("An Act to Provide for the Recapture of Fugitive Slaves," 16 February 1839, in *Laws Made and Passed by the General Assembly of the State of Maryland, at a Session Begun and Held at Annapolis, on Monday, the 30th Day of December, 1838* [Annapolis: Hughes, 1839]).

100. Report of Dr. Eli Ayers, in Minutes of the Board of Managers, 5 August 1831, Maryland Colonization Society Papers, 1827–1871, MS 571, MdHS; *AF,* 16 July 1819.

101. *AF,* 25 May 1827, 15 September 1826; *Niles' Weekly Register* [Baltimore], 15 October 1831.

102. Report of Dr. Eli Ayers, in Minutes of the Board of Managers, 5 August 1831, Maryland Colonization Society Papers; *AF,* 16 July 1819, 8 June 1827.

103. *Genius of Universal Emancipation,* [DATE?] 1823, 90.

104. *AF,* April 1846.

105. Penelope Campbell, "Some Notes on Frederick County's Participation in the Maryland Colonization Scheme," *Maryland Historical Magazine* 66 (Spring 1971): 55.

106. Ibid., 51–59; William McKinney to John B. Latrobe, 30 October 1833, Richard Dorsey to Wm. McKinney, 20 December 1833, James Reid to John B. Latrobe, 31 January 1835, all in Loose Correspondence, Maryland Colonization Society Papers.

107. Joseph M. Getty, ed., *The Carroll Record: Histories of Northwestern Carroll County Communities* (Westminster, Md.: Historical Society of Carroll County, 1994), 65; *Journal of the Proceedings of the House of Delegates of the State of Maryland* (Annapolis: Hughes, 1829), 427; John Switzer and Wm. Hughes to "Sir," 15 September 1831, Davis Richardson Papers, 1720–1885, Special Collections, Duke University, Durham, N.C.

108. *The Liberator,* 14 June 1839.

109. *Hagerstown News,* n.d., quoted in *The National Era* [Washington, D.C.], 28 April 1853.

110. J. H. Cocke Jr. to J. H. Cocke, 29 August 1828, Cocke Family Papers, 1794–1981, Virginia Historical Society, Richmond.

111. *TPA,* 5 April 1832.

112. *HFT,* 8 June 1859; *Middletown Valley Register* [Middletown, Md.], 27 May 1859. For a discussion of the 1859 slaveholders' conventions and their consequences, see Barbara Jeanne Fields, *Slavery and Freedom on the Middle Ground: Maryland during the Nineteenth Century* (New Haven: Yale University Press, 1985), 63–89.

113. *Frederick Examiner,* 1 June 1859; *Middletown Valley Register* [Middletown, Md.], 8 June 1860; "An Act . . . Prohibiting Manumissions of Negro Slaves and Authoriz-

ing Free Negroes to Renounce Their Freedom," 10 March 1860, in *Laws of the State of Maryland, Made and Passed at a Session of the General Assembly, Begun and Held at Annapolis on Wednesday the 4th of January and Ended on Saturday the 10th of March 1860* (Annapolis: Riley, 1860). Of the ninety-six delayed manumissions recorded in 1860, twenty-three specified terms longer than twenty years (FREDERICK COUNTY CIRCUIT COURT [Land Records], Liber BGF 5, MSA T128-26, MdHR).

Chapter 3. "There Are Objections to Black and White, but One Must Be Chosen": Managing Farms and Farmhands in Antebellum Maryland

1. Arthur W. Machen to Lewis H. Machen, 31 December 1845, 3 March 1847, Lewis H. Machen to Arthur W. Machen, 8 July 1846, 8 January 1847, all in Lewis H. Machen Family Papers, 1802–1938, Manuscripts Division, Library of Congress, Washington, D.C. In 1850 Machen's slaveholdings consisted of three men (aged forty-five, thirty-five, and twelve) and two women (aged twenty-two and eighteen) (1850 U.S. Census, Schedule 2 [Slaves], Fairfax County, Va., NARA).

2. Machen's farm did not produce tobacco or any of the traditional plantation staples. In 1850, his 230 improved acres yielded 800 bushels of wheat, 1,200 bushels of Indian corn, 600 bushels of oats, and 40 tons of hay. Machen also owned livestock valued at $2,120 (5 milk cows, 4 oxen, 11 horses, 28 cattle, 150 sheep, and 20 swine) (1850 U.S. Census, Schedule 4 [Agriculture], Fairfax County, Va., NARA).

3. John L. Carey, *Slavery in Maryland Briefly Considered* (Baltimore: Murphy, 1845), 26–30.

4. Carville V. Earle, "A Staple Interpretation of Slavery and Free Labor," *Geographical Review* 68 (January 1978): 51–65. See also Paul G. E. Clemens, *The Atlantic Economy and Colonial Maryland's Eastern Shore: From Tobacco to Grain* (Ithaca: Cornell University Press, 1980). A corollary to this argument is that landowners decided against slavery because it impeded agricultural reform. Proponents of this interpretation argue that farmers could not implement crop rotation, purchase fertilizer, or introduce improved machinery until they sold their unneeded slaves (Avery O. Craven, *Soil Exhaustion as a Factor in the Agricultural History of Maryland and Virginia, 1606–1860* [Urbana: University of Illinois Press, 1925], 114; Eugene D. Genovese, *The Political Economy of Slavery: Studies in the Economy and Society of the Slave South* [New York: Vintage, 1967], 136–41). These interpretations continue to have adherents. See, for example, Todd Harold Barnett, "The Evolution of 'North' and 'South': Settlement and Slavery on America's Sectional Border, 1650–1810" (Ph.D. diss., University of Pennsylvania, 1993), 84–121, 178–204. Still, over the past two decades, a steady trickle of studies has eroded the foundations of the staple interpretation. For studies demonstrating slavery's compatibility with wheat production, see Kenneth E. Koons, "'The Staple of Our Country': Wheat in the Rural Farm Economy of the Nineteenth Century Valley of Virginia," in *After the Backcountry: Rural Life in the Great Valley of Virginia*, ed. Kenneth E. Koons and Warren R. Hofstra (Knoxville: University of Tennessee Press, 2003), 3–15; John T. Schlotterbeck, "Plantation and Farm: Social and Economic Change in Orange and Greene Counties, Virginia, 1717 to 1860"

(Ph.D. diss., Johns Hopkins University, 1980), 161–211; James R. Irwin, "Exploring the Affinity of Wheat and Slavery in the Virginia Piedmont," *Explorations in Economic History* 25 (July 1998): 295–322; Gavin Wright, "Slavery and American Agricultural History," *Agricultural History* 77 (Fall 2003): 527–52.

5. During this eight-year period, Machen augmented his standing force (his family and his slaves) with six white men employed under annual contracts; a free black man and eight white men, who labored under short-term contracts; three white and four enslaved men who worked as day laborers; a free black woman who seems to have been a domestic servant and dairymaid; and at least four slave men hired by the year (Lewis H. Machen Account Book, 1837–1857, Machen Family Papers).

6. John Blackford Journals, 5 October 1837, Headquarters of the Chesapeake and Ohio Canal National Park, Sharpsburg, Md.

7. Arthur W. Machen Jr., *Letters of Arthur W. Machen with Biographical Sketch* (Baltimore: the Author, 1917), 31–33.

8. Ramsey McHenry to James McHenry Boyd, 9 April 1839, James McHenry Boyd Correspondence, 1838–1873, Ms. 1509, MdHS.

9. Over the past two decades, historians have problematized our understanding of free labor, demonstrating that its halting, often uneven development was influenced by a constellation of economic, political, and social forces. For an overview of this literature, see Eric Foner, "The Idea of Free Labor in Nineteenth-Century America," in *Free Soil, Free Labor, Free Men: The Ideology of the Republican Party before the Civil War* (New York: Oxford University Press, 1995), ix–xxxix. The construction of the ideological and legal underpinnings of free labor during the early national period and the antebellum decades is discussed in Robert J. Steinfeld, *The Invention of Free Labor: The Employment Relation in English and American Law and Culture, 1350–1870* (Chapel Hill: University of North Carolina Press, 1991); James D. Schmidt, *Free to Work: Labor Law, Emancipation, and Reconstruction, 1815–1880* (Athens: University of Georgia Press, 1998); Christopher L. Tomlins, *Law, Labor, and Ideology in the Early American Republic* (New York: Cambridge University Press, 1993); Amy Dru Stanley, *From Bondage to Contract: Wage Labor, Marriage, and the Market in the Age of Slave Emancipation* (New York: Cambridge University Press, 1998).

10. James Raymond, *Prize Essay on the Comparative Economy of Free and Slave Labor in Agriculture* (Frederick, Md.: Thomson, 1827), 3–4.

11. Works Progress Administration, *Slave Narratives: A Folk History of Slavery in the United States from Interviews with Former Slaves*, vol. 8, *Maryland Narratives* (Washington, D.C.: U.S. Government Printing Office, 1941), 44.

12. Unless otherwise noted, the discussion of agricultural work routines in the following paragraphs is drawn from James Crawford Neilson, Priestford Farm Journal, 1824–1831, in James Crawford Neilson Record Books, 1798–1900, MS 613, MdHS; Liliendale Farm Diary, 1827–1832, MS 2567, MdHS; Stephen Boyd, Farm Account Book, 1828–1840, Vertical File, MdHS; Fletcher M. Green, ed., *Ferry Hill Plantation Journal, January 4, 1838–January 15, 1839* (Chapel Hill: University of North Carolina Press, 1961); Harry Dorsey Gough, Account Book, 1851–1852, MdHS; Richard Gittings, Roslin Farm Account Book, 1857–1858, in Richard Gittings Account Books, 1764–1888, MS 391, MdHS.

13. *Jacob Gruber's American Farmers' Almanack, for the Year of Our Lord 1833* (Hagerstown, Md.: Gruber, 1833).

14. *Emmitsburg Chronicle*, [January 1908], Vertical File, Emmitsburg Area Historical Society, Emmitsburg, Md.

15. Women's agricultural work routines are discussed in Joan M. Jensen, *Loosening the Bonds: Mid-Atlantic Farm Women, 1750–1850* (New Haven: Yale University Press, 1986), 36–56; John Mack Faragher, *Sugar Creek: Life on the Illinois Prairie* (New Haven: Yale University Press, 1986), 104–18; Donald L. Winters, *Tennessee Farming, Tennessee Farmers: Antebellum Agriculture in the Upper South* (Knoxville: University of Tennessee Press, 1994), 122–27.

16. J. Jakob Rutlinger, "Day Book on a Journey to North America in the Year 1823," in *The Old Land and the New: The Journals of Two Swiss Families in America in the 1820s*, ed. and trans. Robert H. Billigmeier and Fred A. Picard (Minneapolis: University of Minnesota Press, 1965), 224.

17. James Pearre, "Memoirs," n.d., James Pearre Collection, 1831–1880, MS 1038, MdHS.

18. *TPA*, 27 January 1830.

19. *Catoctin Whig*, n.d., quoted in *HFT*, 4 July 1854.

20. *HFT*, 12 July 1854.

21. *Frederick Herald*, 28 June 1859. A Frederick County resident made a similar observation, noting that a mechanical reaper did "the work of a dozen men" at harvest (James Pearre, "Memoirs," n.d., James Pearre Collection).

22. Jacob Miller to Catherine Amelia Houser, 1 July 1859, Miller Family Letter Collection, Antietam National Battlefield, Sharpsburg, Md.

23. Bloomsbury Farm Account Book, 1849–1862, MS 6, MdHS; Gittings Account Books.

24. Such segmentation has been described in the agricultural workforces of New England and the Middle Atlantic. See Winifred B. Rothenberg, "Structural Change in the Farm Labor Force: Contract Labor in Massachusetts Agriculture, 1750–1865," in *Strategic Factors in Nineteenth Century American Economic History: A Volume to Honor Robert W. Fogel*, ed. Claudia Goldin and Hugh Rockoff (Chicago: University of Chicago Press, 1992), 105–32; Richard B. Lyman Jr., "'What Is Done in My Absence?': Levi Lincoln's Oakham, Massachusetts, Farm Workers, 1807–20," *Proceedings of the American Antiquarian Society* 99 (April 1989): 151–87; Jack Larkin, "'Labor Is the Great Thing in Farming': Farm Laborers of the Ward Family of Shrewsbury, Massachusetts, 1787–1860," *Proceedings of the American Antiquarian Society* 99 (April 1989): 189–226; Paul G. E. Clemens and Lucy Simler, "Rural Labor and the Farm Household in Chester County, Pennsylvania, 1750–1820," in *Work and Labor in Early America*, ed. Stephen Innes (Chapel Hill: University of North Carolina Press, 1988), 144–88; Wilma A. Dunaway, *Slavery in the American Mountain South* (New York: Cambridge University Press, 2003), 145–47.

25. W. Faux, *Memorable Days in America: Being a Journal of a Tour to the United States* (London: Simpkin and Marshall, 1823), 144. A wheat farmer in northern Virginia reported that his "regular force" consisted of ten slaves, "occasionally calling in some aid, particularly in harvest, hay-making, fodder saving, &c." (*AF*, 27 July 1821).

26. Richard Gittings, Roslin Farm Account Book, 10 July 1857, Gittings Account Books.

27. Arthur W. Machen to Lewis H. Machen, 16 January 1847, Machen Family Papers.

28. Dr. Robert H. Archer Daybook, John Archer Ledgers, 1786–1852, MS 1502, MdHS.

29. Raymond, *Prize Essay*, 4.

30. Heavy rain seems to have been the greatest danger confronting farmers at harvest. In 1843, persistent storms prevented farmers in Carroll County from gathering their wheat, causing the "entire failure" of some crops. Three years later, floodwaters carried off "large quantities" of freshly cut wheat in Washington County and "injured the standing wheat considerably." A similar catastrophe occurred in 1850, when "heavy dashing rains" left the county's wheat "prostrated and tangled" and resulted in significant losses (*Democrat and Carroll County Republican* [Westminster, Md.], 20 July 1843; *HF*, 7 July 1846; *HFT*, 3 July 1850).

31. *Frederick Herald*, 11 May 1833. The newspaper was warning farmers that the year's promising wheat crops might still be destroyed.

32. Rutlinger, "Day Book," 225. For additional evidence on the size of harvest forces, see *HM*, 27 June 1834.

33. *Frederick Examiner*, 27 June 1855.

34. See, for example, FREDERICK COUNTY COURT (Land Records) Contract between Daniel Main and Michael Zimmerman, 8 March 1845, Liber WBT 2, ff. 42, MSA C814-153, MdHR 40,341-115-1.

35. Franklin Blackford Diary, 3 July 1839, 7 July 1845, Blackford Family Papers, Virginia Historical Society, Richmond.

36. John Blackford Journals, 3 July 1830, MS 1087, MdHS.

37. Massey Diary and Timebook for Bohemian Manor Grassdale Farm, 1861–1904, MS 3044, MdHS.

38. *HFT*, 20 July 1853.

39. *The News* [Shippensburg, Pa.], 17 June 1854.

40. *HFT*, 28 June 1854.

41. Arthur W. Machen to Lewis H. Machen, 14 July 1846, Machen Family Papers.

42. Chester Coleman to Augustus Graham, 15 July 1846, Samuel Cock Papers, 1740–1850, MS 244, MdHS.

43. Chester Coleman to Augustus Graham, 18 October 1846, ibid.

44. Rutlinger, "Day Book," 226.

45. Unsigned Letter, 11 July 1860, Davis Family Papers, UMCP.

46. George F. Heyser, Harvest Rolls, 1783, 1825–1855, 1861–1865, MS 2191, MdHS; Lewis H. Machen Account Book, 1837–1857, Machen Family Papers; James Lawrence Hooff Commonplace Book, 5 July–6 July 1854, Virginia Historical Society, Richmond; Dr. Thomas Johnson Memorandum Book, July 1804, Dr. Thomas Johnson Farm Account Book, 1839, both in Johnson Papers, [unprocessed], MdHS.

47. For a general discussion of the doctrine of entirety in the United States, see Robert J. Steinfeld, *Coercion, Contract, and Free Labor in the Nineteenth Century* (New York: Cambridge University Press, 2001), 290–303. The evolution of entirety clauses in agricultural employment is discussed in Schmidt, *Free to Work*, 38–44.

48. Ramsey McHenry Ledger Book, 1841–1848, in Harford County Record Books, 1750–1901, MS 1516, MdHS.

49. Charles H. Lighter Farm Account Book, Middletown Valley Historical Society, Middletown, Md.

50. *The Compiler* [Gettysburg, Pa.], 26 July 1820.

51. Dr. George Hughes Daybook, John Archer Ledgers.

52. Of the sixteen farmhands who assisted with Feaga's harvest in 1834 and 1835, at least fourteen had accrued debts for having their corn, wheat, and timber processed at Feaga's mills (George Feaga Sawmill and Gristmill Ledger, 1823–1837, HSFC).

53. Jacob Reichard Account Books, 1833–1906, MS 2614, MdHS. Such arrangements had a long history in northern Maryland and southern Pennsylvania. In 1810, several customers of a store and tavern in Sharpsburg, Maryland, squared their accounts by mowing hay and harvesting wheat. Similarly, in 1804 free black Samson Grant settled his debts with a Lancaster County, Pennsylvania, merchant by laboring in the wheat harvest (Untitled Daybook and Ledger, 1809–1812, Washington County Historical Society, Hagerstown, Md.; Little Britain General Store Ledger, 1796–1807, Hagley Museum and Library, Wilmington, Del.).

54. Chauncey P. Holcomb, *Address Delivered before the Montgomery County, Maryland, Agricultural Society, at Its Annual Exhibitions, at Rockville, September 14, 1854* (Washington, D.C.: Globe, 1854), 6.

55. "Some Items in Maryland Farming," *The Cultivator* 16 (December 1860): 375–76.

56. "Agricultural Transactions and Expenses on Elm Grove Farm" Owned by Philip R. J. Friese, 10 July 1834, in William P. Preston Collection, 1799–1913, MS 978, MdHS.

57. William P. Preston, Pleasant Plains Farm Account Book, 1852–1864, Preston Collection.

58. *Transactions of the Agricultural Society and Institute of New Castle, Delaware, at the Ninth Annual Meeting, Held in Wilmington on the 11th and 12th of September 1855* (Wilmington, Del.: Porter and Naff, 1844), 27; "Agricultural Transactions and Expenses on Elm Grove Farm" Owned by Philip R. J. Friese, 8 March 1834, Preston Collection; Sophia McHenry to James Howard McHenry, 1 February 1850, MdHS.

59. "Remarks on Things in General," *Monthly Journal of Agriculture* 3 (September 1847): 101; "The Farm and Farming of Rev. J. H. Turner," *Farmers' Register* 10 (1842): 129; Petition of Mary C. Spence, 18 November 1826, Baltimore City Register of Wills, Petitions, MdHR; Petition of Samuel Lynch Jr., 18 November 1818, Washington County Register of Willis, Petitions, and Orders, MdHR; Arthur W. Machen to Lewis H. Machen, 2 December 1845, Machen Family Papers; Charles A. Worthington to George Fayette Washington, 6 January 1847, Special Collections, Duke University Library, Durham, N.C.

60. Petition of Rachel R. Dell, 6 August 1860, Carroll County Levy Court, Pension Papers, 1852–1879, MdHR; Capt. W. Storer Howe to Col. O. Brown, 8 October 1865, Letters Sent, ser. 4302, Winchester, Va., Superintendent, Records of the Bureau of Refugees, Freedmen, and Abandoned Lands, Record Group 105, NARA.

61. The gendered aspects of slavery in districts that produced corn and wheat

have received scant attention. On the declining value of women's agricultural labor to Chesapeake planters making the transition from tobacco cultivation to general farming, see Lorena S. Walsh, "Work and Resistance in the New Republic: The Case of the Chesapeake, 1770–1820," in *From Chattel Slaves to Wage Slaves: The Dynamics of Labour Bargaining in the Americas,* ed. Mary Turner (Bloomington: Indiana University Press, 1995), 107–8. Joan M. Jensen has offered a mild corrective to this interpretation, arguing that the transition from tobacco to corn and grain production did not necessarily mean a reduction in women's workload. She found that slave women on these properties often assumed additional responsibilities, such as managing dairies and engaging in domestic manufacturing (*Promises to the Land: Essays on Rural Women* [Albuquerque: University of New Mexico Press, 1991], 158–63; John Blackford Journals, September 1836-January 1838, Headquarters of the Chesapeake and Ohio Canal National Park, Sharpsburg, Md.; Charles L. Perdue Jr., Thomas E. Barden, and Robert K. Phillips, eds., *Weevils in the Wheat: Interviews with Virginia Ex-Slaves* (Charlottesville: University Press of Virginia, 1976), 26.

62. *FTH*, 20 March 1824, 2 May 1812; Martha Ogle Forman, *Plantation Life at Rose Hill: The Diaries of Martha Ogle Forman, 1814–1845,* ed. W. Emerson Wilson (Wilmington: Historical Society of Delaware, 1976), 421–22; Alexander Wood to William Lewis, 18 February 1812, Lewis Family Papers, Special Collections, Duke University Library, Durham, N.C.

63. Lewis Charlton, *Sketch of the Life of Mr. Lewis Charlton, and Reminiscences of Slavery,* ed. Edward Everett Brown (Portland, Me.: Daily Press, n.d.), 3–4; James Watkins, *Narrative of the Life of James Watkins, Formerly a Chattel in Maryland; Containing an Account of His Escape from Slavery, Together with an Appeal on Behalf of Three Millions of Such "Pieces of Property," Still Held under the Standard of the Eagle* (Manchester, Eng.: Heywood, 1860), 8–9.

64. James W. C. Pennington, *The Fugitive Blacksmith; or, Events in the History of James W. C. Pennington, Pastor of a Presbyterian Church, New York, Formerly a Slave in the State of Maryland, United States,* 3rd ed. (New York: Gilpin, 1850), 4; Armstrong to Mary, 10 December 1856, Maryland Manuscripts Collection, UMCP; *MH*, 1 February 1820.

65. Green, *Ferry Hill Plantation Journal,* 15 March–27 August 1838; FREDERICK COUNTY REGISTER OF WILLS (Inventories) Inventory of George Fox, 6 February 1843, Inventory of Catherine Willard, 2 June 1843, Liber GME 11, ff. 456, 573, MSA C807-30, MdHR 14,565; FREDERICK COUNTY REGISTER OF WILLS (Inventories) Inventory of Daniel Duval, 17 March 1846, Liber GME 12, ff. 633, MSA C807-31, MdHR 14,566.

66. "An Act to Repeal Certain Parts of an Act, Entitled, An Act to Prevent Disabled and Superannuated Slaves Being Set Free, or the Manumission of Slaves by Any Last Will and Testament," 25 December 1790, in *Laws of Maryland, Made and Passed at a Session of Assembly, Begun and Held at the City of Annapolis, on Monday the First of November, in the Year of Our Lord One Thousand Seven Hundred and Ninety* (Annapolis: Green, 1790); "An Act to Provide for Old and Infirm Negro Slaves Belonging to Deceased Persons' Estates," 10 February 1824, in *Laws Made and Passed by the General Assembly at a Session Begun and Held at the City of Annapolis on Monday, the First Day of December, Eighteen Hundred and Twenty-Three* (Annapolis: Hughes, 1824); FREDERICK

COUNTY REGISTER OF WILLS (Wills) Will of Davis Richardson, 30 October 1858, Liber GME 3, ff. 259–60, MSA C898-13, MdHR 40,285-12; John McClintock Jr. to Mrs. Zeamer, 21 September 1901, Zeamer Family Collection, Cumberland County Historical Society, Carlisle, Pa.; FREDERICK COUNTY REGISTER OF WILLS (Wills) Will of David Shriver, 21 February 1826, Liber HS 3, ff. 458–60, MSA C898-10, MdHR 40,285-9-2.

67. Rutlinger, "Day Book," 227.

68. The connections between the temperance movement, the rise of market economies, and worker discipline have been drawn elsewhere. See, for example, Paul E. Johnson, *A Shopkeeper's Millennium: Society and Revivals in Rochester, New York, 1815–1837* (New York: Hill and Wang, 1978), 79–83.

69. *TPA*, 27 January 1830; Margaret Orr Hering to Dr. Edwin Hering, 16 August 1855, Dr. E. A. Hering Family Correspondence, 1852–1862, MS 3073, MdHS; Joshua Webster Hering, Scrapbooks and Recollections, 1744, 1833–1839, 1951, p. 96, MS 1917, MdHS; "Life in Emmitsburg in the Mid 1800's," Vertical File, Emmitsburg Area Historical Society, Emmitsburg, Md. In Washington County, the average distillery purchased $880 worth of apple, corn, and rye annually (1820 U.S. Census of Manufactures, NARA).

70. "Agricultural Transactions and Expenses on Elm Grove Farm" Owned by Philip R. J. Friese, 28 October, 7 November 1833, in Preston Collection.

71. Anna Maria Shriver Diary, 28 March, 2 May 1830, Steiger-Shriver Family Papers, 1823–1909, Special Collections, Duke University Libraries, Durham, N.C.

72. Green, *Ferry Hill Plantation Journal*, 3 February 1838.

73. "Agricultural Transactions and Expenses on Elm Grove Farm" Owned by Philip R. J. Friese, 5 November 1833, Preston Collection.

74. John Blackford Journals, 30 April, 3 September 1837, Headquarters of the Chesapeake and Ohio Canal National Park, Sharpsburg, Md.; Green, *Ferry Hill Plantation Journal*, 20 August 1838; John Blackford Journals, 18 May 1839, MS 2736, MdHS.

75. John Blackford Journals, 8 January 1831, MS 1087, MdHS; Green, *Ferry Hill Plantation Journal*, 26 August 1838; John Blackford Journals, 8 March 1839, MS 2736, MdHS.

76. William P. Preston, Pleasant Plains Account Books, 3 September 1856, 29 April 1858, Preston Collection.

77. *RB*, 20 February, 17 April 1830.

78. Untitled resolution, 21 April 1838, Frederick City Board of Aldermen, Minutes, 1835–1847, HSFC.

79. GOVERNOR (Miscellaneous Papers) Petition of Stephen Bryan, Thomas Newton, H. P. Worthington, et al., [1856], MSA S1274-33, MdHR 6636.

80. *HM*, 24 January 1840.

81. John Blackford Journals, 22 July 1837, Headquarters of the Chesapeake and Ohio Canal National Park, Sharpsburg, Md.

82. *HM*, 27 June 1834.

83. Joseph R. Stonebraker, *A Rebel of '61* (New York: Wynook Hallenback Crawford, 1899), 31.

84. Such weddings of recreation and work were a prominent feature of prein-

dustrial work routines. See E. P. Thompson, "Time, Work-Discipline, and Industrial Capitalism," *Past and Present* 38 (December 1967): 56–97.

85. *The Family Magazine; or, Monthly Abstract of General Knowledge*, 1 May 1841.

86. Watkins, *Narrative*, 8–9.

87. FREDERICK COUNTY CIRCUIT COURT (Court Papers) Testimony of Dennis Borne, 28 March 1854, enclosed in Maryland vs. Basil Evens, n.d. [1854], Box 154, MSA T176-53, MdHR.

88. FREDERICK COUNTY CIRCUIT COURT (Equity Papers) Affidavits of Enoch Waltz and James Wood, 9 August 1849, enclosed in John H. Stilley vs. Susannah Stilley, filed 14 September 1848, case 2208, MSA T158-131, MdHR.

89. *The Register* [Shepherdstown, Va.], 17 July 1858.

90. *Valley Spirit* [Chambersburg, Pa.], 20 July 1859.

91. John Blackford Journals, 20 June 1830, MS 1087, MdHS.

92. Heyser, Harvest Rolls. Similarly, John Mann recorded that "two Germans" had assisted with the harvest on the lands adjoining his Washington County sawmill (John Mann, Ledger and Miscellaneous Papers, 1835–1840, UMCP).

93. Heyser, Harvest Rolls. A similar pattern prevailed among workers on James Crawford Neilson's Harford County farm. Of the seventy-seven harvesters employed between 1824 and 1827, fifty-nine worked in only one harvest (James Crawford Neilson, Priestford Farm Journals, 1824–1827, Neilson Record Books).

94. Daybook of the Union Temperance Society of Middletown Valley, 1831–1874, UMCP; 1850 U.S. Census, Schedule 1 (Free Population), Frederick County, Md., NARA; 1850 U.S. Census, Schedule 2 (Slaves), Frederick County, Md., NARA.

95. Maryland Sons of Temperance, Carroll Division, Account Book, 1847–1851, MS 1049, MdHS; 1850 U.S. Census, Schedule 1 (Free Population), Carroll County, Md., NARA; 1850 U.S. Census, Schedule 2 (Slaves), Carroll County, Md., NARA.

96. Minutes, 16 May 1833, 20 May 1841, Daybook of the Union Temperance Society of Middletown Valley.

97. *HM*, 3 December 1841.

98. As early as 1819, a newspaper in Gettysburg, Pennsylvania, had reported with great interest that "farmers near Philadelphia are forming associations for the purpose of excluding spirituous liquors altogether from their harvest fields and meadows. . . . Let the experiment be tried here!" (*The Compiler* [Gettysburg, Pa.], 14 July 1819).

99. *TPA*, 25 December 1828.

100. *HM*, 18 May 1832.

101. Ibid., 27 June 1834.

102. *First Annual Report of the Board of Managers of the Union Temperance Society of Harford County, Maryland* (Belle-Air, Md.: Bouldin, 1831), 5; *Third Annual Report of the Board of Managers of the Union Temperance Society of Harford County, Maryland* (Belle-Air, Md.: Bouldin, 1833), 6–7; *Fifth Annual Report of the Board of Managers of the Union Temperance Society of Harford County, Maryland* (Belle-Air, Md.: Bouldin, 1836), 6.

103. *Frederick Herald*, 4 August 1832.

104. *Virginia Free Press* [Charlestown, Va.], 19 July 1832.

105. *HFT*, 20 July 1853.

106. Ibid., 30 July 1856.

107. Dr. William Smith McPherson Jr., Auburn Farm Ledger, 1853–1856, in possession of Clement Gardiner, Frederick, Md.

108. *HFT*, 13 July 1859.

Chapter 4. ". . . How Much of Oursels We Owned": Finding Freedom along the Mason-Dixon Line

1. *The Liberty Bell* (Boston: National Anti-Slavery Bazaar, 1853), 31–36; *FTH*, 17 May 1820. A search through the wills and land records of Frederick County revealed that Hook never filed a will or deeds of manumission (FREDERICK COUNTY REGISTER OF WILLS [Wills] Liber HS 2, MSA C898-8, MdHR 40,285-8). The inventory of Hook's estate confirms that he did not make any arrangements for his slaves' freedom: All of his servants were appraised as slaves for life (FREDERICK COUNTY REGISTER OF WILLS [Inventories], Liber HS 4, ff. 242–43, MSA C807-15, MdHR 14,550). Some parts of Thomas's story cannot be verified. There are no slaves with names similar to Eliza or Josh Gowins in Hook's inventory. Likewise, the account of Hook's estate sale indicates that Samuel Ringgold purchased three male slaves, not a family of seven (FREDERICK COUNTY REGISTER OF WILLS [Accounts of Sales], Liber. HS4, ff. 381–91, MSA C745-6, MdHR 14,573).

2. J. E. Snodgrass, "The Childless Mother," *National Era* [Washington, D.C.], 6 May 1847.

3. Susanna Warfield Diary, 8 January, 29 May–June 7, 1849, Warfield Family Diaries, 1845–1885, MS 760, MdHS.

4. Thomas Price, *Slavery in America: With Notices of the Present State of Slavery and the Slave Trade throughout the World* (London: Wightman, 1837), 215.

5. Testimony of George Ross before the American Freedmen's Inquiry Commission, 1863, Letters Received (Main Series), Series 12, Records of the Adjutant General's Office, Record Group 94, NARA.

6. *American Slavery as It Is: Testimony of a Thousand Witnesses* (New York: American Anti-Slavery Society, 1839), 76.

7. Gerrit Smith to John Thomson Mason, 25 June 1852, Gerrit Smith Papers, Special Collections Research Center, Syracuse University Library, Syracuse, N.Y.

8. Price, *Slavery in America*, 214.

9. James W. C. Pennington, *The Fugitive Blacksmith; or, Events in the Life of James W. C. Pennington, Pastor of a Presbyterian Church, New York, Formerly a Slave in the State of Maryland, United States* (London: Gilpin, 1849), iv–vi.

10. Testimony of George Ross.

11. J. H. Shepherd to Abraham Shepherd Jr., n.d., James H. and Abraham Shepherd Jr. Papers, Special Collections, Duke University Library, Durham, N.C.

12. John W. Blassingame, ed., *Slave Testimony: Two Centuries of Letters, Speeches, Interviews and Autobiographies* (Baton Rouge: Louisiana State University Press, 1977), 167–68.

13. Max L. Grivno, "'There Slavery Cannot Dwell': Agriculture and Labor in Northern Maryland, 1790–1860" (Ph.D. diss., University of Maryland, 2007), 186–87.

14. Barbara Jeanne Fields, *Slavery and Freedom on the Middle Ground: Maryland in the Nineteenth Century* (New Haven: Yale University Press, 1985), 24–25.

15. For a discussion of how the scattering of slave families undermined slaveholders' authority, see Stephanie M. H. Camp, "'I Could Not Stay There': Enslaved Women, Truancy, and the Geography of Everyday Forms of Resistance in the Antebellum Plantation South," *Slavery and Abolition* 23 (December 2002): 1–20.

16. John Goldsborough to R. N. Cronan, 27 May, 15 July 1826, Johnson Papers [unprocessed], MdHS.

17. *MHHWA*, 7 February 1816.

18. Pennington, *Fugitive Blacksmith*, 5.

19. Price, *Slavery in America*, 215.

20. *MH*, 8 January 1822.

21. This configuration was not unique to nonplantation districts. Anthony E. Kaye has identified a similar pattern among slaves on large plantations in Mississippi ("Neighborhoods and Solidarity in the Natchez District of Mississippi: Rethinking the Antebellum Slave Community," *Slavery and Abolition* 23 [April 2002]: 1–24).

22. Rebecca Griffin explores the ambiguous meanings of collective work in "'Goin' over There to See That Girl': Competing Social Spaces in the Lives of the Enslaved in Antebellum North Carolina," *Slavery and Abolition* 25 (April 2004): 94–113.

23. Joshua Webster Hering, Scrapbooks and Recollections, 1744, 1833–1839, 1951, pp. 167–68, MS 1917, MdHS.

24. In 1824, for example, McElroy preached at a "very large funeral for a colored person." Years later, he presided over the "very large funeral of a colored man, Charles, a convert" (Journal of John McElroy, S.J., 15 August 1824, 7 November 1841, Archives of the Maryland Province of the Society of Jesus, Special Collections, Georgetown University, Washington, D.C.).

25. Hering, Scrapbooks and Recollections, 141.

26. Susanna Warfield Diary, 20 May 1849.

27. Hering, Scrapbooks and Recollections, 157.

28. Thomas W. Henry, *From Slavery to Salvation: The Autobiography of Rev. Thomas W. Henry of the A.M.E. Church*, ed. Jean Libby (Jackson: University Press of Mississippi, 1994), 31–32.

29. David Martin, *The Trial of the Rev. Jacob Gruber, Minister in the Methodist Episcopal Church, at the March Term, 1819, in the Frederick County Court, for a Misdemeanor* (Fredericktown, Md.: Martin, 1819), 27.

30. *HFT*, 14 June 1854.

31. *Middletown Valley Register* [Middletown, Md.], 6 August 1858. The meeting was apparently a tremendous success. Later that month, it was reported that "between three and four thousand persons were in attendance at the woods meeting held by the colored folks" (*Middletown Valley Register* [Middletown, Md.], 27 August 1858).

32. Susanna Warfield Diary, 20, 29 May 1849.

33. James Lawrence Hooff Commonplace Book, 9 August 1857, Virginia Historical Society, Richmond.

34. *Frederick Examiner*, 7 June 1854.

35. Ibid., 18 January 1854.

36. John Blackford Journals, 15 November 1835, MS 2736, MdHS; John Blackford Journals, 28 May, 17 September 1837, Headquarters of the Chesapeake and Ohio Canal National Park, Sharpsburg, Md.

37. Hering, Scrapbooks and Recollections, 157.

38. "Pedestrian Tour of a Scottish Emigrant, in the Middle States of America," *Tait's Edinburgh Magazine* 6 (November 1839): 725.

39. Jacob Shriver to Andrew Shriver, 19 May 1821, Shriver Family Papers, 1774–1894, MdHS.

40. *FTH*, 5 December 1818. For a similar warning directed against merchants in the village of New Market, see *FTH*, 20 February 1808.

41. Were the governor to reject their appeal, the slaveholders recommended that the offender be banished to the northern states and "not be allowed to live within forty miles of the Maryland line" (SECRETARY OF STATE [Pardon Papers] Jacob Palmer to Philip F. Thomas, 14 June 1850, Wm. Mantz to Philip F. Thomas, 9 April 1850, MSA S1031-9, MdHR 5401-47).

42. Minutes, 12 June 1835, Records of the Board of Aldermen, HSFC.

43. Ibid., 21 April 1838.

44. Untitled resolutions, 17 May 1851, 20 May 1854, 15 May 1858, Resolutions and Ordinances, Records of the Board of Aldermen, HSFC.

45. *HF*, 14 November 1849.

46. John McClintock Jr., to Mrs. Zeamer, 21 September 1901, Zeamer Family Collection, Cumberland County Historical Society, Carlisle, Pa.

47. William J. Switala, *Underground Railroad in Delaware, Maryland, and West Virginia* (Mechanicsburg, Pa.: Stackpole, 2004), 102.

48. *Daily National Intelligencer* [Washington, D.C.], 2 May 1838. For similar examples of slaves escaping along the canal, see *Daily National Intelligencer* [Washington, D.C.], 26 July 1833; *Montgomery County Sentinel* [Rockville, Md.], 7 September 1860.

49. *Petition of Citizens of Montgomery County, Protesting against Leasing the State's Interest in the Chesapeake and Ohio Canal,* Maryland General Assembly, Public Document "N" (Annapolis: Riley, 1860), 3–4.

50. *Alexandria Gazette,* 11 November 1842.

51. Petition of Noble Beveridge, Wm. Benton, James Smith, et al., January 1836, Legislative Petitions, Legislature of Virginia, Virginia State Archives, Richmond. The petition seems to have been ineffective. Two years later, many of the same slaveholders complained that people of "bad character" were purchasing stolen goods from slaves (Petition of Noble Beveridge, H. B. Powell, H. H. Hamilton, et al., 9 January 1838, Legislative Petitions, Legislature of Virginia).

52. Petition of B. T. Towner, Adam Licklider, Jacob Bernie, et al., December 1841, Legislative Petitions, Legislature of Virginia.

53. *MH*, 7 March 1820.

54. *Report of the Committee on the Colored Population to the Legislature of Maryland,* Maryland General Assembly, Public Document "O" (Annapolis: Riley, 1860), 7.

55. *Commonwealth ex. Rel. Taylor against Hasson* in *Reports of Cases Adjudged in the Supreme Court of Pennsylvania,* comp. Charles B. Penrose and Frederick Watts (Carlisle, Pa.: Fleming, 1833), 3:237–39.

56. "An Act for the Gradual Abolition of Slavery," 1 March 1780, in *The Statutes at Large of Pennsylvania from 1682 to 1801*, comp. James T. Mitchell and Henry Flanders ([Harrisburg, Pa.]: Ray, 1904), 10:72–73; *James M. Russell, Esquire, against the Commonwealth* in *Reports of Cases Adjudged in the Supreme Court of Pennsylvania*, comp. William Rawle Jr., Charles B. Penrose, and Frederick Watts (Harrisburg: Welsh and Miller, 1830), 1:82–83.

57. *Report of the Committee Appointed in the Senate of Pennsylvania to Investigate the Causes of an Increased Number of Slaves Having Returned for That Commonwealth by the Census of 1830, over That of 1820, Read in the Senate February 25, 1833, Samuel Breck, Chairman* (Harrisburg, Pa.: Welsh, 1833), 5–6.

58. Paul Finkelman, *An Imperfect Union: Slavery, Federalism, and Comity* (Chapel Hill: University of North Carolina Press, 1981), 137–45.

59. Paul Finkelman, "*Prigg v. Pennsylvania* and the Northern State Court: Anti-Slavery Uses of a Pro-Slavery Decision," *Civil War History* 25 (March 1979): 5–36.

60. On the passage of Pennsylvania's personal liberty law, see Joseph Nogee, "The Prigg Case and Fugitive Slavery, 1842–1850," *Journal of Negro History* 39 (July 1954): 200–201; Thomas D. Morris, *Free Men All: The Personal Liberty Laws of the North, 1780–1861* (Baltimore: Johns Hopkins University Press, 1974), 117–19.

61. *HF*, 19 January 1848, 14 July 1847; Ann Buchanan to Sophia Buchanan, 6 July 1847, Buchanan Family Papers, Special Collections, Duke University Library, Durham, N.C.

62. *HF*, 31 July, 15, 18 September 1846, 27 October, 24 November 1847. Mass escapes continued into the 1850s. In 1852, for example, sixteen slaves from the vicinity of Funkstown and Hagerstown "ran away for Pennsylvania" (*Frederick Douglass' Paper* [Rochester, N.Y.], 3 December 1852).

63. Hiram Corson, "The Abolitionists of Montgomery County and the Work Done by Them in Favor of Giving Freedom to the Slaves of the Southern States," in *Historical Sketches: A Collection of Papers Prepared for the Historical Society of Montgomery County, Pennsylvania*, 2 vols. (Norristown, Pa.: Herald Printing and Binding, 1900), 2:7; *HF*, 8 May 1845, 19 September 1849; *Baltimore Sun*, 13 September 1849; Elwood L. Brinder Jr., "The Fugitive Slaves of Maryland," *Maryland Historical Magazine* 66 (Spring 1971): 49.

64. Ira Berlin, *Generations of Captivity: A History of African-American Slaves* (Cambridge: Harvard University Press, 2003), 233–44; Steven Hahn, *The Political Worlds of Slavery and Freedom* (Cambridge, Mass.: Harvard University Press, 2009).

65. For a general discussion of how African Americans in southern Pennsylvania thwarted the efforts of Maryland slave owners, see Margaret S. Creighton, *The Colors of Courage: Gettysburg's Forgotten History—Immigrants, Women, and African Americans in the Civil War's Defining Battle* (New York: Basic, 2005), 50–59; *Pennsylvania Freeman*, 10 February 1841; *Westminster Carrolltonian* [Westminster, Md.], 25 June 1841; *Niles' Weekly Register*, 17 May, 25 August 1845; R. C. Smedley, *History of the Underground Railroad in Chester and the Neighboring Counties of Pennsylvania* (Lancaster, Pa.: Hiestand, 1883), 65.

66. *HF*, 9 June 1847; *National Era* [Washington, D.C.], 15 July 1847.

67. T. Stephen Whitman, *Challenging Slavery in the Chesapeake: Black and White Resistance to Human Bondage, 1775–1865* (Baltimore: Maryland Historical Society, 2007), 196–203.

68. In 1807, a Frederick County master offered a cooper on the local market

because he found the young slave "too impudent." Three years later, another Frederick County slave owner offered a family of slaves to local buyers because "they wish to change their master" (*FTH*, 13 June 1807; *The Hornet* [Frederick, Md.], 31 January 1810).

69. Blassingame, *Slave Testimony*, 167.

70. For a description of slave trading routes in northern Maryland, see Wilma A. Dunaway, "Put in Master's Pocket: Cotton Expansion and Interstate Slave Trading in the Upper South," in *Appalachians and Race: The Mountain South from Slavery to Segregation*, ed. John C. Inscoe (Lexington: University Press of Kentucky, 2001), 128. Additional evidence concerning northern Maryland's continued involvement in the domestic slave trade comes from the numerous newspaper advertisements offering the "highest price, in cash, for likely young Negroes." For examples, see *HM*, 20 December 1833, 29 May 1835, 5 January, 22 June 1838, 8 November 1839; *FTH*, 16 October 1830.

71. Charles Watts to Gerrit Smith, 21 December 1841, Smith Papers.

72. Allen Sparrow Diary, n.d., Middletown Valley Historical Society, Middletown, Md.

73. *National Era* [Washington, D.C.], 21 November 1850.

74. Answer of John Lee, 1 November 1837, Remarks of Outerbridge Horsey, Complainant, upon the Answer of John Lee, n.d., Lee Family Papers, Special Collections, Duke University Library, Durham, N.C.

75. Beall's 1847 will identified Knight as his son-in-law and named him inheritor of Beall's southern properties (FREDERICK COUNTY REGISTER OF WILLS [Wills] Will of Wm. M. Beall, 26 April 1847, Liber GME 3, ff. 239–41, MSA C898-14, MdHR 40,285-12). Prior to receiving his father-in-law's lands, Knight had purchased numerous slaves in Frederick County. See, for example, FREDERICK COUNTY COURT (Land Records) Purchase Agreement between John Wilson and John Knight, 27 August 1833, Liber JS 43, ff. 494, MSA C814-121, MdHR 40,341-83-2; FREDERICK COUNTY COURT (Land Records) Purchase Agreement between Geo. Kephart and John Knight, 26 February 1845, Liber WBT 1, ff. 83, MSA C814-152, MdHR 40,341-114-1; FREDERICK COUNTY COURT (Land Records) Purchase Agreement between Greenburry Duke and John Knight, 5 September 1845, Liber WBT 1, ff. 270, MSA 814-152, MdHR 40,341-114-1.

76. W. F. Johnson to Austin Woolfolk, 12 April 1842, Johnson Papers [unprocessed], Correspondence, 1840–1849, MdHS.

77. Priscilla Bond, *A Maryland Bride in the Deep South: The Civil War Diary of Priscilla Bond*, ed. Kimberly Harrison (Baton Rouge: Louisiana State University Press, 2006), 342–43.

78. Jacob Miller to Catherine Amelia Houser, 10 August 1859, Miller Family Letter Collection, Antietam National Battlefield, Sharpsburg, Md.

79. Answer of John Lee, 1 November 1837, Lee Family Papers.

80. W. F. Johnson to Austin Woolfolk, 12 April 1842, Johnson Papers [unprocessed], Correspondence, 1840–1849.

81. Jno. McPherson Brien to Jno. Meredith, 12 June 1848, Jonathan D. Meredith Papers, 1807–1853, MS 1367, MdHS.

82. Michael D. Thompson, *The Iron Industry in Western Maryland* (Hagerstown, Md.:

Washington County Historical association, 1976), 90–91; Jean Libby, "Historical Essay," in Henry, *From Slavery to Salvation*, 86.

83. SECRETARY OF STATE (Pardon Papers) Henry Ankeny to Governor Philip F. Thomas, 2 February 1848, MSA S1031-6, MdHR 5401-44.

84. SECRETARY OF STATE (Pardon Papers) B. T. Johnson to Gov. E. Louis Lowe, 6 September 1853, MSA S1031-12, MdHR 5401-50. For similar examples, see SECRETARY OF STATE (Pardon Papers) Petition of Baker H. Simmons and John Leather, December 1856, MSA S1031-15, MdHR 5401-53.

85. SECRETARY OF STATE (Pardon Papers) Petition of Frederick A. Schley, 14 May 1838, MSA S1031-3, MdHR 5401-41.

86. SECRETARY OF STATE (Pardon Papers) Robt. Fowler to P. F. Thomas, n.d., MSA S1031-6, MdHR 5401-44; SECRETARY OF STATE (Pardon Papers) Petition of Joseph J. Merrick, William T. Hamilton, James Spencer, et al., n.d., MSA S1031-6, MdHR 5401-44; *HM*, 19 August 1842, 13 September 1839.

87. *Daily National Intelligencer* [Washington, D.C.],13 September 1843.

88. *HF*, 28 January 1846; MARYLAND SECRETARY OF STATE (Pardon Papers) Petition of William Freaner, 1848, MSA S1031-6, MdHR 5401-44.

89. *HF*, 28 January 1846; MARYLAND SECRETARY OF STATE (Pardon Papers) Petition of William Freaner, 1848, MSA S1031-6, MdHR 5401-44.

90. Determining the number of term slaves in northern Maryland is a difficult task, as neither the federal census returns nor county tax assessments contain separate headings for term slaves. The low figure (10 percent) is taken from the records of the commissioner of slave statistics. Created in 1868 by the Maryland General Assembly, the county commissioners were charged with collecting data on the age, sex, and value of the state's human chattels in hopes of securing compensation. The commissioner for Frederick County gathered information on 1,663 bondspeople, about half the number enumerated in the 1860 census. Of these, 160 were term slaves. The higher figure (30 percent) is taken from an examination of 722 estates inventoried by the Frederick County register of wills between 1841 and 1850. Of the 1,030 slaves listed in these records, 305 (30 percent) were slaves. See FREDERICK COUNTY COMMISSIONER OF SLAVE STATISTICS (Slave Statistics) MSA CE14-1, MdHR; Grivno, "'There Slavery Cannot Dwell,'" 218–19.

91. J. W. Dixon, "Slave Days on the Farm," *Daily News* [Frederick, Md.], 26 July 1924.

92. Grivno, "'There Slavery Cannot Dwell,'" 239–41.

93. T. Stephen Whitman, *The Price of Freedom: Slavery and Manumission in Baltimore and Early National Maryland* (Lexington: University Press of Kentucky, 1997), 165.

94. FREDERICK COUNTY REGISTER OF WILLS (Inventories) Inventory of Thomas Warfield, 12 November 1855, Liber GH 2, ff. 380, MSA T96-3, MdHR.

95. On the prices of term slaves, see Grivno, "'There Slavery Cannot Dwell,'" 252.

96. FREDERICK COUNTY REGISTER OF WILLS (Wills) Will of Albert Ritchie, 22 October 1857, Liber GH 1, ff. 285, MSA C898-16, MdHR 40,285-14.

97. Susanna Warfield Diary, 6 July 1848.

98. "An Act Relating to Runaway Servants and Slaves," 19 January 1805, in *Laws of Maryland, Made and Passed at a Session of Assembly, Begun and Held at the City of Annapolis on Monday the Fifth of November, in the Year of Our Lord, One Thousand Eight Hundred and Four* (Annapolis: Green, 1805).

99. The statute included provisions guaranteeing the term slaves' eventual freedom. It prohibited nonresident slaveholders from holding convicted slaves indefinitely and required county clerks to provide slaves with copies of their manumission papers ("An Act Relating to Persons of Color, Who Are to Be Free after the Expiration of a Term of Years," 14 March 1834, in *Laws Made and Passed by the General Assembly of the State of Maryland, at a Session Begun and Held at Annapolis, on Monday the 30th Day of December, 1833, and Ended on Saturday the 15th Day of March, 1834* [Annapolis: Hughes, 1834]).

100. "An Act Relating to Servants and Slaves," 23 December 1810, in *Laws of Maryland, Made and Passed at a Session of Assembly, Begun and Held at the City of Annapolis, on Monday the Fifth of November, in the Year of Our Lord One Thousand Eight Hundred and Ten* (Annapolis: Green, 1811).

101. "An Act to Prevent the Unlawful Exportation of Negroes and Mulattoes, and to Alter and Amend the Laws Concerning Runaways," 3 February 1818, in *Laws of Maryland, Made and Passed at a Session of Assembly, Begun and Held at the City of Annapolis, on Monday, the First Day of December, Eighteen Hundred and Seventeen* (Annapolis: Green, 1818).

102. "A Supplement to an Act, Entitled, An Act to Prevent the Unlawful Exportation of Negroes and Mulattoes, and to Alter and Amend the Laws Concerning Runaways," 18 March 1835, in *Laws Made and Passed by the General Assembly of the State of Maryland, at a Session Begun and Held at Annapolis, on Monday, the 29th Day of December, 1834* (Annapolis: Hughes, 1835).

103. FREDERICK COUNTY COURT (Docket), October 1844, MSA C782-141, MdHR 14,501; FREDERICK COUNTY COURT (Docket), February 1845, MSA C782-142, MdHR 14,502. The testimony is recorded in FREDERICK COUNTY CIRCUIT COURT (Court Papers), Papers in State of Maryland vs. David Hargate, Box 89, MSA T176-121, MdHR.

104. GOVERNOR AND COUNCIL (Pardon Record), Pardon of John Ritchie, 12 December 1818, MSA S1107-3, MdHR 1932.

105. Bennett's conviction and sentence are recorded in FREDERICK COUNTY COURT (Docket), February 1830, MSA C782-112, MdHR 14,472. For additional details in his case, see GOVERNOR AND COUNCIL (Pardon Papers), Petition of David Bennett, May 1830, MSA 1061-31, MdHR 5401-31.

106. FREDERICK COUNTY COURT (Docket), October 1830, MSA C7820113, MdHR 14,473.

107. FREDERICK COUNTY CIRCUIT COURT (Court Papers), Indictment of John Hartzock Jr., December 1835, Box 100, MSA T176-112, MdHR.

108. SECRETARY OF STATE (Pardon Papers), Petition of Mary Ann Geasey, [1838], MSA 1031-2, MdHR 5401-40, MdHR.

109. In 1849, a Maryland judge argued that it would be difficult to defraud term slaves of their freedom because they could call on the assistance of white supporters. The instruments of manumission "are exposed on public records, to which all persons have ready access," he opined, adding that "there is very small probability in this age of benevolence and charity, that there will be wanting persons to remind them of their rights, should they be otherwise uninformed" ("Negro Franklin vs. Waters," in Richard W. Gill, comp., *Reports of Cases Argued and Determined in the Court of Appeals of Maryland in 1849* [Annapolis: Bonsall, 1852], 331).

110. *TPA*, 29 July 1818.

111. Petition of "Negro Charles," 1833, Maryland Manuscripts Collection, UMCP.

112. GOVERNOR AND COUNCIL (Pardon Papers), Petition of Upton Wager, [1825], Upton Wager to Joshua Cockey, 16 March 1825, Petition of Sundry Citizens of Frederick County, [1825], all in MSA S1061-25, MdHR 5401-25.

113. "Extract from the Letter of Judge Brice to the Governor of Maryland," *Genius of Universal Emancipation*, 1 March 1828.

114. The court seems to have accepted Jones's explanation. While it acceded to her master's request to extend Jones's term from 1861 to 1863, it denied him permission to sell her outside Maryland (Petition of Henry Shaw and Answer of Mary Jones, 17 November 1857, WASHINGTON COUNTY REGISTER OF WILLS [Petitions and Orders], Box 1, MSA T4501-1, MdHR).

115. William Grammer to A. K. Shriver, 28 July 1849, Shriver Family Papers.

116. FREDERICK COUNTY CIRCUIT COURT (Court Papers), Petition of Roderick Dorsey, 14 November 1842, Box 92, MSA T176-119, MdHR.

117. William Still, *The Underground Rail Road : A Record of Facts, Authentic Narratives, Letters, &c., Narrating the Hardships, Hair-Breadth Escapes, and Death Struggles of the Slaves in Their Efforts for Freedom, as Related by Themselves and Others or Witnessed by the Author: Together with Sketches of Some of the Largest Stockholders and Most Liberal Aiders and Advisers of the Road* (Philadelphia: Still, 1883), 526. Carroll County slave Henry Franklin found himself in similar straits. "He had been frequently promised his freedom at the age of thirty-five," noted a biographer, but "two years before arriving at that age . . . and hearing nothing concerning the subject so dear to him and also fearing that something might occur to prevent his receiving the precious boon, he concluded to take the matter into his own hands." On Whitsunday 1837, he fled into Adams County, Pennsylvania (*A Sketch of Henry Franklin and Family* [Philadelphia: Collins, 1887], 2).

118. *The Trial of Emanuel Myers, of Maryland, for Kidnapping Certain Fugitive Slaves, Had at Carlisle* (Carlisle, Pa.: n.p., 1859), 3–7.

119. John S. Crumbaugh, "The Little Boy and the Slave Lad," *Friends' Intelligencer*, 22 December 1894.

120. Price, *Slavery in America*, 204.

121. FREDERICK COUNTY REGISTER OF WILLS (Wills), Depositions of Rev. John Hickey, John Lefevre, and John Hickey Jr., 24 December 1828, Liber GME 1, ff. 29–30, MSA C898-11, MdHR 40,285-11.

122. Benjamin Drew, *The Refugee; or, The Narratives of Fugitive Slaves in Canada* (Boston: Jewett, 1856), 120.

123. "Freedom for Three," *Pawtucket (R.I.) Times*, 17 April 1899.

124. Helen Tunnicliff Catterall, ed., *Judicial Cases Concerning American Slavery and the Negro*, 4 vols. (Washington, D.C.: Carnegie Institution of Washington, 1936), 4:87.

125. Keyte's story was recorded in the diary of the priest who performed her funeral in 1883 (Eli Washington John Lindersmith, Second Book, Miles City, Montana, Sacred Heart Church and Ursuline Convent, 1883–1886, Department of Archives, Manuscripts, and Museum Collection, Catholic University of America, Washington, D.C.).

126. Henry, *From Slavery to Salvation*, 60–61.

127. John Hope Franklin and Loren Schweninger, *Runaway Slaves: Rebels on the Plantation* (New York: Oxford University Press, 1999), 142–43.

128. Peter Meyler, ed., *Broken Shackles: Old Man Henson from Slavery to Freedom* (Toronto: Natural Heritage, 2001), 49–51.

129. J. C. Lovejoy, *Memoir of Rev. Charles T. Torrey, Who Died in the Penitentiary of Maryland, Where He Was Confined for Showing Mercy to the Poor* (Boston: Jewett, 1847), 106–25.

130. Ibid.

131. Ibid.

132. Kathleen A. Ernst, *Too Afraid to Cry: Maryland Civilians in the Antietam Campaign* (Mechanicsburg, Pa.: Stackpole, 1999), 228.

133. In the Bahamas, for example, the collapse of the cotton economy during the first decade of the 1800s transformed labor arrangements decades before Britain abolished slavery. Unable to employ their bondspeople profitably on their cotton plantations, some owners allowed their slaves to hire themselves, while others divided their estates and employed slaves as tenant farmers. See Howard Johnson, *The Bahamas: From Slavery to Servitude, 1783–1933* (Gainesville: University Press of Florida, 1995), 1–118.

134. Hester's freedom was to commence in fourteen years, on 1 April 1846 (FREDERICK COUNTY COURT [Land Records], Manumission of Hester, 28 February 1832, Liber JS 38, ff. 254–25, MSA C814-116, MdHR 40,341-78).

135. FREDERICK COUNTY REGISTER OF WILLS (Wills), Will of Daniel Boyle, 12 September 1828, Liber GME 1, ff. 189–90, MSA C898-11, MdHR 40,28-5-10. In 1845, Nathan Maynard made similar demands of several slaves who were to receive their freedom at age thirty, stating that their "offspring hereafter [are] to serve like terms" (FREDERICK COUNTY COURT [Land Records], Manumission of Elizabeth, Jane, and Catherine Ann, 6 September 1845, Liber WBT 1, ff. 362–63, MSA C814-152, MdHR 40,341-114-1).

136. FREDERICK COUNTY CIRCUIT COURT (Land Records), Manumission of Savilla, 16 May 1856, Liber ES 7, ff. 424, MSA T128-12, MdHR.

137. Frederick attorney Francis Scott Key advised a client looking to rid himself of two children that although "children cannot be emancipated," they could be sold to their free relations (MARYLAND STATE PAPERS [Scharf Collection], Francis Scott Key to "Dear Sir," 25 June 1824, MSA S1005-128, MdHR 19,999-110-1/79).

138. Susanna Warfield Diary, 22 August 1854.

139. Henry, *From Slavery to Salvation*, 26.

140. "Thomas Anderson vs. Rebecca Garrett et al.," in Richard W. Gill, comp., *Report of Cases Argued and Determined in the Court of Appeals in Maryland in 1850 and 1851* (Annapolis, Md.: Bonsall, 1852), 123–24.

141. *FTH*, 29 April 1819.

142. FREDERICK COUNTY COURT (Land Records), Manumission of Jane Addison, 22 September 1834, Liber JS 47, ff. 210, MSA C814-125, MdHR 40,341-87-1.

143. FREDERICK COUNTY COURT (Land Records), Manumission of William, Eleanor, and Mary, 28 August 1830, Liber JS 34, ff. 463, MSA C814-112, MdHR 40,341-74-1.

144. "James T. Henderson vs. William Jason et al.," in Gill, *Report of Cases . . . in 1850 and 1851*, 483–86.

145. FREDERICK COUNTY CIRCUIT COURT (Court Papers), Papers in the Case of Robert H. Dudderer vs. Zachariah T. Windsor, February 1855, Box 15, MSA T176-116, MdHR.

146. FREDERICK COUNTY CIRCUIT COURT (Land Records), Manumission of Caroline Tyler, 5 May 1855, Liber ES 6, ff. 445, MSA T128-17, MdHR. The following year, Serena Luckett saddled her former slave, Arey, with similar obligations. Although Arey and her two oldest children, aged twenty-one and nineteen, were freed outright, Luckett specified that Arey's sixteen-year-old son, Charles, and eight-year-old son, George, were to remain in bondage until their twenty-first birthdays. Luckett willed that George was "to stay with his mother until age 16, then be hired out by my executors" (FREDERICK COUNTY REGISTER OF WILLS [Wills], Will of Serena Luckett, 14 July 1857, Liber GH 1, ff. 222, MSA C898-16, MdHR 40,285-14).

147. WASHINGTON COUNTY REGISTER OF WILLS (Petitions and Orders), Petition of Nathaniel Summers, 10 November 1854, Box 1, MSA T450-1, MdHR.

148. CARROLL COUNTY BOARD OF COUNTY COMMISSIONERS (Pension Papers), Petition of David Bryan, 23 February 1839, MSA C2131-1, MdHR.

149. FREDERICK COUNTY REGISTER OF WILLS (Wills), Will of Mary Brengle, filed 14 February 1858, Liber GH 1, ff. 18–19, MSA C898-16, MdHR 40,285-14.

150. SECRETARY OF STATE (Pardon Papers), George A. Hanson to Governor T. Watkins Ligon, 21 February 1857, MSA S1031-16, MdHR 5401-54.

Chapter 5. "Chased Out on the Slippery Ice": Rural Wage Laborers in Antebellum Maryland

1. *Carroll County Democrat* [Westminster, Md.], 25 July 1861.

2. Donald R. Adams, "Prices and Wages in Maryland, 1750–1850," *Journal of Economic History* 46 (September 1986): 634–35.

3. GOVERNOR (Miscellaneous Papers), Petition of Peter Middlekauf, Wm. Kemple, Samuel King, et al., 18 March 1856, MSA S1274-33, MdHR 6636; GOVERNOR (Miscellaneous Papers), Geo. Thompson Mason to Governor T. W. Ligon, 11 March 1856, MSA S1274-33, MdHR 6636.

4. Margaret Scholl Hood, *The Diaries of Margaret Scholl Hood, 1851–1861*, ed. Rose Barquist, Mary Frear Keeler, and Ann Lebherz (Camden, Me.: Picton, 1992), 139.

5. *Montgomery County Sentinel* [Rockville, Md.], 17 May 1856.

6. *Farmers' Register and Maryland Herald* [Hagerstown, Md.], 6 July 1830.

7. During the 1838 harvest, Washington County planter John Blackford balked at hiring two "rough blackgardish behaved fellows" who had been scouring the neighborhood for work. Other employers were less discriminating. In 1826, Harford County farmer James Crawford Neilson hired "Bubb, a Drunkard" to help gather his harvest but discharged him after two days (Fletcher M. Green, ed., *Ferry Hill Plantation Journal, January 4, 1838–January 15, 1839* [Chapel Hill: University of North Carolina Press, 1961], 5 July 1838; Priestford Farm Journal, 5 July 1826, James Crawford Neilson Record Books, 1798–1900, MS 613, MdHS).

8. *Hagerstown Courier*, 4 July 1838, quoted in *Virginia Free Press* [Charlestown, Va.], 12 July 1838.

9. *HFT*, 23 July 1856; Joseph R. Stonebraker, *A Rebel of '61* (New York: Wynook Hallenback Crawford, 1899), 31.

10. 1st Lt. A. F. Higgs to Sir, 30 June 1866, Reports Received from the Shenandoah Division, Ser. 1977, Maryland and Delaware Assistant Commissioner, Records of the Bureau of Refugees, Freedmen, and Abandoned Lands, Record Group 105, NARA.

11. Jacob Englebrecht, *The Diary of Jacob Englebrecht, 1818–82*, ed. William R. Quynn, trans. James Lowery, 2 vols. (Frederick, Md.: Historical Society of Frederick County, 2002), 1:469; Joseph M. Wolf Ledgers, 1839–48 and 1849–59, Washington County Historical Society, Hagerstown, Md.; 1850 U.S. Census, Schedule 1 (Population), Washington County, Md., NARA; FREDERICK COUNTY REGISTER OF WILLS (Indentures) Indenture of Joel Stimmel, 24 April 1816, Liber HS 1, ff. 95–97, MSA C799-4, MdHR 14,355; WASHINGTON COUNTY REGISTER OF WILLS (Indentures), Indenture of William Powell, 24 March 1846, [no vol.], ff. 34–36, MSA C1953-6, MdHR 16,361.

12. Stonebraker, *Rebel*, 31. During the 1850 harvest, a Hagerstown newspaper echoed Stonebraker's observations, noting that "the county is alive with the hardy sons of Pennsylvania (commonly called 'Backwooders'), who annually make a pilgrimage from their unproductive fastnesses to the fertile valleys . . . for the purpose of harvesting" (*HFT*, 3 July 1850).

13. *HFT*, 8 July 1858.

14. *Virginia Free Press* [Charlestown, Va.], 24 June 1858.

15. *HF*, 14 July 1846.

16. "Agricultural Transactions and Expenses on Elm Grove Farm" Owned by Philip R. J. Friese, 1833–1834, William P. Preston Collection, 1799–1813, MS 978, MdHS.

17. GOVERNOR AND COUNCIL (Pardon Papers), Thomas Kennedy to Governor Samuel Sprigg, [n.d.], MSA 1061-20, MdHR 5401-20.

18. For the law requiring convicts to serve additional time if they were unable to pay their fines, see "A Further Supplement to the Act, Entitled, An Act concerning Crimes and Punishments," 18 February 1830, in *Laws Made and Passed by the General Assembly of the State of Maryland, at a Session of the Said Assembly, Begun and Held in the State House, in the City of Annapolis, on the Last Monday of December 1830 and Concluded on the Twenty-Fourth Day of February 1831* (Annapolis: Green, 1831).

19. SECRETARY OF STATE (Pardon Papers), Byron Ramam, Thomas Harbine, James Watson, et al. to Governor Philip F. Thomas, n.d. [1850], MSA 1031-9, MdHR 5401-47.

20. Richard Vansant Account Book, 1854–1874, 1896, MS 1054, MdHS.

21. Stockman labored periodically on Charles H. Lighter's Frederick County farm between April 1851 and November 1852 (Charles H. Lighter Account Book, 1851–1852, Middletown Valley Historical Society, Middletown, Md.).

22. Dr. Robert H. Archer Jr. Daybook, 1837–1841, Harford County Business Record Books, 1750–1889, MS 1516, MdHS. These seasonal fluctuations were characteristic of wheat-producing regions throughout the nineteenth century. For a nationwide survey of farm wages, see U.S. Department of Agriculture, Division of

Statistics, *Wages of Farm Labor in the United States: Results of Nine Statistical Investigations, from 1866 to 1892, with Extensive Inquiries concerning Wages from 1840 to 1865* (Washington, D.C.: U.S. Government Printing Office, 1892).

23. James Raymond, *Prize Essay on the Comparative Economy of Free and Slave Labor in Agriculture* (Frederick, Md.: Thomson, 1827), 5.

24. J. Jakob Rutlinger, "Day Book on a Journey to North America in the Year 1823," in *The Old Land and the New: The Journals of Two Swiss Families in America in the 1820s*, ed. and trans. Robert H. Billigmeier and Fred A. Picard (Minneapolis: University of Minnesota Press, 1965), 222–27.

25. Thomas W. Henry, *From Slavery to Salvation: The Autobiography of Rev. Thomas W. Henry of the A.M.E. Church*, ed. Jean Libby (Jackson: University Press of Mississippi, 1994), 43–44.

26. SECRETARY OF STATE (Pardon Papers), Confession of Amos Green, n.d., enclosed in Papers in the Case of Amos Green, 1851, MSA 1031-10, MdHR 5401-48; Admission of John Dougherty, 29 January 1841, Chester County Pauper Records, Admissions, 1841–1851, Chester County Historical Society, West Chester, Pa.; FREDERICK COUNTY COURT (Land Records), Testimony in the Case of David Heim v. Elias Heim, July 1844, Liber HS 23, ff. 587–96, MSA C814-151, MdHR 40,341-113-1.

27. *Third Annual Report of the President and Directors to the Stockholders of the Baltimore and Ohio Railroad Company* (Baltimore: Wooddy, 1829), 22.

28. John Piper Account Book, 1820–1826, Special Collections, UMCP.

29. Susannah Warfield Diary, 8 January 1849, in Warfield Family Diaries, 1845–1885, MS 760, MdHS.

30. GOVERNOR AND COUNCIL (Pardon Papers), Petition of James Brightwell, 12 December 1821, MSA 1061-21, MdHR 5401-21.

31. SECRETARY OF STATE (Pardon Papers), W. Veirs Bowie to Governor T. Watkins Ligon, 19 November 1857, enclosed in Petition of Isaac Mons, n.d. [1857], MSA 1031-16, MdHR 5401-54.

32. FREDERICK COUNTY COURT (Judgment Records), March 1801, MSA C810-18, MdHR 12,968. FREDERICK COUNTY CIRCUIT COURT (Court Papers), Indictment of Prosper Jackson, December 1832, Box 83, MSA T176-106, MdHR.

33. SECRETARY OF STATE (Pardon Papers), Petition of Nelson Carter, n.d. [1837], MSA S1031-1, MdHR 5401-39.

34. GOVERNOR AND COUNCIL (Pardon Papers), Mountjoy Luckett to Governor James Thomas, 18 December 1835, enclosed in Petition of Jane Williams, n.d. [1835], MSA 1061-37, MdHR 5401-37.

35. FREDERICK COUNTY CIRCUIT COURT (Papers) Miscellaneous Papers and Petitions, October 1840, Box 152, MSA T176-17, MdHR.

36. Council Minutes, 24 January 1831, Office of the City Clerk, Williamsport, Md.

37. *HF*, 17 December 1845.

38. Untitled resolution, 17 February 1849, Resolutions of the Board of Aldermen of Frederick, Md., 1840–1880, HSFC.

39. *Frederick Examiner*, 7 February 1855, 14 March 1855, 6 June 1855.

40. Rutlinger, "Day Book," 222; *HF*, 13 September 1848; *The Sentinel* [Clear Spring, Md.], 30 August 1850.

41. *FTH*, 25 December 1830. Less dramatic injuries could be just as crippling, both physically and financially, to woodcutters. Samuel Trine became "so crippled by the cut of an axe upon the foot" that he was "totally incapacitated from obtaining a livelihood for himself and family" (CARROLL COUNTY BOARD OF COUNTY COMMISSIONERS [Pension Papers], Petition of Samuel Trine, n.d., MSA C2131-1, MdHR).

42. CARROLL COUNTY BOARD OF COUNTY COMMISSIONERS (Pension Papers), Petition of George King, n.d. [1847], MSA C2131-1, MdHR.

43. WASHINGTON COUNTY CIRCUIT COURT (Coroners Inquests), Inquest on the Body of Edward Coyle, 17 April 1861, MSA C2937-1, MdHR.

44. CARROLL COUNTY BOARD OF COUNTY COMMISSIONERS (Pension Papers), Petition of Jacob and George Miller, 6 August 1840, MSA C2131-1, MdHR. The Millers' plight was not unique. William Warner and his family became dependent on public relief when he was blinded while quarrying rocks (CARROLL COUNTY BOARD OF COUNTY COMMISSIONERS [Pension Papers], Petition of William Warner, n.d. [1849], MSA C2131-1, MdHR).

45. *FTH*, 1 December 1821; Admission of John Dougherty, 29 January 1841, and Admission of George Eckart, 8 April 1841, both in Chester County Pauper Records.

46. *Frederick Examiner*, 16 January 1856, 27 January 1858; *HF*, 26 July 1848.

47. *HFT*, 21 June 1848.

48. See, for example, Peter Way, *Common Labor: Workers and the Digging of North American Canals, 1770–1810* (Baltimore: Johns Hopkins University Press, 1993).

49. Unless otherwise noted, all statistics on workers' families are drawn from a database culled from the 1850 federal census of Washington County. Because the language used to describe rural workers was often imprecise, the database includes the 2,982 white and free black men identified as farmhands, laborers, day laborers, well diggers, drovers and wagoners, fence makers, woodcutters, and shingle makers. To highlight the plight of rural women, whose occupations were not recorded by census enumerators, the database also includes information on the 626 free black and white women who headed households (1850 U.S. Census, Schedule 1 [Population], Washington County, Md., NARA).

50. On the undervaluing of women's work, see Jeanne Boydston, *Home and Work: Housework, Wages, and the Ideology of Labor in the Early Republic* (New York: Oxford University Press, 1990); Joan M. Jensen, *Loosening the Bonds: Mid-Atlantic Farm Women, 1750–1850* (New Haven: Yale University Press, 1986). On the interdependency of poor households, see Seth Rockman, *Scraping By: Wage Labor, Slavery, and Survival in Early National Baltimore* (Baltimore: Johns Hopkins University Press, 2009), 160–73; Billy G. Smith, *The "Lower Sort": Philadelphia's Laboring People, 1750–1800* (Ithaca: Cornell University Press, 1990), 177–96.

51. *AF*, 14 September 1821.

52. Joseph Pickering, *Inquiries of an Emigrant: Being the Narrative of an English Farmer from the Years 1824 to 1830* (London: Effigham and Wilson, 1832), 29.

53. FREDERICK COUNTY CIRCUIT COURT (Court Papers) Testimony of Dennis Borne, 28 March 1854, enclosed in Maryland vs. Basil Evens, n.d. [1854], Box 154, MSA T-176-53, MdHR.

54. Sidney George Fisher, *The Mount Harmon Diaries of Sidney George Fisher, 1837–1850*, ed. W. Emerson Wilson (Wilmington: Historical Society of Delaware, 1976), 157, 287.

55. Liliendale Farm Diary, 1827–1832, MS 2567, MdHS.

56. FREDERICK COUNTY BOARD OF COUNTY COMMISSIONERS (Levy Papers), Petition of Lewis Jackson, 7 April 1860, Box 2, MSA T191-2, MdHR.

57. Jacob Reichard Account Books, 1833–1906, MS 2614, MdHS.

58. Jeremiah Harlan Papers, 1777–1885, MS 1008, MdHS.

59. WASHINGTON COUNTY CIRCUIT COURT (Equity Papers), Papers in the Case of Otho Snyder vs. Margaret Snyder, Filed 26 January 1848, Case 999, Box 5, MSA T425-5, MdHR.

60. Ibid.

61. The Snyders' case was not unique. Explaining why Agnes and Thomas Finnegan's marriage had unraveled, a witness at the couple's divorce proceedings testified that Thomas was a drunkard and an indifferent provider. "Instead of his keeping her," he swore, "she had to keep him" (WASHINGTON COUNTY CIRCUIT COURT [Equity Papers], Papers in the Case of Agnes Finnegan vs. Thomas Finnegan, Filed 20 March 1856, Case 1364, Box 7, MSA T425-7, MdHR).

62. Unsigned Letter to William Fell Johnson, 11 June 1840, Johnson Papers [unprocessed], MdHS.

63. CARROLL COUNTY BOARD OF COUNTY COMMISSIONERS (Pension Papers), Petition of Hilleary Hillman, n.d. [1844], MSA C2131-1, MdHR.

64. CARROLL COUNTY BOARD OF COUNTY COMMISSIONERS (Pension Papers), Petition of James Spencer, n.d., MSA C2131-1, MdHR.

65. GOVERNOR AND COUNCIL (Pardon Papers), Petition of Peter Snavely, 1827, MSA 1061-28, MdHR 5401-28.

66. SECRETARY OF STATE (Pardon Papers), Petition of Mary Kelly, 1841, MSA 1031-4, MdHR 5401-42.

67. GOVERNOR AND COUNCIL (Pardon Papers), Petition of George Rudy, 14 June 1820, MSA 1061-20, MdHR 5401-20.

68. SECRETARY OF STATE (Pardon Papers), Petition of James Wilson, n.d. [1837], MSA 1031-1, MdHR 5401-39.

69. SECRETARY OF STATE (Pardon Papers), Jacob M. Kunkel et al. to Governor Philip F. Thomas, 15 May 1848, Enclosed in Petition of John H. Miller, n.d. [1848], MSA 1031-6, MdHR 5401-44.

70. GOVERNOR AND COUNCIL (Pardon Papers), John Foxwood to Governor Samuel Stevens, 19 August 1824, enclosed in Petition of Thomas Nixon, n.d. [1824], MSA S1061-24, MdHR 5401-24.

71. CARROLL COUNTY BOARD OF COUNTY COMMISSIONERS (Pension Papers), MSA C2131-1, MdHR. A similar pattern developed in neighboring Frederick County. In 1850, the average age of black pensioners was 70.3 for men and 74.1 for women. Whites who received outdoor relief tended to be younger, but their average ages remained high (60.7 years for men and 61 for women) (1850 U.S. Census, Schedule 1 [Population], Frederick County, Md., NARA).

72. Information on county almshouses was collected from the 1850 U.S. Census, Schedule 1 (Population), Frederick and Washington Counties, Md., NARA.

73. CARROLL COUNTY BOARD OF COUNTY COMMISSIONERS (Pension Papers), Petition of Matilda Brown, 23 December 1846, MSA C2131-1, MdHR.

74. CARROLL COUNTY BOARD OF COUNTY COMMISSIONERS (Pension Papers), Petition of James Edwards, 19 April 1848, MSA C2131-1, MdHR.

75. Unfortunately for Rebecca Haggerty, her first husband, Levi, resurfaced soon after her second marriage and accused her of bigamy (GOVERNOR AND COUNCIL [Pardon Papers], Petition of Rebecca Blaney, 3 August 1822, MSA S1061-22, MdHR 5401-22).

76. WASHINGTON COUNTY REGISTER OF WILLS (Petitions and Orders), Petition of Barney Ohlwine, 22 May 1822, Box 1, MSA T450-1, MdHR.

77. George Alfred Townsend, *Katy of Catoctin; or, The Chain-Breakers: A National Romance* (New York: Appleton, 1886), 273–74.

78. An 1850 survey conducted by an agricultural journal revealed that farmers in Frederick and Washington Counties paid men between $8 and $10 per month, while women received between $2 and $4. A similar discrepancy characterized annual wages, which varied from $80 to $100 for men and from $30 to $40 for women ("Table of the Products of Maryland," *The Plough, the Loom, and the Anvil* 3 [January 1851]: 432–33). The account book of Frederick County farmer Charles H. Lighter confirms these findings. In 1854, his male farmhand received $120 and board for nine months' labor, while the woman he employed as a dairymaid and house servant received a mere $42 for the entire year (Lighter Account Book).

79. James Redpath, *The Roving Editor: or, Talks with Slaves in the Southern States* (New York: Burdick, 1859), 221.

80. Chester Coleman to Mr. and Mrs. Seth Coleman Jr., 25 December 1837, Chester Coleman to Augustus Graham, 9 November 1847, both in Samuel Cock Papers, 1740–1850, MS 244, MdHS.

81. Stephen P. Grove Ledger, 1855–1899, Western Maryland Room, Washington County Free Library, Hagerstown, Md.

82. Joseph M. Wolf Ledgers, 1848–1859.

83. George F. Heyser Harvest Rolls, 1783, 1825–1855, 1861–1865, MS 2191, MdHS.

84. Harvest Book, 1839, Captain William Virdin Papers, MS 866, MdHS.

85. FREDERICK COUNTY CIRCUIT COURT (Court Papers), Papers in the Case of Peter Fogle v. Fred Birely, n.d. [1852], Box 166, MSA T176-113, MdHR.

86. FREDERICK COUNTY CIRCUIT COURT (Court Papers), Affidavit of Samuel Fair, 24 February 1844, Enclosed in State of Maryland vs. John Patterson, Box 89, MSA 176-121, MdHR.

87. James A. Little, *Jacob Hamblin: A Narrative of His Personal Experience, as a Frontiersman, Missionary to the Indians and Explorer* (1881; Freeport, N.Y. Books for Libraries, 1971), 17.

88. WASHINGTON COUNTY CIRCUIT COURT (Equity Papers), Amanda Ann Double vs. Martin Van Double, Filed 16 February 1856, Case 1357, Box 7, MSA T425-7, MdHR.

89. Otho Scott and Hiram McCullough, comp., *The Maryland Code: Public General Laws*, 3 vols. (Baltimore: Murphy, 1860), 1:76.

90. FREDERICK COUNTY CIRCUIT COURT (Equity Papers), Petition of Mary Eaton, Filed 21 January 1846, Case 2044, Box 103, MSA T158-122, MdHR.

91. *Frederick Herald*, 21 June 1859.

92. FREDERICK COUNTY CIRCUIT COURT (Court Papers), Inquest on the Body of Julian Bost, 12 January [n.d.], Box 32, MSA T176-32, MdHR.

93. CARROLL COUNTY BOARD OF COUNTY COMMISSIONERS (Pension Papers), Petition of Julia Patrick, 27 April 1848, MSA C2131-1, MdHR.

94. CARROLL COUNTY BOARD OF COUNTY COMMISSIONERS (Pension Papers), Petition of Eliza Koon, 25 March 1841, MSA C2131-1, MdHR.

95. CARROLL COUNTY BOARD OF COUNTY COMMISSIONERS (Pension Papers), Petition of Catherine Taylor, n.d. [1844], MSA C2131-1, MdHR.

96. CARROLL COUNTY BOARD OF COUNTY COMMISSIONERS (Pension Papers), Petition on Behalf of Betsey Reister, n.d., MSA C2131-1, MdHR.

97. 1850 U.S. Census, Schedule 1 (Population), Frederick and Washington Counties, Md., NARA. Childbearing age is here defined as fifteen to fifty years old. Women who were described as idiotic, insane, blind, deaf, or dumb were excluded from this sample.

98. 1860 U.S. Census, Schedule 1 (Population), Jefferson County, Va., NARA.

99. Franklin Osburn Account Book, Thornton Tayloe Perry Collection, Virginia Historical Society, Richmond.

100. SPECIAL COLLECTIONS (J. Alexis Shriver Collection), Robert Archer Ledger, 1826–1854, MSA SC 162-4-954, MdHR.

101. Neither Sarah nor George Bowers could be located in the 1850 federal census. In the 1860 census, however, they appeared two households away from Joseph M. Wolf's farm. At the time, Sarah was sixty-five and George was twenty-two, placing their respective ages between fifty-three and fifty-nine and ten and sixteen during their dealings with Wolf (1860 U.S. Census, Schedule 1 [Population], Washington County, Md., NARA).

102. Joseph M. Wolf Ledgers, 1848–1859, Washington County Historical Society.

103. Eliza Mercer to Philip E. Thomas, 20 June 1832, Papers of the Baltimore and Ohio Railroad Company, 1827–1866, MdHS.

104. On poor women's involvement in petty production and peddling, see Wilma A. Dunaway, *Women, Work, and Family in the Antebellum Mountain South* (New York: Cambridge University Press, 2008), 186–89, 193–95.

105. FREDERICK COUNTY CIRCUIT COURT (License Record), MSA T181-1, MdHR. A partial list of licenses granted by the Washington County court during the 1820s suggests that these patterns may have persisted throughout the antebellum period. In March 1823, for example, the court granted ordinary licenses to seventy-nine men and seven women. Two years later, the court issued forty-eight licenses to sell spirituous liquors, all to men. In May 1829, the court granted eighty-eight licenses to retailers of dry goods, all but two of which went to men (WASHINGTON COUNTY CIRCUIT COURT (License Record), MSA T427-1, MdHR).

106. The first two laws were "An Act Laying Duties on Licenses to Retailers of Dry Goods, and for Other Purposes," 14 February 1820, in *Laws Made and Passed by the General Assembly of the State of Maryland, at a Session Begun and Held at the City of Annapolis, on Monday the Sixth Day of December, Eighteen Hundred and Nineteen* (Annapolis.: Green, 1820), and "A Supplement to the Act Laying Duties on Licenses to Retailers

of Dry Goods and for Other Purposes," 23 February 1822, in *Laws Made and Passed by the General Assembly of the State of Maryland, at a Session Begun and Held at the City of Annapolis, on Monday the Third Day of December, Eighteen Hundred and Twenty-one* (Annapolis.: Chandler, 1822).

107. "An Act to Regulate the Issuing of Licenses to Traders, Keepers of Ordinaries, and Others," 27 March 1828, in *Laws Made and Passed by the General Assembly of the State of Maryland, at a Session Begun and Held at the City of Annapolis, on the Last Monday of December, Eighteen Hundred and Twenty-seven* (Annapolis: Hughes, 1828).

108. *FTH*, 5 April 1828.

109. *HM*, 20 May 1830.

110. Ibid., 30 March 1832.

111. "An Additional Supplement to the Act of December Session, Eighteen Hundred and Twenty-seven, Entitled, An Act to Regulate the Issuing of Licenses to Traders, Keepers of Ordinaries, and Others," 10 March 1832, in *Laws Made and Passed by the General Assembly of the State of Maryland, at a Session Begun and Held at Annapolis, on Monday the 26th Day of December, 1831, and Ended on Wednesday the 14th Day of March, 1832* (Annapolis: Hughes, 1832).

112. GOVERNOR AND COUNCIL (Pardon Papers), Petition of Anne Hosford, n.d. [1828], MSA S1061-29, MdHR 5401-29.

113. WASHINGTON COUNTY CIRCUIT COURT (Equity Papers), Edward Green v. Matilda Green, Filed 4 October 1856, Case 1361, Box 7, MSA T425-7, MdHR.

114. CARROLL COUNTY BOARD OF COUNTY COMMISSIONERS (Pension Papers), Petition on Behalf of Anne Briscoe and Abraham Ireland, 5 May 1851, MSA C2131-1, MdHR.

115. FREDERICK COUNTY COURT (Land Records), Manumission of Thomas Denby and Catherine Denby, 28 February 1801, Liber WR 20, ff. 495, MSA C814-50, MdHR 40,341-12.

116. FREDERICK COUNTY COURT (Land Records), Purchase Agreement between Malinda Howard and Geo. Souder, 3 March 1845, Liber WBT 2, ff. 13–14, MSA C814-153, MdHR 40,341-115-1.

117. FREDERICK COUNTY CIRCUIT COURT (Land Records), Purchase Agreement between Washington Mitchell and Nathan Nelson, 15 June 1857, Liber ES 10, ff. 409, MSA T128-21, MdHR.

118. The original statute made no reference to a child's race, stating simply that "such children as are suffering through the extreme indigence or poverty of their parents, the children of beggars, and also illegitimate children" could be bound out by county authorities ("An Act for the Better Regulation of Apprentices," 28 December 1793, in *Laws of Maryland, Made and Passed at a Session of Assembly, Begun and Held at the City of Annapolis on Monday the Fourth of November, in the Year of Our Lord One Thousand Seven Hundred and Ninety-three* [Annapolis: Green, 1794]); "A Further Supplement to an Act, Entitled, An Act for the Better Regulation of Apprentices," 23 December 1808, in *The Laws of Maryland*, comp. William Killty et al. (Annapolis: Green, 1815).

119. "An Act Authorizing the Judges of the Orphans Courts to Bind Out the Children of Free Negroes and Mulattoes," 17 February 1819, in *Laws Made and*

Passed by the General Assembly of the State of Maryland, at a Session Begun and Held at the City of Annapolis, on Monday the Seventh Day of December, Eighteen Hundred and Eighteen (Annapolis: Green, 1819).

120. "An Act to Provide for the Better Regulation of Free Negro and Mulatto Children within this State," 20 March 1840, in *Laws Made and Passed by the General Assembly of the State of Maryland, at a Session Begun and Held at Annapolis, on Monday, the 30th Day of December, 1839, and Ended on Saturday, the 21st Day of March, 1840* (Annapolis: McNeir, 1840); "An Act Supplementary to an Act Entitled, An Act to Provide for the Better Regulation of Free Negroes and Mulatto Children within This State," 8 March 1845, in *Laws Made and Passed by the General Assembly of the State of Maryland, at a Session Begun and Held at Annapolis, on Monday, the 30th Day of December, 1844, and Ended on Monday, the 10th Day of March, 1845* (Annapolis: McNeir, 1845).

121. Carroll County Indentures, 1840–1860, Office of the Register of Wills, Westminster, Md.; FREDERICK COUNTY REGISTER OF WILLS (Indentures), Libers GME 2, GME 3, GH 1, MSA C799-5-7, MdHR 14,357–358; HOWARD COUNTY REGISTER OF WILLS (Indentures), Liber WG 1, MSA T2740-1, MdHR; WASHINGTON COUNTY REGISTER OF WILLS (Indentures), MSA C1953-5, MSA C1953-6, MdHR 16,360, 16,361.

122. Shorter was eventually acquitted of the crime (WASHINGTON COUNTY COURT [Docket and Minutes], November 1829, MSA C3004-57, MdHR; WASHINGTON COUNTY COURT [Docket and Minutes], November 1830, MSA C3004-59, MdHR). Such actions may not have been uncommon. In 1819, an enslaved man, Breston Smith, reclaimed his daughter, Mary, from her white master. That same year, "a negro man named Ben" abducted his daughter, Harriet, from her master (Petition of Lane Mathews, 20 August 1820, Petition of John Mauldin, 19 May 1819, both in Baltimore County Orphans Court, Petitions and Orders, MdHR).

123. HOWARD COUNTY REGISTER OF WILLS (Petitions), Petition of Samuel Dorsey, n.d., MSA T1307, MdHR.

124. FREDERICK COUNTY REGISTER OF WILLS (Indentures), Indenture of Lucretia Riggs, 13 June 1849, Liber GME 3, n.p., MSA C799-7, MdHR 14,358.

125. HOWARD COUNTY REGISTER OF WILLS (Petitions), Petition of Sophia Johnson, n.d. [1847], MSA T1307, MdHR. It is unclear how the court responded to Johnson's request.

126. In 1856, for example, Howard County farmer Nicholas Ridgely sold the unexpired twelve years of apprentice James Matthews's term for $120. Three years later, William Lawrence sold the remaining term of a bound farmhand, James Crabb, for $150 (HOWARD COUNTY REGISTER OF WILLS [Indentures], Liber WG 1, ff. 130, 182–84, MSA T2740-1, MdHR).

127. FREDERICK COUNTY REGISTER OF WILLS (Indentures, Original), Indenture of John Francis Reed, 1 March 1841, MSA C800-2, MdHR 9602-2.

128. WASHINGTON COUNTY REGISTER OF WILLS (Indentures), Indentures of John Bryan and Mary Bryan, 2 March 1855, [no vol.], ff. 208–10, MSA C1953-6, MdHR 16,361.

129. WASHINGTON COUNTY REGISTER OF WILLS (Indentures), Indenture of Robert Emory Stewart, 30 June 1853, [no vol.], ff. 176–77, MSA C1953-6, MdHR 16,361.

130. SPECIAL COLLECTIONS (J. Alexis Shriver Collection), Robert Archer Ledger, 1826–1854, MSA SC 162-4-954, MdHR.

131. Lewis Charlton, *Sketch of the Life of Mr. Lewis Charlton, and Reminiscences of Slavery*, ed. Edward Everett Brown (Portland, Me.: Daily Press, n.d.), 6–7.

132. "An Act Relating to Free Negroes and Slaves," 14 March 1832, in *Laws Made and Passed . . . 1832*.

133. *AF*, 25 December 1839.

134. Ibid., 29 January 1840.

135. "An Additional Supplement to the Act of Eighteen Hundred and Thirty-one, Chapter Three Hundred and Twenty-three, Entitled, An Act Relating to Negroes and Slaves," 18 March 1840, in *Laws Made and Passed . . . 1840*.

136. John McClintock Jr. to Mrs. Zeamer, 25 September 1901, Zeamer Family Collection, Cumberland County Historical Society, Carlisle, Pa.; J. C. Lovejoy, *Memoir of Rev. Charles T. Torrey, Who Died in the Penitentiary of Maryland, Where He Was Confined for Showing Mercy to the Poor* (Boston: Jewett, 1847), 166.

137. William Chambers, *American Slavery and Colour* (London: Chambers, 1857), 186–87. Davis's case was not unique. In 1842, a free black from Pennsylvania was arrested in Washington County and assessed thirty-seven dollars in court expenses and fines. To discharge these expenses, he was sold into bondage for nineteen months (*HM*, 12, 26 August 1842).

138. Richard W. Gil and John Johnson, eds., *Reports of Cases Argued and Determined in the Court of Appeals* (Baltimore: Lucas, 1832), 219–33; FREDERICK COUNTY CIRCUIT COURT (Court Papers) Affidavit of John P. [Dowlan], 5 October 1848, Box 91, MSA T176-111, MdHR; Affidavit of John Gleason, 9 December 1840, Maryland Manuscripts Collection, UMCP.

139. *TPA*, 24 May 1827.

140. "An Act Relating to Free Negroes and Slaves," 14 March 1832, in *Laws Made and Passed . . . 1832*. The law did not provide guidelines for determining which blacks should obtain liquor licenses.

141. "An Act to Provide a Remedy against Free Negroes Who May Hire for a Stipulated Period to Any Person, and Quit the Service of Such Person after Entering on the Same, and to Provide a Remedy against Persons Who May Employ Such Free Negroes, with the Knowledge That They Had Previously Hired to Another, or Engage in Another's Service," 10 March 1854, in *Laws Made and Passed by the General Assembly of the State of Maryland, at a Session Begun and Held at Annapolis on Wednesday, the 4th Day of January, 1853, and Ended on Friday, the 10th of March, 1854* (Annapolis: Riley, 1854).

142. *Carroll County Democrat* [Westminster, Md.], 4 March 1847.

143. My thinking on this subject has been influenced by Seth Rockman, who argues that class existed "alongside—and often in dynamic tension with—race, gender, age, nativity, and other categories of social difference" ("The Contours of Class in the Early Republic City," *Labor: Studies in Working-Class history of the Americas* 1 [Winter 2004]: 95).

144. "An Act Entitled, A Further Additional Supplement to the Act, Entitled, An Act Concerning Crimes and Punishments," 10 February 1819, in *Laws Made and Passed by the General Assembly of the State of Maryland, at a Session Begun and Held at the*

City of Annapolis, on Monday the Seventh Day of December, Eighteen Hundred and Eighteen (Annapolis: Green, 1819); *Political Examiner* [Frederick, Md.], 6 January 1819; *The Democrat* [Westminster, Md.], 3 September 1846; William Otter, *History of My Own Times,* ed. Richard B. Scott (Ithaca: Cornell University Press, 1995), 168.

145. Otter, *History,* 112–14.

146. *Baltimore Sun,* 1 July 1850; Otter, *History,* 171.

147. Melville Madison Bigelow, *Reports of All the Published Life and Accident Insurance Cases Determined in the American Courts Prior to January, 1871* (New York: Hurd and Houghton, 1871), 649–62; Otter, *History,* 107–9.

148. On the abduction of free blacks, see Carol Wilson, *Freedom at Risk: The Kidnapping of Free Blacks in America, 1780–1865* (Lexington: University Press of Kentucky, 1994); *FTH,* 13 July 1822; *Torchlight* [Hagerstown, Md.], 25 November 1830; *Phoenix Civilian* [Cumberland, Md.], 5 January 1836.

149. James A. Helman, *History of Emmitsburg, Maryland, with a Prelude of Historical Facts of Frederick County, and a Romance Entitled Disappointed; or, The Recluse of Huckle's Field* (Frederick, Md.: Citizen, 1906), 90–91.

150. *RB,* 27 August 1831; Unsigned Letter to Board of Directors, 17 July 1815, Antietam Woolen Manufacturing Company Records, 1814–1843, Hagley Museum and Library, Wilmington, Del.

151. Henry, *From Slavery to Salvation,* 27–28.

152. *Baltimore Gazette and Daily Advertiser,* 17 September 1838.

153. Englebrecht, *Diary,* 1:284; *Middletown Valley Register* [Middletown, Md.], 17 August 1860.

154. FREDERICK COUNTY COURT (Land Records), Deposition of John H. Manahan, 23 May 1833, Liber JS 43, ff. 96, MSA C814-121, MdHR 40,341-83-2. For a similar example, see FREDERICK COUNTY COURT (Land Records) Deposition of John Michael, 30 December 1818, Liber JS 7, ff. 609–10, MSA C814-85, MdHR 40,341-47.

155. Ramsey McHenry Ledger, 29 June, 7 October 1844, Harford County Record Books.

156. *Middletown Valley Register* [Middletown, Md.], 6 August 1858; *American Sentinel* [Westminster, Md.], 5 February 1858.

157. Jesse Glass, comp., *The Witness: Slavery in Nineteenth-Century Carroll County, Maryland* (Westminster: Historical Society of Carroll County, Maryland, 2004), 17.

158. *Alexandria Gazette,* 21 November 1854.

159. *Baltimore Sun,* 13 March 1861.

160. Otter, *History,* 149.

Conclusion

1. Kathleen A. Ernst, *Too Afraid to Cry: Maryland Civilians in the Antietam Campaign* (Mechanicsburg, Pa.: Stackpole, 1999), 130–33.

2. Ibid., 11–12; Clifton Johnson, *Battleground Adventures in the Civil War* (Boston: Houghton Mifflin, 1915), 104–5.

3. Elizabeth A. Regosin and Donald R. Shaffer, eds., *Voices of Emancipation: Under-*

standing Slavery, the Civil War, and Reconstruction through the U.S. Pension Bureau Files (New York: New York University Press, 2008), 166–68; Frederick Bancroft, "Some Undistinguished Negroes," *Journal of Negro History* 5 (October 1920): 477–78.

4. Philip D. Morgan, "Rethinking American Slavery," in *Inequality in Early America*, ed. Carla Gardina Pestana and Sharon V. Salinger (Hanover, Conn.: University Press of New England, 1999), 241–42. Morgan was not the first to view industrial and urban slavery as safety valves in the plantation system. See, for example, Peter Parish, "The Edges of Slavery in the Old South; or, Do Exceptions Prove Rules?" *Slavery and Abolition* 4 (December 1983): 106–25.

5. Robert Tracy McKenzie, *One South or Many? Plantation Belt and Upcountry in Civil War–Era Tennessee* (New York: Cambridge University Press, 1994), 1–2.

6. Others have suggested the need for integrative or systemic approaches to the study of slavery. See, for example, David Brion Davis, "Looking at Slavery from Broader Perspectives," *American Historical Review* 105 (April 2000): 452–66.

7. The findings here are consistent with those recently presented by Steven Deyle. The domestic trade, he argues, created a "regionwide slave market that tied together all the various slaveowning interests into a common economic concern and help put to rest whatever doubts slave-owners in the Upper South may have had about the future of the institution" ("The Domestic Slave Trade in America: The Lifeblood of the Southern Slave System," in *The Chattel Principle: Internal Slave Trades in the Americas*, ed. Walter Johnson [New Haven: Yale University Press, 2004], 94–95).

8. Eugene D. Genovese identified three categories of slave treatment that must be addressed in any comparative study of slavery: day-to-day living conditions, which include food, clothing, and work routines; conditions of life, such as opportunities for family formation and the creation of independent social and religious organizations; and access to freedom and citizenship ("The Treatment of Slaves in Different Countries: Problems in the Applications of Comparative Method," in *In Red and Black: Marxian Explorations in Southern and Afro-American History*, new ed. [Knoxville: University of Tennessee Press, 1984], 159).

9. See, for example, Steven Deyle, *Carry Me Back: The Domestic Slave Trade in American Life* (New York: Oxford University Press, 2005); Walter Johnson, *Soul by Soul: Life inside the Antebellum Slave Market* (Cambridge: Harvard University Press, 1999); and the essays collected in Johnson, *Chattel Principle.*.

10. For a review of this literature, see John Bezís-Selfa, "A Tale of Two Ironworks: Slavery, Free Labor, Work, and Resistance in the Early Republic," *William and Mary Quarterly*, 3rd ser., 56 (October 1999): 677.

11. John W. Blassingame, ed., *Slave Testimony: Two Centuries of Letters, Speeches, Interviews, and Autobiographies* (Baton Rouge: Louisiana State University Press, 1977), 108, 169.

Index

A *t* after a page reference indicates a table. An *f* after a page reference indicates a figure.

MAX GRIVNO is an associate professor of history at the University of Southern Mississippi.

The Working Class in American History

The University of Illinois Press
is a founding member of the
Association of American University Presses.

University of Illinois Press
1325 South Oak Street
Champaign, IL 61820-6903
www.press.uillinois.edu